Introduction to
COMPUTER GRAPHICS
A Practical Learning Approach

Introduction to
COMPUTER GRAPHICS
A Practical Learning Approach

FABIO GANOVELLI

MASSIMILIANO CORSINI

SUMANTA PATTANAIK

MARCO DI BENEDETTO

CRC Press
Taylor & Francis Group
Boca Raton London New York

CRC Press is an imprint of the
Taylor & Francis Group, an **informa** business

A CHAPMAN & HALL BOOK

CRC Press
Taylor & Francis Group
6000 Broken Sound Parkway NW, Suite 300
Boca Raton, FL 33487-2742

Printed and bound in India by Replika Press Pvt. Ltd.

Printed on acid-free paper
Version Date: 20140714

International Standard Book Number-13: 978-1-4398-5279-8 (Hardback)

Visit the Taylor & Francis Web site at
http://www.taylorandfrancis.com

and the CRC Press Web site at
http://www.crcpress.com

To Reni
F. Ganovelli

To my grandmother, my parents and my wife
M. Corsini

To my parents
S. Pattanaik

To my family
M. Di Benedetto

Contents

List of Figures   xvii

List of Listings   xxvii

Preface   xxxi

1 What Computer Graphics Is   **1**
1.1   Application Domains and Areas of Computer Graphics   . . .   1
     1.1.1   Application Domains 2
     1.1.2   Areas of Computer Graphics 2
1.2   Color and Images   5
     1.2.1   The Human Visual System (HVS) 5
     1.2.2   Color Space 6
         1.2.2.1   CIE XYZ 8
         1.2.2.2   Device-Dependent and Device-Independent
                 Color Space 9
         1.2.2.3   HSL and HSV 10
         1.2.2.4   CIELab 11
     1.2.3   Illuminant 12
     1.2.4   Gamma 13
     1.2.5   Image Representation 13
         1.2.5.1   Vector Images 13
         1.2.5.2   Raster Images 14
1.3   Algorithms to Create a Raster Image from a 3D Scene   . . . 17
     1.3.1   Ray Tracing 17
     1.3.2   Rasterization-Based Pipeline 20
     1.3.3   Ray Tracing vs Rasterization-Based Pipeline 21
         1.3.3.1   Ray Tracing Is Better 21
         1.3.3.2   Rasterization Is Better 22

2 The First Steps   **23**
2.1   The Application Programming Interface 23
2.2   The WebGL Rasterization-Based Pipeline 25
2.3   Programming the Rendering Pipeline: Your First Rendering   28
2.4   WebGL Supporting Libraries 40

2.5   Meet NVMC   40
      2.5.1   The Framework   41
      2.5.2   The Class NVMC to Represent the World   42
      2.5.3   A Very Basic Client   42
      2.5.4   Code Organization   48

3 How a 3D Model Is Represented   51
3.1   Introduction   51
      3.1.1   Digitalization of the Real World   52
      3.1.2   Modeling   52
      3.1.3   Procedural Modeling   53
      3.1.4   Simulation   53
3.2   Polygon Meshes   53
      3.2.1   Fans and Strips   54
      3.2.2   Manifoldness   54
      3.2.3   Orientation   55
      3.2.4   Advantages and Disadvantages   56
3.3   Implicit Surfaces   57
      3.3.1   Advantages and Disadvantages   58
3.4   Parametric Surfaces   58
      3.4.1   Parametric Curve.   59
      3.4.2   Bézier Curves   59
              3.4.2.1   Cubic Bézier Curve   61
      3.4.3   B-Spline Curves   63
      3.4.4   From Parametric Curves to Parametric Surfaces . . .   64
      3.4.5   Bézier Patches   66
      3.4.6   NURBS Surfaces   67
      3.4.7   Advantages and Disadvantages   67
3.5   Voxels   68
      3.5.1   Rendering Voxels   69
      3.5.2   Advantages and Disadvantages   70
3.6   Constructive Solid Geometry (CSG)   70
      3.6.1   Advantages and Disadvantages   71
3.7   Subdivision Surfaces   71
      3.7.1   Chaikin's Algorithm   71
      3.7.2   The 4-Point Algorithm   72
      3.7.3   Subdivision Methods for Surfaces   73
      3.7.4   Classification   73
              3.7.4.1   Triangular or Quadrilateral   73
              3.7.4.2   Primal or Dual   73
              3.7.4.3   Approximation vs Interpolation   74
              3.7.4.4   Smoothness.   75
      3.7.5   Subdivision Schemes   75
              3.7.5.1   Loop Scheme   76
              3.7.5.2   Modified Butterfly Scheme   76

    3.7.6   Advantages and Disadvantages 77
  3.8 Data Structures for Polygon Meshes 78
    3.8.1   Indexed Data Structure 78
    3.8.2   Winged-Edge 80
    3.8.3   Half-Edge 80
  3.9 The First Code: Making and Showing Simple Primitives . . . 81
    3.9.1   The Cube 82
    3.9.2   Cone 83
    3.9.3   Cylinder 86
  3.10 Self-Exercises 89
    3.10.1 General 89

4 Geometric Transformations   **91**
  4.1 Geometric Entities 91
  4.2 Basic Geometric Transformations 92
    4.2.1   Translation 92
    4.2.2   Scaling 93
    4.2.3   Rotation 93
    4.2.4   Expressing Transformation with Matrix Notation . . . 94
  4.3 Affine Transformations 96
    4.3.1   Composition of Geometric Transformations 97
    4.3.2   Rotation and Scaling about a Generic Point 98
    4.3.3   Shearing 99
    4.3.4   Inverse Transformations and Commutative Properties 100
  4.4 Frames 101
    4.4.1   General Frames and Affine Transformations 102
    4.4.2   Hierarchies of Frames 102
    4.4.3   The Third Dimension 103
  4.5 Rotations in Three Dimensions 104
    4.5.1   Axis–Angle Rotation 105
          4.5.1.1   Building Orthogonal 3D Frames from a Single
                  Axis 106
          4.5.1.2   Axis–Angle Rotations without Building the
                  3D Frame 106
    4.5.2   Euler Angles Rotations 108
    4.5.3   Rotations with Quaternions 110
  4.6 Viewing Transformations 111
    4.6.1   Placing the View Reference Frame 111
    4.6.2   Projections 112
          4.6.2.1   Perspective Projection 112
          4.6.2.2   Perspective Division 114
          4.6.2.3   Orthographic Projection 114
    4.6.3   Viewing Volume 115
          4.6.3.1   Canonical Viewing Volume 116

  4.6.4   From Normalized Device Coordinates to Window
          Coordinates   117
       4.6.4.1   Preserving Aspect Ratio   118
       4.6.4.2   Depth Value   119
  4.6.5   Summing Up   119
 4.7 Transformations in the Pipeline   120
 4.8 Upgrade Your Client: Our First 3D Client   120
  4.8.1   Assembling the Tree and the Car   122
  4.8.2   Positioning the Trees and the Cars   123
  4.8.3   Viewing the Scene   123
 4.9 The Code   124
 4.10 Handling the Transformations Matrices with a Matrix Stack   125
   4.10.1 Upgrade Your Client: Add the View from above and
           behind   128
 4.11 Manipulating the View and the Objects   130
   4.11.1 Controlling the View with Keyboard and Mouse . . .   130
   4.11.2 Upgrade Your Client: Add the Photographer View . .   131
   4.11.3 Manipulating the Scene with Keyboard and Mouse: the
           Virtual Trackball   133
 4.12 Upgrade Your Client: Create the Observer Camera   135
 4.13 Self-Exercises   137
   4.13.1 General   137
   4.13.2 Client Related   138

5 Turning Vertices into Pixels   139
 5.1 Rasterization   139
  5.1.1   Lines   139
  5.1.2   Polygons (Triangles)   142
       5.1.2.1   General Polygons   143
       5.1.2.2   Triangles   144
  5.1.3   Attribute Interpolation: Barycentric Coordinates . .   146
  5.1.4   Concluding Remarks   148
 5.2 Hidden Surface Removal   149
  5.2.1   Depth Sort   150
  5.2.2   Scanline   151
  5.2.3   z-Buffer   152
  5.2.4   z-Buffer Precision and z-Fighting   152
 5.3 From Fragments to Pixels   154
  5.3.1   Discard Tests   155
  5.3.2   Blending   156
       5.3.2.1   Blending for Transparent Surfaces   157
  5.3.3   Aliasing and Antialiasing   157
  5.3.4   Upgrade Your Client: View from Driver Perspective .   159
 5.4 Clipping   161
  5.4.1   Clipping Segments   162

      5.4.2   Clipping Polygons 165

  5.5   Culling 165

      5.5.1   Back-Face Culling 166

      5.5.2   Frustum Culling 167

      5.5.3   Occlusion Culling 169

6 Lighting and Shading   **171**

  6.1   Light and Matter Interaction 172

      6.1.1   Ray Optics Basics 174

           6.1.1.1   Diffuse Reflection 174

           6.1.1.2   Specular Reflection 175

           6.1.1.3   Refraction 176

  6.2   Radiometry in a Nutshell 177

  6.3   Reflectance and BRDF 180

  6.4   The Rendering Equation 184

  6.5   Evaluate the Rendering Equation 185

  6.6   Computing the Surface Normal 186

      6.6.1   Crease Angle 189

      6.6.2   Transforming the Surface Normal 190

  6.7   Light Source Types 191

      6.7.1   Directional Lights 192

      6.7.2   Upgrade Your Client: Add the Sun 193

           6.7.2.1   Adding the Surface Normal 193

           6.7.2.2   Loading and Shading a 3D Model 195

      6.7.3   Point Lights 197

      6.7.4   Upgrade Your Client: Add the Street Lamps 198

      6.7.5   Spotlights 200

      6.7.6   Area Lights 201

      6.7.7   Upgrade Your Client: Add the Car's Headlights and Lights in the Tunnel 203

  6.8   Phong Illumination Model 205

      6.8.1   Overview and Motivation 205

      6.8.2   Diffuse Component 205

      6.8.3   Specular Component 206

      6.8.4   Ambient Component 207

      6.8.5   The Complete Model 207

  6.9   Shading Techniques 209

      6.9.1   Flat and Gouraud Shading 209

      6.9.2   Phong Shading 210

      6.9.3   Upgrade Your Client: Use Phong Lighting 210

  6.10 Advanced Reflection Models 211

      6.10.1 Cook-Torrance Model 211

      6.10.2 Oren-Nayar Model 213

      6.10.3 Minnaert Model 214

  6.11 Self-Exercises 215

6.11.1 General   215
6.11.2 Client Related   215

7 Texturing   **217**
7.1   Introduction: Do We Need Texture Mapping?   217
7.2   Basic Concepts   218
      7.2.1   Texturing in the Pipeline   220
7.3   Texture Filtering: from per-Fragment Texture Coordinates to
      per-Fragment Color   220
      7.3.1   Magnification   221
      7.3.2   Minification with Mipmapping   222
7.4   Perspective Correct Interpolation: From per-Vertex to per-
      Fragment Texture Coordinates   225
7.5   Upgrade Your Client: Add Textures to the Terrain, Street and
      Building   227
      7.5.1   Accessing Textures from the Shader Program . . .   229
7.6   Upgrade Your Client: Add the Rear Mirror   230
      7.6.1   Rendering to Texture (RTT)   232
7.7   Texture Coordinates Generation and Environment Mapping   234
      7.7.1   Sphere Mapping   235
              7.7.1.1   Computation of Texture Coordinates . . .   236
              7.7.1.2   Limitations   236
      7.7.2   Cube Mapping   236
      7.7.3   Upgrade Your Client: Add a Skybox for the Horizon .   238
      7.7.4   Upgrade Your Client: Add Reflections to the Car . . .   239
              7.7.4.1   Computing the Cubemap on-the-fly for More
                        Accurate Reflections   240
      7.7.5   Projective Texture Mapping   241
7.8   Texture Mapping for Adding Detail to Geometry   242
      7.8.1   Displacement Mapping   243
      7.8.2   Normal Mapping   243
              7.8.2.1   Object Space Normal Mapping   244
      7.8.3   Upgrade Your Client: Add the Asphalt   245
      7.8.4   Tangent Space Normal Mapping   246
              7.8.4.1   Computing the Tangent Frame for
                        Triangulated Meshes   247
7.9   Notes on Mesh Parametrization   249
      7.9.1   Seams   250
      7.9.2   Quality of a Parametrization   252
7.10 3D Textures and Their Use   254
7.11 Self-Exercises   254
      7.11.1 General   254
      7.11.2 Client   255

8 Shadows   **257**
8.1   The Shadow Phenomenon 257
8.2   Shadow Mapping   259
    8.2.1   Modeling Light Sources 260
       8.2.1.1   Directional Light 260
       8.2.1.2   Point Light 260
       8.2.1.3   Spotlights 261
8.3   Upgrade Your Client: Add Shadows 262
    8.3.1   Encoding the Depth Value in an RGBA Texture . . . 263
8.4   Shadow Mapping Artifacts and Limitations 266
    8.4.1   Limited Numerical Precision: Surface Acne 266
       8.4.1.1   Avoid Acne in Closed Objects 267
    8.4.2   Limited Shadow Map Resolution: Aliasing 268
       8.4.2.1   Percentage Closer Filtering (PCF) 268
8.5   Shadow Volumes 269
    8.5.1   Constructing the Shadow Volumes 271
    8.5.2   The Algorithm 272
8.6   Self-Exercises 273
    8.6.1   General 273
    8.6.2   Client Related 273

9 Image-Based Impostors   **275**
9.1   Sprites   276
9.2   Billboarding   277
    9.2.1   Static Billboards 278
    9.2.2   Screen-Aligned Billboards 278
    9.2.3   Upgrade Your Client: Add Fixed-Screen Gadgets . . . 278
    9.2.4   Upgrade Your Client: Adding Lens Flare Effects . . . 280
       9.2.4.1   Occlusion Query 281
    9.2.5   Axis-Aligned Billboards 284
       9.2.5.1   Upgrade Your Client: Better Trees 285
    9.2.6   On-the-fly Billboarding 287
    9.2.7   Spherical Billboards 288
    9.2.8   Billboard Cloud 289
       9.2.8.1   Upgrade Your Client: Even Better Trees . . . 290
9.3   Ray-Traced Impostors 290
9.4   Self-Exercises 292
    9.4.1   General 292
    9.4.2   Client Related 292

10 Advanced Techniques   **295**
10.1   Image Processing   295
    10.1.1   Blurring 297
    10.1.2   Upgrade Your Client: A Better Photographer with Depth of Field 300

        10.1.2.1 Fullscreen Quad   301
    10.1.3 Edge Detection   306
    10.1.4 Upgrade Your Client: Toon Shading   308
    10.1.5 Upgrade Your Client: A Better Photographer with
            Panning   310
        10.1.5.1 The Velocity Buffer   311
    10.1.6 Sharpen   314
10.2 Ambient Occlusion   316
    10.2.1 Screen-Space Ambient Occlusion (SSAO)   318
10.3 Deferred Shading   320
10.4 Particle Systems   321
    10.4.1 Animating a Particle System   322
    10.4.2 Rendering a Particle System   322
10.5 Self-Exercises   323
    10.5.1 General   323
    10.5.2 Client Related   323

11 Global Illumination   **325**
11.1 Ray Tracing   325
    11.1.1 Ray–Algebraic Surface Intersection   326
        11.1.1.1 Ray–Plane Intersection   326
        11.1.1.2 Ray–Sphere Intersection   327
    11.1.2 Ray–Parametric Surface Intersection   327
    11.1.3 Ray–Scene Intersection   328
        11.1.3.1 Ray–AABB Intersection   328
        11.1.3.2 USS-Based Acceleration Scheme   330
        11.1.3.3 USS Grid Traversal   332
        11.1.3.4 BVH-Based Acceleration Scheme   335
    11.1.4 Ray Tracing for Rendering   337
    11.1.5 Classical Ray Tracing   339
    11.1.6 Path Tracing   341
11.2 Multi-Pass Algorithms   344
    11.2.1 Photon Tracing   344
    11.2.2 Radiosity   345
    11.2.3 Concept of Form Factor   345
    11.2.4 Flux Transport Equation and Radiosity Transport
            Equation   347
        11.2.4.1 Computation of Form Factor   348
    11.2.5 Solution of Radiosity System   351
        11.2.5.1 Rendering from Radiosity Solution   353

A NVMC Class   **355**
A.1 Elements of the Scene   355
A.2 Players   357

B Properties of Vector Products **359**
   B.1 Dot Product 359
   B.2 Vector Product 360

Bibliography **363**

Index **367**

List of Figures

1.1   Structure of a human eye.   5
1.2   (Left) RGB additive primaries. (Right) CMY subtractive primaries.   7
1.3   (Top) CIE 1931 RGB color matching function ($\bar{x}(\lambda)$, $\bar{y}(\lambda)$, $\bar{z}(\lambda)$). (Bottom) CIEXYZ color matching functions ($\bar{r}(\lambda)$, $\bar{g}(\lambda)$, $\bar{b}(\lambda)$).   8
1.4   (Left) Chromaticities diagram. (Right) Gamut of different RGB color systems.   10
1.5   HSL and HSV color space.   11
1.6   Example of specification of a vector image (left) and the corresponding drawing (right).   14
1.7   The image of a house assembled using Lego® pieces.   15
1.8   A grayscale image. (Left) The whole picture with a highlighted area whose detail representation (Right) is shown as a matrix of values.   15
1.9   (Left) Original image with opaque background. (Middle) Background color made transparent by setting alpha to zero (transparency is indicated by the dark gray-light gray squares pattern). (Right) A composition of the transparent image with an image of a brick wall.   16
1.10 Vector vs raster images. (Left) A circle and a line assembled to form a "9." (From Left to Right) The corresponding raster images at increased resolution.   17
1.11 A schematic concept of ray tracing algorithm. Rays are shot from the eye through the image plane and intersections with the scene are found. Each time a ray collides with a surface it bounces off the surface and may reach a light source (ray r_1 after one bounce, ray r_2 after two bounces).   18
1.12 Logical scheme of the rasterization-based pipeline.   20

2.1   The WebGL pipeline.   26
2.2   Illustration of the mirroring of arrays from the system memory, where they can be accessed with JavaScript, to the graphics memory.   32
2.3   The vertex flow.   34

2.4   Architecture of the NVMC framework.   42
2.5   The class NVMC incorporates all the knowledge about the
      world of the race.   43
2.6   A very basic NVMC client.   43
2.7   File organization of the NVMC clients.   49

3.1   An example of polygon mesh (about 22,000 faces).   53
3.2   (Left) A strip of triangles. (Right) A fan of triangles.   54
3.3   Manifolds and non-manifolds. (Left) An example of 2-
      manifold. (Right) Two non-manifold examples.   55
3.4   Mesh orientation.   56
3.5   Mesh is a discrete representation. Curved surfaces are only
      approximated.   56
3.6   Mesh is not a compact representation of a shape: a high-
      detailed surface requires many faces to be represented. . . .   57
3.7   Interpolation vs approximation.   59
3.8   Bernstein polynomials. (Top-Left) Basis of degree 1. (Top-
      Right) Basis of degree 2. (Bottom) Basis of degree 3.   60
3.9   Cubic Bézier curves examples. Note how the order of the con-
      trol points influences the final shape of the curve.   62
3.10 Bézier curves of high degree (degree 5 on the left and degree
      7 on the right).   63
3.11 B-splines blending functions. (Top) Uniform quadratic B-
      spline functions. Knots sequence $t_i = \{0, 1, 2, 3, 4\}$. (Bottom)
      Non-uniform quadratic B-spline function. Knots sequence $t_i =$
      $\{0, 1, 2.6, 3, 4\}$ 64
3.12 Examples of B-splines of increasing order defined on eight
      control points.   65
3.13 Bicubic Bézier patch example. The control points are shown
      as black dots.   66
3.14 Example of parametric surface representation with Bézier
      patches. The Utah teapot.   66
3.15 NURBS surfaces modelling. (Left) NURBS head model from
      the "NURBS Head Modeling Tutorial" by Jeremy Bim.
      (Right) The grid on the final rendered version shows the UV
      parameterization of the surface.   68
3.16 From pixels to voxels.   68
3.17 An example of voxels in medical imaging.   69
3.18 Constructive solid geometry. An example of a CSG tree. . .   70
3.19 Chaikin's subdivision scheme.   72
3.20 Primal and dual schemes for triangular and quadrilateral
      mesh.   74
3.21 Loop subdivision scheme.   76
3.22 Butterfly (modified) subdivision scheme.   77
3.23 An example of indexed data structure.   79

3.24 Winged-edge data structure. The pointers of the edge e_5 are drawn in cyan. 80
3.25 Half-edge data structure. 81
3.26 Cube primitive. 82
3.27 Cone primitive. 84
3.28 Cylinder primitive. 86

4.1   Points and vectors in two dimensions. 92
4.2   Examples of translation (a), uniform scaling (b) and non-uniform scaling (c). 93
4.3   Computation of the rotation of a point around the origin. . 94
4.4   (Left) Three collinear points. (Right) The same points after an affine transformation. 97
4.5   Combining rotation and translation. 97
4.6   How to make an object rotate around a specified point. ... 99
4.7   Example of shearing for $h = 0$ and $k = 2$. 100
4.8   Coordinates of a point are relative to the frame. 101
4.9   (Right) An example of relations among frames. (Left) How it can be represented in a graph. 103
4.10 Handness of a coordinate system. 104
4.11 An example of rotation around an axis. 105
4.12 How to build an orthogonal frame starting with a single axis. 105
4.13 Rotation around an axis without building a frame. 107
4.14 A gimbal and the rotation of its rings. 108
4.15 Scheme of the relations among the three rings of a gimbal. . 109
4.16 Illustration of gimbal lock: when two rings rotate around the same axis one degree of freedom is lost. 109
4.17 View reference frame. 112
4.18 The perspective projection. 113
4.19 The pinhole camera. 113
4.20 The orthographics projection. 115
4.21 All the projections convert the viewing volume in the canonical viewing volume. 116
4.22 From CVV to viewport. 118
4.23 Summary of the geometric properties preserved by the different geometric transformations. 119
4.24 Logic scheme of the transformations in the pipeline. 121
4.25 Using basic primitives and transformations to assemble the race scenario. 122
4.26 Hierarchy of transformations for the whole scene. 126
4.27 A snapshot from the very first working client 128
4.28 A view reference frame for implementing the view from behind the car. 129
4.29 Adding the photographer point of view. 134
4.30 The virtual trackball implemented with a sphere. 134

4.31 A surface made by the union of a hyperbolid and a sphere. . 135
4.32 The virtual trackball implemented with a hyperbolid and a sphere. 136
4.33 Adding the Observer point of view with WASD and Trackball Mode. 137

5.1 Discrete differential analyzer algorithm examples. 140
5.2 Bresenham's algorithm. Schematization. 141
5.3 Scanline algorithm for polygon filling. 143
5.4 Any convex polygon can be expressed as the intersection of the halfspaces built on the polygon edges. 144
5.5 Edge equation explained. 145
5.6 Optimization of inside/outside test for triangle filling. Pixels outside the bounding rectangle do not need to be tested, as well as pixels inside stamp **A**, which are outside the triangle, and pixels inside stamps **C** and **D**, which are all inside the triangle. 146
5.7 Barycentric coordinates: (Top-Left) Barycenter on a segment with two weights at the extremes. (Top-Right) Barycentric coordinates of a point inside a triangle. (Bottom-Left) Lines obtained keeping v_0 constant area parallel to the opposite edge. (Bottom-Right) Barycentric coordinates as a non-orthogonal reference system. 147
5.8 Cases where primitives are not fully visible. 149
5.9 (a) Depth sort example on four segments and a few examples of planes separating them. Note that C and D cannot be separated by a plane aligned with the axis but they are by the plane lying on C. D and E intersect and cannot be ordered without splitting them. (b) A case where, although no intersections exist, the primitives cannot be ordered. 150
5.10 (a) Step of the scanline algorithm for a given plane. (b) The corresponding spans created. 151
5.11 State of the depth buffer during the rasterization of three triangles (the ones shown in Figure 5.9(b)). On each pixel is indicated the value of the depth buffer in $[0, 1]$. The numbers in cyan indicate depth values that have been updated after the last triangle was drawn. 153
5.12 Two truncated cones, one white and one cyan, superimposed with a small translation so that the cyan one is closer to the observer. However, because of z-buffer numerical approximation, part of the fragments of the cyan cones are not drawn due to the depth test against those of the white one. 154
5.13 A plot showing the mapping between z-values in view space and depth buffer space. 155

5.14 Stenciling example: (Left) The rendering from inside the car. (Middle) The stencil mask, that is, the portion of screen that does not need to be redrawn. (Right) The portion that is affected by rendering. 156

5.15 Results of back-to-front rendering of four polygons. A and C have $\alpha = 0.5$, B and D have $\alpha = 1$, and the order, from the closest to the farthest, is A,B,C,D. 157

5.16 (Top-Left) A detail of a line rasterized with DDA rasterization. (Top-Right) The same line with the Average Area antialiasing. (Bottom) Results. 158

5.17 Exemplifying drawings for the cabin. The coordinates are expressed in clip space. 160

5.18 Adding the view from inside. Blending is used for the upper part of the windshield. 162

5.19 Scheme for the Cohen-Sutherland clipping algorithm. 163

5.20 Scheme for the Liang-Barsky clipping algorithm. 164

5.21 Sutherland-Hodgman algorithm. Clipping a polygon against a rectangle is done by clipping on its four edges. 165

5.22 (a) If a normal points toward $-z$ in view space this does not imply that it does the same in clip space. (b) The projection of the vertices on the image plane is counter-clockwise if and only if the triangle is front-facing. 166

5.23 (Left) A bounding sphere for a street lamp: easy to test for intersection but with high chances of false positives. (Right) A bounding box for a street lamp: in this case we have little empty space but we need more operations to test the intersection. 168

5.24 Example of a two-level hierarchy of Axis-Aligned Bounding Boxes for a model of a car, obtained by slitting the bounding box along two axes. 169

6.1 Schematization of the effects that happen when light interacts with matter. 173

6.2 Diffuse reflection. 175

6.3 Specular reflection. (Left) Perfect mirror. (Right) Non-ideal specular material. 175

6.4 Mirror direction equation explained. 176

6.5 Refraction. The direction of the refracted light is regulated by Snell's Law. 177

6.6 Solid angle. 179

6.7 Radiance incoming from the direction ω_i ($L(\omega_i)$). Irradiance (E) is the total radiance arriving from all the possible directions. 180

6.8   Bidirectional Radiance Density Function (BRDF). θ_i and θ_r are the inclination angles and ϕ_i and ϕ_r are the azimuthal angle. These angles define the incident and reflection direction.   182

6.9   Global illumination effects. Shadows, caustics and color bleeding.   186

6.10 How to compute vertex normals from the triangle mesh. . .   187

6.11 Using the known normal.   188

6.12 Crease angle and vertex duplication.   189

6.13 How the normal must be transformed.   190

6.14 (Left) Lighting due to *directional* light source. (Right) Lighting due to *point* or *positional* light source.   192

6.15 Scene illuminated with directional light.   197

6.16 Adding point light for the lamps.   200

6.17 (Left) Lighting due to *spot* light source. (Right) Lighting due to *area* light source.   201

6.18 Adding headlights on the car.   204

6.19 (Left) Specular component of the Phong illumination model. (Right) The variant proposed by Blinn.   207

6.20 (Top-Left) Ambient component. (Top-Right) Diffuse component. (Bottom-Left) Specular component. (Bottom-Right) The components summed up together ($k_A = (0.2, 0.2, 0.2)$, $k_D = (0.0, 0.0, 0.6)$, $k_S = (0.8, 0.8, 0.8)$, $n_s = 1.2$).   208

6.21 Flat and Gouraud shading. As it can be seen, the flat shading emphasizes the perception of the faces that compose the model.   209

6.22 Gouraud shading vs Phong shading. (Left) Gouraud shading. (Right) Phong shading. Note that some details result in a better look with Phong shading (per-pixel) due to the non-dense tessellation.   210

6.23 Masking (left) and shadowing (right) effects.   212

6.24 A car rendered with different reflection models. (Top-Left) Phong. (Top-Right) Cook-Torrance. (Bottom-Left) Oren-Nayar. (Bottom-Right) Minnaert.   213

7.1   A checkerboard can be modeled with 69 colored polygons or with 6 polygons and an 8×8 texture.   218

7.2   Common wrapping of texture coordinates: *clamp* and *repeat*.   219

7.3   Texturing in the rendering pipeline.   220

7.4   Magnification and minification.   221

7.5   Bilinear interpolation. Computation of the color at texture coordinates (u', v').   221

7.6   The simplest mipmapping example: a pixel covers exactly four texels, so we precompute a single texel texture and assign the average color to it.   222

7.7   Example of a mipmap pyramid.   223

7.8 Estimation of pixel size in texture space. 224
7.9 Mipmapping at work. In this picture, false colors are used to show the mipmap level used for each fragment. 224
7.10 Perspective projection and linear interpolation lead to incorrect results for texturing. 225
7.11 Finding the perfect mapping. 226
7.12 (Left) A tileable image on the left and an arrangment with nine copies. (Right) A non-tileable image. Borders have been highlighted to show the borders' correspondence
(or lack of it). 227
7.13 Basic texturing. 231
7.14 Scheme of how the rear mirror is obtained by mirroring the view frame with respect to the plane where the mirror lies. . 232
7.15 Using render to texture for implementing the rear mirror. . 234
7.16 (a) An example of a sphere map. (b) The sphere map is created by taking an orthogonal picture of a reflecting sphere. (c) How reflection rays are mapped to texture space. 235
7.17 A typical artifact produced by sphere mapping. 236
7.18 (a) Six images are taken from the center of the cube. (b) The cube map: the cube is unfolded as six square images on the plane. (c) Mapping from a direction to texture coordinates. 237
7.19 Adding the reflection mapping. 242
7.20 A fine geometry is represented with a simpler base geometry plus the geometric detail encoded in a texture as a
height field. 243
7.21 With normal mapping, the texture encodes the normal. . . 244
7.22 Example of object space normal mapping. (Left) Original mesh made up of 4 million triangles. (Center) A mesh of the same object made of only 500 triangles. (Right) The low resolution mesh with normal mapping applied. 245
7.23 An example of how a normal map may appear if opened with an image viewer. 246
7.24 Deriving the tangential frame from texture coordinates. . . 248
7.25 A parametric plane. 249
7.26 (Top) An extremely trivial way to unwrap a mesh: g is continuous only inside the triangle. (Bottom) Problems with filtering due to discontinuities. 250
7.27 A hemisphere may be mapped without seams. 251
7.28 The model of a car and relative parameterization, computed with Graphite [14]. 252
7.29 (Top) Distorted parameterization. (Bottom) Almost
isometric. 253

8.1   (Left) Shadow caused by a point light. (Middle) Shadow
       caused by a directional light. (Right) Shadow caused by an
       area light.   258
8.2   (Left) A simple scene composed of two parallelepipeds is il-
       luminated by a directional light source. (Right) a rendering
       with the setup.   259
8.3   (Left) Light camera for directional light. (Right) Light camera
       for point light.   261
8.4   Light camera for a spotlight.   262
8.5   Shadow map acne. Effect of the depth bias.   267
8.6   Aliasing due to the magnification of shadow map.   269
8.7   PCF shadow mapping.   270
8.8   (Left) Example of shadow volume cast by a sphere. (Right)
       The shadow volume of multiple objects is the union of their
       shadow volumes.   270
8.9   If the viewer is positioned inside the shadow volume the dis-
       parity test fails.   271
8.10   (Left) Determining silhouette edges. (Right) Extruding sil-
       houette edges and capping.   271

9.1   A categorization of image-based rendering techniques: the
       IBR continuum.   276
9.2   Examples of sprites. (Left) The main character, the ghost and
       the cherry of the famous Pac-Man® game. (Right) Animation
       of the main character.   276
9.3   (Left) Frame of the billboard. (Right) Screen-aligned bill-
       boards.   277
9.4   Client with gadgets added using plane-oriented billboard. .   279
9.5   Lens flare effect. Light scattered inside the optics of the cam-
       era produce flares of light on the final image. Note also the
       increased diameter of the sun, called *blooming* effect.   280
9.6   (Left) Positions of the lens flare in screen space. (Right) Ex-
       amples of textures used to simulate the effect.   281
9.7   A client with the lens flare are in effect.   285
9.8   Alpha channel of a texture for showing a tree with a
       billboard.   286
9.9   (Left) Axis-aligned billboarding. The billboard may only ro-
       tate around the y axis of its frame B. (Right) Spherical bill-
       boarding: the axis z_B always points to the point of view o_V. 288
9.10   Billboard cloud example from the paper [6]. (Left) The orig-
       inal model and a set of polygons resembling it. (Right) The
       texture resulting from the projections of the original model
       on the billboards.   289
9.11   Snapshot of the client using billboard clouds for the trees. .   290
9.12   The way height field is ray traced by the fragment shader. .   291

10.1   Computer graphics, computer vision and image processing are
       often interconnected.   296
10.2   A generic filter of 3×3 kernel size. As we can see, the mask
       of weights of the filter is centered on the pixel to be filtered.   297
10.3   (Left) Original image. (Right) Image blurred with a 9×9 box
       filter ($N = M = 4$).   298
10.4   Weights of a 7×7 Gaussian filter.   299
10.5   (Left) Original image. (Right) Image blurred with a 9×9
       Gaussian filter ($\sigma = 1.5$ pixels).   299
10.6   Out-of-focus example. The scene has been captured such that
       the car is in focus while the rest of the background is out of
       focus. The range of depth where the objects framed are in
       focus is called *depth of field* of the camera.   300
10.7   Depth of field and circle of confusion.   301
10.8   Snapshot of the depth of field client.   305
10.9   (Left) Original image. (Center) Prewitt filter. (Right) Sobel
       filter.   308
10.10 Toon shading client.   310
10.11 Motion blur. Since the car is moving by Δ *during* the expo-
       sure, the pixel value in $x'(t + dt)$ is an accumulation of the
       pixels ahead in the interval $x'(t + dt) + \Delta$.   311
10.12 Velocity vector.   312
10.13 A screenshot of the motion blur client.   315
10.14 (Left) Original image. (Right) Image after unsharp masking.
       The I_{smooth} image is the one depicted in Figure 10.5; λ is set
       to 0.6.   316
10.15 Occlusion examples. (Left) The point **p** receives only certain
       rays of light because it is self-occluded by its surface. (Right)
       The point **p** receives few rays of light because it is occluded
       by the occluders O.   317
10.16 Effect of ambient occlusion. (Left) Phong model. (Right) Am-
       bient occlusion term only. The ambient occlusion term has
       been calculated with Meshlab. The 3D model is a simplified
       version of a scanning model of a capital.   318
10.17 The horizon angle $h(\theta)$ and the tangent angle $t(\theta)$ in a specific
       direction θ.   319

11.1   (Left) Axis-aligned bounding box (AABB). (Right) Oriented
       bounding box (OBB).   329
11.2   The idea of a uniform subdivision grid shown in 2D. Only the
       objects inside the uniform subdivision cells traversed by the
       ray (highlighted in light gray) are tested for intersections. A
       3D grid of AABBs is used in practice.   331

11.3   Efficient ray traversal in USS (shown in 2D). After computing
         the first intersection parameters t_x and t_y, the Δ_x and Δ_y
         values are used to incrementally compute the next t_x and t_y
         values.   334
11.4   An example of bounding volume hierarchy. The room is sub-
         divided according to a tree of depth 3.   335
11.5   Path tracing. Every time a ray hits a surface a new ray is shot
         and a new path is generated.   340
11.6   Form factor.   346

B.1   Dot product. (Left) $\boldsymbol{a}'$ and $\boldsymbol{a}''$ are built from $\boldsymbol{a}$ by swapping
         the coordinates and negating one of the two. (Right) Length
         of the projection of $\boldsymbol{b}$ on the vector $\boldsymbol{a}$.   360
B.2   Cross product. (Top-Left) The cross product of two vectors is
         perpendicular to both and its magnitude is equal to the area
         of the parallelogram built on the two vectors. (Top-Right) The
         cross product to compute the normal of a triangle. (Bottom)
         The cross product to find the orientation of three points on
         the XY plane.   361

List of Listings

1.1 Basic ray tracing. 18
1.2 Classic ray tracing. 19
2.1 HTML page for running the client. 29
2.2 Skeleton code. 29
2.3 Setting up WebGl. 30
2.4 A triangle in JavaScript. 31
2.5 A triangle represented with an array of scalars. 32
2.6 Complete code to set up a triangle. 35
2.7 Complete code to program the vertex and the fragment shader. 37
2.8 The first rendering example using WebGL. 38
2.9 The function onInitialize. This function is called once per
    page loading. 44
2.10 The JavaScript object to represent a geometric primitive made
    of triangles (in this case, a single triangle). 45
2.11 Creating the objects to be drawn. 45
2.12 Creating geometric objects. 46
2.13 Rendering of one geometric object. 47
2.14 Program shader for rendering. 48
2.15 Accessing the elements of the scene. 48
3.1 Cube primitive. 83
3.2 Cone primitive. 84
3.3 Cylinder primitive. 87
4.1 Setting projection and modelview matrix. 126
4.2 Actions performed upon initialization. 127
4.3 A basic shader program. 127
4.4 Setting the ModelView matrix and rendering 128
4.5 The ChaseCamera sets the view from above and behind
    the car. 129
4.6 Setting the view for the photographer camera. 132
5.1 Discrete difference analyzer (DDA) rasterization algorithm. . 140
5.2 Bresenham rasterizer for the case of slope between 0 and 1.
    All the other cases can be written taking into account the
    symmetry of the problem. 142
5.3 The z-buffer algorithm. 152
5.4 Using stenciling for drawing the cabin. 159
5.5 Using blending for drawing a partially opaque windshield. . 161

6.1   Adding a buffer to store normals.   193
6.2   Enabling vertex normal attribute.   193
6.3   Vertex shader.   194
6.4   Fragment shader.   194
6.5   How to load a 3D model with SpiderGl.   195
6.6   The SglTechnique.   195
6.7   Drawing a model with SpiderGl.   196
6.8   Light object.   198
6.9   Light object.   199
6.10   Light object including spotlight.   203
6.11   Bringing headlights in view space.   203
6.12   Area light contribution (fragment shader).   204
6.13   Function computing the Phong shading used in the fragment
       shader.   211
7.1   Create a texture.   228
7.2   Loading images from files and creating corresponding textures.   229
7.3   Minimal vertex and fragment shaders for texturing.   229
7.4   Setting texture access.   230
7.5   Creating a new framebuffer.   233
7.6   Rendering a skybox.   238
7.7   Shader for rendering a skybox.   239
7.8   Shader for reflection mapping.   240
7.9   Creating the reflection map on the y.   241
7.10   Fragment shader for object space normal mapping.   246
8.1   Shadow pass vertex shader.   264
8.2   Shadow pass fragment shader.   264
8.3   Lighting pass vertex shader.   265
8.4   Lighting pass fragment shader.   265
9.1   Definition of a billboard.   278
9.2   Initialization of billboards.   279
9.3   Would-be implementation of a function to test if the point
       at position lightPos is visible. This function should be called
       after the scene has been rendered.   282
9.4   Fragment shader for lens flare accounting for occlusion of light
       source.   283
9.5   Function to draw lens areas.   283
9.6   Rendering axis-aligned billboards with depth sort.   286
10.1   Depth of field implementation (JavaScript side).   303
10.2   Depth of field implementation (shader side).   304
10.3   Code to compute the edge strength.   308
10.4   A simple quantized-diffuse model.   309
10.5   Fragment shader for the second pass.   310
10.6   Storing the modelview matrix at the previous frame.   313
10.7   Shader programs for calculating the velocity buffer.   313
10.8   Shader program for the final rendering of the panning effect.   314

11.1 Ray-AABB intersection finding algorithm. 330
11.2 USS preprocessing algorithm. 331
11.3 Code to take into account the rays originating inside the USS
     bounds. 333
11.4 An incremental algorithm for ray–USS traversal. 333
11.5 BVH creation algorithm. 336
11.6 Ray–BVH intersection-finding algorithm. 337
11.7 Fundamental ray-tracing algorithm. 338
11.8 Algorithm for pixel color computation in classic ray-tracing. 339
11.9 Path tracing algorithm. 341
11.10 Algorithm for uniformly sampling an arbitrarily oriented unit
     hemisphere. 342
11.11 Rejection-based algorithm for uniformly sampling an arbitrar-
     ily oriented unit hemisphere. 343
11.12 Algorithm for cosine importance sampling a hemisphere. . . 343
11.13 Algorithm for computing form factor between two patches us-
     ing Monte Carlo sampling. 349
11.14 Algorithm for computing form factor between a patch and all
     other patches using a method based on projection on hemi-
     sphere. 350
11.15 Initialization for gathering based method. 351
11.16 Jacobi-iteration-based method for computing equilibrium ra-
     diosity. 351
11.17 Gauss-Seidel-iteration-based method for computing equilib-
     rium radiosity. 352
11.18 Southwell-iteration-based method for computing equilibrium
     radiosity. 352

Preface

There are plenty of books on computer graphics. Most of them are at the beginner level, where the emphasis has been on teaching a graphics API to create pretty pictures. There are quite a number of higher level books specializing in narrow areas of computer graphics, for example, global illumination, geometric modeling and non-photorealistic rendering. However, there are few books that cover computer graphics fundamentals in detail and the physical principles behind realistic rendering, so that it is suitable for use by a broader range of audience, say, from beginner to senior level computer graphics classes to those who wish to pursue an ambitious career in a computer graphics-related field and/or wish to carry out research in the field of computer graphics. Also, there are few books addressing theory and practice as the same body of knowledge. We believe that there is a need for such graphics books and in this book we have strived to address this need.

The central theme of the book is real-time rendering, that is, interactive visualization of three-dimensional scenes. About this, we progressively cover a wide range of topics from basic to intermediate level. For each topic, the basic mathematical concepts and/or physical principles are explained, and the relevant methods and algorithms are derived. The book also covers modeling, from polygonal representations to NURBS and subdivision surface representations.

It is almost impossible to teach computer graphics without hands-on examples and interaction. Thus, it is not an accident that many chapters of the book come with examples. What makes our book special is that it follows a teaching-in-context approach, that is, all the examples have been designed for developing a single, large application, providing a context to put the theory into practice. The application that we have chosen is a car racing game where the driver controls the car moving on the track. The example starts with no graphics at all, and we add a little bit of graphics with each chapter; at the end we expect that we will have something close to what one expects in a classical video game.

The book has been designed for a relatively wide audience. We assume a basic knowledge of calculus and some previous skills with a programming language. Even though the book contains a wide range of topics from basic to advanced, the reader will develop the required expertise beyond the basic, as he or she progresses with the chapters of the book. Thus, we believe that both beginner- and senior-level computer graphics students will be the primary audience of the book. Apart from gaining knowledge of various aspects of computer graphics, from an educational point of view, students will be well versed in many essential algorithms useful to understanding in-depth, more advanced algorithms. The book will also be useful to software developers working on any computer graphics interactive application as well as practioners who want to learn more about computer graphics.

Currently, it is impossible to separate real-time rendering from GPU programming, so for real-time algorithms we have accepted the help of GPU compatible API. We have chosen WebGL, the Javascript binding for OpenGL-ES, as the graphics API for the practical examples. The reason for this choice is multi-fold. First, smart phones, tablets and notebooks have become ubiquitous, and almost all these devices support WebGL-enabled browsers. Second, WebGL does not require any specialized developing platform other than a web browser and a simple text editor. Finally, there are also plenty of openly available good quality tutorials to get more information about WebGL.

Finally, thanks to the use of WebGL, the book has a significant on-line component. All the code examples are available online at the book's Website (http://www.envymycarbook.com). We are also commited to providing up-to-date online information on this Website as well as more examples in the future.

Chapter 1

What Computer Graphics Is

Computer graphics is an interdisciplinary field where computer scientists, mathematicians, physicists, engineers, artists and practitioners all gather with the common goal of opening a "window" to the "world". In the previous sentence "window" is the monitor of a computer, the display of a tablet or a smartphone or anything that can show images. The "world" is a digital model, the result of a scientific simulation, or any entity for which we can conceive a visual representation. The goal of this chapter is to provide the first basic knowledge that the reader will need through the rest of the book during the learning of how to develop his/her own interactive graphics application.

1.1 Application Domains and Areas of Computer Graphics

Computer graphics (CG) deals with all the algorithms, methods and techniques that are used to produce a computer-generated image, a *synthetic image*, starting from a collection of data. This data can be the description of a 3D scene, like in a videogame; some physical measures coming from scientific experiments, like in scientific visualization; or statistics collected through the Web visualized in a compact way for summarization purposes, like in an information visualization application. The process of converting the input data into an image is called *rendering*.

During the past twenty years, computer graphics has progressively spread over almost all areas of life. This diffusion has been mainly facilitated by the increasing power and flexibility of the consumer graphics hardware, which provides the capability to a standard PC to render very complex 3D scenes, and by the great effort of the researchers and developers of the computer graphics community to create efficient algorithms, which enable the developer to carry out a wide range of visualization tasks. When you play a computer game, many complex CG algorithms are at work to render your battle-field/space ship/cars, when you go to the cinema you may see your latest movie partly or entirely generated through a computer and a bunch of CG algorithms, when you are writing your business-planning presentation, graphics help you to summarize trends and other information in a easy-to-understand way.

1.1.1 Application Domains

We mentioned just a few examples but CG applications span over a lot of different ambits. Without expecting to be exhaustive, we give here a short list of application fields of CG.

Entertainment Industry: creation of synthetic movies/cartoons, creation of visual special effects, creation of visually pleasant computer games.

Architecture: visualization of how the landscape of a city appears before and after the construction of a building, design optimization of complex architectural structures.

Mechanical Engineering: creation of virtual prototypes of mechanical pieces before the actual realization, for example in the automotive industry.

Design: to enhance/aid the creativity of a designer who can play with several shapes before producing his/her final idea, to test the feasibility of fabricating objects.

Medicine: to train surgeons through virtual surgery simulations, to efficiently visualize data coming from diagnostic instruments, and to plan difficult procedures on a virtual model before the real intervention.

Natural Science: to visualize complex molecules in drugs development, to enhance microscope images, to create a visualization of a theory about a physical phenomenon, to give a visual representation of physical measures coming from an experiment.

Cultural Heritage: to create virtual reconstructions of ancient temples or archeological sites; to show reconstruction hypotheses, for example how ancient Rome appeared in its magnificence, for conservation and documentation purposes.

1.1.2 Areas of Computer Graphics

As mentioned in the introduction, computer graphics is a very general concept encompassing a wide background knowledge. As such, it has naturally evolved into a number of areas of expertise, the most relevant of which are:

Imaging: In recent years many image processing algorithms and techniques have been adopted and extended by the CG community to produce high quality images/videos. Matting, compositing, warping, filtering and editing are common operations of this type. Some advanced tasks of this type are: *texture synthesis*, which deals with the generation of visual patterns of surface such as bricks of a wall, clouds in the sky, skin, facades of buildings, etc.; *intelligent cut-and-paste*, an image editing operation where the user selects a part of interest of an image and modifies it by interactively moving it and integrates it into the surroundings of another part of the same or other image; *media retargeting*, which consists of changing an image so as to optimize its appearance in a specific media. A classic example is how to crop and/or extend an image to show a movie originally shot in a cinematographic 2.39 : 1 format (the usual notation of the *aspect ratio* $x : y$ means that the ratio between the width and the height of the image is $\frac{x}{y}$) to the more TV-like 16 : 9 format.

3D Scanning: The process of converting real world objects into a digital representation than can be used in a CG application. Many devices and algorithms have been developed to acquire the geometry and the visual appearance of a real object.

Geometric Modeling: Geometric modeling concerns the modeling of the 3D object used in the CG application. The 3D models can be generated manually by an expert user with specific tools or semi-automatically by specifying a sketch of the 3D object on some photos of it assisted by a specific drawing application (this process is known as *image-based modeling*).

Geometric Processing: Geometric processing deals with all the algorithms used to manipulate the geometry of the 3D object. The 3D object can be *simplified*, reducing the level of details of the geometry component; *improved*, by removing noise from its surface or other topological anomalies; *re-shaped* to account for certain characteristics; *converted into different types of representation*, as we will see in Chapter 3; and so on. Many of these techniques are related to the field of *computational geometry*.

Animation and Simulation: This area concerns all the techniques and algorithms used to animate a static 3D model, ranging from the techniques to help the artist to define the movement of a character in a movie to the real-time physical simulation of living organs in a surgery simulator. Much of the work in this area is rooted in the domain of mechanical engineering, from where complex algorithms have been adapted to run on low-end computers and in real time, often trading accuracy of physical simulation for execution speed.

Computational Photography: This area includes all the techniques employed to improve the potential of digital photography and the quality of digitally captured images. This CG topic spans optics, image processing and computer vision. It is a growing field that has allowed us to produce low-cost digital photographic devices capable of identifying faces, refocusing images, automatically creating panoramas, capturing images in high dynamic range, estimating the depth of the captured scene, etc.

Rendering: We have just stated that rendering is the process of producing a final image starting from some sort of data. Rendering can be categorized in many ways depending on the property of the rendering algorithm. A commonly used categorization is to subdivide rendering techniques into *photorealistic rendering, non-photorealistic rendering* or *information visualization.* The aim of photorealistic rendering is to produce a synthetic image as realistic as possible starting from a detailed description of the 3D scene in terms of geometry, both at macroscopic and microscopic levels, and materials. Non-photorealistic rendering (NPR) deals with all the rendering techniques that relax the goal of realism. For example, to visualize a car engine, the rendering should emphasize each of its constituent elements; in this sense a realistic visualization is less useful from a perceptual point of view. For this reason sometimes NPR is also referred to as *illustrative rendering. Information visualization* concerns the visualization of huge amounts of data and their relationships, usually it adopts schemes, graphs and charts. The visualization techniques of this type are usually simple; the main goal is to express visually, in a clear way, the data and their underlying relationships.

Another way to classify rendering algorithms is the amount of time they require to produce the synthetic image. The term *real-time rendering* refers to all the algorithms and techniques that can be used to generate the images so fast as to guarantee user interaction with the graphics application. In this ambit, computer game developers have pushed the technologies to become capable of handling scenes of increasing complexity and realism at interactive rates, which means generating the synthetic image in about 40–50 milliseconds, which guarantees that the scene is drawn 20–25 times per second. The number of times a scene is drawn on the screen of a display surface is called *framerate* and it is measured in *frames-per-second* (fps). Many modern computer games can achieve 100 fps or more. *Offline rendering* deals with all the algorithms and techniques to generate photorealistic images of a synthetic scene without the constraint of interactivity. For example, the images produced for an animation movie are usually the result of off-line algorithms that run for hours on a dedicated cluster of PCs (called *render farm*) and simulate the interaction between the light and the matter by means of *global illumination* (GI) techniques. Traditionally the term global-illumination technique implied off-line rendering. Thanks especially to the improvements in CG hardware, this is not entirely true anymore; there are many modern techniques to introduce effects of global illumination in real-time rendering engines.

1.2 Color and Images

Color is a fundamental aspect of computer graphics. Colors are used to communicate visually in several ways, for example an image full of cold colors (blue, gray, green) give us completely different sensations than an image with hot colors (red, yellow, orange). Colors also influence our attention, for example the color orange captures the attention of an observer more than other colors.

When we talk about color we have to think at two levels: a *physical level*, which concerns the physics rules involved in the creation of a color stimulus, given by the light that hits a surface and then reaches our eye, and a *subjective* or *perceptual* level, which concerns how we perceive such color stimulus. Both the physical and perceptual processes involved in how we see colors allow us to manage the color creation process. A complete treatment of colors is beyond the scope of this book. Here, we provide some basic concepts that will be useful to us in understanding how to handle colors in our graphics application.

1.2.1 The Human Visual System (HVS)

The *human visual system (HVS)* is composed of the eyes, which capture the light, the physical color stimuli, and the brain, which interprets the visual stimuli coming from them. Our eyes respond to color stimuli. By *color stimulus* we mean a radiation of energy emitted by some source, reflected by an object that hits the retina, entering into the eye through the cornea (see Figure 1.1). The retina contains the receptors that generate neural signals when stimulated by the energy of the light incident on them. Not all radiation can be perceived by our visual system. Light can be described by its wavelength; *visible light*, the only radiation that is perceived by the human visual system, has a wavelength range from 380 nm to 780 nm. Infrared and microwaves have wavelength greater than 780 nm. Ultraviolet and X-ray have wavelengths less than 380 nm.

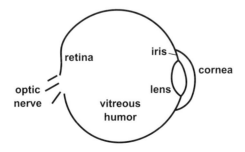

FIGURE 1.1: Structure of a human eye.

The light receptors on the retina are of two types: rods and cones. Rods are capable of detecting very small amounts of light, and produce a signal that is interpreted as monochromatic. Imagine that one is observing the stars during the night: rods are in use at that moment. Cones are less sensitive to light than rods, but they are our color receptors. During the day, light intensities are so high that rods get saturated and become nonfunctional, and that is when cone receptors come into use. There are three types of cones: They are termed long (L), medium (M) and short (S) cones depending on the part of the visible spectrum to which they are sensitive. S cones are sensitive to the lower part of the visible light wavelengths, M cones are sensitive to the middle wavelengths of the visible light and L cones are sensitive to the upper part of the visible spectrum. When the cones receive incident light, they produce signals according to their sensitivity and the intensity of the light, and send them to the brain for interpretation. The three different cones produce three different signals, which gives rise to the *trichromacy* nature of color (in this sense human beings are *trichromats*). Trichromacy is the reason why different color stimuli may be perceived as the same color. This effect is called *metamerism*. Metamerism can be distinguished into *illumination metamerism* when the same color is perceived differently when the illumination changes, and *observer metamerism* when the same color stimulus is perceived differently by two different observers.

The light receptors (rods, cones) do not have a direct specific individual connection to the brain but groups of rods and cones are interconnected to form receptive fields. Signals from these receptive fields reach the brain through the optic nerve. This interconnection influences the results of the signals produced by the light receptors. Three types of receptive fields can be classified: black-white, red-green and yellow-blue. These three receptive fields are called *opponent channels*. It is interesting to point out that the black-white channel is the signal that has the highest spatial resolution on the retina; this is the reason why human eyes are more sensitive to brightness changes of an image than to color changes. This property is used in image compression when color information is compressed in a more aggressive way than luminous information.

1.2.2   Color Space

Since color is influenced by many objective and subjective factors, it is difficult to define a unique way to represent it. We have just stated that color is the result of the trichromatic nature of the HVS, hence the most natural way to represent a color is to define it as a combination of three *primary colors*. These primary colors are typically combined following two models: *additive* and *subtractive*.

With the additive color model, the stimulus is generated by combining different stimuli of three individual colors. If we think of three lamps projecting a set of primary colors, for example, red, green and blue, on a white wall in a completely dark room, then the white wall will reflect the additive combination of the three colors towards our eye. All the colors can be obtained by properly adjusting the intensity of the red, green and blue light.

With the subtractive color model the stimulus is generated by subtracting the wavelengths from the light incident on the reflector. The most well known example of use is the cyan, magenta, yellow and key (black) model for printing. Assume that we are printing on a white paper and we have a white light. If we add no inks to the paper, then we will see the paper as white. If we put cyan ink on the paper then the paper will look cyan because the ink absorbs the red wavelengths. If we also add yellow onto it then the blue wavelengths will also be absorbed and the paper will look green. Finally, if we add the magenta ink we will have a combination of inks that will absorb all the wavelengths so the paper will look black. By modulating the amount of each primary ink or color we put on paper in theory we can express every color of the spectrum. So why the black ink? Since neither the ink nor the paper is ideal, in the real situation you would not actually obtain black, but just a very dark color and hence black ink is used instead. So in general, a certain amount of black is used to absorb *all* the wavelengths, and this amount is the minimum of the three primary components of the color. For example, if we want the color (c, m, y) the printer will combine:

$$
\begin{aligned}
K &= \min(c, m, y) && (1.1) \\
C &= c - K \\
M &= m - K \\
Y &= y - K && (1.2)
\end{aligned}
$$

Figure 1.2 (Left) shows an example of additive primaries while Figure 1.2 (Right) shows a set of subtractive primaries.

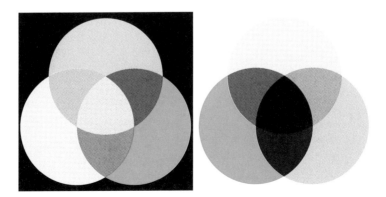

FIGURE 1.2 (SEE COLOR INSERT): (Left) RGB additive primaries. (Right) CMY subtractive primaries.

According to the field of applications and the characteristics of the primaries many color system can be defined. In the following we describe some of the most important color systems.

1.2.2.1 CIE XYZ

One of the most important color systems is the one defined by the *Commission International de l'Eclairage* (CIE) as a standard in 1931. This color system is based on the following experiment: after defining certain viewing conditions, like the distance from the target and the illumination conditions, a subject was asked to match two different colors by tuning certain parameters. The collection of responses to the monochromatic colors of a number of visible wavelengths from many subjects (a total of 17 color-normal observers) was used to define the "mean" response of a human observer, named *standard observer*, to the color stimulus. The response of the standard observer was encoded in a set of functions named *color matching functions*, shown in Figure 1.3. These functions are usually indicated as $\bar{r}(\lambda)$, $\bar{g}(\lambda)$ and $\bar{b}(\lambda)$ and

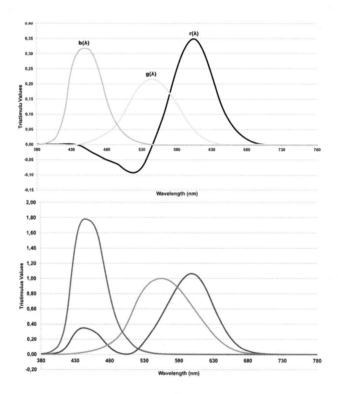

FIGURE 1.3: (Top) CIE 1931 RGB color matching function ($\bar{x}(\lambda)$, $\bar{y}(\lambda)$, $\bar{z}(\lambda)$). (Bottom) CIEXYZ color matching functions ($\bar{r}(\lambda)$, $\bar{g}(\lambda)$, $\bar{b}(\lambda)$).

enable us to define a color by integrating its power spectrum distribution $I(\lambda)$:

$$R = \int_{380}^{780} I(\lambda)\bar{r}(\lambda)d\lambda$$

$$G = \int_{380}^{780} I(\lambda)\bar{g}(\lambda)d\lambda \qquad (1.3)$$

$$B = \int_{380}^{780} I(\lambda)\bar{b}(\lambda)d\lambda$$

The plots on the bottom of Figure 1.3 shows the CIEXYZ primaries $\bar{x}(\lambda)$, $\bar{y}(\lambda)$ and $\bar{z}(\lambda)$. These matching functions are a transformed version of the CIERGB color matching functions in such a way that they are all positive functions and hence are used to simplify the design of devices for color reproduction. The equation to transform the CIERGB color space to the CIEXYZ color space is the following:

$$\begin{bmatrix} X \\ Y \\ Z \end{bmatrix} = \begin{bmatrix} 0.4887180 & 0.3106803 & 0.2006017 \\ 0.1762044 & 0.8129847 & 0.0108109 \\ 0.0000000 & 0.0102048 & 0.9897952 \end{bmatrix} \begin{bmatrix} R \\ G \\ B \end{bmatrix} \qquad (1.4)$$

The normalized version of the XYZ color coordinates can be used to define the so-called *chromaticity coordinates*:

$$x = \frac{X}{X+Y+Z} \quad y = \frac{Y}{X+Y+Z} \quad z = \frac{Z}{X+Y+Z} \qquad (1.5)$$

These coordinates do not completely specify a color since they always sum to one, and hence are specified by only two coordinates, which means a two-dimensional representation. Typically, the Y is added together with x and y to fully define trichromatic color space called xyY. The chromaticity coordinates x and y just mentioned are usually employed to visualize a representation of the colors as in the *chromaticities diagram* shown in Figure 1.4 (on the left). Note that even the ink used in professional printing is not capable of reproducing all the colors of the chromaticities diagram.

1.2.2.2   Device-Dependent and Device-Independent Color Space

So far we talked about *device-independent* color space, that is, color spaces that are able to represent every color and that do not take into account the particular way to physically produce it. In the real world, the color devices, such as printers and monitors, have to deal with the fact that not all the colors are physically reproducible by one system. The *gamut* is the set of colors that a particular device can output. Typically, the color gamut is depicted on the chromaticities diagram just described. Figure 1.4 (on the right) shows an example of the gamut of commonly used RGB color spaces, such as the Adobe RGB, the sRGB system (defined by HP and Microsoft) and the NTSC RGB color system. Pay attention so as not to confuse these RGB

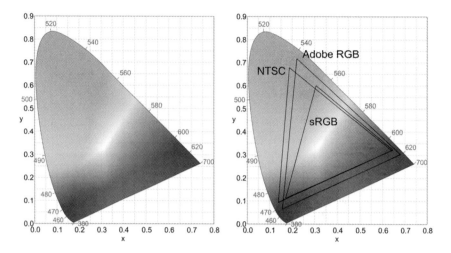

FIGURE 1.4 (SEE COLOR INSERT): (Left) Chromaticities diagram. (Right) Gamut of different RGB color systems.

color spaces with the CIERGB color matching functions described in the previous section. CIERGB is a system of color matching functions that can represent any existing colors while a given RGB color space is a color system that uses RGB additive primaries combined in some way to physically reproduce a certain color. Depending on the particular RGB system, different colors can be reproduced according to its gamut. See color insert for the color version.

1.2.2.3   HSL and HSV

Two color spaces often used in many graphics applications are the *HSL* and the *HSV*. These spaces attempt to use color coordinates that describe colors more intuitively. With HSL a color is described in terms of *hue* (H), *saturation* (S) and *lightness* (L), whereas L is replaced by *value* (V) for the HSV color system. The hue indicates the base chroma of the color to define, the lightness (which is a physical property of the color) is proportional to the brightness of the color (that is how "whitish" we perceive it), and the saturation is somewhat related to the "pureness" of the color to represent.

To better understand what lightness and saturation are, suppose you are a painter and, from your palette, you have chosen a certain hue, say cyan. Then you can choose a shade of gray for the canvas, from black to white, and that is the lightness of the final color. Then you put the color as small dots on the canvas, and the density of the dots gives you the saturation.

A geometric representation of these two spaces is shown in Figure 1.5. As can be seen, the colors of HSL can be naturally mapped on a prism while HSV is mapped on a cone.

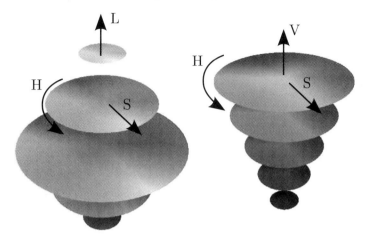

FIGURE 1.5 (SEE COLOR INSERT): HSL and HSV color space.

As we can covert coordinates between CIEXYZ and CIERGB color space, it is also possible to convert between RGB and HSL/HSV color space. As an example, we show here how to convert the sRGB color space to the HSL model:

$$
H = \begin{cases} \text{undefined} & \text{if } \Delta = 0 \\ 60° \left(\frac{G-B}{\Delta} \right) & \text{if } M = R \\ 60° \left(\frac{B-R}{\Delta} \right) + 120° & \text{if } M = G \\ 60° \left(\frac{R-G}{\Delta} \right) + 240° & \text{if } M = B \end{cases} \tag{1.6}
$$

$$
L = \frac{M+m}{2} \tag{1.7}
$$

$$
S = \begin{cases} 0 & \text{if } \Delta = 0 \\ \frac{\Delta}{1-|2L-1|} & \text{otherwise} \end{cases} \tag{1.8}
$$

where $M = \max\{R, G, B\}$, $m = \min\{R, G, B\}$ and $\Delta = M - m$. The degrees in the H formula come from the definition of hue on a hexagonal shape (more details about this can be found here [37]). The HSV conversion is close to the HSL one; the hue is calculated in the same way, while the saturation and the lightness are defined in a slightly different way:

$$
S = \begin{cases} 0 & \text{if } \Delta = 0 \\ \frac{\Delta}{V} & \text{otherwise} \end{cases} \tag{1.9}
$$

$$
V = M \tag{1.10}
$$

1.2.2.4   CIELab

CIELab is another color space defined by the CIE in 1976, with very interesting characteristics. The color coordinates of such systems are usually indicated with L^*, a^* and b^*. L^* stands for lightness and a^* and b^* identify the chromaticity of the color. The peculiarity of this color space is that the distance between colors computed as the Euclidean distance:

$$\Delta Lab = \sqrt{(L_1^* - L_2^*)^2 + (a_1^* - a_2^*)^2 + (b_1^* - b_2^*)^2} \qquad (1.11)$$

is correlated very well with human perception. In other words, while the distance between two colors in other color spaces cannot be perceived proportionally (for example, distant colors can be perceived as similar colors), in the CIELab color space, near colors are perceived as similar colors and distant colors are perceived as different colors.

The equations to convert a color in CIEXYZ color space to a color in CIELab color space are:

$$
\begin{aligned}
L^* &= 116\, f(X/X_n) - 16 \\
a^* &= 500\, f(X/X_n) - f(Y/Y_n) \\
b^* &= 200\, f(Y/Y_n) - f(Z/Z_n)
\end{aligned}
\qquad (1.12)
$$

where X_n, Y_n, Z_n are normalization factors dependent on the *illuminant* (see next section) and $f(.)$ is the following function:

$$
f(x) = \begin{cases} x^{1/3} & \text{if } x > 0.008856 \\ 7.787037x + 0.137931 & \text{otherwise} \end{cases}
\qquad (1.13)
$$

We can see that this formulation is quite complex, reflecting the complex matching between the perception of the stimulus and the color coordinates expressed in the CIEXYZ system.

1.2.3   Illuminant

In the previous section we have seen that the conversion between CIEXYZ and CIELab depends on the particular illuminant assumed. This is always true when we are talking about color conversion between different color spaces.

The different lighting conditions are standardized by the CIE by publishing the spectrum of the light source assumed. These standard lighting conditions are known as *standard illuminants*. For example, Illuminant A corresponds to an average incandescent light, Illuminant B corresponds to the direct sunlight, and so on. The color tristimulus values associated with an illuminant are called *white point*, that is, the chromaticity coordinates of how a white object appears under this light source. For example, the conversion (1.4) between CIERGB and CIEXYZ is defined such that the white point of the CIERGB is $x = y = z = 1/3$ (Illuminant E, equal energy illuminant).

This is the reason why color conversion between different color spaces needs to take into account the illuminant assumed in their definition. It is also possible to convert between different illuminants. For an extensive list of formulas to convert between different color spaces under different illumination conditions, you can take a look at the excellent Web site of Bruce Lindbloom on *http://www.brucelindbloom.com/*, full of useful information, color spaces and related conversions.

1.2.4 Gamma

Concerning the display of colors, once you have chosen a color system to represent the colors, the values of the primaries have to be converted to electrical signals according to the specific display characteristics in order to reproduce the color.

In a CRT monitor, typically, the RGB intensity of the phosphors is a nonlinear function of the voltage applied. More precisely, the power law for a CRT monitor is the applied voltage raised to 2.5. More generally,

$$I = V^\gamma \tag{1.14}$$

where V is the voltage in Volts and I is the light intensity. This equation is also valid for other type of displays. The numerical value of the exponent is known as *gamma*.

This concept is important, because this nonlinearity must be taken into account when we want our display to reproduce a certain color with high fidelity; this is what is intended in *gamma correction*.

1.2.5 Image Representation

Images are fundamental to computer graphics systems, both from a hardware and a software point of view. For this reason it is particularly important to understand how an image is represented, which types of images exist, how the graphics hardware handles them, and so on. Here, we provide some basic knowledge about images and their representation. Basically, two ways to define a 2D image exist: *vector image* and *raster image*.

1.2.5.1 Vector Images

Vector graphics is a way of representing images as a set of basic drawing primitives. Hence, a *vector image* is an image defined by composing a set of points, lines, curves, rectangles, stars and other shapes. Figure 1.6 shows a simple example of how the drawing of number 9 could be obtained by combining a circle and a segment.

The most well-known formats for vector graphics are the SVG and the PS format.

SVG stands for *scalable vector graphics* and it is a family of specifications of an XML-based file format that also supports dynamic content, that is, animated vector graphics. The SVG specification was developed by the World Wide Web Consortium (W3C), which manages many standards for the Web. In fact, all major modern Web browsers, including Mozilla Firefox, Internet Explorer, Google Chrome, Opera and Safari, have at least some degree of direct support and rendering of SVG markup. SVG supports several primitives

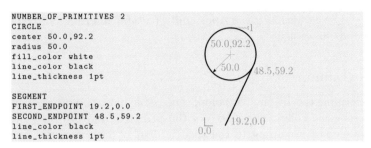

```
NUMBER_OF_PRIMITIVES 2
CIRCLE
center 50.0,92.2
radius 50.0
fill_color white
line_color black
line_thickness 1pt

SEGMENT
FIRST_ENDPOINT 19.2,0.0
SECOND_ENDPOINT 48.5,59.2
line_color black
line_thickness 1pt
```

FIGURE 1.6: Example of specification of a vector image (left) and the corresponding drawing (right).

for the definition of the image, for example paths (as curved or straight lines), basic shapes (as open or closed polylines, rectangles, circles and ellipses), text encoded in unicode, colors, different gradients/pattern to fill shapes, and so on.

PS stands for *PostScript* and it is a programming language for printing illustrations and text. It was originally defined by John Warnock and Charles Geschke in 1982. In 1984 Adobe released the first laser printer driven by the first version of PostScript language and nowadays Adobe PostScript 3 is the de-facto worldwide standard for printing and imaging systems. Since it has been designed to handle the high quality printing of pages it is more than a language to define vector graphics; for example, it allows us to control the ink used to generate the drawing.

1.2.5.2   Raster Images

A *raster image* is, for example, the one you see on the screen of your PC and it is made by a rectangular arrangement of regularly placed small colored tiles, named *pixels* (*pic*ture *el*ements). You can make your own raster image by assembling together some squared Lego® pieces of uniform color and size to form a certain picture, as shown in Figure 1.7. The *size in pixels* of an image is the number of pixels along its width and height. In the Lego example it is 16×10. The size in pixels of an image is often used interchangeably with its *pixel resolution*, or just *resolution*, but there is a quite important difference to underline. Resolution deals with how small are the details an image can represent and it is commonly quantified to how *close* two lines can be on the image without appearing as a single line. The unit of measure of resolution is *pixels per inch*, that is, how many pixels are in one inch. In the example of Figure 1.7 the resolution is $16/3.2 = 5px/in$.

This means that the same image may have different resolutions depending on which media is used to reproduce it. For example, if the size in pixels of both your mobile phone and your TV is 1280×800 it does not mean they have the same resolution because the mobile has the same number of pixels in a much smaller space. However, sometimes the size in pixels is used to indicate

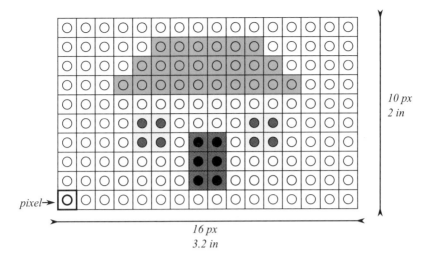

10 px
2 in

pixel→

16 px
3.2 in

FIGURE 1.7: The image of a house assembled using Lego® pieces.

the resolution. This is because media are made to be observed at a certain distance. The mobile phone is made to be seen from 20 cm away, while the TV screen is usually seen at a couple of meters. In other words, they occupy a similar portion of our field of view and this is the reason why it makes sense just to use the number of pixels to indicate the resolution.

A pixel can be defined by a scalar or a vector of values, depending on the nature of the image. For example, in a *grayscale image*, each pixel is a scalar value representing the brightness of the image in that position (see Figure 1.8). In a color image, instead, each element is represented by a vector of multiple

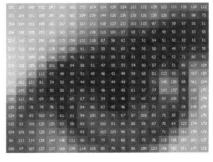

FIGURE 1.8: A grayscale image. (Left) The whole picture with a highlighted area whose detail representation (Right) is shown as a matrix of values.

FIGURE 1.9: (Left) Original image with opaque background. (Middle) Background color made transparent by setting alpha to zero (transparency is indicated by the dark gray-light gray squares pattern). (Right) A composition of the transparent image with an image of a brick wall.

scalar components (typically three) that identifies the color of that image's location.

The length of the vector used to define a pixel defines the number of *image channels* of the image. A color image represented by the RGB color space has three channels; the red channel, the green channel and the blue channel. This is the most common representation of a *color image*. An image can have more than three components; additional components are used to represent additional information, or for certain types of images like multi-spectral images where the color representation requires more than three values to represent multiple wavelength bands. One of the main uses of four-channel images is to handle *transparency*. The transparency channel is usually called *alpha channel*. See Figure 1.9 for an example of an image with a transparent background.

In the comparison of raster images with vector images, the resolution plays an important role. The vector images may be considered to have infinite resolution. In fact, a vector image can be enlarged simply by applying a scale factor to it, without compromising the quality of what it depicts. For example, it is possible to make a print of huge size without compromising its final reproduction quality. Instead, the quality of a raster image depends heavily on its resolution: as shown in Figure 1.10, a high resolution is required to draw smooth curves well, which is natural for a vector image. Additionally, if the resolution is insufficient, the pixels become visible (again see Figure 1.10). This visual effect is called *pixellation*. On the other hand, a vector image has severe limitations to describe a complex image like a natural scene. In this and similar cases, too many primitives of very small granularity are required for a good representation and hence a raster image is a more natural representation of this type of image. This is the reason why vector images are usually employed to design logos, trademarks, stylized drawings, diagrams, and other similar things, and not for natural images or images with rich visual content.

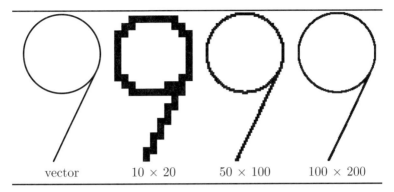

FIGURE 1.10: Vector vs raster images. (Left) A circle and a line assembled to form a "9." (From Left to Right) The corresponding raster images at increased resolution.

1.3 Algorithms to Create a Raster Image from a 3D Scene

When we talk about *rendering algorithm* we mean the method we use to display a 3D scene on the screen. In this section we want to show the two basic *rendering paradigms* that are usually employed to generate synthetic images.

1.3.1 Ray Tracing

As we will see in Chapter 6, we see things because light sources emit *photons*: elementary particles of light travel into space, that hit surfaces, change direction, and finally a part of them reaches our eyes. The color we see depends on the properties of the light sources and the materials.

Suppose we simulate this process and compute all the light-matter interactions to trace the path of each single photon until it possibly reaches our eye. It is obvious that most of them will not reach our eyes at all, they will simply get lost in space. So, why bother doing all the costly computation when we are actually interested only in the photons that follow the paths to our eyes? The idea behind *ray tracing* is to do the reverse process, that is, start from the eye and trace rays into the scene, computing how they interact with the matter to see which ones finally reach a light source. If a ray reaches the light source, it means that a photon will traverse the reverse path from the light to the eye. The idea of ray tracing is illustrated in Figure 1.11.

In its basic form ray tracing can be described by the following algorithm (Listing 1.1):

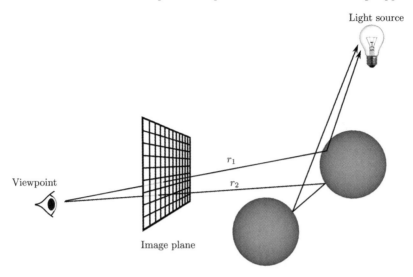

FIGURE 1.11: A schematic concept of ray tracing algorithm. Rays are shot from the eye through the image plane and intersections with the scene are found. Each time a ray collides with a surface it bounces off the surface and may reach a light source (ray r_1 after one bounce, ray r_2 after two bounces).

```
For each pixel of the image:
  1. Construct a ray from the viewpoint through the pixel
  2. For each object in the scene
    2.1. Find its intersection with the ray
  3. Keep the closest of the intersection points
  4. Compute the color at this closest point
```
LISTING 1.1: Basic ray tracing.

The color of the point is computed by taking into account the properties of the material and the characteristics of the light sources. We learn more about this in Chapter 6. Note that it is not required, in this implementation, that the ray must reach a light source. By omitting Step 4 from the above algorithm, what we produce is a *visibility map* of the objects of the scene, that is, a map where for each pixel we have the portion of the 3D scene visible from it. In this case, the algorithm is called *ray casting* and, in practice, it becomes a visibility technique and not a rendering technique, since we simply stop at the first hit of the ray.

The more complete version (see Listing 1.2) is what is normally intended as the *classic ray tracing* algorithm:

```
For each pixel of the image:
  1. Construct a ray from the viewpoint through the pixel
  2. Repeat until TerminationCondition
    2.1. For each object in the scene
      2.1.1. Find its intersection with the ray
    2.2. Keep the closest of the intersection points
    2.3. Compute the change of direction of the ray
  3. Compute the color by taking into account the path of the ↵
     ray
```

LISTING 1.2: Classic ray tracing.

The TerminationCondition at Step 2 may include a number of criteria. If we do not have a time limit it could be simply if the ray hits an emitter or exits the scene. Since we cannot run the algorithm forever we need to add termination conditions to decide to drop the quest for an emitter, putting a limit on the number of iterations (that is, the number of time a ray bounces off a surface), or the distance traveled by the ray, or the time spent on computation for the ray. When the tracing is over, that is, the termination condition is reached, we assign a color to the pixel on the base of the surfaces hit by the ray.

The change of direction computed in Step 2.3 depends on the type of material. The basic case is where the surface is considered perfectly *specular* like an ideal mirror and light is *specularly reflected*. When we want to consider more generic materials, we should consider that when a light ray hits a surface it may be *refracted*, which means that the light ray enters the object, as happens for glass, marble, water or skin; or *diffuses*, that is, it is reflected uniformly in many directions. So, the light ray that reaches our eye is the contribution of all these effects: it is the sum of photons emitted by several emitters that have traveled the scene and have changed their direction many times. The consequence of the algorithm is that each time a ray hits the surface one or more rays may be generated depending on the nature of the material. In this case one ray can generate several paths.

We will learn more details about reflection and refraction, and in general about light–matter interaction in the Lighting and Shading chapter (Chapter 6), and more details about classic ray tracing and path tracing in the Global Illumination chapter (Chapter 11).

The cost of ray tracing can be estimated as follows: for each ray we need to test its intersection with all the m objects, at most for k bounces (where k is the maximum number of bounces allowed) and for each of the n_r rays shot. In general, given n_p as the total number of pixels of the screen, $n_r \geq n_p$ because we want *at least* one ray per pixel. So we have:

$$cost(ray\ tracing) = n_p\ k\ \sum_{i=0}^{m} Int(o_i) \qquad (1.15)$$

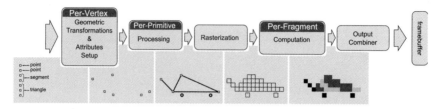

FIGURE 1.12: Logical scheme of the rasterization-based pipeline.

where $Int(o_i)$ is the cost of testing the intersection of a ray with the object o_i. However, it is possible to adopt acceleration data structures that mostly reduce $\sum_{i=0}^{m} Int(o_i)$ to $O(log(m))$ operations.

1.3.2   Rasterization-Based Pipeline

The *rasterization-based* rendering pipeline is the most widely used method to render images at an interactive rate and it is ubiquitously used on all the graphics boards, although the implementations change among different hardware, developers and over time. Here, we describe a logical abstract description of the rendering pipeline that we will refer to through the rest of the book and which is illustrated in Figure 1.12.

The figure shows the sequence of operations that turns the specification of a set of geometric primitives into an image on the screen. We will use a modified version of this scheme throughout the book when necessary for specifying further details. You may find many similar schemes in other texts or on the Web, often specialized to some specific API and/or hardware. We will see one of these in depth in the next chapter.

The *input* to the rendering pipeline is a series of geometric primitives: *points, segments* (which are called *lines* in all the APIs), *triangles* and *polygons*.

All the geometric primitives are defined by vertices (one for the point, two for the segment and so on). When we specify a *vertex*, we will usually provide its coordinates, but there are many other attributes that we may want to use. For example we may associate a color value to the vertex, or a vector indicating the speed, or in general any value that makes sense for our application. The first stage of the pipeline, *per-vertex transformations and attributes setup*, processes all the vertices and transforms their values in a user-specified way. Usually in this stage we decide from where to look at our scene by applying linear transformations (rotations, translations and scaling), but we can also displace all the vertices along a direction by a time dependent value, thus making the car in the example to move.

The next stage is the *primitive processing*, which takes the transformed vertices and the primitive specified by the user and outputs points, segments and triangles to the next stage. The role of this stage may seem minor, because it looks just like it is passing the user input to the next stage. In older schemes of the rasterization-based pipeline you may actually find it collapsed with the *rasterization* stage and/or under the name of *primitive assembly*. Nowadays, this stage not only passes the input to the rasterization stage, but it may also create new primitives from the given input; for example it may take one triangle and output many triangles obtained by subdividing the original one.

The *rasterization* stage converts points, lines and triangles to their raster representation and interpolates the value of the vertex attributes of the primitive being rasterized. The rasterization stage marks the passage from a world made by points, lines and polygons in 3D space to a 2D world made of pixels. However, while a pixel is defined by its coordinates in the image (or in the screen) and its color, the pixels produced by the rasterization may also contain a number of interpolated values other than the color. These "more informative" pixels are called *fragments* and are the input to the next stage, the *per-fragment computation*. Each fragment is processed by the per-fragment computation stage that calculates the final values of the fragment's attributes. Finally, the last stage of the pipeline determines how each fragment is combined with the current value stored in the *framebuffer*, that is, the data buffer that stores the image during its formation, to determine the color of the corresponding pixel. This combination can be a blending of the two colors, the choice of one over the other or simply the elimination of the fragment.

The cost for the rasterization pipeline is given by processing (that is, transforming) all the vertices n_v and rasterizing all the geometric primitives:

$$cost(rasterization) = K_{tr} \; n_v \; + \sum_{i=0}^{m} Ras(p_i) \qquad (1.16)$$

where K_{tr} is the cost of transforming one vertex and $Ras(p_i)$ is the cost of rasterizing a primitive.

1.3.3   Ray Tracing vs Rasterization-Based Pipeline

Which is the better rendering paradigm, ray tracing or rasterization, is a long-running debate that will not end with this section. Here, we want only to highlight advantages and disadvantages of both paradigms.

1.3.3.1   Ray Tracing Is Better

Ray tracing is designed to consider global effects of the illumination, because it follows the bounces of each ray reaching the eye. So, while transparencies, shadows and refractions are "naturally" included in ray tracing, each of them requires an amount of tricks to be done with rasterization, and often the combination of several global effects is hard to achieve. Note that the version of a ray tracer that produces the same result as the rasterization is obtained by limiting the number of bounces to 1, that is, if we do only ray casting.

With ray tracing we may use any kind of surface representation, provided that we are able to test the intersection with a ray. With the rasterization pipeline, every surface is ultimately discretized with a number of geometric primitives and discretization brings approximation. In a practical simple example we may consider a sphere. With ray tracing we have a precise intersection (up to the numerical precision of machine finite arithmetic) of the view ray with an analytic description of the sphere, with the rasterization the sphere approximated with a number of polygons.

Ray tracing is simple to implement, although hard to make efficient, while even the most basic rasterization pipeline requires several algorithms to be implemented.

1.3.3.2   Rasterization Is Better

Although it is the common assumption, it would be unfair to state that rasterization is faster than ray tracing. However, rasterization has a linear and more predictable rendering time because each polygon is processed in the same way and independently of the others. At most, the rasterization time depends on how big each polygon is on screen, but modern hardware is highly parallel and optimized for this task. Ray tracing may be implemented so that the time is logarithmic with the number of primitives (so even less than linear) but we need to know all the elements of the scene in advance in order to build acceleration data structures that allow us to compute ray-primitive intersection in a fast manner. This also means that if the scene is *dynamic*, that is, if the elements in the scene move, these data structures have to be updated.

Rasterization naturally handles *antialiasing*. This is a concept that we will see in detail in Section 5.3.3, but we can give a basic idea by saying that oblique lines will look *jagged* on the screen since pixels discretize it. With rasterization, this problem can be leveraged by modulating the color of the pixels adjacent to the line segments. In ray tracing, instead, we have to shoot multiple rays for a single pixel to cope with aliasing.

Historically the graphics hardware has been developed for the rasterization pipeline, because of its linearity and streamable nature. However, it should be said that current graphics hardware is way more general than rasterization-friendly graphics accelerators. They may be considered more like highly parallel, very fast processors with some limitations on memory access and management, therefore also amenable for a ray tracer implementation.

Chapter 2

The First Steps

In this chapter we deal with the first practical steps that will accompany us for the rest of the book.

First we will show how to set up our first working rendering inside an HTML page by using *WebGL*. More precisely, we will draw a triangle. We advise you that at first it would look like you need to learn an awful lot of information for such a simple task as drawing a triangle, but what we will do in this simple example is the same as what we would do for a huge project. Simply put, you need to learn to drive a car for going 10 miles as well as 100 miles.

Then we will introduce the *EnvyMyCar* (NVMC) framework that we will use for the rest of this book for putting into use the theory we will learn along the way. Briefly, NVMC is a simple car racing game where the gamer controls a car moving on a track. What makes NVMC different from a classic video game is that there is no graphics *at all*, because we are in charge to develop it. Given a complete description of the scene (where is the car, how is it oriented, what is its shape, how is the track made, etc.) we will learn, here and during the rest of the book, how to draw the elements and the effects we need to obtain, at the end, a visually pleasant car racing game.

2.1 The Application Programming Interface

The *rasterization-based* pipeline is one of several possible graphics architectures. As we have seen in Section 1.3.2, the *logical* pipeline is composed of a series of stages, through which data coming from the application is manipulated to obtain a raster image. The logical pipeline will be our desk bench to explain the theory behind graphics structures and techniques.

As it happens for many computer science fields, a particular technology is characterized by having a common substructure. Over this substructure, several interaction *protocols* are defined and, most of the time, standardized. Whoever wants to *comply* with these protocols must respect them. In our context, the technology we are dealing with is the one implemented by computer graphics systems, which may include software components or hardware chips, and the protocol is the *Application Programming Interface*, or API. The API defines the syntax of constant values, data structures and functions (e.g., symbolic names and function signatures), and, more importantly, their semantics (e.g., what they mean and what they do). The graphics API will be our tool to interact with the graphics system and write computer graphics applications.

To clarify these concepts, let us make an example: the car. The Authority specifies how cars have to be made and how they must behave. A car must have wheels, a steering wheel, pedals, levers, and so on. It also specifies what happens if a certain pedal is pushed (e.g., accelerator or brake), or a certain lever is moved (e.g., indicators). A car manufacturer has to follow these instructions to build a vehicle that may be approved by the Authority. Knowing the specifications, a car driver acts on pedals and levers in a certain way to reach his destination. In this example, the Authority *defines* the car specifications, the manufacturer *implements* them, and the driver *uses* them.

For the time being, the most used graphics APIs for real–time rendering are DirectX [42], and OpenGL [17]. Considering OpenGL in the car example, the Authority is the Khronos Groups [19], the manufacturers are NVidia, ATI, or Intel, and we are the drivers.

The original OpenGL API targeted desktops to supercomputers. Given its adoption in academic and industrial contexts, derivatives have been proposed, like OpenGL|SC for safety-critical applications, and OpenGL|ES for embedded systems with lower capabilities with respect to home PCs. The API specifications are language agnostic (that is, they can be implemented in any modern programming language), but are mostly designed to be executed in an unrestricted environment (that is, native executable binary code). This means that using OpenGL in a strictly controlled platform, such as the JavaScript virtual machine of modern Web browsers, is not possible without imposing some additional restrictions.

The OpenGL specifications are defined by the Khronos Group, a *third party* implements the specifications and provides the API, and a graphics programmer uses it to create graphics applications or libraries. From a programmer's point of view, it is not important how the third party actually implements the API (e.g., in the car example, whether the manufacturer uses an oil or an electric engine), as long as it strictly follows the specifications. This means that OpenGL implementations can be both a pure software library, or a system driver that communicates with a hardware device (e.g., a graphics accelerator).

To allow web pages to take advantage of the host system graphics capabilities, the Khronos Group standardized the WebGL graphics API [18]. WebGL is a graphics API written to the OpenGL|ES 2.0 specifications that allows accessing the graphics system, that is, the hardware graphics chip, from within standard HTML pages, with some minor restrictions introduced to address security issues.

As concepts are being developed, we want a comfortable platform that lets us practice on what we learn with as few burdens as possible. For this reason, we will use the WebGL for our code examples. By using the HTML, JavaScript, and WebGL standard technologies we do not have to install and use ad-hoc programming tools. We just need a Web browser that supports WebGL and a text editor, and we will be able to test, run and deploy the code we write on a wide range of devices, from powerful personal computers to smartphones.

2.2   The WebGL Rasterization-Based Pipeline

The WebGL pipeline is the concrete graphics pipeline that we will use throughout this book. Before going into our first rendering example, we must have a big picture of how it works. Figure 2.1 depicts the stages that compose the WebGL pipeline, and which are the entities they involve. The application communicates with the graphics system (e.g., the graphics hardware or the software library) with the WebGL API. When drawing commands are issued, data starts to flow from graphics memory and gets consumed or transformed by each pipeline stage, which we will discuss in the following:

Vertex Puller (VP). The purpose of the vertex puller stage is simply to fetch data associated to vertex attributes from graphics memory, pack them and pass them down to the next stage (the *vertex shader*). The vertex puller represents the first stage of the geometry pipeline, and can manage a maximum fixed number of vertex attributes that depends on the WebGL implementation. Each attribute is identified by an *attribute index*, and only the attributes needed by the vertex shader are actually fetched. For each attribute, the vertex puller must be instructed about where and how the associated data has to be fetched from graphics memory. Once all attributes are fetched, all together they represent a raw data bundle, namely the pipeline *input vertex*. After passing the vertex to the next stage, the process starts again and continues until all required vertices have been assembled and forwarded. For example, we could configure the vertex puller such that the data associated to attribute 0 is a constant four-dimensional value, and the data of attribute 3 is a two-dimensional value that must be fetched from graphics memory, starting at a particular address.

Vertex Shader (VS). The attributes of the input vertex assembled by the vertex puller arrive at the vertex shader, where they will be used to produce new attributes forming the *transformed vertex*. This process is carried out by a *user-defined* procedure, written in the *OpenGL Shading Language* (GLSL). This procedure is referred to as a vertex shader, just

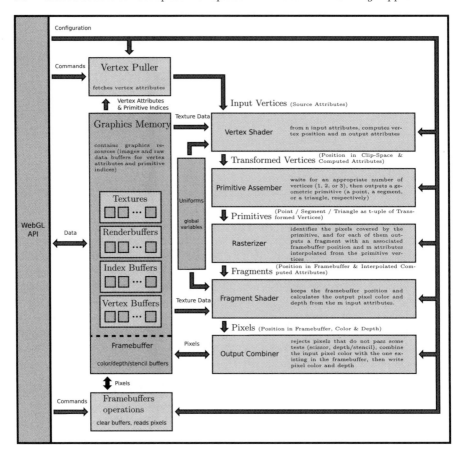

FIGURE 2.1: The WebGL pipeline.

like the pipeline stage name. A vertex shader takes as input n general attributes, coming from the VP, and gives as output m general attributes, plus a special one, namely the vertex position. The resulting transformed vertex is passed to the next stage (primitive assembler). For example, to visualize the temperature of the Earth's surface, a vertex shader could receive in input three scalar attributes, representing a temperature, a latitude and a longitude, and output two 3D attributes, representing an RGB color and a position in space.

Primitive Assembler (PA). The WebGL rasterization pipeline can only draw three basic geometric primitives: points, line segments, and triangles. The primitive assembler, as the name suggests, is in charge of collecting the adequate number of vertices coming from the VS, assembling them in a t-uple, and passing it to the next stage (the rasterizer). The number of vertices (t) depends on the primitive being drawn: 1 for points, 2 for line segments, and 3 for triangles. When an API draw command is issued, we specify which is the primitive that we want the pipeline to draw, and thus configure the primitive assembler.

Rasterizer (RS). The rasterizer stage receives as input a primitive consisting of t transformed vertices, and calculates which are the pixels it covers. It uses a special vertex attribute that represents the vertex position to identify the covered region, then, for each pixel, it interpolates the m attributes of each vertex and creates a packet, called *fragment*, containing the associated pixel position and the m interpolated values. Each assembled fragment is then sent to the next stage (the *Fragment Shader*). For example, if we draw a segment whose vertices have an associated color attribute, e.g., one red and one green, the rasterizer will generate several fragments that, altogether, resemble a line: fragments near the first vertex will have associated a reddish color that becomes yellow at the segment midpoint, and then goes to green while approaching the second vertex.

Fragment Shader (FS). Similarly to the vertex shader, the fragment shader runs a user-defined GLSL procedure that receives as input a fragment with a *read-only* position F_{xy} and m attributes, and uses them to compute the color of the output pixel at location F_{xy}. For example, given two input attributes representing a color and a darkening factor, the output color could be the darkened negative of the input color.

Output Combiner (OC). The last stage of the geometry pipeline is the output combiner. Before writing to the framebuffer the pixels coming out from the fragment shader, the output combiner executes a series of configurable tests that can depend both on the incoming pixel data, and the data already present in the framebuffer at the same pixel location. For example, an incoming pixel could be *discarded* (e.g., not written) if it is not visible. Moreover, after the tests have been performed, the actual color written can be further modified by *blending* the incoming value with the existing one at the same location.

Framebuffer Operations (FO). A special component of the rendering architecture is dedicated to directly access the framebuffer. The framebuffer operations component is not part of the geometry pipeline, and it is used to clear the framebuffer with a particular color, and to read back the framebuffer content (e.g., its pixels).

All the stages of the WebGL pipeline can be configured by using the corresponding API functions. Moreover, the VS and FS stages are programmable, e.g., we write programs that they will execute on their inputs. For this reason, such a system is often referred to as a *programmable pipeline*, in contrast to a *fixed-function pipeline* that does not allow the execution of custom code.

2.3   Programming the Rendering Pipeline: Your First Rendering

Throughout this book we will use simple HTML pages as containers for showing our computer-generated images and for handling general user interface controls. Moreover, we will use JavaScript as our programming language because it is both the primary scripting language to be natively integrated in HTML, and it is the language against which the WebGL specification is written. To this extent, the reader is required to have a well-founded knowledge in general programming, and basic notions of HTML and JavaScript.

In this first practical exercise we will write a very simple HTML page that displays the most basic polygonal primitive, a triangle, using JavaScript and WebGL. We subdivide our goal into the following main steps:

1. define the HTML page that will display our drawing

2. initialize WebGL

3. define *what* to draw

4. define *how* to draw

5. perform the actual drawing

Steps 3 and 4 do not have inter-dependencies, so their order can be exchanged. Even if this is the first rendering example, it will expose some of the fundamental concepts used throughout this book and that will be expanded as new theoretical knowledge is acquired. In the following we will implement the above steps in a top-down fashion, meaning that we will refine our code as steps are examined.

Step 1: The HTML Page
The first thing to do is to define the HTML page that we will use to display our rendering:

```
1   <html>
2     <head>
3       <script type="text/javascript">
4         // ... draw code here ...
5       </script>
6     </head>
7     <body>
8       <canvas
9         id     = "OUTPUT-CANVAS"
10        width  = "500px"
11        height = "500px"
12        style  = "border: 1px solid black"
13      ></canvas>
14    </body>
15  </html>
```

LISTING 2.1: HTML page for running the client.

As just stated we assume that the reader is familiar with basic HTML. In brief, the html root tag (lines 1 to 15) encapsulates the whole page; it is the container of two basic sections, the head section (lines 2 to 6) that contains metadata and scripts, and the body section (lines 7 to 14) that contains the elements shown to the user. A fundamental element of the page is the canvas tag on lines 8 to 13. Introduced in the HTML5 standard, the HTMLCanvasElement represents, as its name suggests, a (rectangular) region of the page that can be used as the target for drawing commands. Like a painter who uses brushes and colors to draw on his or her canvas, we will use WebGL through JavaScript to set the color of the pixels inside our output region. In the HTML code, we also define the id, width and height attributes to set, respectively, the canvas identifier, width and height. With the style attribute we also set up a 1-pixel-wide black border to help us visualize the rectangular region occupied by the canvas inside the page. From now on, our job is to write the JavaScript code inside the script tag, using the code in Listing 2.1 as our base skeleton.

```
1   // <script type="text/javascript">
2   // global variables
3   // ...
4
5   function setupWebGL     () { /* ... */}
6   function setupWhatToDraw () { /* ... */}
7   function setupHowToDraw  () { /* ... */}
8   function draw            () { /* ... */}
9
10  function helloDraw() {
11    setupWebGL();
12    setupWhatToDraw();
13    setupHowToDraw();
14    draw();
15  }
16
17  window.onload = helloDraw;
18  // </script>
```

LISTING 2.2: Skeleton code.

In this example it is important that the code we write will not be executed before the page loading has completed. Otherwise, we would not be able to access the canvas with document.getElementById() simply because the canvas tag has not been parsed yet and thus could not be queried. For this reason we must be notified by the browser whenever the page is ready; by exploiting the native and widely pervasive use of object events in a Web environment, we accomplish our task by simply registering the helloDraw function as the page load event handler, as shown on line 17 in Listing 2.2.

Step 2: Initialize WebGL

As preparatory knowledge, we need to understand how to interact with the WebGL API. In OpenGL and all its derivatives, the graphics pipeline works as a *state machine*: the outcome of every operation (in our case, every API function call) is determined by the internal state of the *machine*. The actual OpenGL machine state is referred to as the *rendering context*, or simply *context*. To help handle this concept more practically, we can think of a context as a car and its state as the state of the car, that is, its position, velocity acceleration, the rotation of the steering wheel, the position of the pedals. The effect of the actions we perform depends on the state: for example the effect we obtain rotating the steering wheel is different if the car is moving or not.

When using OpenGL or OpenGL|ES, once a context is created and activated, it becomes *syntactically hidden* to the API: this means that every function call acts implicitly on the currently active context, which thus needs not to be passed as argument in any of them. WebGL makes the context explicitly available to the programmer, encapsulating it in a JavaScript object with a specific interface, the WebGLRenderingContext: using WebGL thus means creating a context object and then interacting with it by calling its methods.

Every WebGLRenderingContext object is tied to an HTMLCanvasElement that it will use as the output of its rendering commands. The creation of a context is accomplished by requesting it to the canvas, as shown in Listing 2.3.

```
1  // global variables
2  var gl = null; // the rendering context
3
4  function setupWebGL() {
5    var canvas = document.getElementById("OUTPUT-CANVAS");
6    gl = canvas.getContext("webgl");
7  }
```

LISTING 2.3: Setting up WebGl.

The first thing to do is to obtain a reference to the HTMLCanvasElement object: this is done on line 5, where we ask the global document object to retrieve an element whose identifier (its *id*) is OUTPUT-CANVAS, using the method getElementById. As you can argue, the canvas variable is now referencing the canvas element on line 8 in Listing 2.1. Usually, the canvas will provide the rendering context with a framebuffer that contains a color buffer consisting of four 8-bit channels, namely RGBA, plus a depth buffer whose precision would be of 16 to 24 bytes, depending on the host device. It is important to say that the alpha channel of the color buffer will be used by the browser as a *transparency factor*, meaning that the colors written when using WebGL will be *overlaid* on the page in compliance with the HTML specifications.

Now we are ready to create a WebGLRenderingContext. The method get-Context of the canvas object, invoked with the string webgl as its single argument, creates and returns the WebGL context that we will use for rendering. For some browsers, the string webgl has to be replaced with experimental-webgl. Note that there is only one context associated with each canvas: the first invocation of getContext on a canvas causes the context object to be created and returned; every other invocation will simply return the same object. On line 6 we store the created context to the gl variable. Unless otherwise specified, throughout the code in this book the identifier gl will be always and only used for a variable referencing a WebGL rendering context.

Step 3: Define What To Draw

It is important to note that the WebGL specifications, along with other rasterization-based graphics API, are designed to take into account and efficiently exploit the graphics hardware that we find on our devices, from smartphones to powerful personal computers. One of the most important practical effects of the design is that common data structures a programmer would use to describe some entities must be *mirrored* with their corresponding counterpart in the API. That is, before using them, we have to encapsulate their data in an appropriate WebGL structure.

For reasons that we will soon explain, we treat our 500×500 pixels canvas as a region that spans the plane from -1 to 1 both horizontally and vertically, instead of 0 to 499. This means that, in the hypothetical unit of measure we used, the canvas is two units wide and two units tall. As a first example, let's consider the triangle in Figure 2.2 (Top-Left): it is composed by three vertices on the XY plane whose coordinates are $(0.0, 0.0)$, $(1.0, 0.0)$ and $(0.0, 1.0)$. In JavaScript, a straightforward way to express this is indicated in Listing 2.4:

```
1  var triangle = {
2    vertexPositions : [
3      [0.0, 0.0],  // 1st vertex
4      [1.0, 0.0],  // 2nd vertex
5      [0.0, 1.0]   // 3rd vertex
6    ]
7  };
```

LISTING 2.4: A triangle in JavaScript.

The triangle variable refers to an object with a single property named vertexPositions. In turn, vertexPositions refers to an array of three elements, one for each vertex. Each element stores the x and y coordinates of a vertex with an array of two numbers. Although the above representation is clear from

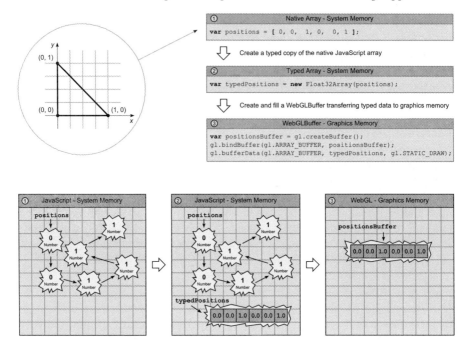

FIGURE 2.2: Illustration of the mirroring of arrays from the system memory, where they can be accessed with JavaScript, to the graphics memory.

a design point of view, it is not very compact in terms of occupied space and data access pattern. To achieve the best performance, we must represent the triangle in a more *raw* way, as shown in Listing 2.5.

```
1  var positions = [
2    0.0, 0.0,  // 1st vertex
3    1.0, 0.0,  // 2nd vertex
4    0.0, 1.0   // 3rd vertex
5  ];
```

LISTING 2.5: A triangle represented with an array of scalars.

As you can notice, the triangle is now represented with a single array of six numbers, where each number pair represents the two-dimensional coordinates of a vertex. Nonetheless, storing the attributes of the vertices that compose a geometric primitive (that is, the positions of the three vertices that form a triangle as in the above example) in a single array of numbers, coordinate after coordinate, and vertex after vertex, is exactly the way WebGL requires us to follow whenever geometric data has to be defined.

Now we have to take a further step to convert the data in a *lower level* representation. Since JavaScript arrays do not represent a contiguous chunk of memory and, moreover, are not homogeneous (e.g., elements can have different types), they cannot be directly delivered to WebGL, which expects a raw, contiguous region of memory. For this reason, the WebGL specifications lead the way to the definition of new JavaScript objects for representing contiguous and strongly-typed arrays. The *typed array* specification defines a series of such objects, i.e., Uint8Array (unsigned, 8-bit integers) and Float32Array (32-bit floating-points), that we will use for creating the low-level version of our native JavaScript array. The following code constructs a 32-bit floating-point typed array from a native array:

```
1    typedPositions =    Float32Array(positions);
```

Alternatively, we could have filled the typed array directly, without passing by a native array:

```
1      typedPositions =    Float32Array(6); // 6 floats
2  typedPositions[0] = 0.0;   typedPositions[1] = 0.0;
3  typedPositions[2] = 1.0;   typedPositions[3] = 0.0;
4  typedPositions[4] = 0.0;   typedPositions[5] = 1.0;
```

The data, laid out as above, is now ready to be *mirrored* (for example by creating an internal WebGL copy) and encapsulated in a WebGL object. As mentioned above, WebGL uses its own counterpart of a *native* data structure: in this case, a JavaScript typed array containing vertex attributes is mirrored by a WebGLBuffer object:

```
1      positionsBuffer = gl.createBuffer();
2  gl.bindBuffer(gl.ARRAY_BUFFER, positionsBuffer);
3  gl.bufferData(gl.ARRAY_BUFFER, typedPositions, gl.STATIC_DRAW);
```

On line 1 an uninitialized, zero-sized WebGLBuffer is created and a reference to it is stored in the positionsBuffer variable. On line 2 we tell WebGL to *bind* positionsBuffer to the ARRAY_BUFFER *target*. This is the first example where the state machine nature of WebGL emerges: once an object O has been bound to a particular target T, every operation addressing T will operate on O. This is actually what happens on line 3: we *send* the data contained in the typed array typedPositions to the object that is bound on target ARRAY_BUFFER, that is, the WebGLBuffer positionsBuffer. The ARRAY_BUFFER target is specific for buffers that store vertex attributes. The third parameter of the method bufferData is a *hint* to the WebGL context that informs it how we are going to use the buffer: by specifying STATIC_DRAW we declare that we are likely to specify the buffer content once but use it many times.

As can be deduced from the above low-level code, from the point of view of the WebGL rendering pipeline a vertex is nothing but a set of vertex attributes. In turn, a vertex attribute is a scalar value (e.g., a *number*), or a two-, three- or four-dimensional vector. The allowed scalar type for both numbers and vectors are integers, fixed- and floating-point values. The WebGL specifications impose restrictions on the number of bits used by each representation. Deciding the most adequate data format for a vertex attribute can be important for both quality and performances, and it has to be evaluated

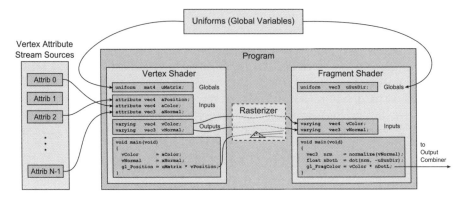

FIGURE 2.3: The vertex flow.

depending on the application and on the software and hardware resources at disposal.

As we have seen when we prepared the buffer, for a WebGL programmer a vertex attribute is a small chunk of memory that contains one to four numbers, and a vertex is formed by a set of attributes. The next step is to tell the context how to fetch the data of each vertex attribute (in our example, only the two-dimensional position attribute). The first operation executed by the pipeline is to gather all the attributes a vertex is composed of, then pass this data bundle to the vertex processing stage. As illustrated in Figure 2.3 (on the left), there are a number of attribute *slots* we can use to compose our vertex (the actual number of slots is implementation dependent).

The next step is to select a slot and tell the context how to fetch data from it. This is accomplished with the following code:

```
1  var positionAttribIndex = 0;
2  gl.enableVertexAttribArray(positionAttribIndex);
3  gl.vertexAttribPointer(positionAttribIndex, 2, gl.FLOAT, false, ←
     0, 0);
```

At line 1, we store the index of the selected slot in a global variable, to be used later. Selecting index zero is completely arbitrary: we can choose whichever indices we want (in case of multiple attributes). At line 2, with the method enableVertexAttribArray we tell the context that vertex attribute from slot positionAttribIndex (zero) has to be fetched from an array of values, meaning that we will *latch* a vertex buffer as the attribute data source. At last, we must specify the context, which is the data type for the attribute and how to fetch it. The method vertexAttribPointer at line 3 solves this purpose; using a C-like syntax, its prototype is:

```
1  void vertexAttribPointer(unsigned int index, int size, int type,
2     bool normalized, unsigned int stride, unsigned int offset);
```

The index parameter is the attribute index that is being specified; size represents the dimensionality of the attribute (two-dimensional vector); type is a symbolic constant indicating the attribute scalar type (gl.FLOAT, e.g., floating point number); normalized is a flag indicating whether an attribute with integral scalar type must be normalized (more on this later, at any rate, the value here is ignored because the attribute scalar type is not an integer type); stride is the number of bytes from the beginning of an item in the vertex attribute stream and the beginning of the next entry in the stream (zero means that there are no gaps, that is the attribute is tightly packed, three floats one after another); offset is the offset in bytes from the beginning of the WebGLBuffer currently bound to the ARRAY_BUFFER target (in our case, positionsBuffer) to the beginning of the first attribute in the array (zero means that our position starts immediately at the beginning of the memory buffer).

The complete shape setup code is resembled in Listing 2.6.

```
1   // global variables
2   // ...
3   var positionAttribIndex = 0;
4
5   function setupWhatToDraw() {
6     var positions = [
7       0.0, 0.0,   // 1st vertex
8       1.0, 0.0,   // 2nd vertex
9       0.0, 1.0    // 3rd vertex
10    ];
11
12    var typedPositions = new Float32Array(positions);
13
14    var positionsBuffer = gl.createBuffer();
15    gl.bindBuffer(gl.ARRAY_BUFFER, positionsBuffer);
16    gl.bufferData(gl.ARRAY_BUFFER, typedPositions, gl.STATIC_DRAW);
17
18    gl.enableVertexAttribArray(positionAttribIndex);
19    gl.vertexAttribPointer(positionAttribIndex, 2, gl.FLOAT, false
20        , 0, 0);
    }
```

LISTING 2.6: Complete code to set up a triangle.

The rendering context is now configured to *feed* the pipeline with the *stream* of vertex attributes we have just set up.

Step 3: Define How to Draw

Once the pipeline has been configured to fetch the triangle vertices, we have to specify the operations we want to execute on each vertex. As just described in Section 2.2, the *vertex shader stage* of the WebGL pipeline corresponds to the per-vertex operations stage of the logical pipeline (seen in Section 1.3.2). In this stage, vertices are processed one by one, without knowledge of their adjacent vertices in the geometric primitive (i.e., the triangle). This stage operates by running a *vertex shader* (VS) on each vertex of the input stream: the VS is a custom program written in a C-like language, namely the OpenGL Shading Language (GLSL), which must be delivered to the rendering context and compiled. Here, we do not provide a complete overview of GLSL; we address the interested reader to a specialized handbook. Instead, as for the WebGL, during the rest of this book, we explain the GLSL commands and features involved in a certain piece of code, instance by instance. The following code sets up our first, simple vertex shader:

```
1  var vsSource = " ... "; // GLSL source code
2  var vertexShader = gl.createShader(gl.VERTEX_SHADER);
3  gl.shaderSource(vertexShader, vsSource);
4  gl.compileShader(vertexShader);
```

As you can notice, once a WebGLShader object is created (line 2), its source code is simply set by passing a native JavaScript string to the method shader-Source() (line 3). Finally, the shader must be compiled (line 4). The GLSL source code vsSource, for this basic example, is:

```
1  attribute vec2 aPosition;
2
3  void main(void)
4  {
5    gl_Position = vec4(aPosition, 0.0, 1.0);
6  }
```

At line 1 we declare a vertex attribute named aPosition whose type is vec2, that is, a two-dimensional vector of floats. As in a C program, the main() function is the shader entry point. Every vertex shader is mandated to write to the global output variable gl_Position, a four-dimensional vector of floats (vec4) representing the vertex position and whose coordinates range from -1 to $+1$. In our first example, we use the two-dimensional positions (x and y) specified at step 2 and use zero and one (more on this later) for the third (z) and fourth (w) coordinates. At line 5 a C++-like constructor is used to create a vec4 from a vec2 and two scalar floats.

The vertex shader processes every vertex in the input stream, calculates its position and sends the output to the Primitive Assembler stage, whose purpose is to assemble vertices to form a geometric primitive. The Primitive Assembler then sends the primitive to the rasterizer, which interpolates the vertex shader output attributes (if any) and generates the fragments of the primitive covers on the screen.

Similarly to vertex processing, we will have to set up a *fragment shader* (FS) to process each generated fragment. The fragment shader setup is analogous to the vertex shader setup:

```
1  var fsSource = " ... "; // GLSL source code
2  var fragmentShader = gl.createShader(gl.FRAGMENT_SHADER);
3  gl.shaderSource(fragmentShader, fsSource);
4  gl.compileShader(fragmentShader);
```

The only change is at line 2 where we pass the FRAGMENT_SHADER symbolic constant to the creation method instead of VERTEX_SHADER.

In our first example the fragment shader simply sets the color of each fragment to blue, as shown in the following GLSL code:

```
1  void main(void)
2  {
3    gl_FragColor = vec4(0.0, 1.0, 0.0, 1.0);
4  }
```

The built-in vec4 output variable gl_FragColor holds the color of the fragment. The vector component represents the red, green, blue and alpha values (RGBA) of the output color, respectively; each component is expressed as a floating point in the range [0.0,1.0].

As illustrated in Figure 2.3, vertex and fragment shaders must be *encapsulated* and *linked* into a *program*, represented by a WebGLProgram object:

```
1  var program = gl.createProgram();
2  gl.attachShader(program, vertexShader);
3  gl.attachShader(program, fragmentShader);
4  gl.bindAttribLocation(program, positionAttribIndex,"aPosition");
5  gl.linkProgram(program);
6  gl.useProgram(program);
```

The WebGLProgram object is created at line 1, and vertex and fragment shaders are attached (lines 2 and 3). A connection between the attribute stream slot and the vertex shader attribute is made at line 4: the bindAttribLocation() method configures the program such that the value assigned to the vertex shader attribute aPosition must be fetched from the attribute slot at index positionAttribIndex, that is, the same slot used when we configured the vertex stream in Step 2. At line 5 the program is *linked*, that is, the connections between the two shaders are established, and then is made as the *current* program at line 6.

The code in Listing 2.7 shows all the operations taken in this step.

```
1   function setupHowToDraw() {
2     // vertex shader
3     var vsSource = "\
4       attribute vec2 aPosition;                          \n\
5                                                          \n\
6       void main(void)                                    \n\
7       {                                                  \n\
8         gl_Position = vec4(aPosition, 0.0, 1.0);         \n\
9       }                                                  \n\
10      ";
11     var vertexShader = gl.createShader(gl.VERTEX_SHADER);
12     gl.shaderSource(vertexShader, vsSource);
13     gl.compileShader(vertexShader);
14
15     // fragment shader
16     var fsSource = "\
17       void main(void)                                    \n\
18       {                                                  \n\
19         gl_FragColor = vec4(0.0, 1.0, 0.0, 1.0);         \n\
```

```
20      }                                                   \n\
21    ";
22    var fragmentShader = gl.createShader(gl.FRAGMENT_SHADER);
23    gl.shaderSource(fragmentShader, fsSource);
24    gl.compileShader(fragmentShader);
25
26    // program
27    var program = gl.createProgram();
28    gl.attachShader(program, vertexShader);
29    gl.attachShader(program, fragmentShader);
30    gl.bindAttribLocation(program, positionAttribIndex,"aPosition"↩
          );
31    gl.linkProgram(program);
32    gl.useProgram(program);
33  }
```

LISTING 2.7: Complete code to program the vertex and the fragment shader.

Having configured the vertex streams and the program that will process vertices and fragments, the pipeline is now ready for drawing.

Step 4: Draw
We are now ready to draw our first triangle to the screen. This is done by the following code:

```
1  function draw() {
2    gl.clearColor(0.0, 0.0, 0.0, 1.0);
3    gl.clear(gl.COLOR_BUFFER_BIT);
4    gl.drawArrays(gl.TRIANGLES, 0, 3);
5  }
```

At line 2 we define the RGBA color to use when clearing the color buffer (line 3). The call to drawArrays() at line 4 performs the actual rendering, creating triangle primitives starting from vertex zero and consuming three vertices.

The resulting JavaScript code of all the parts is shown in Listing 2.8 for recap.

```
1  // global variables
2  var gl                     = null;
3  var positionAttribIndex = 0;
4
5  function setupWebGL() {
6    var canvas = document.getElementById("OUTPUT-CANVAS");
7    gl = canvas.getContext("experimental-webgl");
8  }
9
10 function setupWhatToDraw() {
11   var positions = [
12     0.0, 0.0,    // 1st vertex
13     1.0, 0.0,    // 2nd vertex
14     0.0, 1.0     // 3rd vertex
15   ];
16
```

```
17      typedPositions =    Float32Array(positions);
18
19      positionsBuffer = gl.createBuffer();
20   gl.bindBuffer(gl.ARRAY_BUFFER, positionsBuffer);
21   gl.bufferData(gl.ARRAY_BUFFER, typedPositions,gl.STATIC_DRAW);
22
23   gl.enableVertexAttribArray(positionAttribIndex);
24   gl.vertexAttribPointer(positionAttribIndex,
25     2, gl.FLOAT, false, 0, 0);
26 }
27
28      setupHowToDraw() {
29   // vertex shader
30      vsSource = "\
31     attribute vec2 aPosition;                       \n\
32                                  \n\
33     void main(void)                                 \n\
34     {                                               \n\
35       gl_Position = vec4(aPosition, 0.0, 1.0);  \n\
36     }                                             \n\
37   ";
38      vertexShader = gl.createShader(gl.VERTEX_SHADER);
39   gl.shaderSource(vertexShader, vsSource);
40   gl.compileShader(vertexShader);
41
42   // fragment shader
43      fsSource = "\
44     void main(void)                                 \n\
45     {                                               \n\
46       gl_FragColor = vec4(0.0, 0.0, 1.0, 1.0);  \n\
47     }                                             \n\
48   ";
49      fragmentShader = gl.createShader(gl.FRAGMENT_SHADER);
50   gl.shaderSource(fragmentShader, fsSource);
51   gl.compileShader(fragmentShader);
52
53   // program
54      program = gl.createProgram();
55   gl.attachShader(program, vertexShader);
56   gl.attachShader(program, fragmentShader);
57   gl.bindAttribLocation(program,
58     positionAttribIndex, "aPosition");
59   gl.linkProgram(program);
60   gl.useProgram(program);
61 }
62
63      draw() {
64   gl.clearColor(0.0, 0.0, 0.0, 1.0);
65   gl.clear(gl.COLOR_BUFFER_BIT);
66   gl.drawArrays(gl.TRIANGLES, 0, 3);
67 }
68
69      helloDraw() {
70   setupWebGL();
71   setupWhatToDraw();
72   setupHowToDraw();
73   draw();
```

```
74 }
75
76 window.onload = helloDraw;
```

LISTING 2.8: The first rendering example using WebGL.

As anticipated in the introduction to this chapter, the amount of code necessary for displaying our first triangle seems insanely too much, but, as we will see in the following chapters, understanding these steps means knowing the largest part of every rendering procedure.

2.4 WebGL Supporting Libraries

As of now, we have seen how to set up and draw a simple triangle in WebGL. As you have seen, several lines of code to achieve this simple goal are required. This is the main reason that has motivated the birth of several WebGL libraries to ease the use of WebGL. One of the most famous ones is *Three.js* (*http://threejs.org*). Another interesting WebGL library is *GLGE* (*http://www.glge.org*). In this book, we will use *SpiderGL* (*http://spidergl.org*). SpiderGL, entirely written in Javascript, provides several modules to simplify the development of complex WebGL graphics applications. There is a module to load the content of 3D graphics data, a module of math utilities to handle matrices and vectors entities (Javascript does not provide such mathematical entities and the relative operations between them), a module to simplify the setup of the shaders for the successive rendering, and others. Note that you do not need to master this library to understand and use the code provided in the practical sections, since only very few parts of it are used. More precisely, we use this library to handle matrices and vectors and the operations between them, to handle geometric transformation, and to load and display 3D content. In the rest of the book, we will provide from time to time, some details about SpiderGL commands when they come into play in the code. For readers interested in more in-depth details we refer to the official SpiderGL Web site (http://www.spidergl.org).

2.5 Meet NVMC

The choice of an interactive video game is a fairly straightforward choice for experimenting with computer graphics theory and techniques, and there are several reasons for that:

Interactivity. Implementing a computer game imposes a hard constraint on the time spent for rendering the scene. The more the game is *dynamic* the more the refresh rate has to be high. For a car racing game, if the image is not refreshed at least 40–50 times per second, the game will be too little responsive and hard to play. Therefore we have a strong stimulus to find efficient solutions for rendering the scene as fast as we can.

Natural mapping between theory and practice. Computer graphics concepts are mostly introduced incrementally, that is, the content of a chapter is necessary to understand the next one. Luckily, these concepts can be applied to the construction of our video game right away, chapter after chapter. In other words the code samples that we will show in Chapter 3 will be the building blocks of those in Chapter 4, and so on. We will refer to these code samples in special sections titled "Upgrade Your Client." All together these samples will bring us from an empty screen to a complete and advanced rendering.

Sense of achievement. As aforementioned, we will have the complete description of the scene to render and our goal will be to render it. In doing this there are countless choices to make and it is extremely unlikely that two independent developments would lead to the same result. This means that we are not just making exercises, we are creating something from scratch and shaping it to our taste. In short: Computer graphics is fun!

Completeness. It often happens that students of CG like one specific sub-topic over the others, and consequently choose to make a project on that sub-topic, neglecting the rest. This is a bad practice that cannot be pursued with the proposed car-racing game, because all the fundamentals of computer graphics are required and ineludible.

2.5.1 The Framework

NVMC is an online multi-player car racing game and as such its realization requires us to handle, other than rendering, networking, physical simulation and synchronization issues. However, these topics are beyond the scope of this book and here they are treated as a black box. This means that what follows in this section is *already* implemented and we only need very few notions on how to use it. The only missing part is the rendering of the scene and this is all we will care about. Figure 2.4 illustrates the architecture of the NVMC framework.

The *NVMC server* is in charge of the physical simulation of the race and each *NVMC client* corresponds to one player. The *state of the game* consists of the list of all the players and their state (position, velocity, damages and other per-player attributes) and other general data such as the time of day, the track

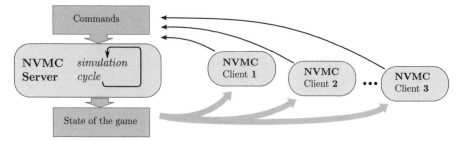

FIGURE 2.4: Architecture of the NVMC framework.

condition (dry, wet, dusty etc.), and so on. A client may send *commands* to the server to control its car, for example TURN_LEFT, TURN_RIGHT, PAUSE etc., and these messages are input to the simulation. At fixed time steps, the server broadcasts to all the clients the state of the race so that they can render it.

2.5.2   The Class **NVMC** to Represent the World

All the interface towards the server is encapsulated in one single class called NVMC. Figure 2.5 shows how the elements of the scene, which are the track, the car, the trees, the buildings, etc., are accessed by the member functions of the class NVMC. The illustration is partial, since there are also other elements (the sunlight direction, the weather conditions, etc.) that are not shown there. For a complete list we refer the reader to Appendix A. Furthermore, this class provides the methods for controlling the car and takes care of the communication with the server. Note that the framework can also be used locally without connecting to any server on the network because the class NVMC also implements the server functionalities.

2.5.3   A Very Basic Client

In this section we will not introduce new WebGL notions—we will simply expand and reorganize the example of Section 2.3 to make it more modular and suitable for further development.

Figure 2.6 shows the very first NVMC client, where the car is represented with a triangle and all the rest is just a blue screen. The client is nothing other than the implementation of a single JavaScript object called NVMCClient.

Everything we will do in the rest of the book is rewriting the methods and/or extending the object NVMCClient to upgrade our client with new rendering features. In the following we will see the main methods of NVMCClient in this first very basic version.

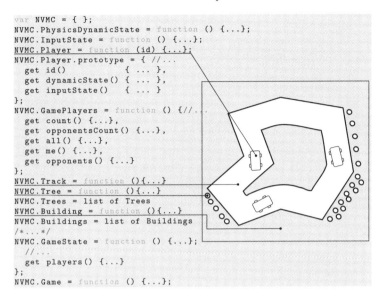

```
var NVMC = { };
NVMC.PhysicsDynamicState = function () {...};
NVMC.InputState = function () {...};
NVMC.Player = function (id) {...};
NVMC.Player.prototype = { //...
  get id()          { ... },
  get dynamicState() { ... },
  get inputState()   { ... }
};
NVMC.GamePlayers = function () {//...
  get count() {...},
  get opponentsCount() {...},
  get all() {...},
  get me() {...},
  get opponents() {...}
};
NVMC.Track = function (){...}
NVMC.Tree = function (){...}
NVMC.Trees = list of Trees
NVMC.Building = function (){...}
NVMC.Buildings = list of Buildings
/*...*/
NVMC.GameState = function () {...};
  //...
  get players() {...}
};
NVMC.Game = function () {...};
```

FIGURE 2.5: The class NVMC incorporates all the knowledge about the world of the race.

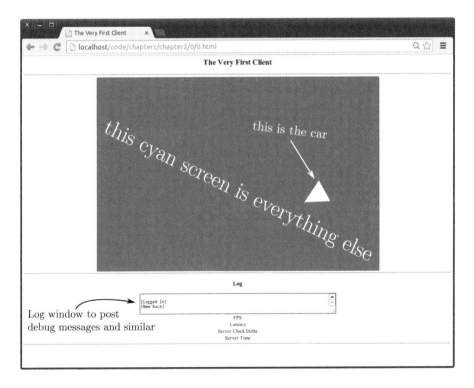

FIGURE 2.6: A very basic NVMC client.

Initializing. The method onInitialize is called once per page loading. Here we will place all the initialization of our graphics resources and data structures that need to be done once and for all. Its implementation in this very basic client is reported in Listing 2.9. The call NVMC.log at line 120 pushes a text message on the log window appearing below the canvas (see Figure 2.6). We will use this window to post information about the current version of the client and as feedback for debugging purposes. Lines 124 to 136 just create a mapping between the key W, A, S, D, and the action to take when one key is pressed. This mapping will involve more and more keys as we will have more input to take from the user (for example, switch the headlights on/off). Then at line 140 we call a function to initialize all the geometric objects we need in the client, which in this case simply means the example triangle shown in Listing 2.6 and finally at line 141 we call the function that creates a shader program.

```
119  NVMCClient.onInitialize = function () {
120    NVMC.log("SpiderGL Version : " + SGL_VERSION_STRING + "\n");
121
122    var game = this.game;
123
124    var handleKey = {};
125    handleKey["W"] = function (on) {
126      game.playerAccelerate = on;
127    };
128    handleKey["S"] = function (on) {
129      game.playerBrake = on;
130    };
131    handleKey["A"] = function (on) {
132      game.playerSteerLeft = on;
133    };
134    handleKey["D"] = function (on) {
135      game.playerSteerRight = on;
136    };
137    this.handleKey = handleKey;
138
139    this.stack = new SglMatrixStack();
140    this.initializeObjects(this.ui.gl);
141    this.uniformShader = new uniformShader(this.ui.gl);
142  };
```

LISTING 2.9: The function onInitialize. This function is called once per page loading. (Code snippet from *http://envymycarbook.com/chapter2/0/0.js.*)

Initializing geometric objects. In these methods we take care of creating the geometric objects needed to represent the scene. We define a JavaScript object to represent a primitive consisting of a set of triangles as shown in Listing 2.10. So every geometric object will have a name, the array of vertices and triangleIndices and their respective cardinalities in numVertices and numTriangles. This representation of the geometry will be detailed later in Section 3.8 and in Section 3.9.

```
1  function Triangle() {
2    this.name = "Triangle";
3    this.vertices = new Float32Array([0,0,0,0.5,0,-1,-0.5,0,-1]);
4    this.triangleIndices = new Uint16Array([0,1,2]);
5    this.numVertices  = 3;
6    this.numTriangles = 1;
7  };
```

LISTING 2.10: The JavaScript object to represent a geometric primitive made of triangles (in this case, a single triangle). (Code snippet from *http:// envymycarbook.com/chapter2/0/triangle.js.*)

Then, we define a function to create the WebGL buffers from these JavaScript objects, as shown in Listing 2.11.

```
35  NVMCClient.createObjectBuffers = function (gl, obj) {
36    obj.vertexBuffer = gl.createBuffer();
37    gl.bindBuffer(gl.ARRAY_BUFFER, obj.vertexBuffer);
38    gl.bufferData(gl.ARRAY_BUFFER, obj.vertices, gl.STATIC_DRAW);
39    gl.bindBuffer(gl.ARRAY_BUFFER, null);
40
41    obj.indexBufferTriangles = gl.createBuffer();
42    gl.bindBuffer(gl.ELEMENT_ARRAY_BUFFER, obj.↩
         indexBufferTriangles);
43    gl.bufferData(gl.ELEMENT_ARRAY_BUFFER, obj.triangleIndices, gl↩
         .STATIC_DRAW);
44    gl.bindBuffer(gl.ELEMENT_ARRAY_BUFFER, null);
45
46    // create edges
47    var edges = new Uint16Array(obj.numTriangles * 3 * 2);
48    for (var i = 0; i < obj.numTriangles; ++i) {
49      edges[i * 6 + 0] = obj.triangleIndices[i * 3 + 0];
50      edges[i * 6 + 1] = obj.triangleIndices[i * 3 + 1];
51      edges[i * 6 + 2] = obj.triangleIndices[i * 3 + 0];
52      edges[i * 6 + 3] = obj.triangleIndices[i * 3 + 2];
53      edges[i * 6 + 4] = obj.triangleIndices[i * 3 + 1];
54      edges[i * 6 + 5] = obj.triangleIndices[i * 3 + 2];
55    }
56
57    obj.indexBufferEdges = gl.createBuffer();
58    gl.bindBuffer(gl.ELEMENT_ARRAY_BUFFER, obj.indexBufferEdges);
59    gl.bufferData(gl.ELEMENT_ARRAY_BUFFER, edges, gl.STATIC_DRAW);
60    gl.bindBuffer(gl.ELEMENT_ARRAY_BUFFER, null);
61  };
```

LISTING 2.11: Creating the objects to be drawn. (Code snippet from *http://envymycarbook.com/chapter2/0/0.js.*)

These two functions are a more modular implementation of the function setupWhatToDraw() in Listing 2.6 to both create the JavaScript objects and their WebGL counterparts. At lines 36, 41 and 57 we extend the JavaScript object passed as input (in this case an object triangle) with the WebGL buffers for vertices, triangles and *edges* of the object. The edges are inferred from a list of triangles, which means that for each triangle indicated with indices (i, j, k), three edges are created: the edge (i, j), the edge (j, k) and the edge

(k, i). In this implementation we do not care that if two triangles share one edge, we will have two copies of the same edge.

In Listing 2.12 we show how the functions above are used for our first client.

```
63  NVMCClient.initializeObjects = function (gl) {
64      this.triangle = new Triangle();
65      this.createObjectBuffers(gl, this.triangle);
66  };
```

LISTING 2.12: Creating geometric objects. (Code snippet from *http://envymycarbook.com/chapter2/0.js*.)

Rendering. In Listing 2.13 we have the function drawObject to actually perform the rendering. The difference from the example in Listing 2.7 is that we render both the triangles and their edges and we pass the color to use (as fillColor and lineColor). So far the only data we passed from our JavaScript code to the program shader were vertex attributes, more specifically the position of the vertices. This time we also want to pass the color to use. This is a global data, meaning that it is the same for all the vertices processed in the vertex shader or for all the fragments of the fragment shader. A variable of this sort must be declared by using the GLSL keyword uniform. Then, when the shader program has been linked, we can query it to know the handle of the variable with the function gl.getUniformLocation (see line 52 in Listing 2.14) and we can use this handle to set its value by using the function gl.uniform (see lines 20 and 25 in Listing 2.13). Note that the gl.uniform function name is followed by a postfix, which indicates the type of parameters the function takes. For example, 4fv means a vector of 4 floating points, 1i means an integer, and so on.

```
10  NVMCClient.drawObject = function (gl, obj, fillColor, lineColor)↩
        {
11      gl.bindBuffer(gl.ARRAY_BUFFER, obj.vertexBuffer);
12      gl.enableVertexAttribArray(this.uniformShader.aPositionIndex);
13      gl.vertexAttribPointer(this.uniformShader.aPositionIndex, 3, ↩
            gl.FLOAT, false, 0, 0);
14
15      gl.enable(gl.POLYGON_OFFSET_FILL);
16
17      gl.polygonOffset(1.0, 1.0);
18
19      gl.bindBuffer(gl.ELEMENT_ARRAY_BUFFER, obj.↩
            indexBufferTriangles);
20      gl.uniform4fv(this.uniformShader.uColorLocation, fillColor);
21      gl.drawElements(gl.TRIANGLES, obj.triangleIndices.length, gl.↩
            UNSIGNED_SHORT, 0);
22
23      gl.disable(gl.POLYGON_OFFSET_FILL);
```

```
24
25      gl.uniform4fv(this.uniformShader.uColorLocation, lineColor);
26      gl.bindBuffer(gl.ELEMENT_ARRAY_BUFFER, obj.indexBufferEdges);
27      gl.drawElements(gl.LINES, obj.numTriangles * 3 * 2, gl.↵
            UNSIGNED_SHORT, 0);
28
29      gl.bindBuffer(gl.ELEMENT_ARRAY_BUFFER, null);
30
31      gl.disableVertexAttribArray(this.uniformShader.aPositionIndex)↵
            ;
32      gl.bindBuffer(gl.ARRAY_BUFFER, null);
33  };
```

LISTING 2.13: Rendering of one geometric object. (Code snippet from *http://envymycarbook.com/chapter2/0.js.*)

In the NVMC clients the shader programs will be encapsulated in JavaScript objects, as you can see in Listing 2.14, so that we can exploit a common interface to access the members (for example, the position of the vertices will always be called **aPositionIndex** on every shader we will write).

```
1   uniformShader = function (gl) {
2       var vertexShaderSource = "\
3         uniform   mat4 uModelViewMatrix;            \n\
4         uniform   mat4 uProjectionMatrix;           \n\
5         attribute vec3 aPosition;                   \n\
6         void main(void)                             \n\
7         {                                           \n\
8           gl_Position = uProjectionMatrix *         \n\
9           uModelViewMatrix * vec4(aPosition, 1.0);  \n\
10        }                                           \n\
11      ";
12
13      var fragmentShaderSource = "\
14        precision highp float;                      \n\
15        uniform vec4 uColor;                        \n\
16        void main(void)                             \n\
17        {                                           \n\
18          gl_FragColor = vec4(uColor);              \n\
19        }                                           \n\
20      ";
21
22      // create the vertex shader
23      var vertexShader = gl.createShader(gl.VERTEX_SHADER);
24      gl.shaderSource(vertexShader, vertexShaderSource);
25      gl.compileShader(vertexShader);
26
27      // create the fragment shader
28      var fragmentShader = gl.createShader(gl.FRAGMENT_SHADER);
29      gl.shaderSource(fragmentShader, fragmentShaderSource);
30      gl.compileShader(fragmentShader);
```

```
31
32    // Create the shader program
33      aPositionIndex = 0;
34      shaderProgram = gl.createProgram();
35    gl.attachShader(shaderProgram, vertexShader);
36    gl.attachShader(shaderProgram, fragmentShader);
37    gl.bindAttribLocation(shaderProgram, aPositionIndex, "↩
         aPosition");
38    gl.linkProgram(shaderProgram);
39
40    // If creating the shader program failed, alert
41      (!gl.getProgramParameter(shaderProgram, gl.LINK_STATUS)) {
42        str = "Unable to initialize the shader program.\n\n";
43      str += "VS:\n" + gl.getShaderInfoLog(vertexShader) + "\n\n";
44      str += "FS:\n" + gl.getShaderInfoLog(fragmentShader) + "\n\n↩
           ";
45      str += "PROG:\n" + gl.getProgramInfoLog(shaderProgram);
46      alert(str);
47    }
48
49    shaderProgram.aPositionIndex = aPositionIndex;
50    shaderProgram.uModelViewMatrixLocation = gl.getUniformLocation↩
         (shaderProgram, "uModelViewMatrix");
51    shaderProgram.uProjectionMatrixLocation = gl.↩
         getUniformLocation(shaderProgram, "uProjectionMatrix");
52    shaderProgram.uColorLocation = gl.getUniformLocation(↩
         shaderProgram, "uColor");
53
54        shaderProgram;
55  };
```

LISTING 2.14: Program shader for rendering. (Code snippet from *http://envymycarbook.com/chapter2/0/0.js*.)

Interface with the game. The class NVMCClient has a member game that refers to the class NVMC and hence gives us access to the world both for giving input to the simulation and for reading information about the scene. In this particular client we only read the position of the player's car in the following line of code (Listing 2.15):

```
94      pos =     .myPos()
```

LISTING 2.15: Accessing the elements of the scene. (Code snippet from *http://envymycarbook.com/chapter2/0/0.js*.)

2.5.4   Code Organization

The various NVMC clients are organized in the following way: each client corresponds to a folder. The clients are separated for each chapter and are numbered starting from 0 in each chapter (see Figure 2.7). So, for example, the second client (that is, the client number is 1) of chapter X corresponds to the folder chapterX/1. Inside the folder of each client we have the HTML file

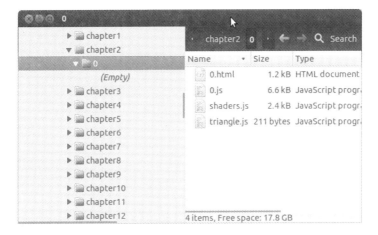

FIGURE 2.7: File organization of the NVMC clients.

[client_number].html, a file named shaders.js for the shaders introduced with the client, one or more javascript files containing the code for new geometric primitives introduced within the client and a file [client_number].js containing the implementation for the class NVMCClient.

Note, and this is **very important**, that each file [client_number].js contains only the modifications with respect to the previous client while in the HTML file we explicitly include the previous versions of the class NVMCClient, so that everything previously defined in each client file will be parsed. This is very handy because it allows us to write only the new parts that enrich our client and/or to redefine existing functions. For example, the function createObject-Buffers will not need to be changed until chapter 5 and so it will not appear in the code of the clients of chapter 4. A reader may argue that many functions can be parsed without actually being called because they are overwritten by more recent versions. Even if this is a useless processing that slows down the loading time of the Web page, we prefer to proceed in this way for didactic purposes. Nothing prevents you from removing overwritten members when a version of the client is finalized.

On the contrary, the shader programs are not written incrementally, since we do not want to always use an *improved* version of the same shader program but, instead, we will often use many of them in the same client. The same goes for the geometric objects. In this first client we introduced the Triangle, in the next chapter we will write the Cube, the Cone and other simple primitives and we will use them in our future clients.

Chapter 3

How a 3D Model Is Represented

In recent years, 3D digital data have gone through a revolution in terms of diffusion and use in several applications, just like it happened before for other digital media such as audio, video and images. This has motivated the development of new ways to represent digital 3D content. In this chapter, we will give an overview of several ways to represent the *geometry of a 3D object* on a computer. Our main goal is to provide insights to the reader about how to handle the geometry of a 3D model in his/her graphics application.

We advise the reader that many details provided about parametric curves and surfaces (Section 3.4) and about subdivision surfaces (Section 3.7) are given only for the sake of completeness but they will not be used in the practical examples and in the development of our game. Readers that prefer to go quickly to the heart of the graphics development, and hence move fast to the next chapters, can read the aforementioned sections considering only the concepts described, skipping the mathematical details. They should put more attention on the polygon meshes (Section 3.2) and their implementation (Section 3.8 plus the practical part), since we will use these types of representation for the rest of the book.

3.1 Introduction

In very general terms a 3D model is a mathematical representation of a physical entity that occupies space. In more practical terms, a 3D model is made of a description of its shape and a description of its color appearance. In this chapter we focus on geometric data representation, providing a panoramic of the most used representations and presenting the peculiarities of each.

One main categorization of 3D object's representation can be done by considering whether the surface or the volume of the object is represented:

- **Boundary-based:** the surface of the 3D object is represented. This representation is also called *b-rep*. Polygon meshes, implicit surfaces and parametric surfaces, which we will describe in the following, are common representations of this type.

- **Volume-based:** the volume of the 3D object is represented. Voxels (described in Section 3.5) and Constructive Solid Geometry (CSG) (described in Section 3.6) are commonly used to represent volumetric data.

The representation of a 3D model depends on the way the model has been created and by its application context. A geometric representation may come from several sources. Just to mention a few:

3.1.1   Digitalization of the Real World

These techniques are what photography is for 2D images: they measure real objects to obtain a digital description of them. Among the most well known we can find the *triangulation-based techniques*. The fundamental idea is that a pattern of light is projected into the surface to be digitalized and a camera takes a photograph of how the light is reflected by the surface. The known relative position of projector and camera (which are usually mounted on the same physical device) make it possible to infer the position of each point of the surface where the light has been projected. Among the triangle-based scanners we find the *laser scanners*, where the pattern of light is simply a thin laser beam swept on the surface (and hence a 3D point per photo is found), or *structured light* scanners, where patterns such as stripes are projected. A well known exmple of this type is the Kinect®, where the pattern projected is on the infrared spectrum and hence not visible to human eyes. *Time-of-light* techniques also project a laser beam on the surface, and detect the time for the light to bounce on the surface and come back to the device. Then the distance is simply obtained with the equation *space = lightspeed · time*.

These techniques are referred to as *active techniques*, because they project light on the surface. In contrast, the *passive techniques* use only cameras (photographic or video). In this case the 3D model is reconstructed from a set of images through the use of modern Computer Vision techniques. In very simple words, the idea is to be able to match the same point on two or more images. If we can do this for many points, it will be possible to estimate both the position of the cameras and the position of the points in 3D. Note that this is also how we perceive depth: our two eyes see two images and the brain finds the correspondences.

3.1.2   Modeling

An artist or a technician interactively designs the 3D model using geometric modeling software such as Maya®, 3D Studio Max®, Rhinoceros®, Blender and others.

3.1.3 Procedural Modeling

The model is automatically generated using procedural methods. A fractal is an example of procedural generation. A common way to generate a 3D model is to use grammar rules to describe in some way the object to generate.

3.1.4 Simulation

Numerical simulations are used for several goals. Winds, temperature and pressure are simulated for weather forecasts, *fluid dynamics*, that is, the study of how liquids behave, is used for designing engines, cardiac pumps, vehicles and so on. Very often the data produced can be naturally mapped on a three-dimensional model, whether a b-rep, for example the wavefront of a low pressure area, or with a volume, for example the fluid velocity.

In the following we analyze several 3D objects' representation by underlining the advantages and the disadvantages of each one.

3.2 Polygon Meshes

Intuitively, a *polygon mesh* is the partition of a continuous surface in polygonal cells, such as triangles, quadrilaterals, etc. Figure 3.1 shows an example of *triangle mesh*. More formally, a mesh $\mathcal{M}$ can be defined as a tuple $(\mathcal{V}, \mathcal{K})$ where $\mathcal{V} = \{v_i \in \mathbb{R}^3 | i = 1 \ldots N_v\}$ is the set of the ver-

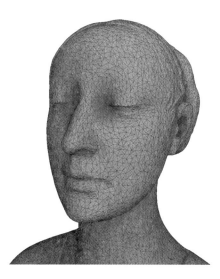

FIGURE 3.1: An example of polygon mesh (about 22,000 faces).

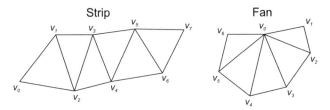

FIGURE 3.2: (Left) A strip of triangles. (Right) A fan of triangles.

tices of the model (points in $\mathbb{R}^3$) and $\mathcal{K}$ contains the *adjacency informa-tion* or, in other words, how the vertices are connected to form edges and faces of the mesh. For example a mesh made by a single triangle would be $(\{v_0, v_1, v_2\}, \{\{v_0, v_1\}, \{v_1, v_2\}, \{v_2, v_0\}, \{v_0, v_1, v_2\}\})$, that is, the three ver-tices, the three edges and the triangle.

The most-used meshes in computer graphics are triangle meshes and quadrilateral meshes (shortened as *quad meshes*). When it comes to render-ing, however, we will always render either points, of segments or triangles, and since a quad mesh can be turned into a triangle mesh just by splitting each quad into two triangles, from now on, when we write mesh we mean triangle mesh.

3.2.1   Fans and Strips

The set of all the neighbors of a vertex v_i is called the *1-ring* of the vertex and is defined as $v_1(i) = \{j | \{i, j\} \in \mathcal{K}\}$. The cardinality of $v_1(i)$ is called *degree* or *valence* of the vertex v_i.

A sequence of adjacent triangles sharing the same vertex is called a *fan* of triangles (see Figure 3.2 (Right)). A *strip* is a sequence of triangles that can be specified by listing its vertices without ambiguity. To be more specific, given an ordered vertex list $\{v_0, v_1, \ldots, v_n\}$, the triangle i is represented by the vertices $\{v_i, v_{i+1}, v_{i+2}\}$ (see Figure 3.2 (Left)). Strips and fans are used to compact the mesh representations. A strip of triangles with n vertices represents $n-2$ triangles. So, a strip of 100 triangle requires 102 vertices to be stored instead of 300. The amount of vertices saved increases with the number of triangles; the average number of vertices $\overline{v_t}$ to represent a triangle in a strip with m triangles is $\overline{v_t} = 1 + 2/m$. In the case of a fan, the triangle i is represented by the vertices $\{v_0, v_{i+1}, v_{i+2}\}$ assuming v_0 is the shared vertex. Fans of triangles have the same performances as strips, that is, the same average number of vertices per triangles.

3.2.2   Manifoldness

A surface is said to be *2-manifold* if the neighborhood of each point **p** on the surface is *homeomorphic* to a disk. Simply put, it means that if we

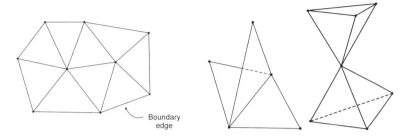

FIGURE 3.3: Manifolds and non-manifolds. (Left) An example of 2-manifold. (Right) Two non-manifold examples.

have a rubber-made disk we can center it on **p** and make it adhere to the surface around it. Figure 3.3 (Right) shows two cases where we cannot do this. This definition of 2-manifold is extended to the surface with boundary by considering cutting away half of the disk and making it adhere to the boundary.

As stated above, manifoldness is a characteristic of general surfaces. When the surface is a polygon mesh, we can determine if it is manifold by checking if the following conditions are true:

- *Edge Manifold.* Every edge is shared by one (that means it is on the boundary of the mesh) or two faces.

- *Vertex Manifold.* If two faces f_a and f_b share a vertex, then we can move from f_a to f_b by traversing only edges in the 1-ring of the vertex. In other words, we can walk over all the neighborhood of the vertex without passing through the vertex itself.

3.2.3 Orientation

Each face is a polygon and hence it has two sides. Let us suppose we paint one side black and one white. If we can paint every face of the mesh so that faces that share an edge are painted the same color, we say the mesh is *orientable* and the *orientation* of a face is how we assigned black and white to its sides. Only we do not need to actually paint the faces, we can assign the orientation by the order in which the vertices are specified. More precisely, if we look at a face and follow its vertices in the order they are specified in $\mathcal{K}$, they can describe a *clockwise* or *anti-clockwise* movement, like that shown in Figure 3.4. Obviously if we look at the same faces from behind, that is, from the back of the page, these orientations will be swapped. We can say that the black side of a face is the side from which the sequence of its vertices is counter-clockwise. Note that two faces f_1 and f_2 have the same orientation if, for each shared edge, its vertices appear in the opposite order in the description of f_1 and f_2.

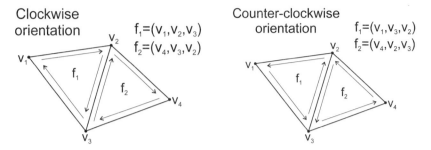

FIGURE 3.4: Mesh orientation.

3.2.4   Advantages and Disadvantages

Polygon meshes suffer from several limitations. First of all, they are a *discrete* representation; curved surfaces can only be piecewise approximated by the planar faces that compose the mesh. The greater the number of faces, the better we can represent the surface, as shown in the example of Figure 3.5 for a sphere.

Another disadvantage is that mesh representation is not compact, that is, a high-detailed model may easily require a huge amount of data to be represented. Again, consider the sphere: we can completely describe its shape mathematically by specifying the radius (one number) while the polygon representation requires much more data to be defined. Figure 3.6 shows an example of a small statue and how even as many as 10,000 faces give a quite poor description of all the details if compared to a version with 100,000 faces. Naturally this data may be compressed and there are many ad hoc techniques for it (see [33] for a survey).

Direct editing is also difficult; designers and artists have to carefully modify each element of the surface in order to obtain the desired result. Although proper user interfaces to edit meshes exist this task still remains problematic.

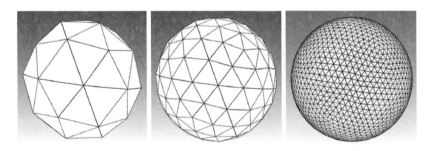

FIGURE 3.5: Mesh is a discrete representation. Curved surfaces are only approximated.

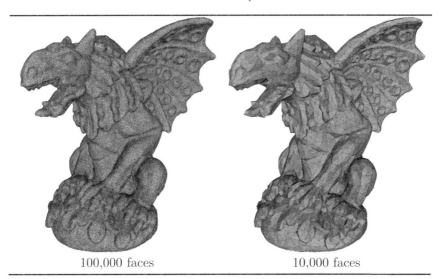

| 100,000 faces | 10,000 faces |

FIGURE 3.6: Mesh is not a compact representation of a shape: a high-detailed surface requires many faces to be represented.

Modeling is more easy and natural with other representations, for example, parametric surfaces such as NURBS (described in Section 3.4) are typically used to this aim. Finally, there is no obvious parameterization (for meshes take a look at Section 7.9 to learn more about the concept of parameterization).

Despite these problems the computer graphics community has put a lot of effort into mesh processing and a huge number of applications use this type of representation. One of the main reasons for this is that meshes are the common denominator of other representations, that is, it is easy to convert other representations to a polygon mesh. Another important motivation is that, as just stated during the description of the rendering pipeline, drawing triangles on the screen is much easier and optimizable than drawing more complex shapes and consequently modern graphics hardware has evolved towards this direction.

3.3 Implicit Surfaces

An implicit surface is defined as the set of points S such that a given trivariate function $f(.)$ is equal to zero. In three dimensions:

$$S = \{(x, y, z) \in \mathbb{R}^3 | f(x, y, z) = 0\} \tag{3.1}$$

where (x, y, z) are cartesian coordinates. The set S is also known as the *zero set* of $f(.)$. For example, a sphere of radius r can be represented by the equation $x^2 + y^2 + z^2 = r^2$, which becomes $x^2 + y^2 + z^2 - r^2 = 0$ in the canonical form. A plane in the space can be represented by the function $ax + by + cz - d = 0$, and so on. So, a 3D object more complex than a basic geometric such as a plane or a sphere can be represented by a set of implicit surface functions, each one describing a part of its shape.

Algebraic surfaces are a particular kind of implicit surface for which $f(.)$ is a polynomial. The degree of an algebraic surface is given by the sum of the maximum powers of all terms $a_m x^{i_m} y^{j_m} z^{k_m}$ of the polynomial. An algebraic surface of degree two describes *quadratic surfaces*, a polynomial of degree three *cubic surfaces*, of degree four *quartic surfaces* and so on. Quadratic surfaces, also called *quadrics*, are very important in geometric modeling. This kind of surface intersects every plane in a proper or degenerate way forming 17 standard-form types of surfaces [40]. To mention some: parallel planes, ellipsoid, elliptic cone, elliptic cylinder, parabolic cylinder, hyperboloid of one sheet, hyperboloid of two sheets can all be obtained as the intersection of a quadric with a plane.

3.3.1   Advantages and Disadvantages

One of the main advantages of implicit representation is their compactness. In their most common implementation the surface is defined as a combination of sphere-like implicit surfaces that form what you usually find under the heading of *blobby surfaces*. These representations can be used for modelling the surface of fluids or even for solid objects. However, they are not very well suited for representing sharp features and for making global modifications to the surface. Implicit surfaces are difficult to render. Either they are tessellated in a polygon mesh or ray tracing is used. In the latter case we need to solve, for each view ray, the problem of finding its intersection with the surface.

3.4   Parametric Surfaces

In order to gently introduce the concepts related to parametric surfaces, we first give a brief description of the generic form of a parametric curve, then we present two important types of parametric curves in computer graphics, the Bézier and B-Spline curves, and finally we describe Bézier patches and NURBS, which are one of the most used parametric surfaces in modern geometric modeling software tools.

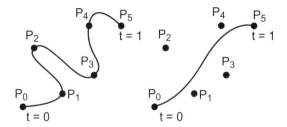

FIGURE 3.7: Interpolation vs approximation.

3.4.1 Parametric Curve

A parametric curve in three-dimensional space is defined by a mapping from the parameter domain, which is a subset of $\mathbb{R}$, to the 3D space $\mathbb{R}^3$:

$$C(t) = (X(t), Y(t), Z(t)) \tag{3.2}$$

where t is the curve parameter. Typically t ranges from 0 to 1, with the starting point of the curve being $C(0)$ and the ending point $C(1)$.

Suppose you want to freely draw a curve and then express it in parametric form. Aside from trivial cases, finding the formulas for $X(t)$, $Y(t)$ and $Y(t)$ directly is a prohibitively difficult task. Fortunately, there are ways that allow us to derive these formulas from an intuitive representation of the curve. For example we can describe the curve as a sequence of points, called *control points*, like those shown in Figure 3.7. We could join these points directly and obtain a piecewise curve but we can do better and obtain a smooth curve by introducing a basis of *blending functions* used to join together the control points in a smooth way. The blending functions define the properties of the final curve/surface such as continuity and differentiability, if the curve/surface is an *approximation* or an *interpolation* of the control points, and so on. We have an interpolation if the curve passes through the control points (see Figure 3.7 (Left)), and an *approximation* if the control points guide the curve but do not necessarily belong to it (see Figure 3.7 (Right)).

The typical formulation of this is:

$$C(t) = \sum_{i=0}^{n} P_i B_i(t) \quad 0 \le t \le 1 \tag{3.3}$$

where P_i are the control points and $\{B_i(.)\}$ are the blending functions. The set of control points is also called the *control polygon*.

3.4.2 Bézier Curves

Béziers curves are one of the parametric curves most frequently used in computer graphics and were independently developed for computer-assisted

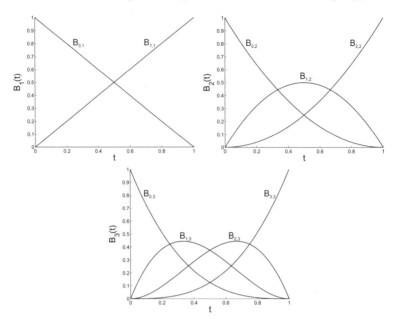

FIGURE 3.8: Bernstein polynomials. (Top-Left) Basis of degree 1. (Top-Right) Basis of degree 2. (Bottom) Basis of degree 3.

car design by two engineers, both working for French automobile companies: Pierre Bézier, who was an engineer for Renault, and Paul de Casteljau, who was an engineer for Citroën. The mathematical definition of a Bézier curve is:

$$P(t) = \sum_{i=0}^{n} P_i B_{i,n}(t) \quad 0 \le t \le 1 \tag{3.4}$$

where P_i are the control points and $B_{i,n}(.)$ are *Bernstein polynomials* of degree n.

A Bernstein polynomial of degree n is defined as:

$$B_{i,n}(t) = \binom{n}{i} t^i (1 - t)^{n-i} \quad i = 0 \ldots n \tag{3.5}$$

where $\binom{n}{i}$ is the binomial coefficient, that is, $\binom{n}{i} = \frac{n!}{i!(n-i)!}$. Figure 3.8 shows the Bernstein basis of degrees 1, 2 and 3.

Bernstein polynomials are widely used as blending functions for parametric curves and surfaces due to their properties:

1. The set of Bernstein polynomials of degree n, $\mathcal{B}_n = \{B_{0,n}(.), B_{1,n}(.), \ldots, B_{n,n}(.)\}$, forms a basis of the vector space of polynomials, called *Bernstein basis*.

2. $\mathcal{B}_n$ is a linear combination of $\mathcal{B}_{n-1}$.

3. They partition the unity (their sum is always one), that is: $\sum_{i=0}^{n} B_{i,n}(t) = 1$.

These properties make them suitable for efficient implementation; polynomials are easy to "treat", a Bernstein basis of degree n can be expressed using the basis of degree $n-1$ (property 2) and so on. Typically, the implementation employs matrix representation of the Bernstein basis, that is, the polynomial basis $\{1, t, t^2, t^3, \dots, t^n\}$ multiplies a matrix of coefficients that defines the Bernstein basis (property 1). For example, considering the basis of degree 2 we can write:

$$B_2(t) = \begin{bmatrix} (1-t)^2 & t(1-t) & t^2 \end{bmatrix} = \begin{bmatrix} 1 & t & t^2 \end{bmatrix} \begin{bmatrix} 1 & 0 & 0 \\ -2 & 2 & 0 \\ 1 & -2 & 1 \end{bmatrix} \qquad (3.6)$$

3.4.2.1 Cubic Bézier Curve

When we talk about Bézier curves, an important aspect, coming from its definition (3.4), is that the number of control points influences the degree of the Bernstein polynomial to use. More precisely $n+1$ control points require a Bernstein basis of degree n. This is not particularly efficient since a curve defined by several control points requires a set of high degree polynomials. For this reason, usually, after specifying the desired degree of the polynomials to use, the control points are grouped into sub-sequences in a way that guarantees the curve continuity. For example, if we want to join three points with a Bernstein polynomial of degree 1 we first join the points P_0 and P_1 and then join the points P_1 and P_2. It is interesting to note that this corresponds with connecting the given points with the corresponding segments, in fact the Bernstein polynomials of degree 1 are $\{(1-t), t\}$ thus resulting in:

$$P(t) = P_0(1-t) + P_1 t \quad 0 \le t \le 1, \qquad (3.7)$$

which corresponds to the linear interpolation between the point P_0 and the point P_1.

Typically, when we have several points to connect, a cubic Bézier curve is used. Following the definition, this curve is formed by the linear combination of 4 control points with the Bernstein basis of degree 3. Taking into account Equation (3.5) the cubic Bézier curve can be written:

$$P(t) = (1-t)^3 P_0 + 3t(1-t)^2 P_1 + 3t^2(1-t)P_2 + t^3 P_3 \qquad (3.8)$$

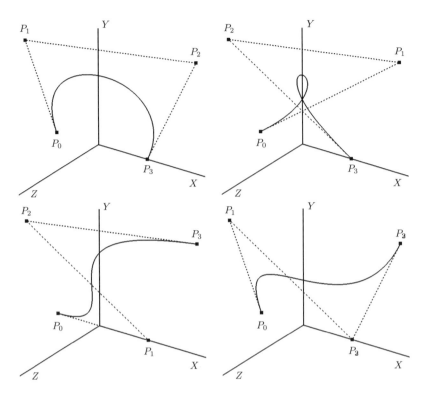

FIGURE 3.9: Cubic Bézier curves examples. Note how the order of the control points influences the final shape of the curve.

By re-arranging this formula in matrix notation it becomes:

$$P(t) = \begin{bmatrix} (1-t)^3 & t(1-t)^2 & t^2(1-t) & t^3 \end{bmatrix} \begin{bmatrix} P_0 \\ P_1 \\ P_2 \\ P_3 \end{bmatrix} =$$

$$= \begin{bmatrix} 1 & t & t^2 & t^3 \end{bmatrix} \begin{bmatrix} 1 & 0 & 0 & 0 \\ -3 & 3 & 0 & 0 \\ 3 & -6 & 3 & 0 \\ 1 & 3 & -3 & 1 \end{bmatrix} \begin{bmatrix} P_0 \\ P_1 \\ P_2 \\ P_3 \end{bmatrix} \tag{3.9}$$

The main characteristics of this curve is that it starts at the point P_0 and ends at the point P_4. The curve in P_0 is tangent to the segment $P_1 - P_0$ and the curve in P_4 is tangent to the segment $P_3 - P_2$. Figure 3.9 shows some examples of cubic Bézier curves. Two examples of Bézier curves with degree higher than 3, and so a number of control points higher than 4, are illustrated in Figure 3.10.

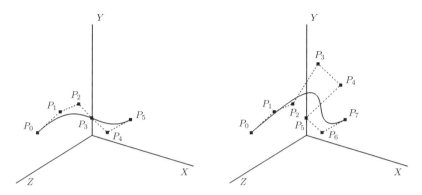

FIGURE 3.10: Bézier curves of high degree (degree 5 on the left and degree 7 on the right).

3.4.3 B-Spline Curves

The definition of a B-spline curve of order k is:

$$P(t) = \sum_{i=0}^{n} P_i N_{i,k}(t) \tag{3.10}$$

where, as usual, P_i are the control points and $N_{i,k}(t)$ are the blending functions defined recursively in the following way:

$$N_{i,k}(t) = \left(\frac{t - t_i}{t_{i+k} - t_i} \right) N_{i,k-1}(t) + \frac{t_{i+k+1} - t}{t_{i+k+1} - t_{i+1}} N_{i+1,k-1}(t) \tag{3.11}$$

for $k > 0$ and

$$N_{i,0}(t) = \left\{ \begin{array}{ll} 1 & t \in [t_i, t_{i+1}) \\ 0 & \text{otherwise} \end{array} \right. \tag{3.12}$$

for $k = 0$. The set $\{t_0, t_1, \ldots, t_{n+k}\}$ is a sequence of values referred to as *knots sequence*. Such sequence influences the shape of the B-spline. In particular, if the knots sequence is uniform, that is, the knots values are equidistant, the B-spline definition becomes $N_{i+1,k}(t) = N_{i,k}(t - t_i)$, that is, the blending functions move along the sequence (see Figure 3.11). A uniform B-spline blending function $N_{i,k}(.)$ is a function of degree k having support in the interval $[t_i, t_{i+k}]$. Note that for B-spline the number of knots k determines the degree of the curve joining the control points and not the number of control points as for the Bézier curves. In other words, B-splines are *local* and the way they locally influence the curve's shape depends on the knots' values; more precisely $N_{i,p}(t) \geq 0$ when $t \in [t_i, t_{i+p+1})$. Another important difference between Bézier curves and B-splines is that Bézier curves must pass through their initial and final control points, making the smoothness between curves joined together more difficult to achieve than in the case of B-splines. For all

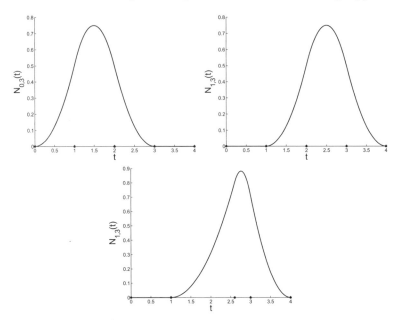

FIGURE 3.11: B-splines blending functions. (Top) Uniform quadratic B-spline functions. Knots sequence $t_i = \{0, 1, 2, 3, 4\}$. (Bottom) Non-uniform quadratic B-spline function. Knots sequence $t_i = \{0, 1, 2.6, 3, 4\}$

of these reasons B-splines are, in general, more flexible than Bézier curves. Some examples of B-splines of different order k defined on the same eight control points of the Bézier curves of Figure 3.10 are shown in Figure 3.12 for comparison. Note the approximating character of the B-spline curves and the fact that the greater k is, the more limited is the support of the curve with respect to the control points. This can be avoided by increasing the multiplicity of the first and last values of the knots (see [11] for more details).

3.4.4   From Parametric Curves to Parametric Surfaces

The extension from parametric curves to parametric surfaces is simple. In this case the parameter domain is a subset of $\mathbb{R}^2$ instead of $\mathbb{R}$ and three bivariate functions ($f : \mathbb{R}^2 \to \mathbb{R}$) defining the mapping between the parameters and the 3D space:

$$S(u, v) = (X(u, v), Y(u, v), Z(u, v)) \qquad (3.13)$$

u and v are the surface parameters. Even in this case the u and v parameters usually range from 0 to 1.

In the case of parametric curves, we have seen that Equation (3.2) can be expressed as a linear combination of control points with some blending

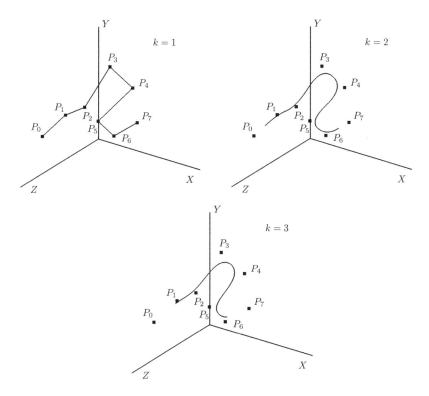

FIGURE 3.12: Examples of B-splines of increasing order defined on eight control points.

functions (3.3). This last equation can be extended to the case of surfaces in several ways. The most used one is the *tensor product surface*, defined as:

$$S(u,v) = \sum_{i=0}^{n}\sum_{j=0}^{m} P_{ij} B_i(u) B_j(v) \qquad (3.14)$$

where P_{ij} are the initial control points and $\{B_i(.)\}$ and $\{B_j(.)\}$ are the blending functions. In this case the control points P_{ij} are referred to as the *control net* of the surface S. Tensor product surfaces are also named *rectangular patches*, since the domain of the parameter (u,v) is a rectangle (in $\mathbb{R}^2$). In the following section we are going to describe two important parametric surfaces: Bézier patches, which are the extension of Bézier curves, and NURBS, which are the extensions of B-splines.

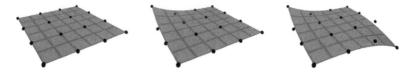

FIGURE 3.13: Bicubic Bézier patch example. The control points are shown as black dots.

3.4.5   Bézier Patches

According to the tensor product surface the definition of Bézier curves can be extended to surfaces in the following way:

$$S(u,v) = \sum_{j=0}^{m} \sum_{i=0}^{n} P_{ij} B_{i,n}(u) B_{j,m}(v) \tag{3.15}$$

where P_{ij} are the points of the control net, $\{B_{i,n}(.)\}$ are Bernstein polynomials of degree n and $\{B_{j,m}(.)\}$ are Bernstein polynomials of degree m. Figure 3.13 shows an example of a bi-cubic Bézier patch. In this case the control net of the patch is formed by 4×4 control points.

The Bézier patches can be assembled together to represent the shape of complex 3D objects. Figure 3.14 shows an example. The model represented in this example is the Utah teapot, a model of a teapot realized in 1975 by Martin Newell, a member of the pioneering graphics program at the University of Utah. Since then, this simple, round, solid, partially concave mathematical model has been a reference object (and something of an inside joke) in the computer graphics community.

FIGURE 3.14: Example of parametric surface representation with Bézier patches. The Utah teapot.

3.4.6 NURBS Surfaces

The non-uniform rational B-splines, or NURBS, are the generalization of the non-rational B-splines (3.10) just seen. Such generalization consists of the use of *ratios of blending functions*. This extends the set of curves that can be represented. Note that Bézier curves are ultimately polynomes and polynomes cannot represent conic curves, that is, curves obtained by intersecting a cone with a plane (such as a circle), but the ratio of polynomials can. So using the ratio of blending functions expands the class of surfaces that can be represented. The term non-uniform refers to the fact that the knots sequence can not be uniform. So, a NURBS curve of order k is defined as:

$$P(t) = \frac{\sum_{i=0}^{n} w_i P_i N_{i,k}(t)}{\sum_{i=0}^{n} w_i N_{i,k}(t)} \qquad (3.16)$$

where n is the number of control points, P_i are the control points, $\{N_{i,k}(t)\}$ is the same blending function as for the B-spline curves and w_i are weights used to alter the shape of the curve. According to the tensor product surface we can extend the definition of NURBS curves in the same manner as Bézier patches to obtain NURBS surfaces:

$$S(u,v) = \frac{\sum_{i=0}^{n} \sum_{j=0}^{m} w_{ij} P_{ij} N_{i,k}(u) N_{j,m}(v)}{\sum_{i=0}^{n} \sum_{j=0}^{m} w_{ij} N_{i,k}(u) N_{j,m}(v)} \qquad (3.17)$$

Thanks to the properties of B-Splines, the local control property still remains valid for the NURBS, that is, the modification of a control point only affects the surface shape in its neighborhood. So, it is easy to control the shape of a large surface. Mainly for this reason NURBS surfaces are the base modeling tool of powerful and famous geometric modellng software such as Maya® and Rhino®. Figure 3.15 depicts an example of a 3D model realized using NURBS.

3.4.7 Advantages and Disadvantages

Parametric surfaces are very flexible representations of 3D objects with a lot of interesting properties; for example, parameterization is just available by definition, geometry processing is analytical (that is, the tangent of the surface in a point is computed by derivation of the parametric equation), they can be easily converted to other representations, and so on. The main limitation of this representation concerns the difficulties in automatically generating a model composed of a set of parametric surfaces. In fact, as just mentioned, the most typical use of parametric surfaces is in geometric modeling software, that is, in the *manual* generation of 3D objects.

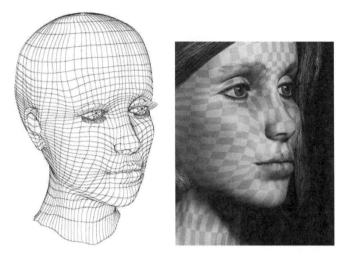

FIGURE 3.15: NURBS surfaces modelling. (Left) NURBS head model from the "NURBS Head Modeling Tutorial" by Jeremy Bim (available at *http://www.3drender.com/jbirn/ea/HeadModel.html.*) (Right) The grid on the final rendered version shows the UV parameterization of the surface.

3.5   Voxels

Voxels are commonly used to represent *volumetric* data. This representation can be seen as the natural extension of two-dimensional images to the third dimension. Like a digital image is represented as a matrix of *picture elements*, called *pixels*, a volumetric image is represented by a set of *volume elements*, called *voxels*, arranged on a regular 3D grid (see Figure 3.16). Each voxel of this 3D grid provides information about the volume. Depending on the specific application, many types of data can be stored into each voxel. Such information could be the density of the volume element, the temperature, the color, etc.

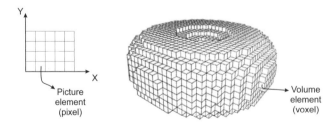

FIGURE 3.16: From pixels to voxels.

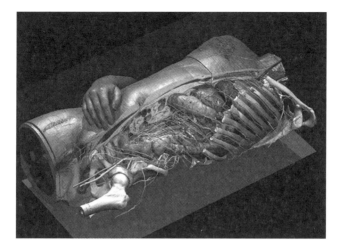

FIGURE 3.17 (SEE COLOR INSERT): An example of voxels in medical imaging. (Courtesy of *Voxel-Man* http://www.voxel-man.com.)

One of the main application domains of the voxels representation is medical imaging, because devices to acquire medical information such as computerized tomography (CT) or magnetic resonance (MR) create a volume of data. For example a voxel may store a code indicating the type of tissue occupying that physical space, so that we can produce an image like the one shown in Figure 3.17.

3.5.1 Rendering Voxels

Unlike the other representations, rendering a volume of data does not have a unique meaning. The reason is that we are just able to see one 2D image at time. Figures 3.17 and 3.16 show two examples where the voxels in the boundary of the objects are shown, because there are representations of solid non-transparent objects. On the other hand, if we store a *pressure value* in each voxel we may want another type of visualization. Typically, we may want to see the region with a specific value of pressure. More formally, if we call $f(x, y, z)$ the function that, given a three-dimensional point, returns the value stored in the voxel grid, and the pressure value we are looking for is c, we want to render the *iso-surface* $S = \{(x, y, z) | f(x, y, z) = c\}$. Note that this is none other than the implicit representation shown in Section 3.3, where the function f is not defined analytically but by samples. The most well established way to do that is to extract from the voxels a polygon representation of the iso-surface S by means of the marching cubes algorithm [26]. Other more recent approaches to extract a mesh from volume data can be found in [20, 44].

Mesh-to-voxels conversion corresponds to the 3D version of polygon rasterization we will see in detail in Chapter 5. Although computationally demanding, it can be efficiently performed by exploiting modern graphics hardware [24].

3.5.2   Advantages and Disadvantages

The voxels representation has several advantages: it is conceptually simple and easy to encode in a data structure; it is easy to test if a point is inside or outside the volume, and the extension of many image processing algorithms to voxels is natural. Voxel representation may also be used for editing if very local modifications are done, such as in the case of *digital sculpting*.

The disadvantages of using voxels compared to polygon meshes or parametric surfaces is the very same as between raster images and vectorial images, that is: the accuracy of the description depends on the resolution of the grid. This means that if our goal is to represent a solid object such as the torus in Figure 3.16, a parametric surface will do a better job than a voxel representation. Furthermore, making global modifications to the shapes or changing their position in space (translating or rotating) is costly.

3.6   Constructive Solid Geometry (CSG)

Constructive solid geometry (or CSG) represents the volume of a 3D object by combining simple solid shapes called *primitives* with boolean operations such as union, difference, and intersection. Common primitives are planes, boxes, tetrahedra, spheres, cylinders, etc. Usually the model is stored as a binary tree where the leaf nodes are the primitives and each branch node is a boolean operator (Figure 3.18 shows an example).

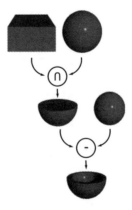

FIGURE 3.18: Constructive solid geometry. An example of a CSG tree.

The primitives can be defined, using implicit equations, as the set of points that satisfy the equation $f(x, y, z) < 0$, where $f(.) = 0$ is an implicit surface function. From this definition the points such that $f(x, y, z) > 0$ are outside the volume bounded by the surface defined through $f(.)$. This last fact is assumed conventionally. Some primitives are defined by more than one implicit equations (e.g., a cube).

3.6.1 Advantages and Disadvantages

The constructive solid geometry finds its main application in the CAD/CAM field where the exact geometric modeling of the parts of the modeled object (e.g., a mechanical piece) is required. Though useful for such applications, in general CSG is not an efficient representation; the rendering must pass through a conversion step into triangle meshes, editing complex shape is difficult, and the compactness of the representation much depends on how the model is created.

3.7 Subdivision Surfaces

The techniques to create curves and surfaces through a process of subdivision are relatively recent. Informally, subdivision surfaces can be thought of as a polygon mesh plus a set of rules that enable it to be refined (through subdivision) to better approximate the surface it represents. In this way subdivision surfaces have the same properties as polygon meshes while alleviating the problem of discrete approximation. This motivates the growing interest in subdivision methods in geometric modeling: subdivision bridges the gap between *discrete* and *continuous* representations of curves and surfaces. In the next section, as for the description of parametric surfaces, we begin to present an example of curves generation through subdivision, and then we describe subdivision surfaces.

3.7.1 Chaikin's Algorithm

The Chaikin's algorithm is a method to generate curves starting from a set of control points by means of subdivision. Let us assume that the initial curve P^0 is represented by the sequence of vertices $\{p_1^0, p_2^0, \ldots, p_n^0\}$ (the superscript of the points indicates the level of subdivision of the curve). The zero level corresponds to the original control polygon. At each subdivision step Chaikin's scheme creates two new vertices between each pair of consecutive ones using

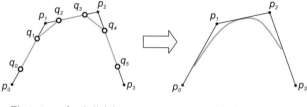

First step of subdivision   Limit curve

FIGURE 3.19: Chaikin's subdivision scheme.

the following subdivision rules:

$$q_{2i}^{k+1} = \frac{3}{4}p_i^k + \frac{1}{4}p_{i+1}^k$$
$$q_{2i+1}^{k+1} = \frac{1}{4}p_i^k + \frac{3}{4}p_{i+1}^k$$

(3.18)

where q_i^{k+1} are the new generated points at level of subdivision $k + 1$. After the generation of the new points the old vertices are discarded and only the new points q_i^{k+1} define the curve at level $k + 1$. Figure 3.19 shows the result of the first step of subdivision on a curve formed by 4 points. By iteratively applying (3.18) we obtain the curves P^1, P^2 and so on. When k approaches infinity a continuous curve is generated. This limit curve is indicated with P^∞. The geometric properties of the limit curve depend on the specific subdivision rules used to generate it. In particular, Chaikin's scheme generates a quadratic B-spline. Like for parametric surfaces, a subdivision scheme may be *interpolating* or *approximating*. If the limit curve interpolates the points of the initial control polygon then the scheme is interpolating. This happens if after each subdivision step both the old and the new generated vertices belong to the curve, and the old vertices remain in the same position. On the other hand, if after each subdivision step the old vertices are discarded or moved according to some rules the limit curve does not interpolate the initial control points and the scheme is approximating. The Chaikin's scheme belongs to the latter category since, after each subdivision step, the old vertices are discarded.

3.7.2   The 4-Point Algorithm

For completeness, we present an example of an interpolating scheme for curve generation called the *4-point algorithm* [8]. This scheme uses the four consequent points in the sequence, p_{i-2}, p_{i-1}, p_i and p_{i+1}, to create a new point. The subdivision rules are:

$$q_{2i}^{k+1} = p_i^k$$
$$q_{2i+1}^{k+1} = \left(\frac{1}{2} + w\right)\left(p_i^k + p_{i+1}^k\right) - w\left(p_{i-1}^k + p_{i+2}^k\right)$$

(3.19)

The first equation in (3.19) means that the original points do not change as required by an interpolating scheme. The second equation is for creating the new points between p_i^k and p_{i+1}^k. The weight w enables us to control the final shape of the curve by increasing or decreasing the "tension" of the curve. When $w = 0$ the resulting curve is a linear interpolation of the starting points. For $w = 1/16$ a cubic interpolation is achieved. For $0 < w < 1/8$ the resulting curve is always continuous and differentiable (C^1).

3.7.3 Subdivision Methods for Surfaces

Subdivision methods for surfaces generation work in a way analogous to those for curves: starting from an initial control mesh (M^0) the subdivision rules that define the subdivision scheme are iteratively applied to obtain a finer mesh (M^k) at level of subdivision k. The initial mesh can also be seen as the equivalent of the control net of the parametric surface. The difference between the two representations relies on the way the surface is generated.

Obviously, different subdivision schemes generate surfaces with different geometric properties. Here, we would like to give a panoramic of such methods and make the reader able to understand how a subdivision method is characterized. In particular we focus on *stationary* schemes. A subdivision scheme is said to be stationary if the subdivision rules do not depend on the level of subdivision but remain the same during all the subdivision steps. Other classes of subdivision schemes, such as *variational subdivision*, are not discussed here.

3.7.4 Classification

In these last years several stationary schemes have been developed. A classification of them related to their basic properties is particularly useful since it helps us to immediately understand how a certain subdivision method works depending on its categorization.

3.7.4.1 Triangular or Quadrilateral

Subdivision schemes work on polygon meshes. Although there are proposals for mesh with arbitrary combinations of cells, the most used and known approaches are designed for triangle mesh and quadrilateral meshes that have their specific subdivision schemes.

3.7.4.2 Primal or Dual

A scheme is said to be *primal* if it proceeds by subdividing the faces of the mesh (*face splitting*), and *dual* if it splits the vertices (*vertex splitting*).

The *1-to-4 split* shown in Figure 3.20 is a common primal scheme: each face is subdivided into four new faces by inserting a new vertex for each edge of

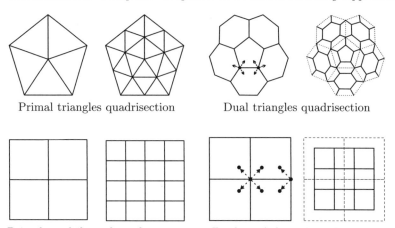

Primal triangles quadrisection   Dual triangles quadrisection

Primal quadrilateral quadrisection   Dual quadrilateral quadrisection

FIGURE 3.20: Primal and dual schemes for triangular and quadrilateral mesh.

the coarse mesh, retaining old vertices, and then connecting the new inserted vertices together.

The dual schemes work on the dual of the polygon mesh, which is obtained by taking the centroids of the faces as vertices, and connecting those in adjacent faces by an edge. Then for each vertex a new one is created inside each face adjacent to the vertex, as shown in the top row of Figure 3.20 (third row from left), and they are connected as shown in the last row of the figure.

Note that for quadrilateral meshes this can be done in such a way that the refined mesh has only quadrilateral faces, while in the case of triangles, vertex split (dual) schemes result in non-nesting hexagonal tilings. In this sense quadrilateral tilings are special: they support both primal and dual subdivision schemes naturally.

3.7.4.3   Approximation vs Interpolation

As previously stated, a subdivision method can produce a curve/surface, that is an interpolation of the initial curve/surface, or that is an approximation of the initial control net. By considering this property we can classify the subdivision schemes into *interpolating* and *approximating*. Primal schemes can be approximating or interpolating. Dual schemes are always intrinsically approximating by definition. Interpolation is an attractive property for several reasons. First, the control points are also points of the limit surface. Second, many algorithms can be considerably simplified improving computational efficiency. Additionally, if needed, the refinement of the mesh can be tuned locally by performing a different number of subdivision steps in different parts of the mesh. Nevertheless, the quality of the surfaces generated by interpolating schemes is lower than that of approximating schemes. Also, the convergence to the limit surface is typically slower with respect to approximating schemes.

3.7.4.4 Smoothness

The smoothness of the limit surface, that is, of the surface obtained applying the subdivision scheme an infinite number of times, is measured by its continuity properties. The limit surface could be continuous and differentiable (C^1), continuous and twice differentiable (C^2) and so on.

Many subdivision schemes with different properties have been proposed, and analyzing them is out of the scope of this book. Just to give you an idea of how such schemes are designed, in the following we show some examples. In particular we will describe the Loop scheme, which is an approximating scheme for triangular meshes, and the (modified) butterfly scheme, which is an interpolation scheme for triangular meshes.

3.7.5 Subdivision Schemes

In this section we present some classical subdivision schemes for triangular meshes to give an idea of how a subdivision scheme is defined. The approximating Loop scheme [25] and the interpolating butterfly scheme [10] are presented. Both these schemes are primal. Often, the subdivision rules of a specific subdivision method are visualized using *masks of weights*. These masks are special drawings that show which control points are used to compute the new ones and the relative weights. This is a standard way to give a compact description of a subdivision scheme. Decoding the subdivision rules for these masks is not difficult, but before explaining it we need to introduce some of the terminology used for the description of the schemes.

We can see from Figure 3.20 that subdivision schemes defined on triangular meshes create new vertices of valence 6 in the interior of the mesh, while subdivision schemes for quadrilateral meshes generate vertices with valence 4. This fact relies on the definition of *semi-regular meshes*, where all the *regular* vertices have valence 6 (for triangle meshes) except the vertices of the initial control mesh, which can have any valence. For a quadrilateral mesh the regular vertices have valence 4. The non-regular vertices are called *extraordinary vertices*. Often, extraordinary vertices require different subdivision rules than the regular ones. The masks of weights can be of two typs: the masks of odd vertices and the masks for even vertices. The *odd vertices* are the ones created at the given level of subdivision while the *even vertices* are the ones inherited from the previous level of subdivision. This notation comes from analyzing the one-dimensional case, when vertices of the control polygon can be enumerated sequentially, thus resulting in odd numbers for the new inserted vertices [48]. The subdivision rules have to be adapted for the boundary of the mesh. The same rules can be used to preserve sharp features of the initial control mesh by tagging the interior edges of interest as boundary edges. Such tagged edges

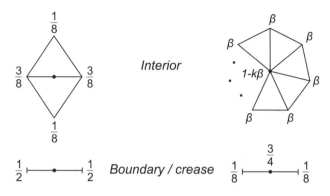

Masks for odd vertices   Masks for even vertices

FIGURE 3.21: Loop subdivision scheme.

are called *creases* (see also Section 6.6.1). Obtaining the subdivision rules for its corresponding mask is not difficult. The new vertices are shown in the mask as a black dot. The edges indicate which neighbor vertices have to be taken into account to calculate the subdivision rules. For example, referring to the masks of the Loop scheme of Figure 3.21, the interior odd vertex v^{j+1}, that is the new inserted vertex, is computed by centering the relative mask over it, obtaining:

$$v^{j+1} = \frac{3}{8}v_1^j + \frac{3}{8}v_2^j + \frac{1}{8}v_3^j + \frac{1}{8}v_4^j \qquad (3.20)$$

where v_1 and v_2 are the immediate neighbors of the new vertex v, and v_3 and v_4 are the other two vertices of the triangles that share the edge where v will be inserted. The mask for the even vertices, which are present only in the approximating schemes, are used to modify the position of the existing vertices.

3.7.5.1   Loop Scheme

The Loop scheme is an approximating scheme for triangle meshes proposed by Charles Loop [25]. This scheme produces surfaces that are C^2 continuous everywhere except at extraordinary vertices where the limit surface is C^1-continuous. The masks of weights for the Loop scheme are shown in Figure 3.21. As proposed by Loop, the parameter β can be computed as $\beta = \frac{1}{n}\left(\frac{5}{8} - \left(\frac{3}{8} + \frac{1}{4}\cos\frac{2\pi}{n}\right)^2\right)$ where n is the number of adjacent vertices.

3.7.5.2   Modified Butterfly Scheme

The butterfly scheme was first proposed by Dyn et al. [10]. The limit surface is not C^1-continuous at extraordinary points of valence $k = 3$ and $k > 7$ [46], while it is C^1 on regular meshes. A modification of the original

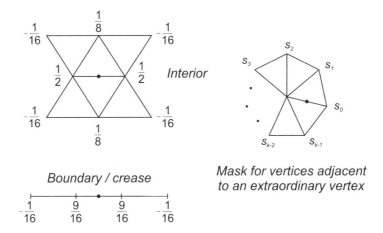

Interior

Mask for vertices adjacent
to an extraordinary vertex

Boundary / crease

Masks for odd vertices

FIGURE 3.22: Butterfly (modified) subdivision scheme.

butterfly scheme was proposed by Zorin et al. [47]. This variant guarantees C^1-continuous surfaces for arbitrary meshes. The masks of this scheme are given in Figure 3.22. The coefficients s_i for the extraordinary vertices are $\{s_0 = \frac{5}{12}, s_1 = -\frac{1}{12}, s_2 = -\frac{1}{12}\}$ for $k = 3$, $\{s_0 = \frac{3}{8}, s_1 = 0, s_2 = -\frac{1}{8}, s_3 = 0\}$ for $k = 4$, and the general formula for $k > 5$ is:

$$s_i = \frac{1}{k}\left(\frac{1}{4} + \cos\left(\frac{2i\pi}{k}\right) + \frac{1}{2}\cos\left(\frac{4i\pi}{k}\right)\right) \tag{3.21}$$

Since this scheme is interpolating, only the masks for the odd vertices are given, and the even vertices preserve its position during each subdivision step.

3.7.6 Advantages and Disadvantages

The subdivision surface attempts to overcome the weak point of meshes representation bridging the gap between a discrete and a continuous representation. Thanks to the subdivision schemes small meshes can be used to represent smooth surfaces, which otherwise require a huge number of triangles to be defined. Moreover, the editing operations are not as complex as in the case of meshes since the effort is only into the drawing of the initial mesh. Hence, this representation is powerful and flexible. In recent years, subdivision surfaces are gaining diffusion and several geometric modeling software tools such as Maya® include them.

3.8   Data Structures for Polygon Meshes

As stated before, polygon meshes are the common denominator of the other representations, and, furthermore, the graphics hardware is especially good in rendering triangle meshes. Therefore it is useful to see what data structures are used to encode this kind of representation. Please note that, although we will use trinagle meshes as examples, the following data structures work for generic polygon meshes.

One of the main factors that influences how a mesh should be implemented is the *queries* the application has to do on it. With the term query we mean the retrieval of information about the connectivity of the mesh elements. Some examples of queries on a mesh are:

- Which are the faces adjacent to a given vertex?

- Which are the edges adjacent to a given vertex?

- Which are the vertices connected with a given vertex v through the set of its adjacent edges (that is, the 1-ring of v)?

Data structures are often tailored to certain types of queries, which in turn are application dependent, so we cannot give a unique general criterion for assessing a data structure. However, we can analyze their performance in several regards:

- *Queries*—How efficient can the main queries listed above be made;

- *Memory footprint*—How much memory the data structure takes;

- *Manifoldness Assumption*—Can non-manifold meshes be encoded?

It will be clear that every data structure is a tradeoff between those three characteristics. Note that the memory footprint (and the description of the data structure) only takes into account the data for storing the mesh adjacencies and not data proper of the vertices, the edges or the faces (such as, for example, the normal) with the only exception being the position of the vertices.

3.8.1   Indexed Data Structure

One of the most intuitive implementations consists of storing the mesh as a sequence of triples of vertices. Typically, each face is stored as a triple of the vertices that define it.

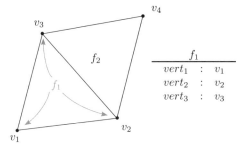

$$
\begin{array}{c|c}
\multicolumn{2}{c}{f_1} \\
\hline
vert_1 \;:\; v_1 \\
vert_2 \;:\; v_2 \\
vert_3 \;:\; v_3 \\
\end{array}
$$

FIGURE 3.23: An example of indexed data structure.

```
class face { float v1[3]; float v2[3];float v3[3];};
```

This data structure is trivial to update but that is the only good quality. No query besides the position of the vertex itself or "which other vertices are in the same face" can be done naturally because there is no explicit information on adjacency. The data stored is redundant, because each vertex must be stored once for each face adjacent to it.

In order to avoid vertices duplication, the vertex data can be stored in two separate arrays, the vertices array and the faces array.

```
class face{ PointerToVertex  v1,   v2,   v3; } ;
class vertex { float x,y,z;};
```

The type **PointerToVertex** indicates some kind of pointer to the vertices. In a C++ implementation they can be actual pointers to memory, while in JavaScript they will be integer indices indicating the position of the vertices in the array of vertices. This is why this data structure is also known as the *Indexed Data Structure* (see Figure 3.23). The Indexed Data Structure is still quite poor on queries. Although it allows us to query for the vertices of a given face in constant time (three pointers to follow), querying for all the faces (or edges, or vertices) adjacent to a vertex requires traversing the vector of the faces. The memory footprint is, on average, the same as the simple sequence of triples. This data structure is still very simple and update operations such as adding/removing one face are easy to do. Furthermore, the Indexed Data Structure can encode non-manifold meshes.

Both these data structures map directly on the WebGL internal format for rendering. This means that when we have the vector of vertices and the vector of faces, we may copy them directly on GPU memory for rendering, as we already did in Section 2.3.

If our application needs to store the edges explicitly, because some kind of value must be associated to them, we can extend the Indexed Data Structure by adding the list of edges and hence have three arrays: the vertices, the edges and the faces array. This time the faces point to edges and the edges point to their vertices. Note that, with respect to the indexed

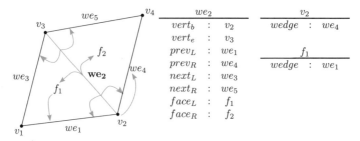

FIGURE 3.24: Winged-edge data structure. The pointers of the edge e_5 are drawn in cyan.

data structure, accessing all the vertices of a face costs twice as much because we need to access the edge first, and from the edge the vertices.

```
class vertex {float x,y,z;};

class edge { PointerToVertex v1, v2; };

class face { PointerToEdge  L1,  L2,  L3;};
```

3.8.2   Winged-Edge

The *winged-edge* is an edge-based representation of polygon meshes. It was introduced by Bruce G. Baumgart [2] in 1975 and it is one of the first data structures for meshes that allows complex queries.

First of all, this data structure assumes that the mesh is two-manifold, so each edge is shared by two faces (or one face if it is a boundary edge). The name comes from the fact that the two faces sharing the edge are its "wings." The main element of this data structure is the edge. As Figure 3.24 illustrates, the edge we_2 stores, for each of the adjacent faces f_1 and f_2, a pointer to each edge that shares one of its two vertices with we_2. Then it also stores the pointers to its two adjacent vertices and to the two adjacent faces. The faces store a single pointer to one (any) of their edges and the vertex stores a pointer to one of its adjacent edges.

The winged edge allows us to perform queries on the 1-ring in linear time because it allows us to jump from one edge to the other by pivoting on the shared vertex. On the average, the memory footprint is three times that of the IDS and updates are more involving, although linear in time.

3.8.3   Half-Edge

The *half-edge* [28] is another edge-based data structure that attempts to simplify the winged-edge while maintaining its flexibility. As the name sug-

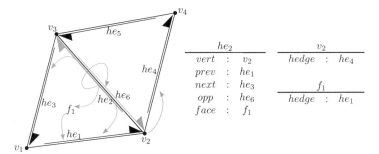

The table shown in the figure:

he_2		v_2	
vert	: v_2	*hedge* :	he_4
prev	: he_1		
next	: he_3	f_1	
opp	: he_6	*hedge* :	he_1
face	: f_1		

FIGURE 3.25: Half-edge data structure.

gests, the half-edge is the "half" of a winged-edge, that is, it is a winged-edge decomposed into two (oriented) half-edges as shown in Figure 3.25.

The half-edge keeps one pointer to the previous half edge and one to the next along the *loop* of half edges that describes the face, plus a pointer to the other half edge on the same edge but oriented in the opposite direction. The half edge has the same characteristics as the winged edge but it is more elegant and introducing the orientation makes it so that the same queries may be done more efficiently.

Other similar data structures include the doubly connected edge list (DCEL) [31] and/or the quad-edge data structure [13]. An overview and comparison of these different data structures together with a description of their implementations can be found in [16].

3.9 The First Code: Making and Showing Simple Primitives

In this section we create the first building block for drawing our scene in 3D.

We will show and explain the code to generate some basic 3D shapes that will be used in the rest of the book. In particular, we will learn how to define a cube, a cone and a cylinder. In the next chapter these basic shapes will be assembled together to form a first sketch of our world with trees (as a combination of cylinders and cones) and cars (as a combination of cubes and cylinders).

We will encode these shapes with an IDS. We do this since, as just described in Chapter 2, in WebGL we sent geometry and other information to the rendering pipeline using typed arrays of data. For each shape we have an

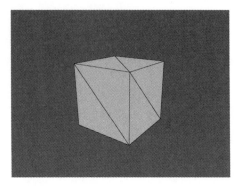

FIGURE 3.26: Cube primitive.

array of vertices:

$$\underbrace{x_0 \ y_0 \ z_0}_{v_0} \ \underbrace{x_1 \ y_1 \ z_1}_{v_1} \ \cdots \ \underbrace{x_{N_v} \ y_{N_v} \ z_{N_v}}_{v_{N_v}} \qquad (3.22)$$

where N_v is the number of vertices of the mesh, and an array of faces, where each face is defined by the indices of three vertex.

$$\underbrace{v0_0 \ v1_0 \ v2_0}_{f_0} \ \underbrace{v0_1 \ v1_1 \ v2_1}_{f_1} \ \cdots \ \underbrace{v0_{N_f} \ v1_{N_f} \ v2_{N_f}}_{f_{N_f}} \qquad (3.23)$$

where N_f is the number of faces (triangles) of the mesh.

3.9.1 The Cube

We first begin creating a cube centered at the origin and with sides of length two.

Listing 3.1 shows the code to define a class that represents a cube primitive. The result is shown in Figure 3.26.

The vertices are stored in the **vertices** array while the index of the triangles are stored in the **triangleIndices** array. The number of vertices and faces are stored explicitly as member variables of the class (**numTriangles** and **numFaces**, respectively). We can see that the definition of the positions of each vertex is given explicitly. The things to pay attention to in this example concern the indices of each face. Since the cube is defined by triangles we need two triangles for each face of the cube. Moreover, each triangle should respect a precise order of definition to account for CW or CCW as explained in Section 3.2.3. The consistency of the triangles' order is particularly important when certain processing is performed on the mesh. If it is wrong, some operations, like navigating the mesh or calculating the exitant normals of the face, for example, could give wrong results.

```
///// CUBE DEFINTION
/////
///// Cube is defined to be centered at the origin of the ↵
   coordinate reference system.
///// Cube size is assumed to be 2.0 x 2.0 x 2.0 .
function Cube () {

  this.name = "cube";

  // vertices definition
  /////////////////////////////////////////////////////////////////

  this.vertices = new Float32Array([
    -1.0, -1.0,  1.0,
     1.0, -1.0,  1.0,
    -1.0,  1.0,  1.0,
     1.0,  1.0,  1.0,
    -1.0, -1.0, -1.0,
     1.0, -1.0, -1.0,
    -1.0,  1.0, -1.0,
     1.0,  1.0, -1.0
  ]);

  // triangles definition
  /////////////////////////////////////////////////////////////////

  this.triangleIndices = new Uint16Array([
    0, 1, 2,   2, 1, 3,   // front
    5, 4, 7,   7, 4, 6,   // back
    4, 0, 6,   6, 0, 2,   // left
    1, 5, 3,   3, 5, 7,   // right
    2, 3, 6,   6, 3, 7,   // top
    4, 5, 0,   0, 5, 1    // bottom
  ]);

  this.numVertices = this.vertices.length/3;
  this.numTriangles = this.triangleIndices.length/3;

}
```

LISTING 3.1: Cube primitive.

3.9.2 Cone

The definition of the cone is a bit more complex than that of the cube. The cone is defined by fixing an apex at a certain height, creating a set of vertices posed on a circle that forms the base of the cone, and connecting them to form the triangle mesh. Our cone is centered at the origin of its coordinate system and has a height of 2 units and a radius of 1 unit, as you can see in Listing 3.2 (Figure 3.27 shows the result).

In this case the generation of the geometric primitive includes the concept of "resolution" of the geometry. For resolution we mean a parameter related to the number of triangles that will compose the final geometric primitive.

FIGURE 3.27: Cone primitive.

The more triangles are used, the more the primitive will look smooth. In this particular case, a resolution of n gives a cone composed by $2n$ triangles.

The vertices that form the circular base are generated in the following way: first, an angle step (Δ_α) is computed by subdividing 2π for the resolution of the cone: $\Delta_\alpha = \frac{2\pi}{n}$. With simple trigonometry the base vertices are calculated as:

$$
\begin{aligned}
x &= \cos \alpha \\
y &= 0 \qquad\qquad\qquad\qquad (3.24)\\
z &= \sin \alpha
\end{aligned}
$$

$$(3.25)$$

where, in this case, y is the up axis and xz form the base plane. α is the angle corresponding to the i-th vertex, that is $\alpha = i\Delta$. Hence, a resolution of n generates a base composed by $n+1$ vertices, the additional vertex corresponds to the origin of the axis and it is used to connect the triangles of the base of the cone. The final cone is composed by $n+2$ vertices, the $n+1$ of the base plus the apex.

The triangles are created by first connecting the base of the cone, and then the lateral surface of the cone. Even in this case we have to pay attention to whether the order of the indices guarantees a consistent CW or CCW orientation. To facilitate the understanding of the connections we point out that the vertices are stored in the **vertices** array in the following way:

$$
\begin{aligned}
\text{index } 0 &\rightarrow \text{ apex} \\
\text{index } 1\ldots n &\rightarrow \text{ base vertices} \\
\text{index } n+1 &\rightarrow \text{ center of the base}
\end{aligned}
$$

where n is the value of **resolution**.

///// CONE DEFINITION

```
/////
///// Resolution is the number of faces used to tesselate the ↩
   cone.
///// Cone is defined to be centered at the origin of the ↩
   coordinate reference system, and lying on the XZ plane.
///// Cone height is assumed to be 2.0. Cone radius is assumed ↩
   to be 1.0 .
function Cone (resolution) {

  this.name = "cone";

  // vertices definition
  ///////////////////////////////////////////////////////////////

  this.vertices = new Float32Array(3*(resolution+2));

  // apex of the cone
  this.vertices[0] = 0.0;
  this.vertices[1] = 2.0;
  this.vertices[2] = 0.0;

  // base of the cone
  var radius = 1.0;
  var angle;
  var step = 6.2831853071795864769252866766559 / resolution;

  var vertexoffset = 3;
  for (var i = 0; i < resolution; i++) {

    angle = step * i;

    this.vertices[vertexoffset] = radius * Math.cos(angle);
    this.vertices[vertexoffset+1] = 0.0;
    this.vertices[vertexoffset+2] = radius * Math.sin(angle);
    vertexoffset += 3;
  }

  this.vertices[vertexoffset] = 0.0;
  this.vertices[vertexoffset+1] = 0.0;
  this.vertices[vertexoffset+2] = 0.0;

  // triangles defition
  ///////////////////////////////////////////////////////////////

  this.triangleIndices = new Uint16Array(3*2*resolution);

  // lateral surface
  var triangleoffset = 0;
  for (var i = 0; i < resolution; i++) {

    this.triangleIndices[triangleoffset] = 0;
    this.triangleIndices[triangleoffset+1] = 1 + (i % resolution↩
      );
    this.triangleIndices[triangleoffset+2] = 1 + ((i+1) % ↩
      resolution);
    triangleoffset += 3;
  }
```

FIGURE 3.28: Cylinder primitive.

```
// bottom part of the cone
for (var i = 0; i < resolution; i++) {

    this.triangleIndices[triangleoffset] = resolution+1;
    this.triangleIndices[triangleoffset+1] = 1 + (i % resolution↩
        );
    this.triangleIndices[triangleoffset+2] = 1 + ((i+1) % ↩
        resolution);
    triangleoffset += 3;
}

this.numVertices = this.vertices.length/3;
this.numTriangles = this.triangleIndices.length/3;
}
```

LISTING 3.2: Cone primitive.

3.9.3   Cylinder

The generation of the cylinder primitive is similar to that of the cone (Listing 3.3). Figure 3.28 shows the resulting primitive. The base of the cylinder lies on the xz plane and it is centered at the origin. The base of the cylinder is generated in the same way as the base of the cone; even in this case the `resolution` parameter corresponds to the number of vertices of the base. The upper part of the cylinder is analogue to the bottom part. Hence, the final cylinder has $2n + 2$ vertices and $4n$ triangles if the value of `resolution` is n. After both the vertices of the bottom and upper part are generated, the triangles are defined, taking care to have a consistent orientation, as usual. In this case the vertices–indices correspondence is:

$$\begin{array}{rcl}
\text{index } 0 \ldots n-1 & \rightarrow & \text{base vertices} \\
\text{index } n \ldots 2n-1 & \rightarrow & \text{upper vertices} \\
\text{index } 2n & \rightarrow & \text{center of the lower circle} \\
\text{index } 2n+1 & \rightarrow & \text{center of the upper circle}
\end{array}$$

```
///// CYLINDER DEFINITION
/////
///// Resolution is the number of faces used to tesselate the ←
   cylinder.
///// Cylinder is defined to be centered at the origin of the ←
   coordinate axis, and lying on the XZ plane.
///// Cylinder height is assumed to be 2.0. Cylinder radius is ←
   assumed to be 1.0 .
function Cylinder (resolution) {

  this.name = "cylinder";

  // vertices definition
  //////////////////////////////////////////////////////////////

  this.vertices = new Float32Array (3*(2*resolution+2));

  var radius = 1.0;
  var angle;
  var step = 6.2831853071795864769252866766559 / resolution;

  // lower circle
  var vertexoffset = 0;
  for (var i = 0; i < resolution; i++) {

    angle = step * i;

    this.vertices[vertexoffset] = radius * Math.cos(angle);
    this.vertices[vertexoffset+1] = 0.0;
    this.vertices[vertexoffset+2] = radius * Math.sin(angle);
    vertexoffset += 3;
  }

  // upper circle
  for (var i = 0; i < resolution; i++) {

    angle = step * i;

    this.vertices[vertexoffset] = radius * Math.cos(angle);
    this.vertices[vertexoffset+1] = 2.0;
    this.vertices[vertexoffset+2] = radius * Math.sin(angle);
    vertexoffset += 3;
  }

  this.vertices[vertexoffset] = 0.0;
  this.vertices[vertexoffset+1] = 0.0;
  this.vertices[vertexoffset+2] = 0.0;
```

```
vertexoffset += 3;

this.vertices[vertexoffset] = 0.0;
this.vertices[vertexoffset+1] = 2.0;
this.vertices[vertexoffset+2] = 0.0;


// triangles definition
/////////////////////////////////////////////////////////////

this.triangleIndices = new Uint16Array(3*4*resolution);

// lateral surface
var triangleoffset = 0;
for (var i = 0; i < resolution; i++)
{
  this.triangleIndices[triangleoffset] = i;
  this.triangleIndices[triangleoffset+1] = (i+1) % resolution;
  this.triangleIndices[triangleoffset+2] = (i % resolution) + ↵
     resolution;
  triangleoffset += 3;

  this.triangleIndices[triangleoffset] = (i % resolution) + ↵
     resolution;
  this.triangleIndices[triangleoffset+1] = (i+1) % resolution;
  this.triangleIndices[triangleoffset+2] = ((i+1) % resolution↵
     ) + resolution;
  triangleoffset += 3;
}

// bottom of the cylinder
for (var i = 0; i < resolution; i++)
{
  this.triangleIndices[triangleoffset] = i;
  this.triangleIndices[triangleoffset+1] = (i+1) % resolution;
  this.triangleIndices[triangleoffset+2] = 2*resolution;
  triangleoffset += 3;
}

// top of the cylinder
for (var i = 0; i < resolution; i++)
{
  this.triangleIndices[triangleoffset] = resolution + i;
  this.triangleIndices[triangleoffset+1] = ((i+1) % resolution↵
     ) + resolution;
  this.triangleIndices[triangleoffset+2] = 2*resolution+1;
  triangleoffset += 3;
}

this.numVertices = this.vertices.length/3;
this.numTriangles = this.triangleIndices.length/3;
}
```

LISTING 3.3: Cylinder primitive.

3.10 Self-Exercises

3.10.1 General

1. Which is the most compact surface representation to describe sphere? And for the intersection of three spheres? And for a statue?

2. What are the main differences between the Bézier curves and the B-Splines curves?

3. In what way can we represent volumetric data?

4. What is the main weak point of polygon meshes representation?

5. What are the goals of the subdivision surfaces?

6. In what way can we represent volumes?

7. Define a 3D object that represents an $N \times M$ grid of equi-spaced points.

8. Define a 3D object that represents the surface defined by the function $F(x, y) = sin(x)cos(y)$ $x, y \in [0, 1]$.

9. Consider the code example of the cube and try to subdivide each face of the cube in four faces.

Chapter 4

Geometric Transformations

Geometric transformations come into play all the time in computer graphics, and to learn how to manipulate them correctly will save you hours of painful debugging. In this chapter, we will take an informal approach, starting from simple intuitive examples and then generalizing.

4.1 Geometric Entities

In computer graphics we deal with three entities: scalars, points and vectors. A **scalar** is a one-dimensional entity that we use to express the magnitude of something, for example the temperature of a body or the weight of a car. A **point** is a location in space, for example the tip of your nose, and a **vector** is a direction, for example the direction in which you are walking or the orientation of a satellite antenna. We did not specify the dimensions of points and vectors because they depend on the dimension of the space we are dealing with. If we work with bidimensional space, then points and vectors will have 2 dimensions, if we are in three-dimensional space (as we will in most practical cases) then they will have 3 dimensions, and so on. In this book we will use the *italic* for scalars, **bold** for points and ***italic bold*** for vectors:

- scalars $a, b, \alpha \ldots$

- points $\mathbf{p} = \begin{bmatrix} p_x \\ p_y \\ \ldots \\ p_w \end{bmatrix}, \mathbf{q} = \begin{bmatrix} q_x \\ q_y \\ \ldots \\ q_w \end{bmatrix} \ldots$

- vectors $\boldsymbol{v} = \begin{bmatrix} v_x \\ v_y \\ \ldots \\ v_w \end{bmatrix}, \boldsymbol{u} = \begin{bmatrix} u_x \\ u_y \\ \ldots \\ u_w \end{bmatrix} \ldots$

Also, in general we will often use $\mathbf{p}$ and $\mathbf{q}$ to indicate points. We will use a set of operations on these entities to express transformation of the objects they represent. These operations, shown in Figure 4.1, are:

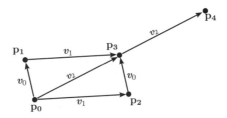

FIGURE 4.1: Points and vectors in two dimensions.

- *point–vector sum*: we can add vector v_0 to point $\mathbf{p}_0$ and obtain point $\mathbf{p}_1$. We can think of this operation as moving, or translating, point $\mathbf{p}_0$ by v_0;

- *point–point subtraction*: in the same way, we can subtract point $\mathbf{p}_0$ from point $\mathbf{p}_1$ and obtain vector v_0. We can think of this as the method of finding the translation required to move point $\mathbf{p}_0$ to point $\mathbf{p}_1$.

- *vector–vector sum*: again, if we think of a vector as a translation then it will be obvious that the result of two consecutive translations is also a translation. That means $v_0 + v_1 = v_1 + v_0 = v_2$.

- *scalar–vector multiplication*: this operation maintains the direction of the vector but scales its length by a factor. So instead of writing $\mathbf{p}_4 = \mathbf{p}_0 + v_2 + v_2$ we can write $\mathbf{p}_4 = \mathbf{p}_0 + 2v_2$

4.2   Basic Geometric Transformations

A generic **geometric transformation** is a function that maps points to points or/and vectors to vectors. In the computer graphics domain we are only interested in a small subclass of transformations that, luckily, are the easiest to handle.

From now on, when we talk about transformation of an object, the intended meaning is that we apply a transformation to all the points of that object.

We will start by looking at transformations in 2D because they are easier to understand with the help of our intuition, and then we will move onto their 3D counterparts.

4.2.1   Translation

A **translation** is a transformation applied to a point defined as:

$$T_v(\mathbf{p}) = \mathbf{p} + v$$

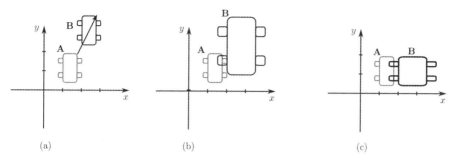

FIGURE 4.2: Examples of translation (a), uniform scaling (b) and non-uniform scaling (c).

We have already seen an example of translation in the previous section when considering point–vector sum. Figure 4.2.(a) shows the (very basic) drawing of a car as seen from above and its translation by $v = [1, 2]^T$.

4.2.2 Scaling

A **scaling** is a transformation applied to a point or a vector defined as:

$$S_{(s_x, s_y)}(\mathbf{p}) = \left[\begin{array}{c} s_x p_x \\ s_y p_y \end{array} \right]$$

A scale multiplies each coordinate of a point by a scalar value, named scaling factor. As the word implies, the effect of scaling is to change the size of the object. Figure 4.2.(b) shows the effect of applying $S_{2,2}$ to our car. When all the scaling factors are equal, in this case when $s_x = s_y$, the scale is said to be **uniform**, **non-uniform** otherwise (see Figure 4.2.(c)).

4.2.3 Rotation

A **rotation** is a transformation applied to a point or a vector defined as:

$$R_\alpha(\mathbf{p}) = \left[\begin{array}{c} p_x \cos\alpha - p_y \sin\alpha \\ p_x \sin\alpha + p_y \cos\alpha \end{array} \right]$$

where α is the rotation angle, that is the angle by which the point or vector is rotated around the origin. This formula for rotation is less trivial and needs a small proof. Referring to Figure 4.3, consider the point $\mathbf{p}$ at distance ρ from the origin. The vector connecting the point $\mathbf{p}$ to the origin makes an angle β with the X-axis. The coordinates of $\mathbf{p}$ can be written as:

$$\mathbf{p} = \left[\begin{array}{c} p_x \\ p_y \end{array} \right] = \left[\begin{array}{c} \rho \cos\beta \\ \rho \sin\beta \end{array} \right]$$

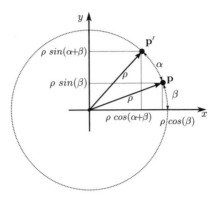

FIGURE 4.3: Computation of the rotation of a point around the origin.

If we rotate the point **p** with respect to the origin by an angle α in the counterclockwise direction we obtain a new point **p**′, which is still at a distance ρ from the origin and such that the vector **p**′ − **0** forms an angle α with **p** − **0**, where **0** is the origin, that is, the vector $[0, 0]^T$. Again, let us express the coordinates of **p**′ in terms of the angle **p**′ − **0** forms with the x axis:

$$\mathbf{p}' = \left[\begin{array}{c} \rho \ \cos{(\beta + \alpha)} \\ \rho \ \sin{(\beta + \alpha)} \end{array} \right]$$

Using the trigonometric equality $\cos{(\beta + \alpha)} = \cos \beta \cos \alpha - \sin \beta \sin \alpha$ we get:

$$\begin{aligned} p_x{}' &= \rho \ \cos{(\beta + \alpha)} \\ &= \rho \cos \beta \cos \alpha - \rho \sin \beta \sin \alpha = \\ &= p_x \cos \alpha - p_y \sin \alpha \end{aligned}$$

A very similar derivation, using the equality $\sin{(\beta + \alpha)} = \sin \beta \cos \alpha + \cos \beta \sin \alpha$, completes the proof.

4.2.4   Expressing Transformation with Matrix Notation

If we want to express a series of consecutive transformations, even a simple translation followed by a rotation, the expressions easily become very long and practically unmanageable. Here we show how things may be simplified using matrix notation. You may have noticed how both scaling and rotation are expressed as a *linear combination* of coordinates:

$$\begin{aligned} p'_x &= a_{xx} \ p_x + a_{xy} \ p_y \\ p'_y &= a_{yx} \ p_x + a_{yy} \ p_y \end{aligned}$$

Thus, we could conveniently write these transformations in a more compact way:

$$\mathbf{p}' = \begin{bmatrix} a_{xx} & a_{xy} \\ a_{yx} & a_{yy} \end{bmatrix} \mathbf{p}$$

with:

$$S_{(s_x,s_y)}(\mathbf{p}) = S_{(s_x,s_y)}\mathbf{p} = \begin{bmatrix} s_x & 0 \\ 0 & s_y \end{bmatrix} \mathbf{p}$$

$$R_\alpha(\mathbf{p}) = R_\alpha \mathbf{p} = \begin{bmatrix} \cos\alpha & -\sin\alpha \\ \sin\alpha & \cos\alpha \end{bmatrix} \mathbf{p}$$

Note that we indicate with the same symbol of the function the matrix corresponding to that geometric transformation. Also note that, this does not capture translation, which is an addition to the point coordinates and not a combination of them. So, if we want to write a rotation followed by a translation, we still have to write $R_\alpha p + v$.

In order to extend the use of matrix notation to translation we have to express points and vectors in **homogeneous coordinates**. Homogeneous coordinates will be explained in more detail in Section 4.6.2.2; here we only need to know that a point in Cartesian coordinates $\mathbf{p} = [p_x, p_y]^T$ can be written in homogeneous coordinates as $\bar{\mathbf{p}} = [p_x, p_y, 1]^T$, while a vector $\bar{\mathbf{v}} = [v_x, v_y]^T$ can be written as $\bar{\mathbf{v}} = [v_x, v_y, 0]^T$. The first thing to notice is that now we can distinguish between points and vectors just by looking at whether the last coordinate is 1 or 0, respectively. Also note that the sum of two vectors in homogeneous coordinates gives a vector $(0 + 0 = 0)$, the sum of a point and a vector gives a point $(1 + 0 = 1)$ and the subtraction of two points gives a vector $(1 - 1 = 0)$, just like we saw earlier in this section.

In order to simplify notation, we define the following equivalences:

$$p = \mathbf{p} - \begin{bmatrix} 0 \\ 0 \\ 1 \end{bmatrix}, \mathbf{p} = \begin{bmatrix} 0 \\ 0 \\ 1 \end{bmatrix} + p$$

that is, if we have a point $\mathbf{p}$ we write as p the vector from the origin to $\mathbf{p}$ and, vice versa, if we have a vector p we write as $\mathbf{p}$ the point obtained adding the vector to the origin.

With homogeneous coordinates, we only need one more column and one more row for matrix vector multiplication. In particular, we will use matrices of the form:

$$\begin{bmatrix} a_{xx} & a_{xy} & v_x \\ a_{yx} & a_{yy} & v_y \\ 0 & 0 & 1 \end{bmatrix} \tag{4.1}$$

Notice what the product of such a matrix by the point $\bar{\mathbf{p}}$ looks like:

$$
\begin{bmatrix} a_{xx} & a_{xy} & v_x \\ a_{yx} & a_{yy} & v_y \\ 0 & 0 & 1 \end{bmatrix} \begin{bmatrix} p_x \\ p_y \\ 1 \end{bmatrix} = \begin{bmatrix} a_{xx}p_x + a_{xy}p_y + v_x \\ a_{yx}p_x + a_{yy}p_y + v_y \\ 1 \end{bmatrix}
$$

$$
= \begin{bmatrix} \begin{bmatrix} a_{xx} & a_{xy} \\ a_{yx} & a_{yy} \end{bmatrix} \mathbf{p} + \boldsymbol{v} \\ 1 \end{bmatrix}
$$

In other words, now we are also able to express the translation of a point in our matrix notation, by arranging the translation vector in the upper part of the last column of the matrix. Note that if we multiply the matrix with a vector $[v'_x, v'_y, 0]$ the translation part will have no effect because the elements of $\boldsymbol{v}$ are multiplied by 0. This is coherent with the fact that vectors represent a *direction* and a *magnitudo* (the length of the vector, hence a scalar value): the direction can be changed by a rotation or by a non-uniform scaling, the magnitude can be changed by a scaling but neither of them is affected by translation.

4.3   Affine Transformations

So far we have seen three types of transformations: translation, scaling and rotation, and we have seen how they can conveniently be expressed with a 3×3 matrix by using homogeneous coordinates. You may wonder if the matrices like the one in Equation (4.1) may also represent other kinds of transformations and how they are characterized. In fact the matrix in (4.1) expresses the class of **affine transformations**. A transformation is said to be *affine* if:

- It preserves *collinearity*. This means that points that lie on a line before being transformed also do so after being transformed.

- It preserves *proportions*. This menas that, given three points p_1, p_2 and p_3 that lie on a line, the ratio $\|p_2 - p_1\|/\|p_3 - p_1\|$ is preserved after the transformation. Here $\|v\|$ represents the norm (that is, magnitude or length) of vector v.

Figure 4.4 shows an example of an affine transformation applied to three points. Among the affine transformations, the rotation and the translation are called **rigid transformations** because they only *move* the object they are applied to, preserving all the angles and lengths. The scaling is not rigid, but if uniform it preserves the angles. Also, parallel lines are mapped to parallel lines.

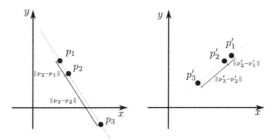

FIGURE 4.4: (Left) Three collinear points. (Right) The same points after an affine transformation.

4.3.1   Composition of Geometric Transformations

Suppose you want to move the car in Figure 4.5 from position A to position B. To do so, you can first rotate the car clockwise by $45°$ and then translate by $(3, 2)$. The matrix for a clockwise rotation by $45°$ is:

$$R_{-45°} = \begin{bmatrix} \cos(-45°) & -\sin(-45°) & 0 \\ \sin(-45°) & \cos(-45°) & 0 \\ 0 & 0 & 1 \end{bmatrix} = \begin{bmatrix} \frac{1}{\sqrt{2}} & -\frac{1}{\sqrt{2}} & 0 \\ \frac{1}{\sqrt{2}} & \frac{1}{\sqrt{2}} & 0 \\ 0 & 0 & 1 \end{bmatrix}$$

and the matrix for a translation by $(3, 2)$ is:

$$T_{(3,2)} = \begin{bmatrix} 1 & 0 & 3 \\ 0 & 1 & 2 \\ 0 & 0 & 1 \end{bmatrix}$$

so you can apply the rotation $R_{-45°}$ to all the points of the car and bring it to the position marked with A', then apply the translation $T_{(3,2)}$:

$$T_{(3,2)}(R_{-45°}\mathbf{p}) = \begin{bmatrix} 1 & 0 & 3 \\ 0 & 1 & 2 \\ 0 & 0 & 1 \end{bmatrix} \left(\begin{bmatrix} \frac{1}{\sqrt{2}} & -\frac{1}{\sqrt{2}} & 0 \\ \frac{1}{\sqrt{2}} & \frac{1}{\sqrt{2}} & 0 \\ 0 & 0 & 1 \end{bmatrix} \mathbf{p} \right)$$

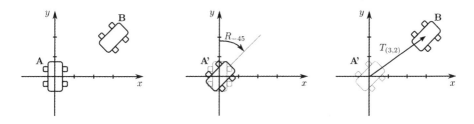

FIGURE 4.5: Combining rotation and translation.

since the matrix product is associative, that is $A\ (B\ C) = (A\ B)\ C$, where every term of the product can be either a matrix or a vector with compatible dimensions, we can multiply the two matrices first and so obtain a matrix that will be applied to $\mathbf{p}$:

$$T_{(3,2)}(R_{-45^\circ}\mathbf{p}) = (T_{(3,2)}R_{-45^\circ})\mathbf{p} = \left(\begin{bmatrix} 1 & 0 & 3 \\ 0 & 1 & 2 \\ 0 & 0 & 1 \end{bmatrix} \begin{bmatrix} \frac{1}{\sqrt{2}} & -\frac{1}{\sqrt{2}} & 0 \\ \frac{1}{\sqrt{2}} & \frac{1}{\sqrt{2}} & 0 \\ 0 & 0 & 1 \end{bmatrix} \right) \mathbf{p} =$$

$$\begin{bmatrix} \frac{1}{\sqrt{2}} & -\frac{1}{\sqrt{2}} & 3 \\ \frac{1}{\sqrt{2}} & \frac{1}{\sqrt{2}} & 2 \\ 0 & 0 & 1 \end{bmatrix} \mathbf{p} = M\mathbf{p}$$

Matrices of this form, containing a rotation and a translation, are often referred to as *roto-translation* matrices. They are very common since they are the tools you have to use to move things around, keeping their shape intact.

In general we can apply any number of affine transformations and obtain a single corresponding matrix as we did above. We will now see that some of them are especially useful in practical situations.

4.3.2   Rotation and Scaling about a Generic Point

The rotation matrix we have used so far performs a rotation about the origin, that is about the point $[0, 0, 1]^T$. Very often you want to rotate an object about a point different from the origin, for example you may want to rotate the car about its barycenter. Note that in the example in Figure 4.5 we just hide this fact by placing the car so that its barycenter coincided with the origin.

A rotation by α about a generic point $\mathbf{c}$ is obtained as the composition of three transformations, illustrated in Figure 4.6.

1. Apply the translation $T_{-\mathbf{c}}$ so that the point $\mathbf{c}$ coincides with the origin.

2. Apply the rotation R_α.

3. Apply the translation $T_{\mathbf{c}} = T_{\mathbf{c}}^{-1}$ so that the point $\mathbf{c}$ returns in its initial position.

In one formula:

$$R_{\alpha,\mathbf{c}} = T_{-\mathbf{c}}^{-1}R_\alpha T_{-\mathbf{c}}$$

where we indicate with $R_{\alpha,\mathbf{c}}$ the matrix corresponding to the rotation by α about the point $\mathbf{c}$.

It is interesting here to see what the matrix $R_{\alpha,\mathbf{c}}$ looks like. To do so we may do the whole product or we can switch back to Cartesian coordinates and write the transformation of point $\mathbf{p}$ (let us drop the pedices to simplify

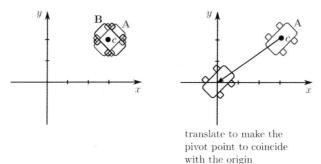

translate to make the
pivot point to coincide
with the origin

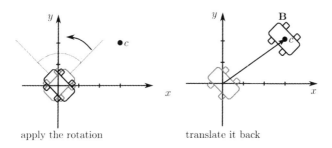

apply the rotation   translate it back

FIGURE 4.6: How to make an object rotate around a specified point.

the notation):

$$\mathbf{p}' = (R(\mathbf{p} - \mathbf{c})) + \mathbf{c} = R\,\mathbf{p} - R\,\mathbf{c} + \mathbf{c} =$$
$$\underbrace{R\,\mathbf{p}}_{\text{rotation}} + \underbrace{(\mathbf{I} - R)\mathbf{c}}_{\text{translation}}$$

so that after all, we have a roto-translation matrix:

$$R_{\alpha,\mathbf{c}} = \left[\begin{array}{cc} R & (I - R)\mathbf{c} \\ \mathbf{0} & 1 \end{array} \right] \qquad (4.2)$$

The very same considerations hold for the scaling, just putting a scaling matrix $S_{(s_x,s_y)}$ in place of the rotation matrix R_α, thus:

$$S_{(s_x,s_y),\mathbf{c}} = \left[\begin{array}{cc} S & (I - S)\mathbf{c} \\ \mathbf{0} & 1 \end{array} \right] \qquad (4.3)$$

4.3.3 Shearing

Shearing is an affine transformation where the point p is scaled along one dimension by an amount proportional to its coordinate in another dimension (see the example in Figure 4.7).

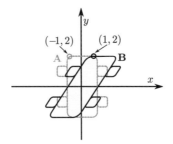

FIGURE 4.7: Example of shearing for $h = 0$ and $k = 2$.

$$Sh_{(h,k)}(\mathbf{p}) = \begin{bmatrix} 1 & k & 0 \\ h & 1 & 0 \\ 0 & 0 & 1 \end{bmatrix} \mathbf{p} = \begin{bmatrix} x + ky \\ hx + y \\ 1 \end{bmatrix}$$

Note that shearing can also be obtained as a composition of a rotation and a non-uniform scaling (see Exercise 5, Section 4.13).

4.3.4   Inverse Transformations and Commutative Properties

The *inverse* of an affine transformation is easily computed as:

$$\begin{bmatrix} A & \mathbf{v} \\ \mathbf{0} & 1 \end{bmatrix}^{-1} = \begin{bmatrix} A^{-1} & -A^{-1}\mathbf{v} \\ \mathbf{0} & 1 \end{bmatrix}$$

The meaning of the inverse of an affine transformation is to restore a transformed object into its original shape. For example it is geometrically intuitive that $T_v^{-1} = T_{-v}$, $R_\alpha^{-1} = R_{-\alpha}$ and $S_{(s_x,s_y)}^{-1} = S_{(1/s_x,1/s_y)}$ (the proof of these equivalences is left for the exercises). As a side note, we anticipate here that the rotation matrices are *orthonormal*, meaning that $R^{-1} = R^T$. So the inverse of a rototranslation is simply obtained as:

$$\begin{bmatrix} R & \mathbf{c} \\ \mathbf{0} & 1 \end{bmatrix}^{-1} = \begin{bmatrix} R^T & -R^T\mathbf{c} \\ \mathbf{0} & 1 \end{bmatrix} \tag{4.4}$$

Matrix product is associative, which means that $A\,(B\,C) = (A\,B)\,C$, but, in general, not commutative, which means that $A\,B \neq B\,A$. Among the affine transformations the commutative property holds only between two translations and between uniform scaling and rotation (and of course always if at least one of the two transformations is the identity or if the two are equal). The general non-commutativity of matrix multiplication means, in other words, that "the order of multiplication matters". And it matters a lot, and remembering this will save us a lot of debugging time.

4.4   Frames

A *frame* is a way to assign values to the component of geometric entities. In two dimensions, a frame is defined by a point and two non-collinear axes. Figure 4.8 shows our car and two distinct frames. If you were given only frame F_0 and were asked to write the coordinates of the point **p** on the front of the car, it would be obvious to say $(2.5, 1.5)$. The presence of the other frame implies the *relative* nature of coordinates of point **p**, which are $(1.4, 2.1)$ with respect to frame F_1.

Note that the origin and axis of these frames are themselves expressed in a frame. The frame we use to express all other frames is called a **canonical frame** and has origin in $[0, 0, 1]^T$ and axes $\boldsymbol{u} = [1, 0, 0]^T$ and $\boldsymbol{v} = [0, 1, 0]$. To **change frame** means to express the value of the components of points and vectors given in a frame into another, which is what we have just done visually in the previous example. Here we want to show how to compute the transformation required to change frame from F_0 to F_1. Let us start with changing the coordinates of a point given in one frame F_0 into the canonical frame. We can do this geometrically by starting from the origin of F_0, moving p_{0x} units along vector $\boldsymbol{u}_0$ and p_{0y} units along vector $\boldsymbol{v}_0$:

$$\mathbf{p} = O_0 + p_{0x}\boldsymbol{u}_0 + p_{0y}\boldsymbol{v}_0$$

Note that we can write this formula in matrix notation by arranging the axes as column vectors and the origin as the last column of a matrix (that we will call M_0):

$$\mathbf{p} = \underbrace{\left[\begin{array}{ccc} u_{0x} & v_{0x} & O_{0x} \\ u_{0y} & v_{0y} & O_{0y} \\ 0 & 0 & 1 \end{array} \right]}_{M_0} \mathbf{p_0}$$

It should not be a surprise that this matrix is just another affine transformation, because we have just applied two scalings and two point-vector sums. In

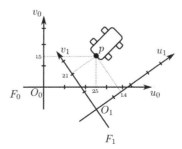

FIGURE 4.8: Coordinates of a point are relative to the frame.

fact there is more: the upper left 2×2 matrix obtained by the axes of F_0 is the *rotation* matrix that brings the canonical axes to coincide with the F_0 axes and the last column is the translation that brings the origin of the canonical frame to coincide with F_0. So the matrix that expresses the coordinates $\mathbf{p_0}$ in the canonical frame is just a rototranslation.

$$\mathbf{p} = \begin{bmatrix} R_{uv} & O_0 \\ \mathbf{0} & 1 \end{bmatrix} \mathbf{p_0}$$

If we apply the same steps to $\mathbf{p_1}$ in frame F_1 we obtain:

$$\mathbf{p} = \underbrace{\begin{bmatrix} R_0 & O_0 \\ \mathbf{0} & 1 \end{bmatrix}}_{M_0} \mathbf{p_0} = \underbrace{\begin{bmatrix} R_1 & O_1 \\ \mathbf{0} & 1 \end{bmatrix}}_{M_1} \mathbf{p_1}$$

therefore:

$$M_1^{-1} M_0 \mathbf{p_0} = \mathbf{p_1}$$

The matrix $M_1^{-1} M_0$ transforms a point (or a vector) given in the frame F_0 into the frame F_1. Note that from Section 4.3.4 we know how to invert rototranslation matrices like M_1 without resorting to algorithms for the inversion of generic matrices.

4.4.1   General Frames and Affine Transformations

So far we have only seen orthonormal frames, which are characterized by having normalized and orthogonal axes. In general, the axes of a frame do not have to be orthogonal or normalized, and then any affine transformation may be considered a change of frame. The direct implication is that applying an affine transformation to an object is the same as changing the frame in which it is expressed. Whether we refer to an affine transformation as a transformation of the coordinates of the object or transformation of the reference frame is a mere matter of what is more intuitive for our inner representation of reality. If, for example, we are asked to find the transformation that brings our car *forward* we think of it as an object transformation and not as bringing the reference frame *backward*, but, if we go down to the math, there is no difference.

4.4.2   Hierarchies of Frames

A very important concept to grasp when using frames is the hierarchical way they can be arranged for an intuitive and practical description of the scene. We could describe the drawing in Figure 4.9 as a car with four frames: one centered in the middle of the car, one on a corner of the driver cabin, one on the center of the steering wheel and one on the keyhole. Now consider the following sentences:

- The keyhole is **on the right** of the steering wheel.

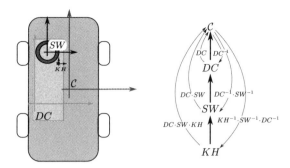

FIGURE 4.9: (Right) An example of relations among frames. (Left) How it can be represented in a graph.

 - The steering wheel is **inside** the driver cabin.

 - The driver cabin is **on the left side** of the car.

In these sentences we have expressed the position of the keyhole in the frame of the steering wheel, the position of the steering wheel in the frame of the driver cabin and the position of the driver cabin in the frame of the car. In the above description we first established a hierarchical relationship between the frames where the parent of a frame F is the frame in which the values of F, its origin and its axes, are expressed.

The hierarchy and the relations among the frames can be conveniently illustrated with a directed graph as in Figure 4.9. Each node corresponds to a frame, each arc corresponds to the transformation that converts the coordinates from the *tail* frame to the *head* frame and the thick arrows show the hierarchical relation among the frames. The matrix representing the frame and the matrix, which transforms the coordinates of the current frame to the coordinates of the parent frame, are the same thing, so the arc (KH, SW) is associated with matrix KH and consequently its opposite arc, (SW, KH), is associated with the inverse KH^{-1}.

Note that if we apply a transformation to one of the frames, such a transformation will also have an effect on all the nodes of the subtree rooted at that node. So, if we translate the frame C the frames DC, SW and KH will be translated in the same way, although C will be the only matrix to change.

4.4.3 The Third Dimension

Everything we learned so far about transformations in two dimensions holds in any dimension. To extend the formulas to the 3D case we only need to add the z component to points and vectors and a fourth row and column to the matrices. This is true for all the transformations except for rotations, which need some more explanation, provided in the next section.

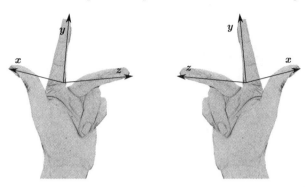

FIGURE 4.10: Handness of a coordinate system.

Here we start extending the notion of frames in 3D space. Since we have shown all our examples with the axis x and y in the plane, it is straighforward to add a third axis z orthogonal to the plane XY to obtain a reference frame for the 3D space. There are two possible verses for the vector: one pointing *upward* and one *downward*. This determines the orientation of the frame, or *handness* of the coordinate system.

The term *handness* derives from the rule illustrated in Figure 4.10. If we set our hands as shown in the figure and assign the x, y and z to the thumb, index and middle fingers, respectively, we will obtain a *left-handed* reference system (LSH) with the left hand and a *right-handed* reference system (RHS) with the right hand.

The right-handed system is somehow a more common choice. Just consider when you draw the x an y axis on paper. If you want to add a third axis to make a three-dimensional frame it would be coming out of the paper towards you (RHS), and not through the table (LHS).

The RHS also gives us a mnemonic rule for the cross product between two vectors, that is: $x \times y = z$. So if you have two generic vectors a and b and assign a to your right thumb and b to your right index-finger, the middle finger gives you the direction of $a \times b$.

4.5   Rotations in Three Dimensions

In Section 4.2.3 we showed how to compute a rotation around the origin of the bidimensional plane. If we consider the bidimensional plane as an infinitely thin slice of 3D space passing through the origin $[0, 0, 0, 1]^T$ and perpendicular to the z-axis (the axis $[0, 0, 1, 0]^T$) then we can see how the rotation in two

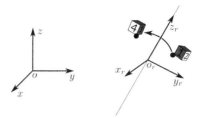

FIGURE 4.11: An example of rotation around an axis.

dimensions is also a rotation in 3D around the $\boldsymbol{z}$ axis:

$$
R_{\alpha,\boldsymbol{z}} = \left[\begin{array}{cccc} \cos\alpha & -\sin\alpha & 0 & 0 \\ \sin\alpha & \cos\alpha & 0 & 0 \\ 0 & 0 & 1 & 0 \\ 0 & 0 & 0 & 1 \end{array}\right] \tag{4.5}
$$

Note that applying a rotation about the z axis only changes the x and y coordinates. In other words a point rotated around an axis always lies on the plane passing through the point and orthogonal to that axis. In fact, the rotation in $3D$ is defined with respect to an axis, called the **axis of rotation**, which is usually specified as $\boldsymbol{r} = \mathbf{o}_r + t\boldsymbol{d}_{ir}$, $t \in (-\infty, \infty)$. All the techniques to implement a rotation that we will see consider the case where the rotation axis passes through the origin, which means $\boldsymbol{r} = [0,0,0,1]^T + t\ \boldsymbol{d}_{ir}$ (see Figure 4.11). This is not a limitation, since, as we did in Section 4.3.2, we can compose the transformations to find the rotation around a generic axis. This can be achieved by applying a translation to make the generic axis pass through the origin, applying the rotation and then translating it back.

4.5.1 Axis–Angle Rotation

The first technique to find the rotation around an axis of rotation $\boldsymbol{r}$ (defined as previously specified) is a composition of transformations:

1. Apply the transformation that makes the rotation axis $\boldsymbol{r}$ coincide with the $\boldsymbol{z}$ axis.

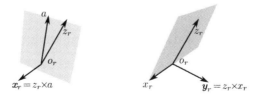

FIGURE 4.12: How to build an orthogonal frame starting with a single axis.

2. Apply the rotation $R_{\alpha,z}$ using the matrix in equation (4.5).

3. Apply the transformation that makes the z axis coincide with the rotation axis r.

We know how to rotate a point about the z axis, but what about the first transformation (and its inverse)? Suppose that we have a whole frame F_r whose z axis coincides with r. The affine transformation F_r^{-1} brings the frame F_r to coincide with the canonical frame, which means the axis r is transformed to the axis z, just like we wanted. In matrix form:

$$R_{\alpha,r} = F_r R_{\alpha,z} F_r^{-1} \qquad (4.6)$$

So what we miss is just the x and y axis of the frame F_r, which we will calculate in the next section.

4.5.1.1   Building Orthogonal 3D Frames from a Single Axis

As stated in the previous section, it is useful to see how we can build a $3D$ orthogonal frame starting from a partial specification of it, say the axis z_F (that we want corresponding to r). The x_r axis will have to be orthogonal to z_F. We use the property of **vector (or cross) product**: given two vectors a and b, the vector $c = a \times b$ is orthogonal to both, that is, $c \cdot a = 0$ and $c \cdot b = 0$ (see Appendix B). If we take any vector a, we can define the x_r axis as:

$$x_r = r \times a$$

and then do the same operation to obtain y

$$y_r = r \times x_r$$

It should be clear that the choice of a determines the frame. We must be careful about choosing a vector a not collinear with vector r, because the vector product of two collinear vectors gives a null vector. If we pick three random numbers to build the vector a, the chances of creating a vector collinear to r are infinitely small, but not zero. Furthermore the finite precision of the computer representation of real numbers also degrades the quality of the vector product for *quasi* collinear vectors. So, instead of taking the chance, we consider the position of the smallest component of vector r, let us call it i, and define a as the vector with value 1 for the component i and 0 for the other components. In other words, we take the canonical axis "most orthogonal" to r.

4.5.1.2   Axis–Angle Rotations without Building the 3D Frame

Note that there are infinite orthogonal frames having z_r as their z axis and they all can be used for our rotation. This means that whatever choice for vector a we make, we will always end up in the same rotation matrix, which in turn means that if we simplify the expression we will see that a disappears from it, which will then be written only in terms of r and α.

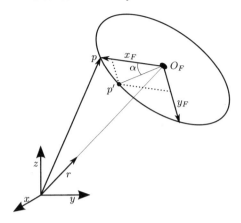

FIGURE 4.13: Rotation around an axis without building a frame.

Instead of performing the tedious algebraic simplification we will now show it with a geometric approach. Considering Figure 4.13, let **p** be the point we want to rotate by α around the axis r and let **p**$'$ be the arrival position. **p** and **p**$'$ line on a plane orthogonal to the rotation axis r: let us build a new frame F taking the intersection of such a plane with the axis r as the origin $\mathbf{O}_F$, the vectors r, $x_F = \mathbf{p} - \mathbf{O}_F$ and $y_F = r \times x_F$ as axes. The coordinates of point **p**$'$ with respect to the frame F are $[\cos\alpha, \sin\alpha, 0]^T$, which means that the coordinates of the point **p**$'$ in the canonical frame are:

$$\mathbf{p}' = \left[\begin{array}{ccc|c} & & & O_{Fx} \\ x_F & y_F & r & O_{Fy} \\ & & & O_{Fz} \\ \hline & 0 & & 1 \end{array} \right] \left[\begin{array}{c} \cos\alpha \\ \sin\alpha \\ 0 \\ 1 \end{array} \right] = \cos\alpha \; x_F + \sin\alpha \; y_F + 0 \; r + \mathbf{O}_F$$

$\mathbf{O}_F$ is the projection of p on axis t r, which is:

$$\mathbf{O}_F = (\mathbf{p} \; r) \; r$$

and thus:

$$\begin{aligned} x_F &= \mathbf{p} - \mathbf{O}_F = \mathbf{p} - (\mathbf{p} \; \cdot r) \; r \\ y_F &= r \times x_F = r \times (\mathbf{p} - \mathbf{O}_F) = \\ &= r \times (\mathbf{p} - \mathbf{O}_F) = r \times \mathbf{p} - r \times (\mathbf{p} \; \cdot r) \; r = r \times \mathbf{p} \end{aligned}$$

so we have the formula for rotating the point **p** around the axis r_{dir} by α:

$$\mathbf{p}' = \cos\alpha \; \mathbf{p} + (1 - \cos\alpha)(\mathbf{p} \; \cdot r)r + \sin\alpha \; (r \times \mathbf{p}) \tag{4.7}$$

4.5.2   Euler Angles Rotations

For some applications it is convenient to specify a rotation as a combination of rotations around the canonical axes. The most well known example is the control of an aircraft in a flight simulator: referring to Figure 4.14, consider the three possible rotations of the aircraft. The rotation around the Y axis is called *yaw* (aircraft turning left or right), the rotation around the X axis is called *pitch* (head up or down) and the rotation around the Z axis is called *roll* (inclination to left or right). Every possible orientation of the aircraft (which means every possible rotation) may be obtained by properly specifying the angles for yaw, pitch and roll, that we call α, β and γ respectively, and composing the three rotations.

With the name *Euler angles* we usually refer to the angles by means of which we specify a rotation. *How* they specify a rotation, that is which axes are used, in which order the axis rotations are applied and if they are intrinsic or extrinsic, is a matter of convention.

Here we show a classic example: the aircraft mounted on a *gimbal*. A gimbal is a system of three concentric rings, r_1, r_2 and r_3, where each ring is bound to the first outer ring through a support that allows rotation. We may associate a frame to each ring, F_1, F_2 and F_3, that coincides with the canonical frame if $\alpha = \beta = \gamma = 0$.

As shown in Figure 4.14 the ring r_1 lies on the plane XY of frame F_1, which rotates around the canonical Y axis, the ring r_2 lies on the plane XZ of frame F_2 which rotates around the X axis of the frame F_1, and the ring r_3 lies on the plane YZ of frame F_3, which rotates around the Z axis of the frame F_2. Figure 4.15 shows the corresponding hierarchy of frames and the transformations/changes of coordinates between them (which are all rotations around a canonical axis).

So the values of α, β and γ determine the frame F_3 as:

$$F_3 = R_{z\gamma} \, R_{x\beta} \, R_{y\alpha} \, C$$

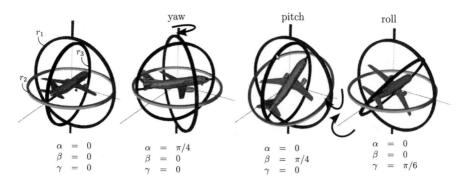

yaw	pitch	roll

$$\begin{array}{lll} \alpha = 0 & \alpha = \pi/4 & \alpha = 0 & \alpha = 0 \\ \beta = 0 & \beta = 0 & \beta = \pi/4 & \beta = 0 \\ \gamma = 0 & \gamma = 0 & \gamma = 0 & \gamma = \pi/6 \end{array}$$

FIGURE 4.14: A gimbal and the rotation of its rings.

FIGURE 4.15: Scheme of the relations among the three rings of a gimbal.

Note that rotation $R_{x\beta}$ is specified with respect to its outer frame, that is, the canonical frame transformed by rotation $R_{y\alpha}$, as well as rotation $R_{z\gamma}$ is expressed in the canonical frame rotated by $R_{x\beta}\,R_{y\alpha}$. In this case we speak of *intrinsic* rotations while if all the rotations were expressed with respect to the canonical frame we would have *extrinsic* rotations.

The mapping between angles and resulting rotations is not bijective, in fact the same rotation can be obtained with a combination of different angles.

Figure 4.16 illustrates a very annoying phenomenon: the *gimbal lock*. If $\beta = \pi/2$ rotation is applied with rings r_1 and r_3 both make the aircraft roll by an angle $\alpha + \gamma$ so we have infinite values for α and β leading to the same rotation, and one degree of freedom is lost: more precisely, the gimbal is no longer able to make the aircraft *yaw* and the rotation is *locked* in 2 dimensions (pitch and roll). This means that when we are using euler angles we need to take into account these degenerate configurations, for example, making it so that the discontinuity points correspond to rotations we are not interested in.

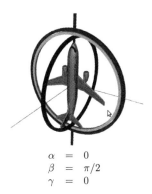

$$\alpha = 0$$
$$\beta = \pi/2$$
$$\gamma = 0$$

FIGURE 4.16: Illustration of gimbal lock: when two rings rotate around the same axis one degree of freedom is lost.

4.5.3   Rotations with Quaternions

The *quaternions* are a mathematical entity that can be used to represent rotations in a way more efficient than with matrices and more robust than Euler angles. They provide a sound way to interpolate rotations and are easy to implement. The only bad news is that quaternions are a bit more difficult to understand.

The quaternions are an extension of complex numbers with two more imaginary parts:

$$a = a_w + \mathbf{i}a_x + \mathbf{j}a_y + \mathbf{k}a_z$$

usually found in short form as

$$a = (a_w, \boldsymbol{a})$$

with $\boldsymbol{a} = (a_x, a_y, a_z)$. So, quaternions can also be seen as points in four dimensions.

Quaternions can be summed component by component just like point in two or three dimensions:

$$a + b = (a_w + b_w, \boldsymbol{i}\,(a_x + b_x) + \boldsymbol{j}(a_y + b_y) + \boldsymbol{k}(a_z + b_z))$$

The multiplication is done using the following rules:

$$\boldsymbol{i}^2 = \boldsymbol{j}^2 = \boldsymbol{k}^2 = \boldsymbol{ijk} = -1$$

which gives:

$$ab = (a_w b_w - \boldsymbol{a} \cdot \boldsymbol{b}, a_w \boldsymbol{b} + b_w \boldsymbol{a} + \boldsymbol{a} \times \boldsymbol{b})$$

The identity is $\boldsymbol{1} = (1, 0, 0, 0)$ and the inverse can be calculated as:

$$a^{-1} = \frac{1}{\|a\|^2}(a_w, -\boldsymbol{a})$$

while the *magnitude* of a quaternion is $\|a\|^2 = a_w^2 + a_x^2 + a_y^2 + a_z^2$.

Finally, the quaternions in the form $(0, x, y, z)$ represent the points (x, y, z) in 3D space.

Concerning rotation, the following quaternion:

$$q = (\cos \frac{\alpha}{2}, \sin \frac{\alpha}{2}\,\boldsymbol{r})$$

with $\|\boldsymbol{r}\| = 1$ may be used to rotate a point $\mathbf{p} = (0, p_x, p_y, p_z)$ around the axis $\boldsymbol{r}$ by α. More precisely, back to the example of Figure 4.13, we can demonstrate that:

$$\mathbf{p}' = q\mathbf{p}q^{-1} \tag{4.8}$$

The proof can be obtained in a few simple derivations.

$$
\begin{aligned}
q\,\mathbf{p}q^{-1} &= (\cos\frac{\alpha}{2}, \sin\frac{\alpha}{2}\,\boldsymbol{r})\,(0, \boldsymbol{p})\,(\cos\frac{\alpha}{2}, -\sin\frac{\alpha}{2}\,\boldsymbol{r}) \\
&= \left(\cos\frac{\alpha}{2}, \sin\frac{\alpha}{2}\,\boldsymbol{r}\right)\left(\sin\frac{\alpha}{2}(\boldsymbol{p}\cdot\boldsymbol{r}), \cos\frac{\alpha}{2}\,\boldsymbol{p} - \sin\frac{\alpha}{2}\,(\boldsymbol{p}\times\boldsymbol{r})\right) \\
&= \left(0, (\cos^2\frac{\alpha}{2} - \sin^2\frac{\alpha}{2})\,\boldsymbol{p} + 2\,\sin^2\frac{\alpha}{2}\,\boldsymbol{r}\,(\boldsymbol{p}\cdot\boldsymbol{r}) + 2\,\sin\frac{\alpha}{2}\cos\frac{\alpha}{2}\,(\boldsymbol{r}\times\boldsymbol{p})\right)
\end{aligned}
$$

Now, using the following trigonometric equivalences:

$$
\cos^2\frac{\alpha}{2} - \sin^2\frac{\alpha}{2} = \cos\alpha
$$

$$
2\,\sin^2\frac{\alpha}{2} = (1 - \cos\alpha)
$$

$$
2\,\cos\frac{\alpha}{2}\sin\frac{\alpha}{2} = \sin\alpha
$$

we obtain precisely the equation 4.7.

4.6 Viewing Transformations

At this point we know how to manipulate objects to create our 3D scene but we did not say anything about how these objects will be projected to the 2D screen by the rasterization-based pipeline. Let us imagine that you are in the scene with a camera: are you looking at our car from the front, from the back, from far away? Are you using a zoom or a wide angle lens?

4.6.1 Placing the View Reference Frame

We can specify our view on a scene by answering three questions: from what position are we looking, called the *view point*, towards which direction are we looking, called the *viewing direction* and towards which direction is pointing the spike of the "pickelhaube helmet" we are wearing, called the *up direction* (see Figure 4.17). Conventionally we express these data with a frame, called *view reference frame*, whose origin is at the view point, the $\boldsymbol{y}$ axis oriented like the up direction and the $\boldsymbol{z}$ axis point as the opposite of viewing direction, while the $\boldsymbol{x}$ axis, pointing toward the right of the viewer, is found as $\boldsymbol{x} = \boldsymbol{y} \times \boldsymbol{z}$ (again see Figure 4.17). With the term *view transformation* we indicate the transformation that expresses all the coordinates with respect to the view reference frame.

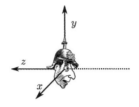

FIGURE 4.17: View reference frame.

So we can write our view frame in matrix form as:

$$V = \begin{bmatrix} x_x & y_x & z_x & o_x \\ x_y & y_y & z_y & o_y \\ x_z & y_z & z_z & o_z \\ 0 & 0 & 0 & 1 \end{bmatrix}$$

Hence, the inverse of the V matrix allows us to transform the coordinates of our scene to the view reference frame. Since V describes an orthogonal frame, we know, from Section 4.3.4, that V^{-1} can be computed by:

$$V^{-1} = \begin{bmatrix} R_{xyz}^T & (-R_{xyz}^T \, \mathbf{o}) \\ 0 & 1 \end{bmatrix} \, , \quad R_{xyz} = \begin{bmatrix} x_x & y_x & z_x \\ x_y & y_y & z_y \\ x_z & y_z & z_z \end{bmatrix}$$

4.6.2   Projections

Establishing the projection means describing the type of camera we are using to observe the scene. In the following we will assume that the scene is expressed in the view reference frame, therefore the point of view is centered at the origin, the camera is looking toward the negative z axis and its up direction is y.

4.6.2.1   Perspective Projection

Suppose you are standing beyond an infinitely large window and looking outside with only one eye. You can draw a line from each point to your eye and, for every point you see, the corresponding line will pass through the window. This example describes the *perspective projection*: the point of view (your eye) is called *center of projection* C, the plane of the window *plane of projection* (or *image plane*) VP and the lines are *projectors*. So, given a 3D point $\mathbf{p}$, a center of projection $\mathbf{C}$ and a plane of projection VP, its perspective projection $\mathbf{p}'$ is the intersection between the line passing through $\mathbf{p}$ and $\mathbf{C}$, and the plane VP. In our case $\mathbf{C} = [0, 0, 0, 1]^T$ and plane VP is orthogonal to the z axis. Figure 4.18 shows an example where the plane VP is $(z = -d)$. In this case it is easy to find the formula for the projection of the point $\mathbf{p}$ by

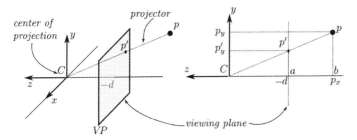

FIGURE 4.18: The perspective projection.

observing that the triangles Cap' and Cbp are *similar* and hence the ratios between corresponding sides are equal:

$$p'_y : d = p_y : p_z \Rightarrow p'_y = \frac{p_y}{p_z/d}$$

the same holds for the x coordinate, therefore

$$\mathbf{p}' = \begin{bmatrix} \frac{p_x}{p_z/d} \\ \frac{p_y}{p_z/d} \\ d \\ 1 \end{bmatrix} \tag{4.9}$$

Note that our example is only an ideal description, since the eye is not a zero-dimensional point. Another, more common, way to introduce perspective projection is by means of the *pinhole camera*, represented in Figure 4.19. The pinhole camera consists of a light-proof box with a single *infinitely small* hole so that each point in front of the camera projects on the side opposite to the hole. Note that in this way the image formed is inverted (*up* becomes *down*, *left* become *right*) and this is why we prefer the eye-in-front-of-the-window example.

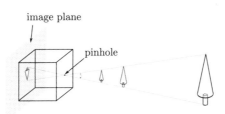

FIGURE 4.19: The pinhole camera.

4.6.2.2   Perspective Division

We introduced homogeneous coordinates in section 4.2.4 almost like a trick to be able to express translations in matrix notation. In fact homogeneous coordinates do more: they allow us to express the equivalence of points with respect to their projections. Referring to Figure 4.18, note that not just point **p** but *all* the points that lie on the line passing through **C** and **p** project onto the point **p**′, with the single exception of the center of projection. In homogeneous coordinates we can write this equivalence as:

$$
p' = \begin{bmatrix} p_x \\ p_y \\ p_z \\ 1 \end{bmatrix} = \begin{bmatrix} \lambda_0 p_x \\ \lambda_0 p_y \\ \lambda_0 p_z \\ \lambda_0 \end{bmatrix} = \begin{bmatrix} \lambda_1 p_x \\ \lambda_1 p_y \\ \lambda_1 p_z \\ \lambda_1 \end{bmatrix} = \begin{bmatrix} \lambda_2 p_x \\ \lambda_2 p_y \\ \lambda_2 p_z \\ \lambda_2 \end{bmatrix} = \cdots
$$

Note that the fourth component can be any real number $\lambda_i \neq 0$ but when it is 1 the coordinates are said to be in the canonical form. When a point is in *canonical form* we can represent it in 3D space by simply considering its first three coordinates. Consider again our point **p**′ in equation 4.9: if we multiply all the components by $\frac{p_z}{d}$ we have the following equivalence:

$$
\mathbf{p}' = \begin{bmatrix} \frac{p_x}{p_z/d} \\ \frac{p_y}{p_z/d} \\ d \\ 1 \end{bmatrix} = \begin{bmatrix} p_x \\ p_y \\ p_z \\ \frac{p_z}{d} \end{bmatrix}
$$

Note that the difference is that now no component of **p**′ appears in the denominator and so the perspective projection can be written in matrix form:

$$
P_{rsp}\, \mathbf{p} = \overbrace{\begin{bmatrix} 1 & 0 & 0 & 0 \\ 0 & 1 & 0 & 0 \\ 0 & 0 & 1 & 0 \\ 0 & 0 & \frac{1}{d} & 1 \end{bmatrix}}^{\text{perspective projection}} \begin{bmatrix} p_x \\ p_y \\ p_z \\ 1 \end{bmatrix} = \begin{bmatrix} p_x \\ p_y \\ p_z \\ \frac{p_z}{d} \end{bmatrix} = \begin{bmatrix} \frac{p_x}{p_z/d} \\ \frac{p_y}{p_z/d} \\ d \\ 1 \end{bmatrix}
$$

The operation of turning a point in homogeneous coordinates in its canonical form consists of dividing each component by the fourth one and it is called *perspective division*. There is a fundamental difference between the projection matrix and all the matrices we have encountered so far: the last row of the projection matrix is not $[0, 0, 0, 1]$ like for the affine transformations. In fact, perspective transformation **is not affine** in that, although it preserves collinearity, it does not preserve ratios between distances.

4.6.2.3   Orthographic Projection

The projections where all the projectors are parallel are called *parallel projections*. If the projectors are also orthogonal to the projection plane we

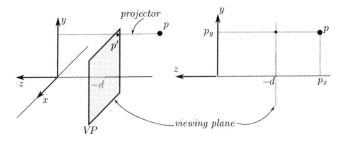

FIGURE 4.20: The orthographics projection.

have **orthographic projections** (see Figure 4.20). In this case the projection matrix is trivially obtained by setting the z coordinate to d. To be more precise, the x and y values of the projected points are independent from d, so we just consider the projection plane $z = 0$. In matrix notation:

$$O_{rth}\, \mathbf{p} = \overbrace{\begin{bmatrix} 1 & 0 & 0 & 0 \\ 0 & 1 & 0 & 0 \\ 0 & 0 & 0 & 0 \\ 0 & 0 & 0 & 1 \end{bmatrix}}^{\text{orthographic projection}} \begin{bmatrix} p_x \\ p_y \\ p_z \\ 1 \end{bmatrix} = \begin{bmatrix} p_x \\ p_y \\ 0 \\ 1 \end{bmatrix}$$

Unlike the perspective projection, the orthographic projection is an affine transformation (although not invertible). The orthogonal projection can also be seen as an extreme case of perspective projection, where the distance between the center of projection and the projection plane is ∞.

4.6.3   Viewing Volume

The term *viewing volume* indicates the portion of 3D space that is seen from our ideal camera. For example, if we take one of the projections above and a specified rectangular region of the viewing plane, called *viewing window*, the *viewing volume* consists of the portion of space whose projection falls inside such viewing windows. By this definition, the viewing volume has infinite extent, because points that fall inside the viewing window may be infinitely far to the view point. However, in computer graphics we bound the viewing volume with two other planes, called *near plane* and *far plane*. Figure 4.21 (Top) shows two examples of viewing volume, one obtained with a perspective projection and one with an orthographics projection. The planes that bound the viewing volume are called *clipping planes* because they are used to "clip" the geometric primitives against it so as to discard from the rest of the pipeline the parts of the objects that would not be visible (details on this process will be given later in Section 5.4).

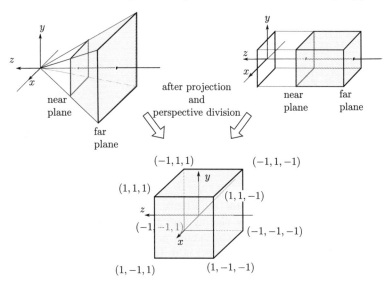

FIGURE 4.21: All the projections convert the viewing volume in the canonical viewing volume.

4.6.3.1 Canonical Viewing Volume

We have seen that, depending on the projection, the viewing volumes can be either a parallelepiped or a trunk of a pyramid.

As we know from Chapter 1.3.2, projection is not the last operation of the rendering pipeline, but many other operations such as clipping, rasterization, and so on, are at work. This means that at a certain point of the rasterization-based pipeline the algorithms should be "parametric" on the specific viewing volume. A more elegant and efficient option to account for this is to establish a *common interface* between the projection and the rest of the pipeline. In fact, in the pipeline it is imposed that the projection always transforms its corresponding viewing volume into a *Canonical Viewing Volume (CVV)*, which is by definition the cube aligned with the axis and with corners $[-1, -1, -1]$ and $[1, 1, 1]$.

Figure 4.21 shows the viewing volumes corresponding to an orthographic projection and a perspective projection and their mapping to the canonical viewing volume. The orthogonal and perspective projections taking into account this mapping become:

$$
\overbrace{
P_{orth} = \begin{bmatrix}
\frac{2}{r-l} & 0 & 0 & \frac{r+l}{r-l} \\
0 & \frac{2}{t-b} & 0 & \frac{t+b}{t-b} \\
0 & 0 & \frac{-2}{f-n} & -\frac{f+n}{f-n} \\
0 & 0 & 0 & 0
\end{bmatrix}
}^{\text{orthographic projection}}
\qquad
\overbrace{
P_{persp} = \begin{bmatrix}
\frac{2n}{r-l} & 0 & \frac{r+l}{r-l} & 0 \\
0 & \frac{2n}{t-b} & \frac{t+b}{t-b} & 0 \\
0 & 0 & \frac{-(f+n)}{f-n} & \frac{-2fn}{f-n} \\
0 & 0 & -1 & 0
\end{bmatrix}
}^{\text{perspective projection}}
$$

$$(4.10)$$

In these transformations, n indicates the distance of the near plane, f the distance of the far planes, and t, b, l, r are the values that define the *top*, the *bottom*, the *left*, and the *right* delimitation of the viewing window, respectively, all expressed with respect to the observer (that is, in view space).

Be aware that a point transformed by the projection matrix is not yet in its canonical form: it will be so only after its normalization. So, the projection matrix does not bring points from view space to CVV but to a four-dimensional space called *clip space* because it is the space where clipping is done. The Canonical Viewing Volume is also referred to as *Normalized Device Context* (NDC) to indicate the normalization applied to the homogeneous coordinates. Coordinates in NDC space are called *normalized device coordinates*.

4.6.4 From Normalized Device Coordinates to Window Coordinates

We have seen how, after projection and perspective division, the viewing volume is mapped to the canonical viewing volume. More specifically, the viewing window is mapped to the face $(-1, -1, -1), (1, -1, -1), (1, 1, -1),$ $(-1, 1, -1)$ of the canonical viewing volume. The last transformation we need is to map from such a face to the rectangular portion of the screen we designated for rendering, called the *viewport*. Figure 4.22 shows the face of the canonical viewing volume (in the middle) and the viewport (on the right). Note that the viewport is a portion of a bigger rectangle, called *application windows*, which is the region of the screen your application can draw into. In order to transform the face of the CVV to the viewport, we may do the followings: (see Figure 4.22): 1) apply a translation of $[1, 1]^T$ to bring the Bottom-Left corner to $(0, 0)^T$; 2) scale by $(v_X - v_x)/2$ along the x axis and by $(v_Y - v_y)/2$ along the y axis; 3) translate by $(v_x, v_y)^T$. In matrix form:

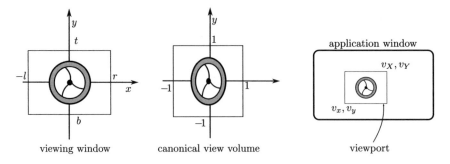

FIGURE 4.22: From CVV to viewport.

$$W = \begin{bmatrix} 1 & 0 & v_x \\ 0 & 1 & v_x \\ 0 & 0 & 1 \end{bmatrix} \begin{bmatrix} \frac{v_X - v_x}{2} & 0 & 0 \\ 0 & \frac{v_Y - v_y}{2} & 0 \\ 0 & 0 & 1 \end{bmatrix} \begin{bmatrix} 1 & 0 & 1 \\ 0 & 1 & 1 \\ 0 & 0 & 1 \end{bmatrix}$$

$$= \begin{bmatrix} \frac{v_X - v_x}{2} & 0 & \frac{v_X - v_x}{2} v_x \\ 0 & \frac{v_Y - v_y}{2} & \frac{v_Y - v_y}{2} v_y \\ 0 & 0 & 1 \end{bmatrix}$$

4.6.4.1   Preserving Aspect Ratio

The aspect ratio of a window is the ratio between width and height. If the aspect ratio of the viewing window (which is defined in world space) and the aspect ratio of the viewport (which is defined in screen coordinates) are different, we will see our scene deformed because the matrix PW will produce a non-uniform scaling.

The most common situation is that the viewport is fixed and coincides with the canvas size and we would like to set a viewing window that does not have the same aspect ratio. If we do not want to see a distorted image (and usually we don't) we have to set a viewing window that is as close as possible to the one we had in mind and that has the same aspect ratio as the viewport.

Let V_w, V_h the sizes of the viewing window we would like to set and W_w and W_h the sizes of the vieport. We have different aspect ratios, so:

$$\frac{V_w}{V_h} \neq \frac{W_w}{W_h}$$

and we want to change V_w and V_h so that the aspect ratios are the same. We can easily express all the ways to modify these values by introducing two scaling factors k_w and k_h and writing:

$$V'_w = V_w \, k_w$$
$$V'_h = V_h \, k_h$$

so that

$$\frac{V'_w}{V'_h} = \frac{W_w}{W_h}$$

Note that in order to change the aspect ratio just one coefficient would be enough, but we also want to choose *how* to change width and height of the viewing window. For example, we may want to keep the width fixed, so: $k_w = 1$ and $k_h = \frac{W_h}{W_w}\frac{V_w}{V_h}$.

A fairly common choice is not to cut anything from our intended projection and enlarge one of the two sizes. This is achieved by setting $k_w = 1$ and solving for k_h if $\frac{V_w}{V_h} > \frac{W_w}{W_h}$. We set $k_h = 1$ and we solve for k_w otherwise. You may easily verify both geometrically and algebraically that the unknown coefficient is greater than 1, that is, we enlarge the viewing window.

4.6.4.2 Depth Value

Note that the transformation from clip space to window coordinates does not involve the z component, so the distance of the point to the near plane is apparently lost. Although this topic will be treated in section 5.2, here we anticipate that a memory buffer of the same size as the viewport, called *depth buffer* or *z-buffer*, is used to store depth value of the object points visible through each pixel. Conventionally, the value of $z \in [-1, +1]$ (in clip space) is linearly mapped to the range $z \in [0, 1]$. However, we must note that the mapping of z from the $[near, far]$ to the CVV **is not** linear (more details about this will be given in Section 5.2.4).

4.6.5 Summing Up

Figure 4.23 summarizes the various properties preserved by all the transformations discussed in this chapter.

Transformations	Length	Angles	Ratio	Collinearity
Translation	Yes	Yes	Yes	Yes
Rotation	Yes	Yes	Yes	Yes
Uniform scaling	No	Yes	Yes	Yes
Non-uniform scaling	No	No	Yes	Yes
Shearing	No	No	Yes	Yes
Orthogonal projection	No	No	Yes	Yes
Generic affine transformation	No	No	Yes	Yes
Perspective transformation	No	No	No	Yes

FIGURE 4.23: Summary of the geometric properties preserved by the different geometric transformations.

4.7 Transformations in the Pipeline

As we learned in Chapter 1.3.2, when vertices enter the pipeline, their position is the one specified by the application. The vertex shader processes one vertex at a time and transforms its position into its clip space coordinates. The transformation applied by the shader may be obtained as the concatenation of transformations as shown in Figure 4.24. The first transformation is conventionally called *model* transformation and it is used to place the object in the scene. For example, the primitive cube created in Section 3.9 is centered at the origin, but if in our scene we want it to be centered at coordinates $[20, 10, 20]^T$, our model transformation will have to be a translation. So, the vertices of every object will be subjected to a proper model transformation to bring the object in the right position and with the right proportions. The next transformation is the *view* transformation and that is the one that transforms all the coordinates so that they are expressed in the view reference frame, like we saw in Section 4.6.1. Finally we apply the *projection* transformation that transforms all the coordinates in clip space, like we saw in Section 4.6.2.

Please note that this decomposition of the transformation applied to the vertices coordinates is purely logical and it is not encoded in the WebGL API in any way. We may program the vertex shader to output coordinates of the vertex in any way we want; it does not have to be done by means of a matrix multiplication or even to be linear. We make this point because it marks an important difference with respect to the old fixed pipeline. In the fixed pipeline, the state of the API only exposed two 4×4 matrices that you could use to specify the transformation to apply: the MODELVIEW matrix and the PROJECTION matrix. Each vertex was then transformed by the concatenation of these transformations.

4.8 Upgrade Your Client: Our First 3D Client

In Section 3.9 we have seen how to specify a polygonal shape and we created some JavaScript objects for them: the Box, the Cylinder, the Cone and the Track. Now we will use these shapes to assemble all the elements of our first working client.

Figure 4.25 shows a scheme of how to create a simple model both for a tree and the car and gives names to these transformations $(M_0, \ldots M_9)$. The first task is to compute these transformations.

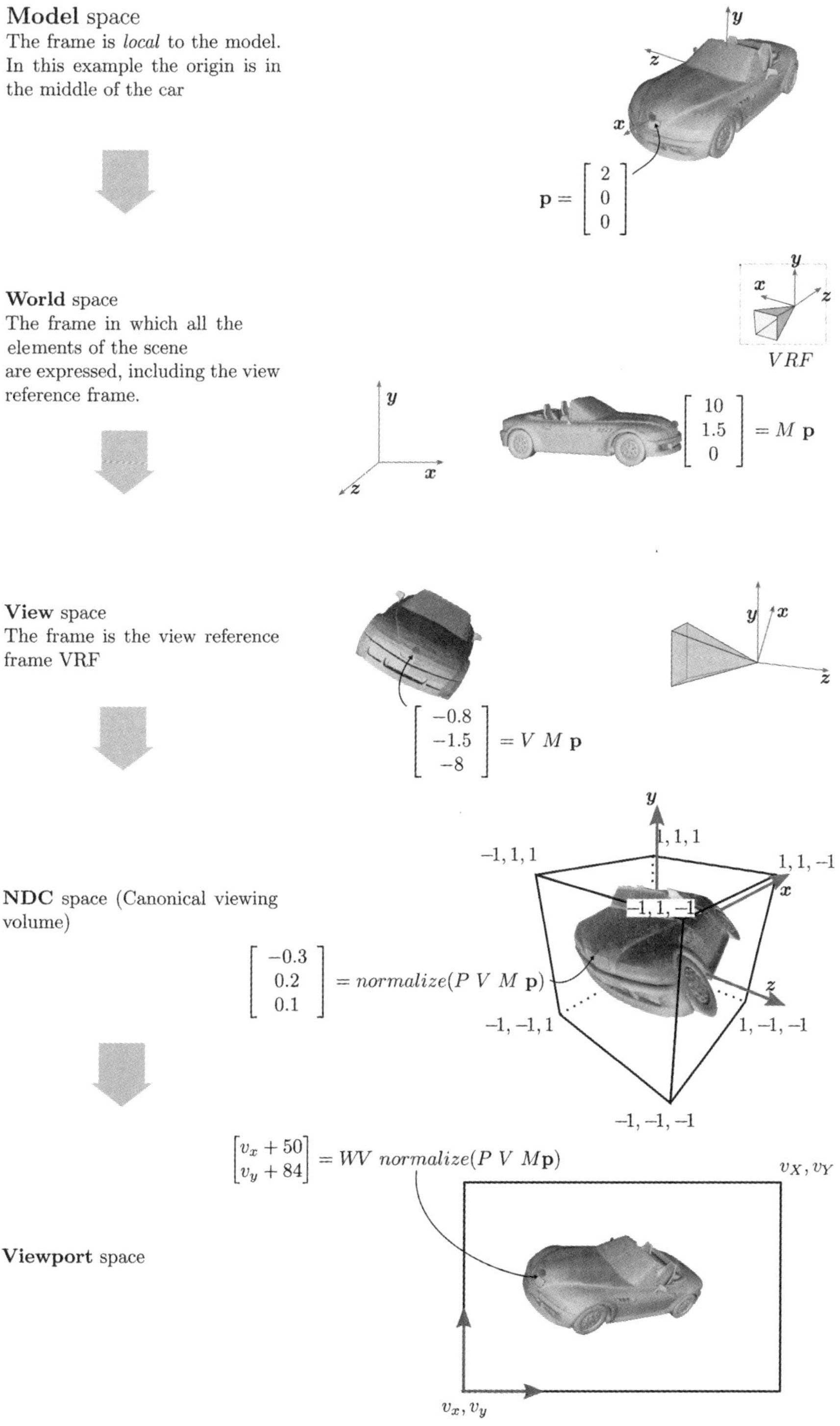

Model space
The frame is *local* to the model.
In this example the origin is in
the middle of the car

$$\mathbf{p} = \begin{bmatrix} 2 \\ 0 \\ 0 \end{bmatrix}$$

World space
The frame in which all the
elements of the scene
are expressed, including the view
reference frame.

$$\begin{bmatrix} 10 \\ 1.5 \\ 0 \end{bmatrix} = M\,\mathbf{p}$$

View space
The frame is the view reference
frame VRF

$$\begin{bmatrix} -0.8 \\ -1.5 \\ -8 \end{bmatrix} = V\,M\,\mathbf{p}$$

NDC space (Canonical viewing
volume)

$$\begin{bmatrix} -0.3 \\ 0.2 \\ 0.1 \end{bmatrix} = normalize(P\,V\,M\,\mathbf{p})$$

$$\begin{bmatrix} v_x + 50 \\ v_y + 84 \end{bmatrix} = WV\;normalize(P\,V\,M\mathbf{p})$$

Viewport space

FIGURE 4.24: Logic scheme of the transformations in the pipeline.

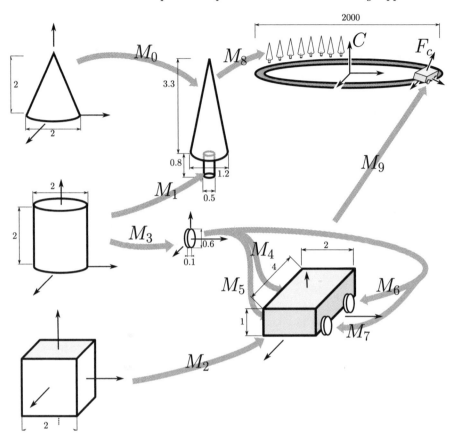

FIGURE 4.25: Using basic primitives and transformations to assemble the race scenario.

4.8.1   Assembling the Tree and the Car

As shown in Figure 4.25, the trunk of the tree is obtained by transforming the cylinder with diameter 2 and height 2 into one with diameter 0.5 and height 0.8, so we only need a non-uniform scaling:

$$M_1 = S_{(0.25, 0.4, 0.25)} = \begin{bmatrix} 0.25 & 0 & 0 & 0 \\ 0 & 0.4 & 0 & 0 \\ 0 & 0 & 0.25 & 0 \\ 0 & 0 & 0 & 1 \end{bmatrix}$$

The upper part of the tree is also obtained by a non-uniform scaling, this time of the cone. However, the scaled cone must also be translated along the Y axis by 0.8 units in order to be put onto the trunk. Therefore:

$$M_0 = T_{(0,0.8,0)} \; S_{(0.6,1.65,0.6)} = \begin{bmatrix} 1 & 0 & 0 & 0 \\ 0 & 1 & 0 & 0.8 \\ 0 & 0 & 1 & 0 \\ 0 & 0 & 0 & 1 \end{bmatrix} \begin{bmatrix} 0.6 & 0 & 0 & 0 \\ 0 & 1.65 & 0 & 0 \\ 0 & 0 & 0.6 & 0 \\ 0 & 0 & 0 & 1 \end{bmatrix}$$

Our first car will be a very simple one, made by a box for the car's body and four cylinders for the wheels. We want to transform the cube centered in $(0,0,0)$ with side 2 into the box with sizes $(2,1,4)$ and with its bottom face on the plane $y = 0.3$. We first apply a translation by 1 along the Y axis to make the bottom face of the cube to lie on the plane $y = 0$. In this way we can apply the scaling transformation $S_{(1,0.5,2)}$ to have the box with the right proportions while keeping the bottom face on the plane $y = 0$. Finally we translate again along Y by the radius of the wheel. All together:

$$M_6 = T_{(0,0.3,0)} \; S_{(1,0.5,2)} \; T_{(0,1,0)}$$

The transformation M_3 turns the cylinder into a wheel centered at the origin. We can first translate along Y by -1 to have the cylinder centered at the origin, then rotate by $90°$ around the Z axis, then scale to obtain the 0.6 diameter and 0.1 width:

$$M_3 = S_{(0.05,0.3,0.3)} \; R_{90Z} \; T_{(0,-1,0)}$$

The matrices from M_4 to M_7 are simply translations that bring the wheels to their place on the side of the car.

4.8.2   Positioning the Trees and the Cars

At this point we have assembled a tree and a car in their right proportions so no scaling will be involved in M_8 and M_9. Transformation M_8 brings the assembled tree on its position along the circuit. The transformation will be a simple translation $T_{(tx,ty,tz)}$, where $[tx, ty, tz]^T$ is the position of the tree (if the ground is all flat ty will be 0). Transformation M_9 brings the car onto its position and orientation in the track. In the NVMC framework, the position and rotation of the car is specified by a frame F_c, which, as we have seen in Section 4.4.1, corresponds to a roto-translation matrix.

4.8.3   Viewing the Scene

Now that we have found all the matrices to build the scene from the given primitives, we have to specify from where we are looking at the scene and what kind of projection we are using. As a first example we decide to watch the whole scene from above with an orthogonal projection (an *over-head view*). So let us say we are positioned at $[0.0, 10, 0.0]$ and looking down along the y

axis. The corresponding viewing frame is described by the following matrix:

$$
V = \begin{bmatrix} u_x & v_x & w_x & O_x \\ u_y & u_y & w_y & O_y \\ u_z & u_z & w_z & O_z \\ 0 & 0 & 0 & 1 \end{bmatrix} = \begin{bmatrix} 1 & 0 & 0 & 0 \\ 0 & 0 & -1 & 10 \\ 0 & -1 & 0 & 0 \\ 0 & 0 & 0 & 1 \end{bmatrix}
$$

Let us say that the projection is such that it includes the whole circuit, which is a square of $200m \times 200m$. Since we have set the point of view along the y axis, we will need to include $100m$ on each side (left, right, top and bottom) in the viewing volme. So we take the matrix in 4.10 and replace r, l, t and b with 100. The near plane n may be set to 0 and the far plane f so that it includes the ground. Since we are looking from $[0, 10, 0]^T$, f may be set to a value greater than 10 (we will see in Section 5.2 how to choose the far plane correctly to avoid artifacts due to limited numerical representation).

$$
P = \begin{bmatrix} 2/200 & 0 & 0 & 0 \\ 0 & 2/200 & 0 & 0 \\ 0 & 0 & -2/11 & -11/11 \\ 0 & 0 & 0 & 1 \end{bmatrix}
$$

As explained in Section 4.6.4.1, these values may need to be changed according to the viewport chosen.

4.9   The Code

At this point the problem of writing the necessary code to show our simple scene may be put as follows: we have the function drawObject that activates the rendering of a primitive and four kinds of primitives: Cube, Cone, Cylinder and Street. Furthermore, we have the matrices which transform each instance of each primitive in order to compose our scene. We know from Chapter 1 that the coordinates of every vertex are transformed in the vertex transformation and attribute setup phases, and more precisely in the vertex shader. So what we have to do is to make it so that when a primitive is rendered the vertex shader will apply the right transformation. We use Figure 4.26, which shows the whole hierarchy of frames/transformation of our scene, as a reference. This is essentially the same as Figure 4.25 but this time we put in evidence the hierarchy and also add the viewing transformations. What you find in this hierarchy is similar to what you find when you consider a scene described with a *scene graph*, which is in fact a hierarchical organization of a scene commonly used to model and optimize the rendering of complex scenes. A detailed description of a scene graph is beyond the scope of this book, so we mention it only to give the intuitive idea of it.

4.10 Handling the Transformations Matrices with a Matrix Stack

The code can be just a sequence of three steps: 1) compute the proper transformation; 2) set the vertex shader to apply it; 3) render the primitive. Let us consider how the code would look for drawing the first two wheels:

```
// draw the wheel 1 (w1)
M = P * Inverse(V) * M_9 * M_4 * M_3;
SetMatrixInTheVertexShader(M);
draw(w1);
// draw the wheel 2 (w2)
M = P * Inverse(V) * M_9 * M_5 * M_3;
SetMatrixInTheVertexShader(M);
draw(w2);
// ...
```

Although this way to apply transformations is correct, we can see it requires unnecessary computation. Specifically, the first three matrices of the multiplication, P, V^{-1} and M_9 are the same for all the wheels, so the obvious thing to do is to compute their product in advance and store it in a variable. We may apply the same idea to avoid computing PV^{-1} three times (for the car, the trees and the track).

In order to generalize this mechanism we note from Figure 4.26 that the order in which the matrices are multiplied before drawing any shape describes a path from the clip space node to the shape node. In the figure we use a path of cyan arrows for the case of the first wheel. With this interpretation if two or more paths share a subpath, it is convenient to compute and store the product of the matrices corresponding to that subpath.

The simple and elegant way to implement this mechanism is by assuming to access directly the transformation matrix used by the vertex shader, which we will call **current**, and to keep this matrix updated with the value resulting from the composition of transformations applied. Furthermore, we use a *stack* (that is, a last-in first-out data structure) of matrices that stores all the values of *current* that we want to save for later use, which we will call a *matrix stack*. The table in Figure 4.9 shows the sequence of matrix operations we do to draw the first wheel. Note that every time we traverse a node with more than one child we make a push of the matrix on the stack, because we know we will need it again for all the other children.

In the example, when we draw the cylinder for the first wheel (w_1), we can see that $current = P\ V^{-1}\ M_9\ M_4\ M_3$. Then we make a pop from the stack and reset *current* to the last value pushed on the stack, which is $P\ V^{-1}\ M_9$.

We are now ready to comment the code in Listing 4.2. At line **295** we create a **SpiderGL** object **SglMatrixStack**. Like the name suggests, this object implements a stack of matrices, so it provides the methods **push** and **pop**. The

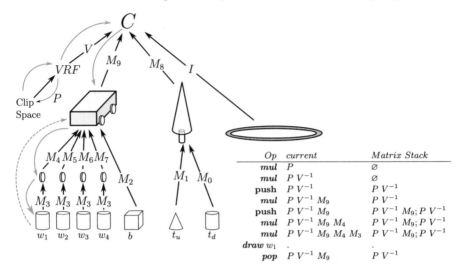

The table in the figure:

Op	current	Matrix Stack
mul	P	$\varnothing$
mul	$P\,V^{-1}$	$\varnothing$
push	$P\,V^{-1}$	$P\,V^{-1}$
mul	$P\,V^{-1}\,M_9$	$P\,V^{-1}$
push	$P\,V^{-1}\,M_9$	$P\,V^{-1}\,M_9; P\,V^{-1}$
mul	$P\,V^{-1}\,M_9\,M_4$	$P\,V^{-1}\,M_9; P\,V^{-1}$
mul	$P\,V^{-1}\,M_9\,M_4\,M_3$	$P\,V^{-1}\,M_9; P\,V^{-1}$
draw w_1	.	.
pop	$P\,V^{-1}\,M_9$	$P\,V^{-1}$

FIGURE 4.26: Hierarchy of transformations for the whole scene.

matrix we referred to as current is a member of the object SglMatrixStack. The function multiply(P) right-multiplies the matrix current, which means it performs *current = current P*.

The lines between 229 and 240 (Listing 4.1) set the projection matrix and the view matrix. Although we can manually set these matrices as those shown in Section 4.8.3, SpiderGL provides the utilities to build these matrices by specifying a few intuitive parameters. SglMat4.ortho builds an orthogonal projection matrix by specifying the extremes of the viewing volume. SglMat4.lookAt creates the view matrix (that is, the inverse of the view frame) by passing the eye position, the point towards which we are looking and the *up* direction.

Note that we set the viewing volume taking into account the ratio between width and height of the viewport (which in this case has the same size as the canvas) to preserve the aspect ratio, as explained in Section 4.6.4.1.

At line 242 we push the current matrix, which is now *P invV*, and then we multiply by the car frame (returned by function myFrame).

```
229   var ratio = width / height;
230   var bbox = this.game.race.bbox;
231   var winW = (bbox[3] - bbox[0]);
232   var winH = (bbox[5] - bbox[2]);
233   winW = winW * ratio * (winH / winW);
234   var P = SglMat4.ortho([-winW / 2, -winH / 2, 0.0], [winW / 2, ↵
          winH / 2, 21.0]);
235   gl.uniformMatrix4fv(this.uniformShader.↵
          uProjectionMatrixLocation, false, P);
236
237   var stack = this.stack;
238   stack.loadIdentity();
```

```
239  // create the inverse of V
240  var invV = SglMat4.lookAt([0, 20, 0], [0, 0, 0], [1, 0, 0]);
241  stack.multiply(invV);
242  stack.push();
```

LISTING 4.1: Setting projection and modelview matrix.

```
290  NVMCClient.onInitialize = function () {
291    var gl = this.ui.gl;
292    NVMC.log("SpiderGL Version : " + SGL_VERSION_STRING + "\n");
293    this.game.player.color = [1.0, 0.0, 0.0, 1.0];
294    this.initMotionKeyHandlers();
295    this.stack = new SglMatrixStack();
296    this.initializeObjects(gl);
297    this.uniformShader = new uniformShader(gl);
```

LISTING 4.2: Actions performed upon initialization.

```
2   var vertexShaderSource = "\
3     uniform    mat4 uModelViewMatrix;  \n\
4     uniform    mat4 uProjectionMatrix; \n\
5     attribute vec3 aPosition;          \n\
6     void main(void)                    \n\
7     {                                  \n\
8     gl_Position = uProjectionMatrix * uModelViewMatrix  \n\
9       * vec4(aPosition, 1.0);          \n\
10    }";
11
12  var fragmentShaderSource = "\
13    precision highp float;             \n\
14    uniform vec4 uColor;               \n\
15    void main(void)                    \n\
16    {                                  \n\
17      gl_FragColor = vec4(uColor);  \n\
18    } ";
```

LISTING 4.3: A basic shader program.

Listing 4.3 shows the vertex and the fragment shader. With respect to the shader shown in Listing 2.8 we added a uniform variable for the color, so that every render call will output fragments of color uColor and the matrices uProjectionMatrix (that we set at line 235 of Listing 4.1) and uModelViewMatrix (that we set to stack.matrix before rendering any shape) to transform the vertex position from object space to clip space.

Lines 147-148 of Listing 4.4 show the typical pattern for drawing a shape: we first set the uModeViewMatrix the value of the current matrix in the stack (stack.matrix) and then make the render call. A snapshot from the resulting client is shown in Figure 4.27.

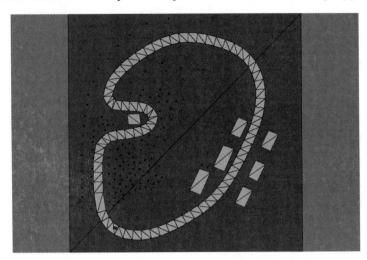

FIGURE 4.27: A snapshot from the very first working client. (See client *http://envymycarbook.com/chapter4/0/0.html.*)

```
147    gl.uniformMatrix4fv(      .uniformShader.↩
          uModelViewMatrixLocation,          , stack.matrix);
148       .drawObject(gl,         .cylinder, [0.8, 0.2, 0.2, 1.0], [0, ↩
          0, 0, 1.0]);
```

LISTING 4.4: Setting the ModelView matrix and rendering

4.10.1 Upgrade Your Client: Add the View from above and behind

To make things more interesting, suppose we want to place the view reference frame as in Figure 4.28, which is the classic view from up-behind where you see part of your car and the street ahead. This reference frame cannot be a constant because it is **behind** the car and so it is expressed in the frame of the car F_0, which changes as the car moves. In terms of our hierarchy, this view reference frame is a child of the car's frame F_0. In terms of transformations, the view reference frame can be easily expressed in the frame of the car by rotating the canonical frame around the x axis by $-30°$ and then translating by $(0, 3, 1.5)$.

$$V_{c_0} = T_{(0,3.0,1.5)} \, R_x(-20°)$$

Please note that V_{c_0} is expressed in the frame of the car F_0, and not (yet) in the world reference frame. As for the wheels and the car's body, to know the view reference frame in the world coordinates we just need to multiply it by F_0:

$$V_0 = F_0 \, V_{c_0}$$

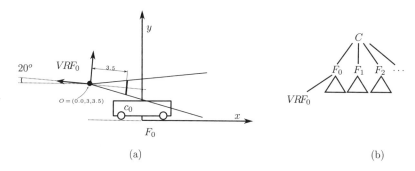

FIGURE 4.28: A view reference frame for implementing the view from behind the car.

Since we will create more view frames and we want to give some structure to the code we create an object that represents a specific view frame and the way we manipulate it. In this case we call this object ChaseCamera, and show its implementation in Listing 4.5.

```
74  function ChaseCamera() {
75    this.position          = [0.0,0.0,0.0];
76    this.keyDown           = function (keyCode) {}
77    this.keyUp             = function (keyCode) {}
78    this.mouseMove         = function (event) {};
79    this.mouseButtonDown   = function (event) {};
80    this.mouseButtonUp     = function () {}
81    this.setView           = function ( stack, F_0) {
82      var Rx = SglMat4.rotationAngleAxis(sglDegToRad(-20), [1.0, ↵
         0.0, 0.0]);
83      var T = SglMat4.translation([0.0, 3.0, 1.5]);
84      var Vc_0 = SglMat4.mul(T, Rx);
85      var V_0 = SglMat4.mul(F_0, Vc_0);
86      this.position = SglMat4.col(V_0,3);
87      var invV = SglMat4.inverse(V_0);
88      stack.multiply(invV);
89    };
90  };
```

LISTING 4.5: The ChaseCamera sets the view from above and behind the car. (Code snippet from *http://envymycarbook.com/chapter4/1/1.js.*)

The lines from 76 to 80 define functions to handle key and mouse events. For this specific camera they do nothing, since the camera simply depends on the car position and orientation, which is passed to the function setView in line 81. The goal of this function is to update the matrix stack (passed as parameter stack) with the viewing transformation. In this case the lines from 82 to 88 simply build the frame as defined by the equations above and finally its inverse is right multiplied to the stack's current matrix.

4.11   Manipulating the View and the Objects

In every interactive application the user must be enabled to manipulate the scene and/or change the point of view using some input interface such as the mouse, the keyboard, the touch screen or a combination of them. This means translating some events (e.g., click and/or movement of the mouse) into a modification to the transformations in the pipeline shown in Figure 4.24. In a 3D scene this is typically done following one of the following paradigms: *camera-in-hand* (CIH) and *world-in-hand* (WIH). The CIH paradigm corresponds to the idea that the user moves in the scene holding a camera, like in a *first person shooter* video game or like any subjective sequence in a movie. It is useful when the 3D scene is "big" with respect to the user (for example, a building or our circuit). The WIH paradigm is applied when the scene is something that can virtually be held in the palm of one's hand and observed from *outside*, such as a model of a car. In this case the view is fixed and the scene is rotated, scaled and translated to be observed.

In terms of our transformations pipeline, we can think that the CIH is implemented by changing the **view** transformation, while the WIH is implemented by adding one more transformation between the **model** and the **view** transformations, that is, transforming the scene in view space.

4.11.1   Controlling the View with Keyboard and Mouse

If you ever played a first person shooting game you are already familiar with the so called *WASD* mode, where the keys **w**, **a**, **s** and **d** are used to move forward, left, backward and right, respectively, and the mouse is used to rotate the view (most often to aim at some enemy).

All we need to do to move the point of view is to add a vector to the origin of the view refererence frame V towards the direction we want to move along. Note that we usually want to specify such a direction, let us call it t_V, in the view reference frame itself (e.g.,"move to my right") so we will need to express t_V in the world reference frame and then add to the current origin of the frame V:

$$\mathbf{v}'_o = \mathbf{v}_o + V_R\, t_V \qquad (4.11)$$

In order to change the orientation of the view reference frame using the mouse, a common strategy is to map mouse movements into Euler angles and rotate the frame axis (V_R) accordingly. Typically, the change of orientation is limited to yaw and pitch, therefore we can store the current direction as α and β (following notation of Section 4.5.2) and obtain the z axis of the view reference frame as:

$$\boldsymbol{v}'_{oz} = R_{x\beta}\, R_{y\alpha} \boldsymbol{v}_{oz} \qquad (4.12)$$

Then we can build the reference frame as shown in Section 4.5.1.1

$$\begin{aligned} \boldsymbol{v}'_{ox} &= [0,1,0]^T \times \boldsymbol{v}'_{oz} \\ \boldsymbol{v}'_{oy} &= \boldsymbol{v}'_{oz} \times \boldsymbol{v}'_{ox} \end{aligned} \tag{4.13}$$

The values for α and β are obtained by converting the mouse movement from pixels, as it is returned by onMouseMove function, to degrees:

$$\alpha = d_x \frac{maxYaw}{width}, \beta = d_y \frac{maxPitch}{height}$$

Note that the choice of $[0,1,0]^T$ guarantees that $\boldsymbol{v}'_{ox}$ will be parallel to plane XZ, which is what we want in this kind of interaction (no roll). Also note that this choice does not work if we are aiming straight up, which means when $\boldsymbol{v}'_{oz} = [0,1,0]^T$. This problem is usually avoided by limiting the pitch to $89.9°$.

A more elegant implementation is to always update the original view reference frame (and not build a new one). Instead of keeping the total rotation angles α and β we keep the increment $d\alpha$ and $d\beta$. Then we first rotate V_R around the *(y)* axis of the world reference frame:

$$V'_R = R_{y\,d\alpha}\, V_R$$

Note that rotating a frame (or, more generally, applying any affine transformation to it) is simply done by rotating each of its axes. Then we apply a rotation to V'_R around its $\boldsymbol{x}$ axis, which is done as shown in Section 4.4:

$$V''_R = \underbrace{V'_R\, R_{xd\beta}\, {V'_R}^{-1}}_{rotation\ around\ V'_{R\,x}}\, V'_R = R_{yd\alpha}\, V_R\, R_{xd\beta} \tag{4.14}$$

4.11.2 Upgrade Your Client: Add the Photographer View

The photographer stays at a position alongside the track and takes pictures of the race. So what we want is the ability to control a view reference frame whose origin is between $50cm$ to $180cm$ from the ground. We also want to enable the photographer to lock the camera target to a specific car, which will be very useful to make photos with the technique called *panning photography* (more on this in Section 10.1.5). Like we did with the ChaseCamera, we create another object that we call PhotographerCamera, but this time the keys and mouse events will affect the camera position and orientation.

Listing 4.6 shows the properties of the camera. Note that this time we do not store the view frame as 4×4 matrix. Instead, we have the property this.position (a three-dimensional point) for the origin of the frame and the property this.orientation (a 4×4 matrix) for the axes. The only reason for this is that we will always handle position and orientation separately, so it is just more handy to store them explicitly.

The position is updated by the function **updatePosition**, which is called at every frame. At line 58 we convert the direction of movement from photographer to world space and then add it to the current position, as shown in Equation (4.11), and then clamp the y value (that is, the height) between 0.5 and 1.8. The direction is determined by the mouse movement in the function **mouseMove**. At lines 35 and 36 we compute the angles **alpha** and **beta** as the horizontal and vertical mouse movements, respectively, and lines 40 to 42 are the implementation of Equation (4.14).

The function **setView** simply uses the **lookAt** function to compute the viewing transformation. If the variable **lockToCar** is true we use the car position as target for the **lookaAt** function; otherwise we use the colums of the matrix **orientation** to define the target and the up vector.

```
7   function PhotographerCamera() {
8     this.position = [0, 0, 0];
9     this.orientation = [1, 0, 0, 0, 0, 1, 0, 0, 0, 0, 1, 0, 0, 0, ↩
          0, 1];
10    this.t_V = [0, 0, 0];
11    this.orienting_view = false;
12    this.lockToCar = false;
13    this.start_x = 0;
14    this.start_y = 0;
15
16    var me = this;
17    this.handleKey = {};
18    this.handleKey["Q"] = function () {me.t_V = [0, 0.1, 0];};
19    this.handleKey["E"] = function () {me.t_V = [0, -0.1, 0];};
20    this.handleKey["L"] = function () {me.lockToCar= true;};
21    this.handleKey["U"] = function () {me.lockToCar= false;};
22
23    this.keyDown = function (keyCode) {
24      if (this.handleKey[keyCode])
25        this.handleKey[keyCode](true);
26    }
27
28    this.keyUp = function (keyCode) {
29      this.delta = [0, 0, 0];
30    }
31
32    this.mouseMove = function (event) {
33      if (!this.orienting_view) return;
34
35      var alpha = (event.offsetX - this.start_x)/10.0;
36      var beta  = (event.offsetY - this.start_y)/10.0;
37      this.start_x = event.offsetX;
38      this.start_y = event.offsetY;
39
40      var R_alpha = SglMat4.rotationAngleAxis(sglDegToRad( alpha ↩
          ), [0, 1, 0]);
41      var R_beta = SglMat4.rotationAngleAxis(sglDegToRad (beta  ),↩
          [1, 0, 0]);
42      this.orientation = SglMat4.mul(SglMat4.mul(R_alpha, this.↩
          orientation), R_beta);
```

```
43    };
44
45    this.mouseButtonDown = function (event) {
46      if (!this.lock_to_car) {
47        this.orienting_view = true;
48        this.start_x = event.offsetX;
49        this.start_y = event.offsetY;
50      }
51    };
52
53    this.mouseButtonUp = function () {
54      this.orienting_view = false;
55    }
56
57    this.updatePosition = function ( t_V ){
58      this.position = SglVec3.add(this.position, SglMat4.mul3(this.
           .orientation, t_V));
59      if (this.position[1] > 1.8) this.position[1] = 1.8;
60      if (this.position[1] < 0.5) this.position[1] = 0.5;
61    }
62
63    this.setView = function (stack, carFrame) {
64      this.updatePosition (this.t_V )
65      var car_position = SglMat4.col(carFrame,3);
66      if (this.lockToCar)
67        var invV = SglMat4.lookAt(this.position, car_position, [0,
             1, 0]);
68      else
69        var invV = SglMat4.lookAt(this.position, SglVec3.sub(this.
             position, SglMat4.col(this.orientation, 2)), SglMat4.
             col(this.orientation, 1));
70      stack.multiply(invV);
71    };
72 };
```

LISTING 4.6: Setting the view for the photographer camera. (Code snippet from *http://envymycarbook.com/chapter4/1/1.js.*)

Figure 4.29 shows a snapshot from the client while viewing from the photographer's point of view.

4.11.3   Manipulating the Scene with Keyboard and Mouse: the Virtual Trackball

The virtual trackball is a convenient way to map mouse movements to rotation of the scene (or to a single object). The idea is that we have a sphere centered to a fixed point in world space, and we can grab any point of its visible surface and drag it in order to make the sphere and the scene rotate accordingly around the sphere's center. Figure 4.30 shows how a virtual trackball can be implemented. p_0 and p_1 are two consecutive positions on screen during mouse movement, and p_0' and p_1' their projections on the sphere. The corresponding rotation is obtained bringing p_0' to p_1' throught the shortest path on the sphere's surface, which is done by rotating p_0' around the axis

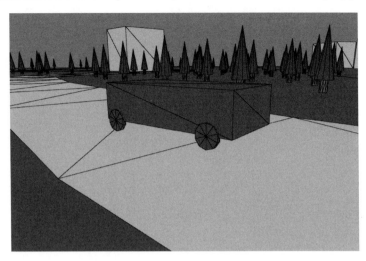

FIGURE 4.29: Adding the photographer point of view. (See client *http://envymycarbook.com/chapter4/1/1.html.*)

$(p_0' - c) \times (p_1' - c)$ by an angle

$$\theta = asin \left(\frac{\|(p_0' - c))\|\|(p_1' - c))\|}{\|(p_0' - c)\ (p_1' - c)\|} \right) \tag{4.15}$$

We can see several problems with this implementation. The first one is that nothing happens when the projection of the mouse position does not intersect the sphere, which is both unpleasant to see and a source of jolty movements when the projection leaves the sphere on one point to reappear on a faraway point. Furthermore, when the projection approaches the border of the sphere the surface becomes very steep and small mouse movements correspond to big angles. Also, it is not possible to obtain a rotation around the **z** axis (roll) because all the points will always be in the z positive halfspace.

A naive solution to the first two problems would be to use a sphere so big that its projection covers the whole viewing window. Apart from the fact that

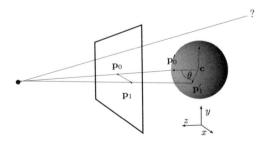

FIGURE 4.30: The virtual trackball implemented with a sphere.

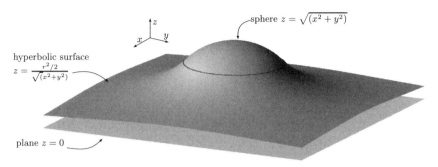

FIGURE 4.31: A surface made by the union of a hyperbolid and a sphere.

this is not always possible because the center of the sphere may be too close to the viewing plane, note that the ratio between mouse movement and angle depends on sphere radius: if it is too big large mouse movements will result in small angle rotation and make the trackball nearly useless.

A common and effective solution consists of using as surface a combination of the sphere and a hyperbolic surface as shown in Figure 4.31:

$$S = \begin{cases} \sqrt{r^2 - (x^2 + y^2)} & x^2 + y^2 < r^2/2 \\ \frac{r^2/2}{\sqrt{x^2+y^2}} & x^2 + y^2 >= r^2/2 \end{cases}$$

This surface coincides with the sphere around the center of the trackball and then smoothly approximates the plane XY. The amount of rotation can still be determined by Equation (4.15) although the more the points p_0' and p_1' are off the center the smaller the angle will be with respect to their distance. Instead we can use:

$$\theta = \frac{\|p_1' - p_0'\|}{r}$$

that is, the angle covered by the arc length $\|p_1' - p_0'\|$ (see Figure 4.32, left side).

4.12 Upgrade Your Client: Create the Observer Camera

The improvement we are about to make to our client will be very helpful for the rest of the development. We will add the *Observer Camera*, a view that allows us to freely fly around with WASD mode and switch to a trackball mode when we want to examine some detail. This is a tool that, during the development of the game, will enable us to examine details of the scene from a privileged point of view. Suppose we want to use WASD mode to move the point of view near the car, then use a virtual trackball to make the world

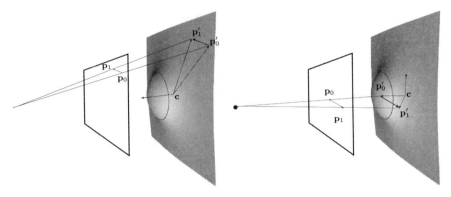

FIGURE 4.32: The virtual trackball implemented with a hyperbolid and a sphere.

rotate about the car center, to examine it, and then to switch back to WASD mode to go to see some other detail of the scene.

We define the object **ObserverCamera**, which has all the same member functions as the **ChaseCamera** and the **PhotographerCamera**. The implementation of the camera is a mere implementation of the formulas in Sections 4.11.1 and 4.11.3. The only detail left out is what happens when we switch from the trackball mode to the WASD mode. Note the WASD mode works by changing the view frame while the trackball makes *the world* rotate about a pivot point, that is, *without* changing the view frame. Such rotation is stored in the matrix **tbMatrix**, which multiplies the stack matrix right after the view transformation, so that all the scene is rotated. If we use the virtual trackball and then switch to WASD mode we cannot simply ignore the matrix **tbMatrix** because our view frame has not changed since the beginning of the rotation and it would be like if we did not use the trackball mode at all.

What we do is the following: every time a mouse movement controlling the trackball has ended, we convert the trackball rotation into a camera transformation and reset the trackball transformation to the identity. In other words, we change the view frame to obtain exactly the same transformation as with the trackball. Let us see how this is done. During the trackball manipulation, the generic point p of the scene is brought in view space by:

$$\mathbf{p}' = V^{-1} \ tbMatrix \ \mathbf{p}$$

When we switch to WASD mode we want to forget about *tbMatrix*, but keep the same global transformation, so we need a new view reference frame V_{wasd} such that:

$$\mathbf{p}' = V_{wasd}^{-1}\mathbf{p} = V^{-1} \ tbMatrix \ \mathbf{p}$$

so we have:

$$V_{wasd}^{-1} = V^{-1} \ tbMatrix \rightarrow V_{new} = tbMatrix^{-1} \ V$$

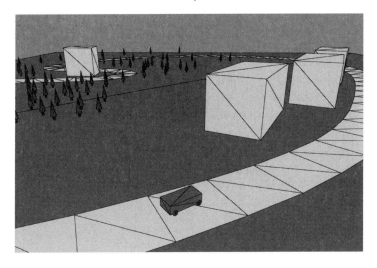

FIGURE 4.33: Adding the Observer point of view with WASD and Trackball Mode. (See client *http://envymycarbook.com/chapter4/2/2.html.*)

The listing below shows the implementation of the **mouseUp** function. orbiting is a Boolean variable that is set to true when the camera is in trackball mode and the mouse button is pressed, and to false when the mouse button is released.

```
144    this.mouseButtonUp = function (event) {
145        if (this.orbiting) {
146            var invTbMatrix = SglMat4.inverse(this.tbMatrix);
147            this.V   = SglMat4.mul(invTbMatrix, this.V);
148            this.tbMatrix = SglMat4.identity();
149            this.rotMatrix = SglMat4.identity();
150            this.orbiting = false;
151        }else
152            this.aiming = false;
153    };
```

Figure 4.33 shows a snapshot from the client while viewing the scene with the Observer Camera.

4.13 Self-Exercises

4.13.1 General

1. Find the affine 2D transformation that transforms the square centered at $(0,0)$ with sides of length 2 into the square with corners $\{(2,0),(0,2),(-2,0),(0,-2)\}$ and find its inverse transformation.

2. Provide a counter example to the following statements: a non-affine transformation is not invertible; translation and rotation are commutative transformations.

3. Prove that affine transformation maps parallel lines to parallel lines. *Hint*: express the lines in parametric form as $L = \mathbf{p} + t\ \mathbf{d}$ and then apply an affine transformation to both.

4. Consider the square with unitary sides centered at $(0.5, 0.5)$ and apply the following transformations:

   - rotation by $45°$
   - scaling by 0.5 along the $\mathbf{y}$ axis
   - rotation by $-30°$

   Write down the shear transformation that gives the same result.

5. Describe what happens to the image formed in a pinhole camera when the hole is not punctiform.

4.13.2   Client Related

1. In order to improve the visualization of the steering of the car, allow the front wheels of the car to rotate by $30°$ about the y axis on the left and on the right.

2. In order to tell the front of the car from its back, apply a transformation along the z axis so that the front will look half as wide and half as high as the back. Can you do it with an affine transformation? *Hint*: draw the transformed version of the box and answer to the question: do parallel lines stay parallel after this transformation?

3. Add the *front view*, which is the view looking forward from the car (so the car is no longer visible).

4. In Listing 4.1 we show how to set the projection matrix so to preserve the aspect ratio. Note that the way we did it works on the assumptions that *width/height* ratio was greater for the viewport than the wanted viewing window. What happens if we set the viewport to 300×400? Will we still see the whole circuit? Fix the code in Listing 4.1 so that it works in every case.

Chapter 5

Turning Vertices into Pixels

In the previous chapters we learned the basic algorithms for turning a specification of a three-dimensional scene (vertices, polygons, etc.) into a picture on the screen. In the following sections we show the details of how a geometric primitive becomes a region of colored pixels and also several optimizations that are commonly used for making it an efficient operation.

5.1 Rasterization

Rasterization comes into play after the vertex positions are expressed in viewport space (see Section 4.6.4). Unlike all the previous reference systems (in order: object space, world space, view space, NDC) this one is discrete and we have to decide how many fragments belong to the primitive and which discrete coordinates have to be assigned to the corresponding fragments.

5.1.1 Lines

What is called *line* in CG is actually a *segment* specified by the two endpoints (x_0, y_0) and (x_1, y_1), and for the sake of simplicity we assume that the coordinates are integers. The segment can be expressed as:

$$y = y_0 + m\,(x - x_0) \tag{5.1}$$
$$m = \frac{y_1 - y_0}{x_1 - x_0}$$

From Equation (5.1) we can see that if x is incremented to $x + 1$, y is incremented to $y + m$. Note that if $-1 \le m < 1$ and we round to the closest integer the values of y, for all the values of x between x_0 and x_1 we will have a series of pixels such that there is exactly one pixel for each column and two consecutive pixels are always adjacent, as shown in Figure 5.1. If $m > 1$ or $m < -1$ we can invert the roles of x and y and write the equation as:

$$x = x_0 + \frac{1}{m}(y - y_0) \tag{5.2}$$

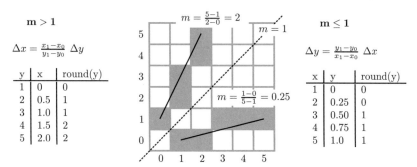

FIGURE 5.1: Discrete differential analyzer algorithm examples.

and compute the values of x for y going from y_0 to y_1. This algorithm is called *discrete difference analyzer (DDA)* and is reported in Listing 5.1.

```
DDARasterizer(x₀,y₀,x₁,y₁) {
    float m = (y₁ - y₀) / (x₁ - x₀)
    if ((m >= -1) && (m <= 1)) {
        Δy = m;
        Δx = 1;
    }
    else {
        Δy = 1;
        Δx = 1/m;
    }

    x = x₀; y = y₀;

    do {
        OutputPixel(round(x),round(y));
        x = x + Δx;
        y = y + Δy;
    }
}
```

LISTING 5.1: Discrete difference analyzer (DDA) rasterization algorithm.

The weakness of the DDA rasterization is that Δx and Δy are fractionary numbers, which at the same time slows down computation, and since the floating point representation has finite precision, causes error accumulation.

The *Bresenham's algorithm* solves both problems with a formulation that only involves integer numbers. Figure 5.2 shows 4 lines with different slopes but all passing through the same pixel.

Let us assume the case $0 \leq m \leq 1$, that we are performing the DDA rasterization and that we have just outputted pixel (i, j), so we are now computing the y value for $i + 1$. We can see that:

$$
\begin{aligned}
&\text{if } j + \Delta y \geq j + \tfrac{1}{2} \rightarrow OutputPixel(i+1, j+1) \\
&\text{if } j + \Delta y < j + \tfrac{1}{2} \rightarrow OutputPixel(i+1, j)
\end{aligned}
\tag{5.3}
$$

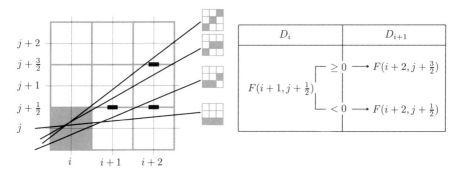

FIGURE 5.2: Bresenham's algorithm. Schematization.

or, stated in other words, if the lines pass over $(i+1, j+\frac{1}{2})$ the next pixel will be $(i+1, j+1)$, otherwise it will be $(i+1, j)$. It is useful to write the line equation

$$y = \frac{\Delta y}{\Delta x}\, x + c \tag{5.4}$$

with the implicit formulation:

$$y\Delta x - x\Delta y - c\Delta x = 0. \tag{5.5}$$

For compactness we define the function $F(x, y) = -\Delta y\, x + \Delta x\, y - c$. Note that

$$F(x, y) = \begin{cases} 0 & \text{if } (x, y) \text{ belongs to the line} \\ > 0 & \text{if } (x, y) \text{ is above the line} \\ < 0 & \text{if } (x, y) \text{ is below the line} \end{cases} \tag{5.6}$$

We define a boolean variable $D_i = F(i+1, j+\frac{1}{2})$, called *decision variable*, and replace the condition in Equation (5.3) to get the following relations:

$$\begin{aligned} &\text{if } D_i \geq 0 \rightarrow OutputPixel(i+1, j+1) \\ &\text{if } D_i < 0 \rightarrow OutputPixel(i+1, j) \end{aligned} \tag{5.7}$$

Up to now we are still dealing with the DDA rasterization, we just wrote the formulas in a slightly different way. The good news is that, as shown in the table in Figure 5.2, the decision variable for $i+1$ depends only on the decision variable for i. Let us have a look at how the decision variable changes between two consecutive pixels:

$$\Delta D_i = D_{i+1} - D_i = \begin{cases} \Delta x - \Delta y & \text{if } D_i \geq 0 \\ -\Delta y & \text{if } D_i < 0 \end{cases} \tag{5.8}$$

This means that we do not have to recompute D for each value of x, but we can just update its value at each step. Note that even though all ΔD_i's are integers, the first value for F is still a fraction:

$$F(i+1, j+\frac{1}{2}) = -\Delta y\, (i+1)\Delta x\, (j+\frac{1}{2}) - \Delta x\, c \tag{5.9}$$

However, since we only use the sign of F, we simply multiply both F and ΔD_i by 2 and obtain integer-only operations:

$$F(i,j) = 2\,\Delta x j - 2\,\Delta y\, i - 2\,\Delta x\, c \qquad (5.10)$$

So, if our line starts from pixel (i_0, j_0) and ends at pixel (i_1, j_1) we can compute the initial value of the decision variable:

$$
\begin{aligned}
F(i_0 + 1, j_0 + \tfrac{1}{2}) &= 2\,\Delta x (j_0 + \tfrac{1}{2}) - 2\,\Delta y\,(i_0 + 1) - 2\,\Delta x\, c \\
&= \underline{2\,\Delta x j_0} + \Delta x - \underline{2\,\Delta y\, i_0} - 2\,\Delta y - \underline{2\,\Delta x\, c} \\
&= F(i_0, j_0) + \Delta x - 2\,\Delta y \\
&= 0 + \Delta x - 2\,\Delta y
\end{aligned}
$$

Note that, according to Equation (5.6), $F(i_0, j_0) = 0$ because (i_0, j_0) belongs to the line. This allows us to write a rasterization algorithm that uses integer coordinates only and simple updates of the decision variable as shown in Listing 5.2. Since $\Delta y / \Delta x$ are related to the slope of the line we can simply set them as the width and the height of the line, respectively.

```
BresenhamRasterizer(i0,j0,i1,j1) {
    int Δy = j1 - j0;
    int Δx = i1 - i0;
    int D = Δx - 2 * Δy;
    int i = i0;
    int j = j0;
    OutputPixel(i,j);
    while(i < i1)
    {
        if (D >= 0) {
            i = i + 1;
            j = j + 1;
            D = D + (Δx - Δy);
        }
        else {
            i = i + 1;
            D = D + (-Δy);
        }

        OutputPixel(i,j);
    }
}
```

LISTING 5.2: Bresenham rasterizer for the case of slope between 0 and 1. All the other cases can be written taking into account the symmetry of the problem.

5.1.2   Polygons (Triangles)

Rasterizing a polygon is usually referred to as *polygon filling*. We will not go very deep into technicalities about general polygons because usually polygons are tessellated into triangles before being rasterized.

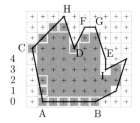

FIGURE 5.3: Scanline algorithm for polygon filling.

5.1.2.1 General Polygons

The *scanline* algorithm fills a polygon by proceeding line by line, from the bottom to the top and from left to right with each line, outputting pixels inside the polygon, just like an inkjet printer. This is done by finding the intersections between each scanline and the edges of the polygon and sorting them on their y values (ascending). Then the interior pixels are found by the *disparity test*, that is: on every *odd* intersection we are going from outside to inside the polygon, on every *even* intersection we are going from inside to outside.

To make this very simple algorithm actually work we must consider the following requirement for the filling: if two polygons share the same edge, no pixel should be outputted by both, that is, there must be no overlapping.

The basic problem is due to the intersection on integer values. Referring to Figure 5.3, consider the scanline passing though vertex C and the scanline passing through E. Both vertices are in a scanline, but while pixel at C is considered part of the polygon, pixel at E is not. This is because, in the case of intersection with integer coordinates, the scanline algorithm chooses to consider the pixel inside if it is an odd intersection (entering) and outside otherwise. This guarantees that if a non-horizontal edge is shared by two polygons, all the pixels crossed by the edges will belong only to one of the two.

The same kind of choice is done for horizontal edges: note that the pixels on the horizontal edge AB are considered inside while those on FG are not. Finally, note that the intersections with the edge DH and the edge DF concide with the vertex D but must be considered separately, the first as an even/exiting intersection, the second as an odd/entering intersection. Note that this strategy would cause a problem with vertex E, which instead should be counted only as an even/exiting intersection. The problem is solved by not considering the maximum y coordinate in the intersection test, which means that the edge IE does not intersect scanline 4.

The intersection tests of the scanlines with the edges are not computed from scratch for each scanline. Instead, the same considerations used for the DDA rasterizer are used: if a segment is expressed as $y = m\,x + b$, that is,

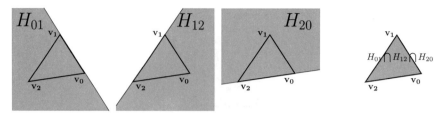

FIGURE 5.4: Any convex polygon can be expressed as the intersection of the halfspaces built on the polygon edges.

$x = (y - b)\frac{1}{m}$, it means that the intersection point moves by $\frac{1}{m}$ at every scanline.

5.1.2.2   Triangles

The modern graphics hardware are massively parallel and designed to process the pixels in groups, but if we consider the rasterization algorithms seen so far we can notice they are quite linear in that they process one pixel after the other and update quantities. The scanline algorithm for polygon filling works for every type of polygon (even non-convex or with holes) but proceeds line after line.

A more *parallel* approach is just to give up on incremental computation and test in a parallel group of pixels to see if they are inside or outside the polygon. As will be made clear in a moment, this test can be done efficiently for convex polygons without holes. The only thing we need is to be able to know if a point is inside a triangle or not.

A useful characteristics of the convex polygons, and hence of triangles, is that they can be seen as the intersection of a finite number of halfspaces. If, for each edge of the triangle, we take the line passing through it, one of the two halfspaces will include the inside of the triangle, as shown in Figure 5.4.

Let us consider again the implicit formulation of the line used in Equation (5.6). In this case, we can think that the line divides the 2D space in two halfspaces, one where the function $F(.)$ is positive and one where it is negative. In principle we could just find the implicit definition for each of the three lines but then we are left with an ambiguity: how do we know, for a given line, if the points inside the triangle are those in the positive or in the negative halfspace? Just to make it clearer, note that if F is the implicit formulation of a line, $-F$ also is.

What we need is a conventional way to define the implicit formulation that depends on the order in which we consider the two vertices defining the line. Consider the edge $\overline{v_0 v_1}$: the line passing through it can be written as:

$$\begin{bmatrix} x \\ y \end{bmatrix} = \begin{bmatrix} x_0 \\ y_0 \end{bmatrix} + t \left(\begin{bmatrix} x_1 \\ y_1 \end{bmatrix} - \begin{bmatrix} x_0 \\ y_0 \end{bmatrix} \right) \qquad (5.11)$$

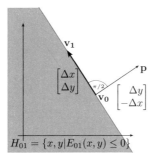

FIGURE 5.5: Edge equation explained.

so when t increases we move on the line in the direction $(\mathbf{v}_1 - \mathbf{v}_0)$. We can solve these two equations for t, for any $[x, y]^T$ on the line (horizontal and vertical lines are not considered since they are trivial cases to treat):

$$t = \frac{x - x_0}{x_1 - x_0} \tag{5.12}$$

$$t = \frac{y - y_0}{y_1 - y_0}$$

hence:

$$\frac{x - x_0}{x_1 - x_0} = \frac{y - y_0}{y_1 - y_0} \tag{5.13}$$

upon which, after few simplification steps and factoring out x and y, we obtain the so called *edge equation* for the edge $\overline{\mathbf{v}_0\mathbf{v}_1}$:

$$E_{01}(x, y) = \Delta y \; x - \Delta x \; y + (y_0 x_1 - y_1 x_0) = 0 \tag{5.14}$$

Note that if we consider the vector made of x and y coefficients $[\Delta y, -\Delta x]^T$ we will find that it is orthogonal to the line direction $[\Delta x, \Delta y]^T$ (their dot product is 0, see Appendix B) and it indicates the halfspace where the implicit function is positive. To test that this is true, we can simply write E_{01} for point p (see Figure 5.5):

$$E_{01}\left(\mathbf{v}_0 + \begin{bmatrix} \Delta y \\ -\Delta x \end{bmatrix}\right) = \ldots = \Delta y^2 + \Delta x^2 > 0$$

In other words, if we walk on the line along direction $\mathbf{v}_1 - \mathbf{v}_0$ the positive halfspace is on our right. Note that if we write the edge equation swapping the order of the two points we will see that $E_{10} = -E_{01}$ and, again, the positive halfspace will be on our right (walking along $\mathbf{v}_0 - \mathbf{v}_1$). So if we specify the triangle as three vertices $\mathbf{v}_0\mathbf{v}_1\mathbf{v}_2$ counterclockwise, it means that if we walk from $\mathbf{v}_0$ to $\mathbf{v}_1$, and then from $\mathbf{v}_1$ to $\mathbf{v}_2$, the space outside the triangle is on our right all the time. According to this, we can test if a point p is inside the triangle in this way:

$$\mathbf{p} \text{ is inside } T \Leftrightarrow (E_{01}(\mathbf{p}) \leq 0) \; \wedge \; (E_{12}(\mathbf{p}) \leq 0) \; \wedge \; (E_{20}(\mathbf{p}) \leq 0) \tag{5.15}$$

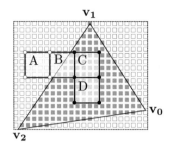

FIGURE 5.6: Optimization of inside/outside test for triangle filling. Pixels outside the bounding rectangle do not need to be tested, as well as pixels inside stamp **A**, which are outside the triangle, and pixels inside stamps **C** and **D**, which are all inside the triangle.

This means that an algorithm for the rasterization of a triangle could be just to test all the pixels of the viewport against the condition (5.15), but that would not be very efficient.

A straightforward optimization consists of reducing the space of the pixels to test those inside the smallest rectangle that include the triangle, named *bounding rectangle*. Another optimization consists of testing a square group of pixels, often named *stamp*, to test if it is entirely inside (outside) the triangle, in which case all the pixels in the stamp are surely inside (outside) the triangle. Figure 5.6 shows an example of a triangle with its bounding rectangle and some stamps: **A**,**C** and **D** save us the cost of testing their inside pixels individually while the stamp **B** is neither entirely outside nor entirely inside. In this case, we may think to have a second level of smaller stamps or we simply test all the pixels individually. The number of levels of the stamps, the size of the stamps, etc., are a matter of implementation and vary with the graphics hardware.

5.1.3   Attribute Interpolation: Barycentric Coordinates

We already know from Section 2.2 that to each vertex we may assign attributes other than its position. For example, we may assign a color attribute to each vertex. Now the question is: which color should we assign to the pixels rasterized by the primitive? For example, if we have a line segment going from $\mathbf{v}_0$ to $\mathbf{v}_1$ and we assign the color *Red* to $\mathbf{v}_0$ and the color *Blue* to $\mathbf{v}_1$, which color will be assigned to the pixels outputted by the rasterization? One intuitive answer is that the color should *fade* from red to blue as we follow the rasterization of the segment from $\mathbf{v}_0$ to $\mathbf{v}_1$. This is obtained by a linear combination of the two colors:

$$c(i,j) = Red\ \lambda_0(i,j) + Blue\ \lambda_1(i,j) \qquad (5.16)$$

where we indicate with $c(i,j)$ the color of pixel (i,j) and with $\lambda_0(i,j)$ and $\lambda_1(i,j)$ the coefficients of the linear combination. Let us assume the position of pixel (i',j') is exactly middle way between $\mathbf{v}_0$ and $\mathbf{v}_1$. Then we would have

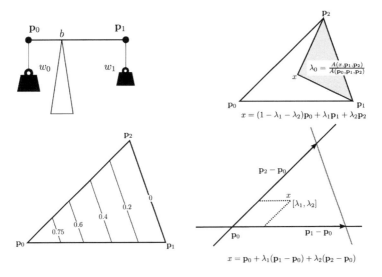

FIGURE 5.7: Barycentric coordinates: (Top-Left) Barycenter on a segment with two weights at the extremes. (Top-Right) Barycentric coordinates of a point inside a triangle. (Bottom-Left) Lines obtained keeping v_0 constant area parallel to the opposite edge. (Bottom-Right) Barycentric coordinates as a non-orthogonal reference system.

no doubt that both the coefficients should be $\frac{1}{2}$. This concept is extended to a generic point on the segment (or triangle) by means of *barycentric coordinates*.

Barycentric coordinates are a practical and elegant way to express points inside a simplex, as our segments and triangles are (see the definition of simplex in Section 3.2), as a function of the simplex vertex positions.

Let us see how they are found. Suppose we have a segment with no mass with two weights w_0 and w_1 hanging at the extremes $\mathbf{p}_0$ and $\mathbf{p}_1$, respectively. The barycenter is the point along the segment so that the segment will stay in equilibrium, as shown in Figure 5.7. We know from very basic notions of physics that the barycenter is the point where the sum of all the forces is 0, so:

$$(\mathbf{p}_0 - \mathbf{b})w_0 + (\mathbf{p}_1 - \mathbf{b})w_1 = 0 \qquad (5.17)$$

which means that we can find the barycenter as:

$$\mathbf{b} = \mathbf{p}_0 \frac{w_1}{w_0 + w_1} + \mathbf{p}_1 \frac{w_0}{w_0 + w_1} \qquad (5.18)$$

which is in fact the general formula for the barycenter applied to the case of two points. Let us define

$$\lambda = \frac{w_0}{w_0 + w_1} \qquad (5.19)$$

Note that $0 \leq \lambda \leq 1$ and also that $\frac{w_1}{w_0 + w_1} = 1 - \lambda$, so that we can rewrite equation 5.18 as:

$$\mathbf{b} = \mathbf{p}_0(1 - \lambda) + \mathbf{p}_1\lambda \qquad (5.20)$$

where λ and $1 - \lambda$ are called the *barycentric coordinates* of point $\mathbf{b}$. We point out that we do not need any weights to find the barycentric coordinates, since they only depend on the proportion between them (if we multiply w_0 and w_1 by any non-zero factor $\mathbf{b}$ does not change).

Computing the barycentric coordinates of any point $\mathbf{x}$ along the segment is straightforward, since according to Equation (5.20) we can write:

$$(\mathbf{p}_1 - \mathbf{p}_0)\lambda = (\mathbf{x} - \mathbf{p}_0)$$

and hence, solving from λ by simply considering the fraction of the length of $\mathbf{x} - \mathbf{p}_0$ over the whole length of the segment:

$$\lambda = \frac{\|\mathbf{x} - \mathbf{p}_0\|}{\|\mathbf{p}_1 - \mathbf{p}_0\|} \qquad (5.21)$$

Barycentric Coordinates of a Triangle

We can extend the same reasoning to the triangle and reach a similar conclusion. Given a point $\mathbf{x}$ inside the triangle we can express it as a linear combination of the vertices position: $\mathbf{x} = \lambda_0\mathbf{p}_0 + \lambda_1\mathbf{p}_1 + \mathbf{p}_2\lambda_2$, where $0 \leq \lambda_0, \lambda_1, \lambda_2 \leq 1$ and $\lambda_0 + \lambda_1 + \lambda_2 = 1$. The weight associated to the point p_n is obtained as the ratio between the area of the triangle formed by the point $\mathbf{x}$ and the other two points of the triangle except p_n and the area of the whole triangle. So, for example, for λ_0:

$$\lambda_0 = \frac{Area(\mathbf{x}, \mathbf{p}_1, \mathbf{p}_2)}{Area(\mathbf{p}_0, \mathbf{p}_1, \mathbf{p}_2)} = \frac{(\mathbf{p}_1 - \mathbf{x}) \times (\mathbf{p}_2 - \mathbf{x})}{(\mathbf{p}_1 - \mathbf{p}_0) \times (\mathbf{p}_2 - \mathbf{p}_0)} \qquad (5.22)$$

We can see that as $\mathbf{x}$ approaches $\mathbf{p}_0$, λ_0 approaches 1, and λ_1 and λ_2 go to 0.

Also note that we can see the triangle itself as a non-orthogonal reference system, with origin in $\mathbf{p}_0$ and axis $\mathbf{p}_1 - \mathbf{p}_0$ and $\mathbf{p}_2 - \mathbf{p}_0$. In fact, if we consider that $\lambda_0 = 1 - \lambda_1 - \lambda_2$ we can write

$$\mathbf{x} = \mathbf{p}_0 + \lambda_1(\mathbf{p}_1 - \mathbf{p}_0) + \lambda_2(\mathbf{p}_2 - \mathbf{p}_0)$$

where $\mathbf{x}$ is inside the triangles if and only if $0 \leq \lambda_1, \lambda_2 \leq 1$ and $\lambda_1 + \lambda_2 \leq 1$. This also explains the constraint $\lambda_0 + \lambda_1 + \lambda_2 = 1$ given before. Also $\lambda_1 + \lambda_2$ is constant over all the lines parallel to the edge opposite to the vertex $\mathbf{p}_0$, as shown in Figure 5.7.

5.1.4 Concluding Remarks

In this section we have seen how to rasterize the primitives of which our scene is composed, such as segments and triangles. When a scene is made of many primitives it may happen that not all of them are entirely visible at the same time. This may happen for three reasons (see Figure 5.8):

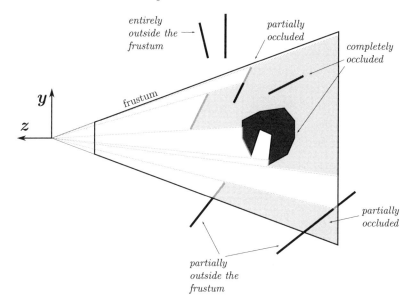

FIGURE 5.8: Cases where primitives are not fully visible.

- because a primitive is partially or entirely covered by another with respect to the viewer, and then we need a *Hidden Surface Removal* algorithm to avoid rasterizing it;

- because the primitive is partially outside the view volume, in which case
  we have to *clip* it, which means to determine which part of the primitive
  is inside the view volume;

- because the primitive is entirely outside the view volume, in which case
  we should simply avoid rasterizing it.

In the next two sections we will deal with exactly these problems, how to
avoid rasterizing hidden primitives and how to clip them.

5.2   Hidden Surface Removal

Many computer graphics algorithms are subdivided into *object space* and
image space, depending on whether they work on the 3D space where vertices
are defined or on the raster domain after the primitives are rasterized. In the
case of hidden surface removal, the most well-known object-space algorithm
is called *depth sorting*, which is an improvement on the *painter's algorithm*.
The idea is that the primitives are sorted on the basis of their distance from

the viewer and then drawn from the farthest to the nearest (which is referred to as *back-to-front* drawing), as is done in some painting techniques, where the painter paints the background and then draws on it the objects starting from the far ones and proceeding with the ones closer to the viewer. In this manner, if more primitives overlap on a pixel the nearest will be rasterized as the last one and will determine the pixel value.

5.2.1 Depth Sort

When the painter's algorithm was first proposed, the distance of a primitive from the viewer was taken as the distance of its barycenter from the viewer. The problem is that if the barycenter of a primitive A is closer to the viewer than the barycenter of another polygon B, this does not imply that the whole of A is closer than the whole of B. The depth sort algorithm attempts to find a correct back-to-front order by looking for a *separating plane* between couples of primitives. As the name suggests, a separating plane is a plane that separates entities (primitives in this case) into two groups: one in the positive halfspace and one in the negative halfspace. Consider a separating plane with a normal having positive z (in view space, that is, pointing towards the viewer) as in the example in Figure 5.9. We can safely say that the primitive in the negative halfspace is on the back of the primitive that is in the positive halfspace and hence must be drawn first.

The depth sort algorithm simply tries to sort the primitives using the separating plane to establish the order between each couple. For example, if the nearest vertex of B is farther away than the farthest vertex of A, then any plane parallel to XY and with z between the two values is a separating plane. If this is not the case, the same test can be done for the x (y) values to find a separating plane parallel to YZ (XZ). In essence, we are doing a series of

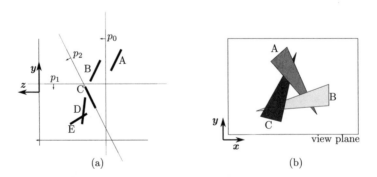

(a)   (b)

FIGURE 5.9: (a) Depth sort example on four segments and a few examples of planes separating them. Note that C and D cannot be separated by a plane aligned with the axis but they are by the plane lying on C. D and E intersect and cannot be ordered without splitting them. (b) A case where, although no intersections exist, the primitives cannot be ordered.

tests to look for a separating plane, and we start with planes parallel to the principal planes because the tests are simply comparisons of one coordinate. Note that for a couple of non-intersecting convex polygons one of the planes that contains one of the primitives is the separating plane.

Unfortunately, if the primitives intersect they cannot be ordered and, in general, it is not possible to draw first one and then the other and get the correct result. Even if no intersections exist, it may be not possible to find a correct back-to-front order. Figure 5.9(b) shows a case where this happens: a part of A is behind B, a part of B is behind C, and a part of C is behind A.

5.2.2 Scanline

Note that the cyclic ordering of Figure 5.9(b) would never happen in the bidimensional case; that is, for segments in the plane. The *scanline* algorithm rasterizes the scene line-by-line along the y axis, therefore each iteration concerns the intersection of a plane $y = k$ with the scene. The result of a scanline pass produces a set of segments whose vertices are at the intersection of the plane with the edges of the primitives. In this manner the problem is scaled down by one dimension and it becomes a matter of correctly rendering a set of segments.

If we project the vertices on the current scanline, we obtain a series of spans with the following obvious property: in each span the back-to-front order does not change (see Figure 5.10). So, for each span, we find out the nearest portion of segment and rasterize it until the end of the span.

The scanline may also be used for intersecting polygons, although we need a more complicated approach to define the spans (and which is also beyond our interest for this technique).

Although both depth sort and scanline approaches are widely known in the CG community, they are not part of the rasterization-based pipeline, for

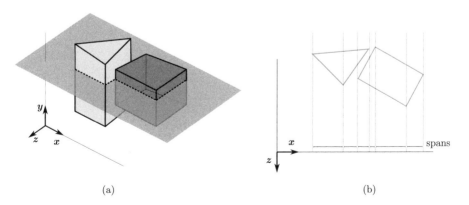

(a)   (b)

FIGURE 5.10: (a) Step of the scanline algorithm for a given plane. (b) The corresponding spans created.

the simple reason that they do not fit the pipeline architecture well, where primitives are processed one-by-one through the stages of the pipeline. Instead, these algorithms need to store all the primitives to be rendered and order them before drawing. Furthermore, they are not well suited for implementation on parallel machines, like current GPUs are.

5.2.3   z-Buffer

The *z-Buffer* is a *de facto* standard solution for hidden surface removal. We explained in Section 5.1 that when a primitive is rasterized, a number of interpolated attributes are written in the output buffers. One of the attributes is the z value of the vertex coordinate, which is written in the buffer called z-buffer (or *depth buffer*). The algorithm is very simple and it is shown in Listing 5.3. At the beginning the z-buffer is initialized with the maximum possible value (line 2), which is the value of the *far* plane of the view frustum (note that the z-buffer operates in NDC and hence this value is 1). Then each primitive is rasterized and for each pixel covered (line 4) its z value is calculated. If this value is smaller than the value currently written in the z-buffer, the latter is replaced with the new value (line 6).

```
1   ZBufferAlgorithm () {
2     forall i,j ZBuffer[i,j] = 1.0;
3       for each primitive pr
4         for each pixel (i,j) covered by pr
5           if (Z[i,j] < ZBuffer[i,j])
6             ZBuffer[i,j] = Z[i,j];
7   }
```

LISTING 5.3: The z-buffer algorithm.

The advantages of the z-buffer in the rasterization-based pipeline are many. The primitives are processed *as they are sent* to the pipeline and no previous ordering operations are needed. The computation is *per-pixel* and adjacent pixels can be processed *independently* and in *parallel*.

5.2.4   z-Buffer Precision and z-Fighting

One issue that must be considered carefully is the depth buffer *granularity*, that is, how well close values of z are distinguished. Simply put, the problem is that the projection and the rasterization may not preserve the original relation among depth values: it may happen that two values z_a and z_b where $z_a < z_b$ are stored as the same value in the depth buffer. This is simply because of finite numerical precision. Let us see how this may happen.

Vertex coordinates are transformed from view space to NDC and then the z coordinates are remapped from $[-1, 1]$ to $[0, 1]$ to be compared with the value in the depth buffer and possibly written. Let us call this mapping

$$f(z) : \text{view space} \to \text{depth buffer space}$$

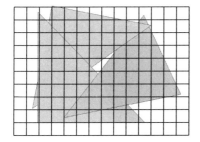
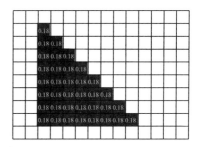

FIGURE 5.11: State of the depth buffer during the rasterization of three triangles (the ones shown in Figure 5.9(b)). On each pixel is indicated the value of the depth buffer in $[0, 1]$. The numbers in cyan indicate depth values that have been updated after the last triangle was drawn.

If the projection is orthogonal (see Section 4.6.3.1) we have:

$$f_o(z) = \frac{1}{2}\left(z\frac{-2}{f-n} - \frac{f+n}{f-n} + 1\right) \tag{5.23}$$

So the mapping is of the form $f_o(z) = az + b$, that is, just a scaling and a translation. Note that typically the depth buffer stores values in *fixed-point representation*. In a fixed-point representation the number is simply an integer with a common denominator. For example, the fixed-point 16-bits numbers between 0 and 1 are $i/(2^{16} - 1) : i = 0 \ldots 2^{16} - 1$, which means that all the consecutive numbers represented are at the same distance, $(2^{16} - 1)^{-1}$. Conversely, coordinates are expressed in floating-point numbers, which are distributed more densely around 0. This means that if we have a 32-bit depth buffer, there will be multiple depth values in view space that, when transformed, will map to the same value in depth buffer space. Figure 5.12 shows an example of artifacts we see. The cyan truncated cone is closer but because of this approximation some fragments lost the contest. This problem is called *z-fighting*.

FIGURE 5.12: Two truncated cones, one white and one cyan, superimposed with a small translation so that the cyan one is closer to the observer. However, because of z-buffer numerical approximation, part of the fragments of the cyan cones are not drawn due to the depth test against those of the white one.

Things get worse for perspective projection, for which we have:

$$f_p(z) = \frac{1}{2}\left(\frac{f+n}{f-n} - \frac{1}{z}\frac{2fn}{f-n} + 1\right) = \left(\frac{1}{2}\frac{f+n}{f-n} + \frac{1}{2}\right) - \frac{fn}{z(f-n)} \quad (5.24)$$

Unlike for orthogonal projection, this time the depth value is proportional to the reciprocal of the z value in view space. Figure 5.13 shows a plot where the abscissa corresponds to the value of z from n to f and the ordinate to the value in depth buffer space for $f_p(z)$ and $f_o(z)$. We may see how with perspective projection, the first 30% of the interval maps on the 80% of the interval in depth space, that is, values close to the near plane n are mapped more uniformly in depth buffer space. Therefore, the farther away from the near plane, the less the precision.

5.3   From Fragments to Pixels

After rasterization we are in the domain of fragments, which are integer coordinates with color and z-value attached. Before they become pixels on the screen, some *per-fragment operations*, included in any graphics API and implemented in many rasterization-based pipelines, are applied.

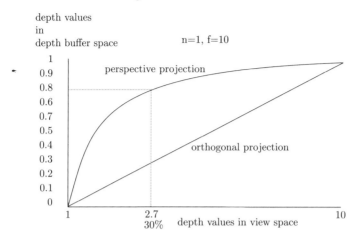

FIGURE 5.13: A plot showing the mapping between z-values in view space and depth buffer space.

5.3.1 Discard Tests

These tests do not modify the fragment values, only decide whether to *discard* it or let it pass to the next stage. We will introduce them in the order they are found along the pipeline.

The *scissor test* discards any fragment whose coordinates fall outside a specified *scissor rectangle*. Suppose that we want to show some scrolling text on a bar at the bottom of the screen, while rendering our complex and time-consuming 3D scene on the rest. A moving text is a very simple rendering, but in order to animate it we would need to redraw the whole scene even if not needed. With the scissor test we can select the only rectangle of the screen that will be affected by rendering, treating it like a screen inside the screen.

The scissor test is somewhat limited because we can only specify a rectangular region. Suppose we want a point of view fixed inside the car as shown in Figure 5.14, an option present in many racing games. In this case we would like to draw in a region whose shape is not simply a rectangle. The *stencil buffer* is a buffer of integer values that can be written during rasterization and used to mask out fragments. In the example above, which is a classic usage pattern, we would first render the interior of the car and set to 1, in the stencil buffer, all the pixels involved in the rasterization. Then we would render the rest of the scene enabling the *stencil test* to discard all the fragments whose corresponding position in the stencil buffer contains 1.

The next test is the *depth test*, the HSR removal solution we just explained in Section 5.2.3. Note that the stencil and the depth test are very similar: both use a buffer that is read, written and then tested to decide whether to discard or keep the fragment. Also note that we do not need a stencil buffer

FIGURE 5.14 (SEE COLOR INSERT): Stenciling example: (Left) The rendering from inside the car. (Middle) The stencil mask, that is, the portion of screen that does not need to be redrawn. (Right) The portion that is affected by rendering.

to implement the view from inside the car: if at each frame we render both the interior and then the rest of the scene we obtain the same result. The difference is in efficiency: using stenciling, we only draw the interior once and avoid executing the z-buffer algorithm (reading from the z-buffer, comparing and writing) for all those fragments that would never be drawn anyway.

5.3.2   Blending

When a fragment passes the z-test, its color can be written into the color buffer. Until now, we assumed that the color already present is replaced by the color of the fragment, but this is not necessarily the case: the color of the fragment (referred to as *source color*) can be *blended* with that in the color buffer (referred to as *destination color*) to model things such as transparent surfaces. A key role in blending is played by the alpha component, which is used to specify the opacity of a surface, that is, how much light passes through it.

The CG APIs such as WebGL offer the possibility of making a linear combination of each color component to obtain a wide range of effects. More precisely, let:

$$s = [s_R, s_G, s_B, s_a]$$
$$d = [d_R, d_G, d_B, d_a]$$

s be the source and d the destination color; the new destination color (d') is computed as:

$$d' = \underbrace{\begin{bmatrix} b_R \\ b_G \\ b_B \\ b_A \end{bmatrix}}_{b} \begin{bmatrix} s_R \\ s_G \\ s_B \\ s_a \end{bmatrix} + \underbrace{\begin{bmatrix} c_R \\ c_G \\ c_B \\ c_A \end{bmatrix}}_{c} \begin{bmatrix} d_R \\ d_G \\ d_B \\ d_a \end{bmatrix} \tag{5.25}$$

where b and c are coefficients, referred to as *blending factors* that can be set to produce different visual effects. The resulting value is clamped in the interval in which the color is encoded. The most common uses of blending are handling transparent surfaces and improving antialiasing.

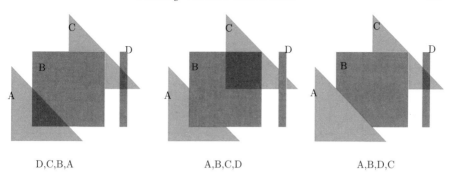

D,C,B,A   A,B,C,D   A,B,D,C

FIGURE 5.15: Results of back-to-front rendering of four polygons. A and C have $\alpha = 0.5$, B and D have $\alpha = 1$, and the order, from the closest to the farthest, is A,B,C,D.

5.3.2.1   Blending for Transparent Surfaces

The algorithms for hidden surface removal we have seen in Section 5.2 are all based on the assumption that if one surface is in front of another, the latter is hidden from view, that is, we cannot see *through* things. Thanks to this assumption we can use the depth buffer technique and do not worry about the order in which the primitives are rendered. This is no more true if the occluding surface is not opaque.

The most common way to handle transparent surfaces consists of rendering the primitives in back-to-front order, that is, from the farthest to the closest, and using blending for showing the contribution of non-opaque surfaces with blending factors $b = [s_a, s_a, s_a, s_a]$ and $c = [1 - s_a, 1 - s_a, 1 - s_a, 1 - s_a]$. The effect is that the surface being rendered contributes to the color proportionally to its opacity (for $s_a = 1$ it simply replaces the color currently in the color buffer). This simple setting is very effective. Note that the destination α value is not used.

5.3.3   Aliasing and Antialiasing

When we rasterize a segment or a polygon, we take a real domain and break it into discrete parts, the pixels. If we go back to Figure 5.1 and look at the two segments, we may agree that the pixels we use to represent them are the closest approximation we can find, but if you had no previous knowledge that those pixels are supposed to be segments, you probably would never identify them as two segments, because they just look like a series of adjacent pixels. Another way to say it is that there are infinite segments that would be rasterized, which pass on the very same set of pixels. This ambiguity is what we call the phenomenon of *aliasing*. The visual look of this effect is that segments and borders of polygons look *jagged* and are not quite believable as such.

Aliasing is intrinsic to the discretization, but there are techniques to make it less perceivable. Let us consider line rasterization and assume that the width

Without antialiasing   Average Area Antialiasing

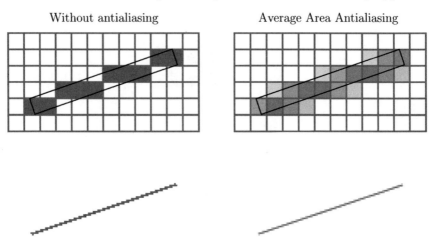

FIGURE 5.16: (Top-Left) A detail of a line rasterized with DDA rasterization. (Top-Right) The same line with the Average Area antialiasing. (Bottom) Results.

of the line is one pixel, which is the minimum size we can handle with our raster device. So, the rasterizer computes a set of pixels to represent the line. However, we can still play with the color of the surrounding pixels to reduce the aliasing effect. If we consider the segment as a polygon having width 1 pixel and length equal to the segment's length, we see that such a polygon partially covers some pixels. The *area averaging technique* or *unweighted area sampling* consists of shading each pixel intersected by this polygon with a color whose intensity is scaled down by the percentage of the area of the pixel covered by the polygon, as shown in Figure 5.16. The intuition behind this technique is that if only half a pixel is inside the line, we halve its color and, at a proper viewing distance, we will obtain a convincing result. Considering the color space HSV (hue, saturation and value), what happens is that the saturation is scaled down while H and V remain the same.

However, what about the color of the other half of the pixel? What if more lines and polygons cover the same pixel? If we use blending, we can composite our *half color* by using the alpha channel with the color already in the color buffer.

To implement this technique we could just compute the area of intersection between the thick line and the pixels during the rasterization process and output the color depending on the area value. We can try to do this as an exercise by passing the segments' endpoints in the fragment shader and making the computation. However, the exact intersection between a polygon and a square (the pixel) requires several floating point operations and we want to avoid that.

An alternative implementation consists of using *super sampling*, that is, considering each pixel as a grid of smaller pixels (for example a 2 × 2 grid) and approximating the area of the pixel covered with the number of these smaller pixels covered by the line. A finer grid leads to a better approximation but requires more computation. Super sampling can also be applied to the whole scene by *full-screen anti-aliasing* (FSSA). In its naive implementation, the rendering is performed with a higher resolution and then converted to the desired resolution by averaging the fragments values obtained.

5.3.4 Upgrade Your Client: View from Driver Perspective

In principle we could implement the view from the driver just by placing the view frame on the driver's head, in the assumption that the 3D model of the car also includes the cockpit.

It is common in many games where the character is inside something (a car, plane, starship, robot, helmet, etc.) that this something does not move with respect to the point of view of the player. In the case of the car, for example, the cockpit will always be occupying the same portion of the screen. So let us suppose we render the cockpit normally, that is, as a 3D model. The vertices of cockpit will go through all the transformations of the pipeline (object space → world space→ view space → clip space → NDC space) to finally produce the same image always. Moreover, we need to model all of the car's interior.

In its simplicity, this is something of a crucial point in rendering: the fact that we want to produce an image of a 3D scene, it does not mean that we have to actually model all the scene in three dimensions. We will explore this concept in detail in Chapter 9; for now we only want to say that we do not need to model the cockpit and then render it if in the end we just need one specific image of it. Instead, let us assume that we have placed a glass screen on the near plane of our view frustum. What we are going to do is to *paint* the inside of the car as seen by the driver directly on the glass. In more practical terms, we set the view transformation as the identity and draw the polygons expressing the coordinates directly in NDC space (that is, in $[-1, 1]^3$) as shown in Figure 5.17. This way we simply skip all the transformations and draw all the interior as an overlay on everything outside.

```
130    gl.enable(gl.STENCIL_TEST);
131    gl.clearStencil(0);
132    gl.stencilMask(~0);
133    gl.stencilFunc(gl.ALWAYS, 1, 0xFF);
134    gl.stencilOp(gl.REPLACE, gl.REPLACE, gl.REPLACE);
135
136    gl.useProgram(this.perVertexColorShader);
137    gl.uniformMatrix4fv(this.perVertexColorShader.↵
           uModelViewMatrixLocation, false, SglMat4.identity());
138    gl.uniformMatrix4fv(this.perVertexColorShader.↵
           uProjectionMatrixLocation, false, SglMat4.identity());
```

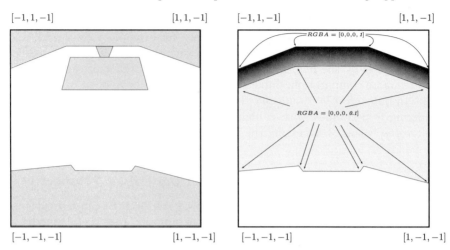

FIGURE 5.17: Exemplifying drawings for the cabin. The coordinates are expressed in clip space. (See code at *http://envymycarbook.com/chapter5/0/cabin.js.*)

```
139        this.drawColoredObject(gl, this.cabin, [0.4, 0.8, 0.9, 1.0]);
140
141        gl.stencilFunc(gl.EQUAL, 0, 0xFF);
142        gl.stencilOp(gl.KEEP, gl.KEEP, gl.KEEP);
143        gl.stencilMask(0);
```

LISTING 5.4: Using stenciling for drawing the cabin.

The changes to our client to include the view from inside the car are very few. First we add a new camera that we call **DriverCamera** placed inside the car, which is easily done as in Section 4.10.1. Then we need to introduce the code shown in Listing 5.4 at the beginning of the rendering cycle. These few lines simply prepare the stencil buffer by drawing the polygons shown in Figure 5.17 (on the left) and thus inhibit the writing in the frame buffer of the pixels covered by such polygons.

With gl.clearStencil(0) we tell WebGl that the value to use to clear the stencil buffer is 0 and with gl.stencilMask(~0) we indicate that all bits of the stencil are enabled for writing (these are also the default values anyway).

How the stencil test behaves is determined by the calls at lines 133-134. Function gl.stencilFunc(func,ref,mask) sets the condition for discarding a fragment as the outcome of the comparison between the value already in the stencil buffer; and the reference value **ref**. func specifies the kind of test; and mask is a bit mask that is applied to both values. In this very simple example by passing gl.ALWAYS we say that all fragments will pass no matter what the stencil, the reference and the mask values are.

Function gl.stencilOp(sfail,dpfail,dppass) tells how to update the stencil buffer depending on the outcome of the stencil test and the depth test. Since we draw the polygon with the depth buffer cleared and make all the fragments pass, the only meaningful value is dppass, that is, what to do when both stencil and depth test pass. By setting this parameter to gl.REPLACE we tell WebGL to replace the current value on the stencil with the reference value specified in gl.stencilFunc (1 in this example). After the drawing (lines 136-139) we will have a stencil buffer that contains 1 in all the positions covered by the drawing and 0 elsewhere. This is our mask.

Then, at lines (141-143) we change the way to do the stencil test so that only those fragments for which the value in the stencil buffer is 0 pass and that no modification is done to the stencil buffer in any case. The final result is that no subsequent fragments will pass the stencil test for the pixels rasterized by the cockpit.

We also want to add the windshield with a partially opaque upper band (see Figure 5.17 on the right), that is, we want to see *through* a dark windshield. We can use blending by adding the code shown in Listing 5.5 at the end of function drawScene.

The function gl.blendFunction determines how the color of the fragment is computed, that is, the blending factors introduced in Section 5.3.2 and used in Formula (5.25). Again, we specified the coordinates of the windshield in clip space.

```
188     gl.enable(gl.BLEND);
189     gl.blendFunc(gl.SRC_ALPHA, gl.ONE_MINUS_SRC_ALPHA);
190     gl.useProgram(     .perVertexColorShader);
191     gl.uniformMatrix4fv(     .perVertexColorShader.↩
            uModelViewMatrixLocation,     , SglMat4.identity());
192     gl.uniformMatrix4fv(     .perVertexColorShader.↩
            uProjectionLocation,     , SglMat4.identity());
193         .drawColoredObject(gl,     .windshield, [0.4, 0.8, 0.9, ↩
            1.0]);
194     gl.disable(gl.BLEND);
```

LISTING 5.5: Using blending for drawing a partially opaque windshield.

Figure 5.18 shows a snapshot from the client showing the driver's point of view.

5.4 Clipping

A clipping algorithm takes as input a primitive and returns the portion of it *inside* the view frustum. Clipping is not strictly necessary to produce a correct output. We could simply rasterize the whole primitive and ignore the fragments outside the viewport, but rasterization has a cost.

Clipping is done in clip space (which we introduced in Section 4.6.3.1) so the problem is posed as finding the portion of a primitive (that is, a line

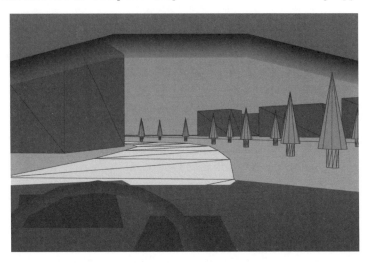

FIGURE 5.18 (SEE COLOR INSERT): Adding the view from inside. Blending is used for the upper part of the windshield. (See client *http://envymycarbook.com/chapter5/0/0.html*.)

segment or a polygon) inside the cube $[x_{min}, y_{min}, z_{min}] \times [x_{max}, y_{max}, z_{max}]$ with as few operations as possible.

5.4.1 Clipping Segments

We start with the *Cohen-Sutherland* algorithm for the bidimensional case. The idea is to perform a test that only requires a few operations to check if the segment is fully outside or fully inside the view volume. If it is fully inside, the output is the segment itself, and if it is fully outside, the output is empty (the segment is discarded).

As shown in Figure 5.19, we can see the view volume as the intersection of four half spaces defined by the planes, p_{+x}, p_{-x}, p_{+y} and p_{-y}. The algorithm finds in which part of each plane the end points are to check if one of the planes is a separating plane for the segment and the view volume or if the segment is entirely inside the view volume. Let us call $\mathbf{p}_0$ and $\mathbf{p}_1$ the two end points of any of the segments in the figure (which end point is $\mathbf{p}_0$ and which is $\mathbf{p}_1$ is not important here) For example, if $\mathbf{p}_{0,x} > x_{max}$ and $\mathbf{p}_{1,x} > x_{max}$ then p_{+x} is a separating plane (segments A and B). Suppose we define a function $R(\mathbf{p})$ returning a four-digit binary code $b_{+y}b_{-y}b_{+x}b_{-x}$ where each bit corresponds

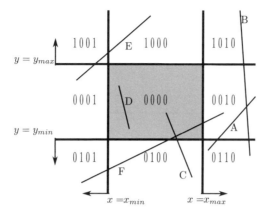

FIGURE 5.19: Scheme for the Cohen-Sutherland clipping algorithm.

to one of the planes and it is 1 if **p** lies in its positive halfspace:

$$b_{+x}(\mathbf{p}) = \begin{cases} 1 & \mathbf{p}_x > x_{max} \\ 0 & \mathbf{p}_x <= x_{max} \end{cases} \qquad b_{-x}(\mathbf{p}) = \begin{cases} 1 & \mathbf{p}_x < x_{min} \\ 0 & \mathbf{p}_x >= x_{min} \end{cases}$$

$$b_{+y}(\mathbf{p}) = \begin{cases} 1 & \mathbf{p}_x > y_{max} \\ 0 & \mathbf{p}_x <= y_{max} \end{cases} \qquad b_{-x}(\mathbf{p}) = \begin{cases} 1 & \mathbf{p}_x < y_{min} \\ 0 & \mathbf{p}_x >= y_{min} \end{cases}$$

Note that if $\mathbf{p}_0$ and $\mathbf{p}_1$ lie in the positive halfspace of any of the four planes, and so such a plane is a separating plane, the corresponding bit will be 1 for both endpoints. Therefore we have a simple test to determine if one of the planes is a separating plane, which is:

$$R(\mathbf{p}_0) \ \& \ R(\mathbf{p}_1) \neq 0$$

where & is the bitwise AND operator. Also, we have another test to check if the segment is fully inside the view volume

$$R(\mathbf{p}_0) \mid R(\mathbf{p}_1) = 0$$

where | is the bitwise OR operator. This means $(R(\mathbf{p}_0) = 0) \wedge (R(\mathbf{p}_1) = 0)$.

If these two tests fail some intersection computation between the segment and the planes will need to be done.

If $R(\mathbf{p}_0) = 0 \vee R(\mathbf{p}_1) \neq 0$ (or vice versa) then one endpoint is inside and the other is outside and one intersection has to be computed. Otherwise both endpoints are outside the view volume but none of the four planes is a separating plane. In this case the segment may be intersecting, like segment E, or not, like segment D, so the algorithm computes the intersection of the segment with one of the planes and the test is executed again with the new endpoints.

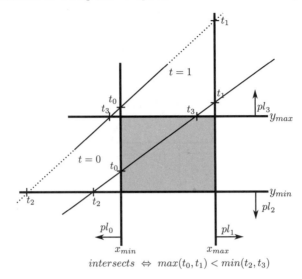

$$intersects \Leftrightarrow max(t_0, t_1) < min(t_2, t_3)$$

FIGURE 5.20: Scheme for the Liang-Barsky clipping algorithm.

The *Liang-Barsky* algorithm avoids making divisions by working with a parametric definition of the segment. The points on the segment $(\mathbf{p}_0, \mathbf{p}_1)$ may be written as:

$$s(t) = \mathbf{p}_0 + t(\mathbf{p}_1 - \mathbf{p}_0) = \mathbf{p}_0 + t\mathbf{v} \tag{5.26}$$

As shown in Figure 5.20, $s(t)$ is a point in the segment for t in the interval $[0, 1]$, if $t < 0$ $s(t)$ is outside the segment on the side of $\mathbf{p}_0$ and if $t > 1$ $s(t)$ is outside the segment on the side of $\mathbf{p}_1$. We can easily calculate the values of t for which the line intersects each of the plane's boundaries. For example for plane $pl_0(x = x_{min})$ we have:

$$(\mathbf{p_0} + \mathbf{v}\,t)_x = x_{min} \Rightarrow t = \frac{x_{min} - \mathbf{p_0}_x}{v_x}$$

So we can replace t in Equation (5.26) to find the intersection t_k with each of the planes pl_k. Now consider walking along the line in the direction indicated by $\mathbf{v}$, starting from the smallest t to the largest. We can label each t_k as *entry* point if we move from the positive halfspace of plane pl_k to the negative, *exit* otherwise:

$$t_0 \text{ is an entry if } \mathbf{v}_x > 0, \text{ exit otherwise}$$
$$t_1 \text{ is an entry if } \mathbf{v}_x < 0, \text{ exit otherwise}$$
$$t_2 \text{ is an entry if } \mathbf{v}_y > 0, \text{ exit otherwise}$$
$$t_3 \text{ is an entry if } \mathbf{v}_y < 0, \text{ exit otherwise}$$

The extremes of our clipped segment are the last one entering the clip rectangle and belonging to the segment and the first one leaving the clip

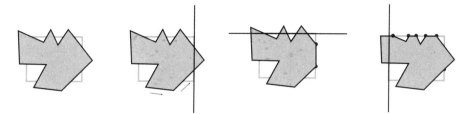

FIGURE 5.21: Sutherland-Hodgman algorithm. Clipping a polygon against a rectangle is done by clipping on its four edges.

rectangle and belonging to the segment:

$$t_{min} = \max(0, \text{largest entry value})$$
$$t_{max} = \min(1, \text{smallest exit value})$$

Note that if $t_{min} > t_{max}$ this means there is no intersection, otherwise the new extremes are $\mathbf{p}'_0 = s(t_{min})$ and $\mathbf{p}'_1 = s(t_{max})$.

5.4.2 Clipping Polygons

The most well-known algorithm for clipping a polygon P against a convex polygon, which in our case is a rectangle, is the *Sutherland-Hodgman* algorithm. The idea is that we use a pair of scissors to cut the polygon P along the edge of the clipping polygon. If the clipping polygon has k edges, after k cuts we have our clipped version of P (see Figure 5.21). Making a cut means clipping a polygon against a halfspace, which is the basic step of this algorithm.

We recall that a polygon is specified as a list of n vertices where each consecutive vertex plus the last and the first define a segment. The algorithm for clipping a polygon against a halfspace pl_{k_-} starts from a vertex of P and walks along the polygon edges (p_i, p_{i+1}). If p_i is in the negative halfspace (inside), then it is added to the output polygon. If the segment intersects the plane, the intersection point is also added.

5.5 Culling

A primitive is *culled* when there is no chance that any part of it will be visible. This may happen in three cases:

- *Back-face culling*: when it is oriented away from the viewer.

- *Frustum culling*: when it is entirely outside the view volume.

- *Occlusion culling*: when it is not visible because it is occluded by other primitives (referred to as *occluder*).

As for clipping, we do not need culling for obtaining a correct result, we need it for eliminating unnecessary computation, which means to avoid rasterization of primitives that, at the end, will not determine any of the final pixel.

5.5.1   Back-Face Culling

When we use polygons to describe objects, we can choose whether only their front side or also their back side can be seen. If we have modeled a flag or a piece of paper or any other object so thin that we consider it bidimensional, then we want to see both sides of the polygons. On the other hand, if we modeled the surface of a tridimensional object (as we do most of the time) usually, it is not possible to see the back of the polygons, so what is the point of rasterizing them? Back-face culling is a filter that discards polygons that are *facing away* from the point of view. Does it matter that much? Yes — consider that if we orbit around an object with back-face culling enabled, at the end we avoid rasterizing 50% of the faces, on average.

Determining if a polygon is facing away from the viewer is simple and consists of checking if the angle between the normal of the polygon and the line passing through the point of view and any point on the polygon (for example, one of its vertices) is greater that $\frac{\pi}{2}$, which can be done by checking if the dot product is positive $(\mathbf{c} - \mathbf{p})\boldsymbol{n} > 0$ (see Figure 5.22). Note that here the *normal* of the polygon is the vector orthogonal to the polygon surface and not the interpolated normal attribute. One may be tempted to replace $(\mathbf{p} - \mathbf{c})$ with the view direction (in order to avoid the subtraction) but consider that this leads to incorrect results for perspective projection (while it would

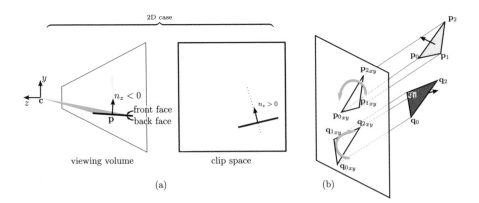

(a)   (b)

FIGURE 5.22: (a) If a normal points toward $-z$ in view space this does not imply that it does the same in clip space. (b) The projection of the vertices on the image plane is counter-clockwise if and only if the triangle is front-facing.

be correct for a parallel projection). To ensure this, the rasterization-based pipeline performs the back-face culling after the projection, in the canonical viewing volume. Thus, the test becomes checking the sign of the z component of the polygon's normal.

Let us consider the case of the triangle $\mathcal{T}$. Its normal direction is:

$$N(\mathcal{T}) = (\mathbf{p_1} - \mathbf{p_0}) \times (\mathbf{p_2} - \mathbf{p_1}) \tag{5.27}$$

where $\|N(\mathcal{T})\| = 2\, Area(\mathcal{T})$ (see Appendix B). If we project the point on the view plane we can write:

$$N(\mathcal{T})_z = (\mathbf{p_1}_{xy} - \mathbf{p_0}_{xy}) \times (\mathbf{p_2}_{xy} - \mathbf{p_1}_{xy}) = 2\, Area(\mathcal{T}_{xy})$$

that is, the double area of the projection of $\mathcal{T}$ on the view plane xy. So if $Area(\mathcal{T}_{xy})$ is negative, it means $N(\mathcal{T})_z$ is negative and hence the triangle is facing away, while if it is positive it is facing the viewer.

You may find mentioned elsewhere that back-face culling works only for convex objects. This needs more clarification: even if the object is not convex, faces are culled correctly. What can happen for non-convex objects is that there can be other faces that are front-facing, but are not visible because they are occluded by other parts of the surface. So, we would have unnecessary rasterization computation. Another common misunderstanding is that the object has to be *watertight* for back-face culling to produce correct results. Watertight means that if we could fill the inside of the object with water none would spill out, because there are no holes. This is a sufficient but not a necessary assumption: it is enough that there is no configuration (for example, viewer position, orientation, application conditions) where the user can possibly see the back of the surface. A straightforward example is the terrain and the street of our circuit: it is not a watertight surface but we can use back-face culling since we do not want to allow the point of view to go underground.

5.5.2 Frustum Culling

So far, all the algorithms we have seen work on a per-primitive basis and are hard-wired in the fixed functionality pipeline. However, in many cases we can save a lot of computation by making choices at a higher level. For example, if we are in front of a building made of 10,000 triangles but we are looking so that the building is behind us, we do not really need to check every single triangle to find out that they are all outside the view frustum. The same happens if there is a big wall between us and the building.

In this case, it comes into play a very common tool of CG: the *bounding volume*. A bounding volume for a set of geometric objects is a solid that encloses them all. For example, we could have a large cuboid (generally called a *box*) enclosing a whole building. Then, in the case of frustum culling, we could test the box against the view frustum and if there is no intersection among the two, we can conclude that there will be no intersection between the frustum and the primitives inside the box.

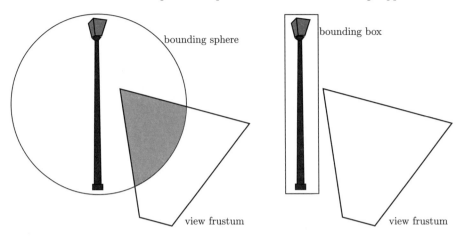

FIGURE 5.23: (Left) A bounding sphere for a street lamp: easy to test for intersection but with high chances of false positives. (Right) A bounding box for a street lamp: in this case we have little empty space but we need more operations to test the intersection.

The choice between the types of volume to use as bounding volume is always a tradeoff between two factors:

- how tightly it encloses the set of primitives

- how easy it is to test its intersection against the view frustum

Let us consider the sphere. The sphere is an easy volume to test for intersection, but if we use it for a street lamp, as shown in Figure 5.23, we will have a lot of empty space. This means that it will often happen that the sphere intersects the view frustum but the lamp does not. A box would make a tighter bounding volume than the sphere, but the intersection test between a freely oriented box and the frustum requires more operations than for a sphere. What can we do when the bounding box intersects the view frustum? Either we go ahead and process all the primitives within or we use a *divide et impera* solution. This solution consists of using smaller bounding volumes that, all together, enclose all the primitives contained in the original bounding volume. This can be done recursively creating a *hierarchy of bounding volumes*. Figure 5.24 shows an example of hierarchy of bounding boxes for a model of a car.

The type of hierarchy with the strategy to handle it are other choices that, along with the type of bounding volumes, gave rise to hundreds of algorithms and data structures to do this task. This topic is well beyond the scope of this book. Anyway, we will come back to this concept, providing some more details, in Chapter 11, when we discuss efficient implementation of ray tracing.

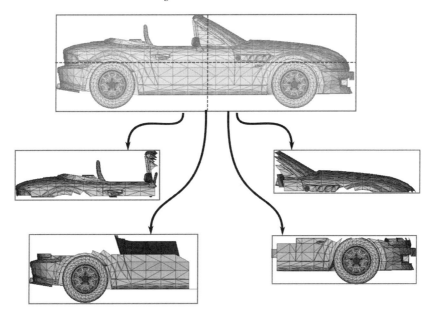

FIGURE 5.24: Example of a two-level hierachy of Axis-Aligned Bounding Boxes for a model of a car, obtained by slitting the bounding box along two axes.

Note that frustum culling is just one specific use of the hierarchies of bounding volumes. They are in general used for speeding the process of testing if two moving objects collide (*collision detection*), in which parts they do (*contact determination*) so to compute the correct (or physically plausible) behavior (*collision handling*).

5.5.3 Occlusion Culling

As stated, occlusion culling deals with *visibility*; the idea is to avoid rasterizing primitives that are not visible because they are occluded.

Several solutions for occlusion culling are context specific. If the viewer is inside a room with a window and a door, then the outside space will only be visible through the window and the door. In this case we can precompute the *potentially visible set* (*PVS*), that is, the set of primitives that may be visible when the point of view is located inside the room. A similar example could also be implemented in our game, by building a PVS for each part of the track and using it to avoid rasterizing all the items of the track every time (as we do now).

A well-known algorithm for implementing occlusion culling in the general case is *hierarchical visibility*, which uses the same idea of the bounding volumes for frustum culling, that is: if a set of primitives is enclosed in a bounding volume and the bounding volume itself is occluded, then none of what is inside can be visible. We point out that, in general, the difference between occlusion culling and frustum culling is simply that we replaced *is inside the view frustum* with *is visible*.

In general, an efficient algorithm for occlusion culling may give a dramatic speedup to the rendering of the whole 3D scene. How much this speedup is depends mainly on the *depth complexity* of the scene, which means how many primitives overlap on the same pixels. Note that with the z-buffer algorithm each and every primitive in the frustum is rasterized, even if it is completely occluded from the viewer, because the conflict is resolved at pixel level.

Chapter 6

Lighting and Shading

We see objects in the real world only if light from their surface or volume reaches our eye. Cameras capture the images of the objects only when light coming from them falls on their sensors. The appearance of an object in a scene, as seen by the eye or as captured in photographs, depends on the amount and the type of light coming out of the object towards the eye or the camera, respectively. So to create realistic looking images of our virtual scene we must learn how to compute the amount of light coming out from every 3D object of our synthetic world.

Light coming from an object may originate from the object itself. In such a case, light is said to be *emitted* from the object, the process is called *emission*, and the object is called an *emitter*. An emitter is a primary source of light of the scene, like a lamp or the sun; an essential component of the visible world. However, only a few objects in a scene are emitters. Most objects redirect light reaching them from elsewhere. The most common form of light redirection is *reflection*. Light is said to be *reflected* from the surfaces of objects, and objects are called *reflectors*. For an emitter, its shape and its inherent emission property determine the appearance. But, for a reflector its appearance not only depends on its shape, but also on the reflection property of its surface, the amount and the type of light incident on the surface, and the direction from which the light is incident.

In the following, after a brief introduction about what happens when light interacts with the surface of an object and is reflected by them, we will describe in depth the physics concepts that help us to better understand such interaction from a mathematical point of view. Then, we will show how such complex mathematical formulation can be simplified in order to implement it more easily, for example with the local Phong illumination model. After this, more advanced reflection models will be presented. As usual, after the theoretical explanation, we will put into practice all that we explain by putting our client under a new light, so to speak.

6.1   Light and Matter Interaction

By light we mean visible electromagnetic radiation in the wavelength range 400 to 700 nm. We have seen in Chapter 1 that this is the *visible range* of the light. The visible light may contain radiation of only one wavelength, in which case it is also called *monochromatic* light, or it may be composed of many wavelengths in the visible range; then it is called *polychromatic* light. In the real world mostly lasers are monochromatic in nature. No other emitter emits light in a single wavelength. There are emitters, such as gas discharge light, that emit light that is composed of a finite number of wavelengths, but emission from most emitters have wavelengths in the whole visible range. Reflectors can be nonselective in reflection, for example: white surfaces, or can be selective, for example: colored surfaces. So, unless specified otherwise, by light we mean polychromatic light and hence it must be specified as a spectrum, that is, the amount of electromagnetic radiation at every wavelength of the visible range. The spectrum is more or less continuous in wavelengths. Spectral representation of light can be expensive for rendering. If visible wavelength is discretized at 1 nm intervals then 300 pieces of information must be stored for every pixel of the image. Fortunately, as we have already discussed in Chapter 1, the color of a visible spectrum can be very well approximated by a linear combination of three primary light sources. So, it is a common practice in computer graphics to represent everything related to a visible spectrum as a (R, G, B) triplet. We will follow such a practice in the rest of this chapter.

Light, like any other electromagnetic radiation, is a form of energy. More precisely, it is a flow of radiant energy, where the energy is transported or propagated from one place (source) to another (receiver). The source could be an emitter, also called *primary source*, or a reflector, called *secondary source*. The energy flows at a speed close to 3×10^8 m/sec. Because of its high speed, independent of the size of the scene in the real world, light takes an insignificant amount of time to reach from one place to another. Hence, the light transport is considered instantaneous. Light travels from the source to the receiver in a straight line. Because of its nature, light is often represented as straight rays. In this representation, light travels in straight rays, and changes direction only when redirected by its interaction with matter. Though the ray representation of light is an approximation, such a representation is conceptually and computationally simple, and hence is a widely accepted nature of light. The area of physics that uses the ray representation for light is known as *ray optics* or *geometric optics*. Most of the properties of light are well and easily explained by ray optics.

As previously stated, for rendering realistic-looking images, we must learn how to compute the amount of light reflected by the objects that enters in the camera/eye after a certain number of direct or indirect reflections. Typically, we distinguish the reflected light into two types: the *direct light*, the light

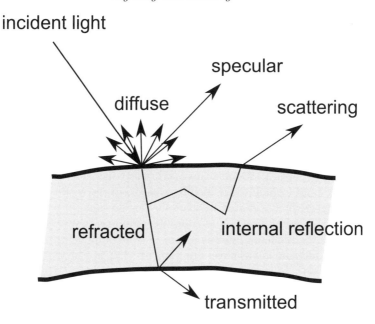

FIGURE **6.1**: Schematization of the effects that happen when light interacts with matter.

due to the reflection of light reaching from one or more primary sources, and *indirect light*, the light due to the reflection light from one or more secondary sources.

When light hits the surface of an object, it interacts with the matter and, depending on the specific properties of the material, different types of interaction can take place. Figure 6.1 summarizes most of the light–matter interaction effects. A part of the light reflected from a surface point is generally distributed in all the directions uniformly; this type of reflection is called *diffuse* reflection and it is typical of the matte and dull materials such as wood, stone, paper, etc. When the material reflects the light received in a preferred direction that depends on the direction of the incident light, then it is called *specular* reflection. This is the typical reflection behavior of metals. A certain amount of light may travel into the material; this phenomenon is called *transmission*. A part of the transmitted light can reach the opposite side of the object and ultimately leave the material; this is the case with a transparent object and this light is named *refracted* light. A part of the transmitted light can also be scattered in random directions depending on the internal composition of the material; this is the *scattered* light. Sometime a certain amount of scattered light leaves the material at points away from the point at which the light enters the surface; this phenomenon is called *sub-surface scattering* and makes the object look as if a certain amount of light is suspended inside the material. Our skin exhibits this phenomenon: if you try to illuminate your ear at a point from behind you will notice that the area around that point gets a reddish glow, particularly noticeable at the front. This reddish glow is due to sub-surface scattering.

6.1.1   Ray Optics Basics

Before discussing in detail the mathematical and physical aspects behind the lighting computation, and how to simplify the related complex formulas in order to include lighting in our rendering algorithms, we give here a brief introduction about the computational aspects of diffuse and specular reflection according to ray optics. We also give a brief treatment of refraction. The basic concepts and formulas provided here can help the reader to get a better understanding of what is stated in the following sections.

It has been common practice in computer graphics to express the complex distribution of the reflected light as a sum of two components only: one is the directionally independent uniform component, that is, the *diffuse reflection*, and the other is the directionally dependent component, that is, *the specular reflection.* So the amount of reflected light $L_{\text{reflected}}$ reaching the synthetic camera is a combination of diffusely reflected light, L_{diffuse}, and specularly reflected light, L_{specular}:

$$L_{\text{reflected}} = L_{\text{diffuse}} + L_{\text{specular}} \qquad (6.1)$$

A part of the incident light could also be transmitted inside the material, in this case the equation (6.1) can be written as an equilibrium of energy:

$$L_{\text{outgoing}} = L_{\text{reflected}} + L_{\text{refracted}} = L_{\text{diffuse}} + L_{\text{specular}} + L_{\text{refracted}} \ . \qquad (6.2)$$

These three components of the reflected light will be treated in the next paragraphs.

6.1.1.1   Diffuse Reflection

Diffuse reflection is the directionally independent component of the reflected light. This means that the fraction of the incident light reflected is independent of the direction of reflection. So, diffusely reflecting surfaces look equally bright from any direction. A purely diffusive material is said to be a material that exhibits a *Lambertian* reflection. The amount of the light reflected in this way only depends on the direction of light incidence. In fact, a diffusive surface reflects the most when the incident light direction is perpendicular to the surface, and the reflection reduces as a function of inclination of the incident light direction to the surface normal. This reduction is modeled as the cosine of the angle between the normal and the direction of incidence. So the amount of reflected light, L_{diffuse} from this type of surface is given by the following equation:

$$L_{\text{diffuse}} = L_{\text{incident}} k_{\text{diffuse}} \cos \theta \qquad (6.3)$$

Diffuse Model

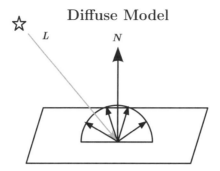

FIGURE 6.2: Diffuse reflection.

where L_{incident} is the amount of the incident light, θ is the angle of inclination of the incident light vector, that is, the angle between the normal N, which indicates the surface orientation, and the incident light direction L_{incident} (see Figure 6.2); k_{diffuse} is a constant term indicating how much the surface is diffusive. Using the relation of dot product of two normalized vectors and the cosine of angle between them we can express the cosine term in Equation (6.3) as:

$$\cos \theta = \boldsymbol{N} \cdot \boldsymbol{L}_{\text{incident}} \tag{6.4}$$

and this leads to the standard expression for the Lambertian reflection:

$$L_{\text{diffuse}} = L_{\text{incident}} k_{\text{diffuse}} (\boldsymbol{N} \cdot \boldsymbol{L}_{\text{incident}}). \tag{6.5}$$

6.1.1.2 Specular Reflection

Specular reflection is the directionally dependent component of the reflected light. The amount of specularly reflected light depends both on the

Ideal Specular Surface   Non-Ideal Specular Surface

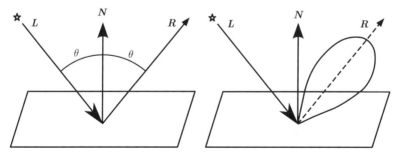

FIGURE 6.3: Specular reflection. (Left) Perfect mirror. (Right) Non-ideal specular material.

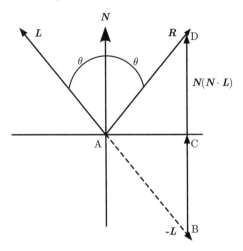

FIGURE 6.4: Mirror direction equation explained.

incident and on the reflection direction. Figure 6.3 shows the specular reflection for an ideal specular surface, that is, a *mirror*. In this case the material reflects the incident light with exactly the same angle of incidence. In the non-ideal case the specular reflection is partially diffused around the mirror direction (see Figure 6.3, on the right). The mirror direction is computed taking into account the geometry between the normalized vector forming the isosceles triangle. Using simple vector algebra, we can express the mirror reflection direction $\boldsymbol{R}$, as:

$$\boldsymbol{R} = 2\boldsymbol{N}(\boldsymbol{N} \cdot \boldsymbol{L}) - \boldsymbol{L} \tag{6.6}$$

The vectors used in Equation (6.6) are shown in Figure 6.4. The equation is easily understood by noting that the direction $\boldsymbol{R}$ can be obtained by adding to the normalized vector $-\boldsymbol{L}$ two times the vector $\boldsymbol{x} = \boldsymbol{N}(\boldsymbol{N} \cdot \boldsymbol{L})$, which corresponds to the edge BC of the triangle ABC shown in the figure.

6.1.1.3 Refraction

Refraction happens when a part of the light is not reflected but passes through the material surface. The difference in the material properties cause light direction to change when the light crosses from one material to the other. The amount of refracted light depends strictly on the material properties of the surface hit, the modification of the light direction depends on both the material in which the light travels (e.g., the air, the vacuum, the water) and on the material of the surface hit. *Snell's Law* (Figure 6.5), also called *reflectance law*, models this optical phenomenon. The name of the law derives from the Dutch astronomer Willebrord Snellius (1580–1626), but it was first accurately described by the Arab scientist Ibn Sahl, who in 984 used it to derive lens

Refraction

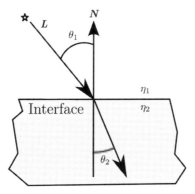

FIGURE 6.5: Refraction. The direction of the refracted light is regulated by Snell's Law.

shapes that focus light with no geometric aberrations [36, 43]. Snell's Law stated that:

$$\eta_1 \sin \theta_1 = \eta_2 \sin \theta_2 \qquad (6.7)$$

where η_1 and η_2 are the refractive indices of the material 1 and the material 2, respectively. The *refractive index* is a number that characterizes the speed of the light inside a medium. Hence, according to Equation (6.7), it is possible to evaluate the direction change when a ray of light passes from a medium to another one. It is possible to see this phenomenon directly by putting a straw inside a glass of water and taking a look at the glass from the side. We see the straw appears to have different inclinations in the air and in the water, as if it was formed by two pieces. This visual effect is caused because of the difference in the refractive indices of the air and the water.

6.2 Radiometry in a Nutshell

In the previous section we wrote equations for a quantity of light L without actually defining the quantity. Light is the flow of radiant energy. So the fundamental measurable quantity of light is *radiant flux* or simply *flux* (conventionally indicated with Φ). This is the total amount of light passing through (reaching or leaving) an area or a volume. It is the flow of energy per unit of time, as Watt (W) is the unit of flux. It is understandable that more flux means more and hence brighter light. However, flux in itself is not indicative of the extent of area or volume through which the radiant energy is flowing. If the same amount of flux is flowing out from one square millimeter of area and from one square meter of area, then the smaller area must be much brighter than the larger area. Similarly, flux is also not indicative of the direction towards which the light is flowing. Light flux may be flowing through or from the area uniformly in all directions, or may be preferentially more in some directions and less in other directions, or may even be flowing along only one direction. In the case where the light is flowing out of the surface uniformly in all directions, then the area would look equally bright from every direction; this is the case with matte or diffuse surfaces. But in the nonuniform case, the surface will look much brighter from some directions compared to the other directions. Hence, we have to be more selective in terms of specifying the distribution of the flow in space and in direction. So we have to specify the exact area, or the direction, or better define density terms that specify flux per unit area and/or per unit direction. Here we introduce three density terms: irradiance, radiance and intensity.

The first density term we introduce is the area density, or flux per unit area. To distinguish light that is arriving or incident at the surface from the light that is leaving the surface, two different terms are used to specify area density. They are: *irradiance* and *exitance*. The conventional symbol for either of the quantities is E. Irradiance represents the amount of flux incident on or arriving at the surface per unit area, and exitance represents the flux leaving or passing though per unit area. They are expressed as the ratio $d\Phi/dA$. So irradiance and exitance are related to flux by the expression

$$d\Phi = E \, dA, \tag{6.8}$$

where $d\Phi$ is the amount of flux reaching or leaving a sufficiently small (or differential) area dA. Light from a surface with nonuniform flux distribution is mostly represented by the function $E(x)$, where x represents a point on the surface. For a surface with uniform flux, irradiance is simply the ratio of total flux and surface area, that is,

$$E = \frac{\Phi}{A}. \tag{6.9}$$

The unit of irradiance (or exitance) is Watt per meter squared (W· M^{-2}). *Radiosity* (B), a term borrowed from the heat transfer field, is also used to represent areal density. To distinguish between irradiance and exitance, radiosity is often qualified with additional terms, for example *incident radiosity* and *exiting radiosity*.

The next density term is directional density, which is known as *intensity* (I). It represents the flux per unit solid angle exiting from a point around a direction. The *solid angle* (ω) represents a cone of directions originating from a point x (Figure 6.6). The base of the cone can have any shape. The unit of solid angle is *Steradian* (Sr). A solid angle measures 1 Steradian if the area of the cone intercepted by a sphere of radius r is r^2. For example, a solid angle that intercepts one meter squared of a sphere of 1 meter of radius measures 1

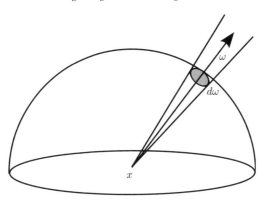

FIGURE 6.6: Solid angle.

Steradian. Intensity is related to flux as:

$$I = \frac{d\Phi}{d\omega}. \tag{6.10}$$

The unit of intensity is Watt per Steradian (W·Sr^{-1}). From the definition of Steradian we can say that the sphere of directions around a point subtends a solid angle that measures 4π Steradians. So the intensity of a point light source emitting radiant flux Φ Watt uniformly around all the directions around the point is $\Phi/4\pi$ W·Sr^{-1}, since the surface area of a sphere of radius r is $4\pi r^2$. The intensity can be dependent on the direction ω, in which case it will be represented as function $I(\omega)$. We would like to bring to the attention of the reader that the term intensity is frequently used improperly to represent more or less intense light coming out of an object and is also incorrectly used in the lighting equation. The correct use of intensity is to represent directional flux density of a point light source and it is often not the quantity of interest in lighting computation.

Flux leaving a surface may vary over the surface and along the directions. So we introduce the final density term, actually a double density term, which is the area and direction density of flux. It is known as *radiance* (L). It represents the flow of radiation from a surface per unit of projected area and per unit of solid angle along the direction of the flow. The term *projected area* in the definition of radiance indicates that the area is to be projected along the direction of flow. Depending on the orientation of the surface, the same projected area may refer to different amounts of actual area of the surface. So with exitance remaining the same, the flux leaving along a direction will be different depending on the flow direction. The projected area term in the denominator takes into account this dependance of the light flow on the surface orientation. With this definition radiance can be related to flux as:

$$L(\omega) = \frac{d^2\Phi}{dA_\perp d\omega} = \frac{d^2\Phi}{dA\cos\theta d\omega}. \tag{6.11}$$

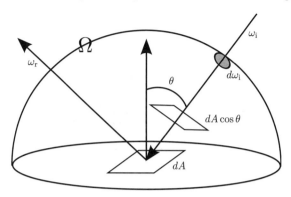

FIGURE 6.7: Radiance incoming from the direction ω_i ($L(\omega_i)$). Irradiance (E) is the total radiance arriving from all the possible directions.

where θ is the angle the normal to the surface makes with the direction of light flow (see Figure 6.7). The unit of radiance is Watt per meter squared per Steradian (W·M^{-2} ·Sr^{-1}). The integral of the incoming radiance on the hemisphere corresponds to the irradiance:

$$E = \int_{\Omega} L(\omega) \cos \theta d\omega. \tag{6.12}$$

Radiance is the quantity of actual interest in rendering. The value of a pixel in a rendered image is directly proportional to the radiance of the surface point visible through that pixel. So to compute the color of a pixel we must compute the radiance from the surface point visible to the camera through that pixel. This is the reason we used the symbol L in the previous section, and provided the equation for computing radiance from a point on the reflector surface.

6.3   Reflectance and BRDF

Most objects we come across are opaque and reflect light incident on their surfaces. The reflection property determines whether the object surface is bright or dark, colored or gray. So the designer of the synthetic world must specify the reflection property of every synthetic object in the scene. We use this property and the incident light on it to compute reflected radiance from every visible surface of the scene. There are two commonly used specifications of the surface reflection property: *reflectance* and *BRDF*. Both these properties are wavelength dependent; despite this, they are usually specified per color channel.

Reflectance, also known as hemispherical surface reflectance, is a fraction that specifies the ratio of the reflected flux to the incident flux, that is, Φ_r/Φ_i, or equivalently, the ratio of the reflected exitance to the incident irradiance, that is, E_r/E_i. Notice that we use the subscripts **r** and **i** to distinguish between reflected and incident radiation. ρ and **k** are the two commonly used symbols of reflectance. Reflectance, by definition, does not take direction into account. Incident flux may be due to light incident from any one direction or from the whole hemisphere of directions[1], or part of it. Similarly, the reflected flux may be the flux leaving towards an any one direction, or the hemisphere of directions, or towards a selected few directions. Because of its independence from incident and reflected direction, it is a useful property only for dull matte surfaces that emit light almost uniformly in all directions.

Most real world reflectors have directional dependence. *Directional-Hemispherical* reflectance is used to represent this incident direction dependent reflection. Keeping the same symbols of reflectance, the dependence of incident direction is specified by making it a function of incident direction ω_i. So we use $\rho(\omega_i)$ or $\mathbf{k}(\omega_i)$ to represent directional-hemispherical reflectance, and we define it as:

$$\rho(\omega_i) = \frac{E_r}{E_i(\omega_i)}, \tag{6.13}$$

where $E_i(\omega_i)$ is the irradiance due to radiation incident from a single direction ω_i.

For most reflectors, the reflected radiance around the hemisphere of directions are non-uniform and vary with the direction of incidence. So the general surface reflection function is actually a bidirectional function of incident and reflected directions. We use *bidirectional reflectance distribution function* or *BRDF* to represent this function. The commonly used symbol for such a function is f_r. It is defined as the ratio of directional radiance to directional irradiance, that is,

$$f_r(\omega_i, \omega_r) = \frac{dL(\omega_r)}{dE(\omega_i)} \tag{6.14}$$

where ω_i is an incident direction and ω_r is the reflection direction originating at the point of incidence. So the domain of each of the directions in the function is the hemisphere around the surface point, and is defined with respect to the local coordinate system set-up at the point of incidence of light (see Figure 6.8). By exploiting the relation between directional radiance and directional irradiance, that is

$$E_i(\omega_i) = L(\omega_i)cos\theta_i d\omega_i \tag{6.15}$$

we can rewrite the BRDF definition in terms of the radiance only:

$$f_r(\omega_i, \omega_r) = \frac{dL(\omega_r)}{L(\omega_i)\cos\theta_i d\omega} \tag{6.16}$$

---

[1]Note that there is only a hemisphere of directions around every point on an opaque surface. We will use symbol Ω to represent the hemisphere. Where it is not obvious from the context, we may use subscripting to distinguish the hemisphere of incoming directions from the hemisphere of outgoing directions, for example: Ω_{in} and Ω_{out}.

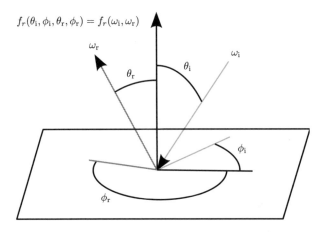

$$f_r(\theta_i, \phi_i, \theta_r, \phi_r) = f_r(\omega_i, \omega_r)$$

FIGURE 6.8: Bidirectional Radiance Density Function (BRDF). θ_i and θ_r are the inclination angles and ϕ_i and ϕ_r are the azimuthal angle. These angles define the incident and reflection direction.

The direction vectors may be specified in terms of inclination angle, θ, and azimuth angle, ϕ. This means that a direction is a function of two angular dimensions, and hence the BRDF at a certain surface point is a 4D function.

Using the definitions of the directional reflectance (6.13) and of the BRDF (6.14), we can derive the following relation between them:

$$
\begin{aligned}
\rho(\omega_i) &= \frac{\int_{\omega_r \in \Omega} L(\omega_r) \cos\theta_r d\omega}{E(\omega_i)} \\
&= \frac{E(\omega_i) \int_{\omega_r \in \Omega} f_r(\omega_i, \omega_r) \cos\theta_r d\omega}{E(\omega_i)} \\
&= \int_{\omega_r \in \Omega} f_r(\omega_i, \omega_r) \cos\theta_r d\omega. \quad (6.17)
\end{aligned}
$$

Earlier we mentioned that reflectance ρ is mostly used to specify direction-independent reflections, particularly, from matte and dull surfaces. We recall that the ideal diffusive surfaces are called Lambertian surfaces. For such reflectors, reflected radiance is constant in all reflection directions, that is, $f_r(\omega_i, \omega_r) = f_r = $ constant. Very few surfaces in the real world are exactly Lambertian in nature. However, surfaces of many real-world objects approximate the Lambertian reflection property well. Diffuse or matte surfaces are widely used in rendering. We can use the directional independence to simplify the relation between reflectance and BRDF as

$$
\begin{aligned}
\rho = \rho(\omega_i) &= \int_{\omega_i \in \Omega} f_r(\omega_i, \omega_r) \cos\theta_r d\omega \\
&= f_r \int_{\omega_i \in \Omega} \cos\theta_r d\omega = f_r \pi \quad (6.18)
\end{aligned}
$$

or simply,

$$f_r = \frac{\rho}{\pi}. \tag{6.19}$$

So, for Lambertian surfaces BRDF is only a constant factor of the surface reflectance and hence is a zero-dimensional function.

Another ideal reflection property is exhibited by optically *smooth* surfaces. Such a reflection is also known as *mirror reflection*. From such surfaces reflection is governed by *Fresnel's law* of reflection:

$$L(\omega_r) = \begin{cases} R(\omega_i) L(\omega_i) & \text{if } \theta_i = \theta_r \\ 0 & \text{otherwise} \end{cases} \tag{6.20}$$

where θ_i and θ_r are inclination angles of the incident and reflection vectors, and the two vectors and normal to the point of the incidence are all in one plane. $R(\omega_i)$ is the Fresnel function of the material. We provide more detail about the Fresnel function later. Note that the direction of the reflected light $\theta_i = \theta_r$ is the same as the mirror direction just discussed for the ideal specular material treated in Section 6.1.1. Hence, BRDF for a perfect mirror is a delta function of incident directions, and hence is a one-dimensional function.

A number of real world surfaces exhibit invariance with respect to the rotation of the surface around the normal vector at the incident point. For such surfaces, BRDFs are dependent only on three parameters θ_i, θ_r and $\phi = \phi_i - \phi_r$, thus they are three-dimensional in nature. To distinguish such reflectors from general four-dimensional BRDFs we call the former *isotropic* BRDFs and the latter as *anisotropic* BRDFs.

Light is a form of energy. So all reflection-related functions must satisfy the *law of energy conservation*. That means, unless a material is an emitting source, the total reflected flux must be less than or equal to the flux incident on the surface. As a consequence, $\rho \leq 1$ and

$$\int_{\omega_r \in \Omega} f_r(\omega_i, \omega_r) \cos \theta_r d\omega \leq 1. \tag{6.21}$$

The latter expression uses the relation between BRDF and reflectance. Note that while reflectance must always be less than one, the above expressions do not restrict the BRDF values to less than one. Surface BRDF values can be more than one for certain incident and outgoing directions. In fact, as we just noted, BRDF for a mirror reflector is a delta function, that is, it is infinity along the mirror reflection direction and zero otherwise. In addition to the energy conservation property, BRDF satisfies a reciprocity property according to which the function value is identical if we interchange the incidence and reflection directions. This property is known as *Helmholtz Reciprocity*.

Concluding, we point out that the BRDF function can be generalized to account for subsurface scattering effects. In this case the light incident from any direction at a surface point x_i gives rise to reflected radiance at another point of the surface x_o along its hemispherical directions. In this case the reflection property is a function of incident point and direction, and exiting point and direction, $f_r(x_i, x_o, \omega_i, \omega_o)$, and gets the name of *bidirectional scattering surface reflectance distribution function (BSSRDF)*. The BSSRDF is a function of eight variables instead of four assuming that the surface is parameterized and thus that each surface point can be identified with two variables.

6.4   The Rendering Equation

We now know that for computing images we must compute radiance of the surfaces visible to the synthetic camera through each pixel. We also know that the surface reflection properties of the reflectors are mostly specified by their surface BRDF. So now all we need is an equation to compute the reflected surface radiance along the view direction. The equation for radiance reflected towards any direction ω_r due to light incident from a single direction ω_i is easily derived from the BRDF definition:

$$dL\left(\omega_r\right) = f_r\left(\omega_i, \omega_r\right) E\left(\omega_i\right) = f_r\left(\omega_i, \omega_r\right) L\left(\omega_i\right) \cos\theta_i d\omega. \qquad (6.22)$$

In a real-world scene light reaches every surface point of a reflector from all the directions of the hemisphere around that point. So the total reflected radiance along ω_r is:

$$L\left(\omega_r\right) = \int_{\omega_i \in \Omega} dL\left(\omega_r\right) = \int_{\omega_i \in \Omega} f_r\left(\omega_i, \omega_r\right) L\left(\omega_i\right) \cos\theta_i d\omega. \qquad (6.23)$$

This latter equation is referred to as *radiance equation* or *rendering equation*. We may generalize this equation to include emitters in the scene and express the outgoing radiance from a surface along any outgoing direction ω_o as a sum of radiance due to emission and radiance due to reflection. So the generalized rendering equation is:

$$
\begin{aligned}
L\left(\omega_o\right) &= L_e\left(\omega_o\right) + L_r\left(\omega_o\right) \\
&= L_e\left(\omega_o\right) + \int_{\omega_i \in \Omega} f_r\left(\omega_i, \omega_o\right) L\left(\omega_i\right) \cos\theta_i d\omega \qquad (6.24)
\end{aligned}
$$

where L_e and L_r are respectively radiance due to emission and reflection. We would like to point out that in this equation we replace the subscript **r** by **o** to emphasize the fact that the outgoing radiance is not restricted to reflection alone.

According to the definition of the BSSRDF previously given the rendering equation in the most general case becomes:

$$L\left(x_o, \omega_o\right) = L_e\left(x_o, \omega_o\right) + \int_A \int_{\omega_i \in \Omega} f_r\left(x_i, x_o, \omega_i, \omega_o\right) L\left(\omega_i\right) \cos\theta_i d\omega dA \qquad (6.25)$$

We can see to account for sub-surface scattering we need to evaluate it on the area $\mathcal{A}$ around x_o.

6.5   Evaluate the Rendering Equation

A fundamental goal in any photo-realistic rendering system is to accurately evaluate the rendering equation previously derived. At the very least, the evaluation of this equation requires that we know $L\left(\omega_\mathrm{i}\right)$ from all incident directions. $L\left(\omega_\mathrm{i}\right)$ in the scene may originate from an emitter, or from another reflector, that is, an object of the scene. Evaluating radiance coming from another reflector would require evaluation of radiance at some other reflector, and so on, making it a *recursive* process. This process is made more complicated by the shadowing effect, that is, objects that could occlude other objects. Finally, for an accurate evaluation, we need to know for each point of the surface the BRDF (or the BSSRDF, for translucent materials or materials that exhibit scattering) function.

In the rest of this chapter we will use some restrictions in order to make the evaluation of the rendering equation, and so the lighting computation of our scene, simpler. First, we use the restriction that $L\left(\omega_\mathrm{i}\right)$ originates only from an emitter. In other words we do not consider effects of the *indirect light*, that is, the light reflected by other objects of the scene. Second, we do not take into account the visibility of the emitters, every emitter is considered visible from any surface of the scene. Another restriction we do is the use of relatively simple mathematical reflection models for the BRDF. *Global lighting* computation methods, which account for the recursive nature of the rendering equation and for visibility allowing a very accurate evaluation, will be treated in Chapter 11. We concentrate here on *local lighting computation* in order to focus more on the basic aspects of the lighting computation such as the *illumination models* and the *light source type*. To better visualize the differences between local and global lighting effects we refer to Figure 6.9. Some global lighting effects that cannot be obtained with local lighting computation are:

Indirect light: As just stated, this is the amount of light received by a surface through the reflection (or diffusion) by another object.

Soft shadows: Shadows are global effects since they depend on the position of the objects with respect to each other. Real shadows are usually "soft" due do the fact that real light sources have a certain area extent and are not points.

Color bleeding: This particular effect of the indirect light corresponds to the fact that the color of an object is influenced by the color of the

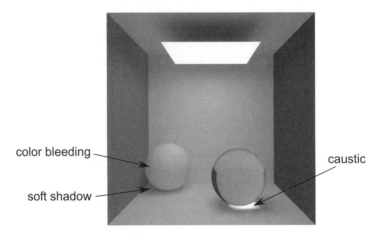

FIGURE 6.9 (SEE COLOR INSERT): Global illumination effects. Shadows, caustics and color bleeding. (Courtesy of Francesco Banterle *http://www.banterle.com/francesco.*)

neighboring objects. In Figure 6.9 we can see that the sphere is green because of the neighboring green wall.

Caustics: The caustics are regions of the scene where the reflected light is concentrated. An example is the light concentrated around the base of the glass sphere (Bottom-Right of Figure 6.9).

In Section 6.7 we will derive simplified versions of local lighting equations for a few simple light sources: *directional* source, *point* or *positional* source, *spotlight* source, *area* source, and *environment* source, whose evaluations will be mostly straightforward. Then, we will describe some reflection models, starting from the basic Phong illumination model, and going to more advanced ones such as the Cook-Torrance model for metallic surfaces, the Oren-Nayar model for retro-reflective materials and the Minneart model for velvet.

6.6   Computing the Surface Normal

As we have seen, light-matter interaction involves the normal to the surface. The normal at point $\mathbf{p}$ is a unitary vector $\boldsymbol{n}_p$ perpendicular to the plane tangent to the surface at point $\mathbf{p}$.

The problem with triangle meshes (and with any discrete representation) is that they are not *smooth* at the vertices and edges (except for the trivial case of a flat surface), which means that if we move on the surface around a vertex the tangent plane does not change in a continuous way. As a practical

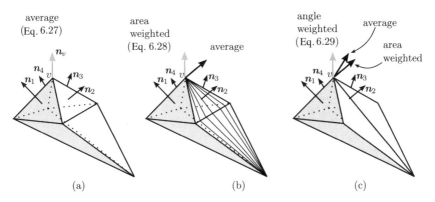

FIGURE 6.10: How to compute vertex normals from the triangle mesh.

example consider vertex v in Figure 6.10. If we move away a little bit from v we see that we have four different tangent planes. So which is the normal (and hence the tangent plane) at vertex v? The answer to this question is "there is no correct normal at vertex v," so what we do is to find a *reasonable* vector to use as normal. Here "reasonable" means two things:

- that it is close to the normal we would have on the continuous surface we are approximating with the triangle mesh;

- that it is as much as possible *independent* of the specific triangulation.

The most obvious way to assign the normal at vertex v is by taking the *average* value of the normals of all the triangles sharing vertex v:

$$n_v = \frac{1}{|S^*(v)|} \sum_{i \in S^*(v)} n_{f_i} \qquad (6.26)$$

This intuitive solution is widely used but it is easy to see that it is highly dependent on the specific triangulation. Figure 6.10.(b) shows the very same surface as Figure 6.10.(a), but normal n_2 contributes more than the others to the average computation and therefore the result consequently changes. An improvement over Equation (6.26) is to weight the contribution with the triangle areas:

$$n_v = \frac{1}{\sum_{i \in S^*(v)} Area(f_i)} \sum_{i \in S^*(v)} Area(f_i) n_{v_i} \qquad (6.27)$$

However, if we consider the triangulation in Figure 6.10.(c) we may see that very long triangles may have a large area and, again, influence the normal. The problem with Formula (6.27) is that parts that are far away from v contribute to the areas and hence influence its normal, while the normal should depend only on the immediate neighborhood (infinitely small in the continous case).

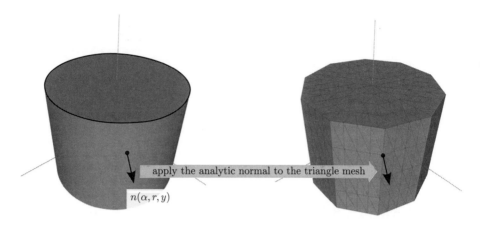

FIGURE 6.11: Using the known normal.

This problem is avoided if we weight the normals with the angle formed by the triangle at v:

$$n_v = \frac{1}{\sum_{i \in S^*(v)} \alpha(f_i, v)} \sum_{i \in S^*(v)} \alpha(f_i, v) n_{v_i} \qquad (6.28)$$

That said, please note that in the average situation we do not create bad tessellation just for the fun of breaking the algorithms, so even the Formula (6.26) generally produces good results.

Note that if the triangle mesh is created by connecting vertices placed on a *known* continuous surface, that is, a surface of which we know the analytic formulation, we do not need to approximate the normal from the faces, we may simply use the normal of the continuous surface computed analytically.

For example, consider the cylinder in Figure 6.11. We know the parametric function for the points on the sides:

$$Cyl(\alpha, r, y) = \begin{bmatrix} r\ cos\alpha \\ y \\ r\ sin\alpha \end{bmatrix}$$

and the normal to the surface is none other than

$$n(\alpha, r, y) = \frac{Cyl(\alpha, r, y) - [0.0, y, 0.0]^T}{\|Cyl(\alpha, r, y) - [0.0, y, 0.0]^T\|}$$

So we can use it directly without approximating it from the triangulated surface.

Please note that this is the first example of a process called *redetail*, that is, re-adding *original* information on the approximation of a surface. We will see a more complex example of redetail in Chapter 7.

6.6.1 Crease Angle

With Equations (6.26), (6.27) and (6.28), we have shown how to compute the normal at a vertex v of a triangle mesh, overcoming the problem that the surface of the triangle mesh is not smooth at the vertices. However, there may be points where the surface is not smooth itself and not because of the tessellation, for example at the points along the bases of the cylinder in Figure 6.11. In these points one normal is simply not enough, because we do not want to *hide* the discontinuity but represent the two (or more) orientations of the surface in the neighboorhood of the vertex. So there are two questions. The first is how do we decide which vertices are not smooth because of the tessellation and which ones are not smooth because of the surface itself. This is commonly done by checking the *dihedral angle* between edge-adjacent faces and deciding that if the angle is too big then the edge must be along a *crease* of the surface (see Figure 6.12). This technique works well on the assumption that the surface is tessellated finer and well enough not to create big dihedral

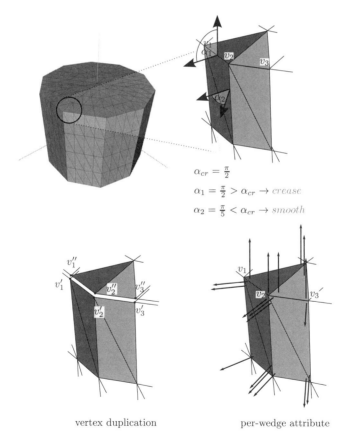

$$\alpha_{cr} = \frac{\pi}{2}$$

$$\alpha_1 = \frac{\pi}{2} > \alpha_{cr} \rightarrow crease$$

$$\alpha_2 = \frac{\pi}{5} < \alpha_{cr} \rightarrow smooth$$

vertex duplication   per-wedge attribute

FIGURE 6.12: Crease angle and vertex duplication.

angles where the surface should be smooth. The second question is how to encode this in the data structure shown in Section 3.9. This is typically done in two alternative ways: the first way is to simply *duplicate* the vertices along a crease, assign them the same position but different normals, and this is what we will do. The second way is to encode the normal attribute on the face data, so that each face stores the normal at its vertices. This involves a useless duplication of all the normal values for all the vertices that are on smooth points (usually the vast majority) but it does not change the connectivity of the mesh.

6.6.2   Transforming the Surface Normal

We know from Section 4.3 that generic affine transformations do not preserve angles and lengths. Consider the normal $\boldsymbol{n}$ and a tangent vector $\boldsymbol{u}$ at a point $\mathbf{p}$. Those two vectors are orthogonal, hence:

$$\boldsymbol{n}\boldsymbol{u}^T = 0$$

But if we appy an affine transformation M to both we have no guarantees that $(M\boldsymbol{n})(M\boldsymbol{u}^T) = 0$. Figure 6.13 shows a practical example where a non-uniform scaling is applied. So the normal should be transformed so that it stays perpendicular to the tranformed surface.

$$\boldsymbol{n}M^{-1}M\boldsymbol{u}^T = 0 \tag{6.29}$$

$$(\boldsymbol{n}M^{-1})(M\boldsymbol{u}^T) = 0 \tag{6.30}$$

Since we multiply the matrices on the left we will write:

$$(\boldsymbol{n}M^{-1})^T = M^{-1^T}\boldsymbol{n}^T$$

Hence the normal must be transformed by the inverse trasposense of the matrix applied to the positions.

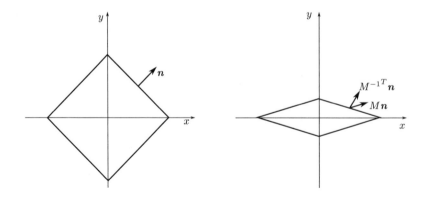

FIGURE 6.13: How the normal must be transformed.

6.7   Light Source Types

Here, we present different types of light sources and we learn how to compute lighting for each of them. In all cases we assume the material to be Lambertian. How to put the theory in practice is presented during the light-source-type description.

We remind the reader that for Lambertian surfaces, radiance is independent of direction. For spatially uniform emitters, radiance is independent of the position on the emitting surface. This directional and positional independence of radiance gives rise to a simple relationship between radiance from a uniform Lambertian emitter, and its radiosity (or exitance), and flux. The relation is:

$$E = \pi L \ , \quad \Phi = EA = \pi LA. \tag{6.31}$$

The derivation of this relationship is as follows. For a spatially uniform emitter the surface emits flux uniformly over the whole area of the emitter. So E, the flux per unit area, is constant over the whole surface; from Equation (6.8) this is $\Phi = \int d\Phi = \int E dA = E \int dA = EA$. From the definition of radiance (6.11), $d^2\phi = LdA \cos\theta d\omega$. The total flux from the emitter surface area is then the double integration:

$$
\begin{aligned}
\Phi &= \int\int d^2\phi = \int\int LdA \cos\theta d\omega \\
&= \left(\int \cos\theta d\omega\right)\left(\int LdA\right) = \pi LA = EA. \tag{6.32}
\end{aligned}
$$

The relations are also the same for a reflector if the surface is Lambertian, and the reflected light is spatially uniform over the surface of the reflector.

We will now proceed to derive equations for carrying out the computation of this exiting radiance from Lambertian reflectors because of the lighting coming from various light sources. In the derivation we will use subscripts **out** and **in** to distinguish light exiting and light incident on the reflector surface. Before doing this, we summarize below the property of a Lambertian reflector:

- The reflected radiance from the surface of the reflector is direction independent, i.e., L_{out} is constant along any direction.

- The relation between exitance (E_{out}), i.e., the areal density of reflected flux, and the outgoing radiance L_{out} due to reflection, is $L_{\text{out}} = \frac{E_{\text{out}}}{\pi}$.

- The relation between irradiance (E_{in}), i.e., the area density of incident flux, and the outgoing radiance L_{out} is $L_{\text{out}} = k_D \frac{E_{\text{in}}}{\pi}$ where k_D is the ratio of exiting flux to the incident flux at the surface, also known as the diffuse surface reflectance.

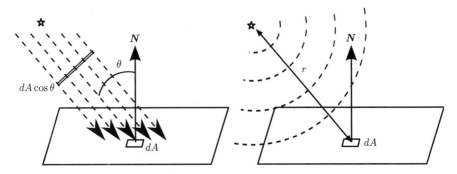

FIGURE 6.14: (Left) Lighting due to *directional* light source. (Right) Lighting due to *point* or *positional* light source.

6.7.1   Directional Lights

Directional lights are the simplest to specify. All we have to do is define the direction from which the light will reach a surface. Then light flows from that direction to every surface point in the scene. The origin of such a light could be an emitter positioned at a very far distance, for example the stars, the sun, the moon, and so on. Along with the direction, we specify the exitance, E_0, of such light sources. As the light flows only from one direction, along the path of the flow the incident irradiance on any surface area perpendicular to the path is the same as the exitance, that is,

$$E_i = E_0 \tag{6.33}$$

To compute the incident irradiance on surface areas with other orientations, we must project them and use their projected area (see Figure 6.14). Thus the incident irradiance on a surface of arbitrary orientations is

$$E_i = E_0 \cos \theta_i \tag{6.34}$$

Substituting the value of E_i in the rendering equation and using the fact that light is incident from only one direction we get:

$$L(\omega_r) = f_r(\omega_i, \omega_r) E_0 \cos \theta_i \tag{6.35}$$

For Lambertian surfaces BRDF is a constant, independent of incident and reflection direction. We can then use the relation between BRDF and reflectance, obtaining:

$$L(\omega_r) = \frac{\rho}{\pi} E_0 \cos \theta_i \tag{6.36}$$

6.7.2 Upgrade Your Client: Add the Sun

Until now we did not care about light in our client; we simply drew the primitives with a constant color. By adding the sun we are taking the first (small) step towards photorealism.

6.7.2.1 Adding the Surface Normal

Here we will add the attribute *normal* to every object in the scene for which we want to compute lighting. In order to add the normal to our objects we will simply add the lines in Listing 6.1 to the function createObjectBuffers.

```
25    if (createNormalBuffer) {
26      obj.normalBuffer = gl.createBuffer();
27      gl.bindBuffer(gl.ARRAY_BUFFER, obj.normalBuffer);
28      gl.bufferData(gl.ARRAY_BUFFER, obj.vertex_normal, gl.↵
            STATIC_DRAW);
29      gl.bindBuffer(gl.ARRAY_BUFFER, null);
30    }
```

LISTING 6.1: Adding a buffer to store normals. (Code snippet from *http://envymycarbook.com/chapter6/0/0.js.*)

Similarly, we modify the function drawObject by adding the lines in Listing 6.2:

```
91    if (shader.aNormalIndex && obj.normalBuffer && shader.↵
            uViewSpaceNormalMatrixLocation) {
92      gl.bindBuffer(gl.ARRAY_BUFFER, obj.normalBuffer);
93      gl.enableVertexAttribArray(shader.aNormalIndex);
94      gl.vertexAttribPointer(shader.aNormalIndex, 3, gl.FLOAT, ↵
            false, 0, 0);
95      gl.uniformMatrix3fv(shader.uViewSpaceNormalMatrixLocation, ↵
            false, SglMat4.to33(this.stack.matrix));
96    }
```

LISTING 6.2: Enabling vertex normal attribute. (Code snippet from *http://envymycarbook.com/chapter6/0/0.js.*)

We saw in Section 6.6 how normals can be derived by the definition of surface (for example for isosurfaces) or derived from the tessellation. In this client we use the function computeNormals(obj) (see file code/chapters/chapters3/0/compute-normals.js), which takes an object, computes the normal per vertex as the average of the normals to the faces incident on it and creates a Float32Array called vertex-normal. In this way we can test if an object has the normal per vertex by writing:

```
1    if (obj.vertex_normal) then ...
```

So we can have objects with normal per vertex. Now all we need is a program shader that uses the normal per vertex to compute lighting, which we will call lambertianShader. The vertex shader is shown in Listing 6.3.

```
6   precision highp float;                                    \n\
7                                                             \n\
8   uniform mat4 uProjectionMatrix;                          \n\
9   uniform mat4 uModelViewMatrix;                           \n\
10  uniform mat3 uViewSpaceNormalMatrix;                     \n\
11  attribute vec3 aPosition;                                \n\
12  attribute vec3 aNormal;                                  \n\
13  attribute vec4 aDiffuse;                                 \n\
14  varying vec3 vpos;                                       \n\
15  varying vec3 vnormal;                                    \n\
16  varying vec4 vdiffuse;                                    \n\
17                                                             \n\
18  void main()                                              \n\
19  {                                                        \n\
20    // vertex normal (in view space)                       \n\
21    vnormal = normalize(uViewSpaceNormalMatrix * aNormal); \n\
22                                                             \n\
23    // color (in view space)                               \n\
24    vdiffuse = aDiffuse;                                   \n\
25                                                             \n\
26  // vertex position (in view space)                       \n\
27    vec4 position = vec4(aPosition, 1.0);                  \n\
28    vpos = vec3(uModelViewMatrix * position);              \n\
29                                                             \n\
30    // output                                              \n\
31    gl_Position = uProjectionMatrix *uModelViewMatrix *    \n\
32      position;                                            \n\
```

LISTING 6.3: Vertex shader. (Code snippet from *http:// envymycarbook.com/chapter6/0/shader.js.*)

Note that, with respect to that shader we wrote in Section 5.3.4, we added the varying vpos and vnormal to have these values interpolated per fragment. See fragment shader code in Listing 6.4. Both these variables are assigned to coordinates in view space. For the position this means that only uModelViewMatrix is applied to aPosition, while the normal is transformed by the matrix aViewSpaceNormalMatrix. This also means that the light direction must be expressed in the same reference system (that is, in view space). We use the uniform variable uLightDirection to pass the view direction expressed in view space, which means that we take the variable this.sunLightDirection and transform it by the normal matrix.

```
36  shaderProgram.fragment_shader = "\
37  precision highp float;                                   \n\
38                                                            \n\
39  varying vec3 vnormal;                                    \n\
40  varying vec3 vpos;                                       \n\
41  varying vec4 vdiffuse;                                   \n\
42  uniform vec4 uLightDirection;                            \n\
43                                                            \n\
44  // positional light: position and color                  \n\
45  uniform vec3 uLightColor;                                \n\
46                                                            \n\
47  void main()                                              \n\
```

```
48  {                                                        \n\
49    // normalize interpolated normal                       \n\
50    vec3 N = normalize(vnormal);                           \n\
51                                                            \n\
52    // light vector (positional light)                     \n\
53    vec3 L = normalize(-uLightDirection.xyz);              \n\
54                                                            \n\
55    // diffuse component                                   \n\
56    float NdotL = max(0.0, dot(N, L));                     \n\
57    vec3 lambert = (vdiffuse.xyz * uLightColor) * NdotL;   \n\
58                                                            \n\
59    gl_FragColor = vec4( lambert, 1.0);                    \n\
60  } ";
```

LISTING 6.4: Fragment shader. (Code snippet from *http:// envymycarbook.com/chapter6/0/shaders.js*.)

6.7.2.2 Loading and Shading a 3D Model

Even if we got attached to our boxy car, we may want to introduce in the scene some nicer 3D model. SpiderGl implements the concept of tessellated 3D model as SglModel and also provides a function to load it from a file and to enable the attributes it finds in it (color, normal and so on). This can be done with the lines shown in Listing 6.5:

```
158  NVMCClient.loadCarModel = function (gl, data) {
159    if (!data)
160      data = "../../../media/models/cars/ferrari.obj";
161    var that = this;
162    this.sgl_car_model = null;
163    sglRequestObj(data, function (modelDescriptor) {
164      that.sgl_car_model = new SglModel(that.ui.gl, ↵
             modelDescriptor);
165      that.ui.postDrawEvent();
166    });
167  };
```

LISTING 6.5: How to load a 3D model with SpiderGl. (Code snippet from *http://envymycarbook.com/chapter6/0/0.js*.)

SpiderGl also provides a way to specify the shaders to use for rendering a SglModel and the values that must be passed to such shaders with an object called SglTechnique. Line 170 in Listing 6.6 shows the creation of a SglTechnique for our simple single light shader.

```
169  NVMCClient.createCarTechnique = function (gl) {
170    this.sgl_technique = new SglTechnique(gl, {
171      vertexShader: this.lambertianShader.vertex_shader,
172      fragmentShader: this.lambertianShader.fragment_shader,
173      vertexStreams: {
174        "aPosition": [0.0, 0.0, 0.0, 1.0],
175        "aNormal":   [1.0, 0.0, 0.0, 0.0],
176        "aDiffuse":  [0.4, 0.8, 0.8, 1.0],
```

```
177      },
178      globals: {
179        "uProjectionMatrix": {
180          semantic: "PROJECTION_MATRIX",
181          value: this.projectionMatrix
182        },
183        "uModelViewMatrix": {
184          semantic: "WORLD_VIEW_MATRIX",
185          value: this.stack.matrix
186        },
187        "uViewSpaceNormalMatrix": {
188          semantic: "VIEW_SPACE_NORMAL_MATRIX",
189          value: SglMat4.to33(this.stack.matrix)
190        },
191        "uLightDirection": {
192          semantic: "LIGHT0_LIGHT_DIRECTION",
193          value: this.sunLightDirectionViewSpace
194        },
195        "uLightColor": {
196          semantic: "LIGHT0_LIGHT_COLOR",
197          value: [0.9, 0.9, 0.9]
198        },}})); };
```

LISTING 6.6: The SglTechnique. (Code snippet from *http:// envymycarbook.com/chapter6/0/0.js.*)

The parameters of the function SglTechnique are fairly self-explanatory: it takes a WebGl context and all it takes to render the model, that is: the vertex and fragment shader sources, the attributes and the list of uniform variables. Furthermore, it allows us to assign names to the uniform variables to be used in the program (referred to as semantic). In this manner we can create a correspondence between the set of names we use in our JavaScript code and the name of the uniform variables in the program shader. This will become useful when we want to use shaders written by third parties with their own naming convention: instead of going to look for all gl.getUniformLocations in our code and change the name of the uniform variable, we just define a technique for the program shader and set all the correspondences with our name set.

Now we are ready to redefine the function drawCar (See Listing 6.7):

```
142  NVMCClient.drawCar = function (gl) {
143    this.sgl_renderer.begin();
144    this.sgl_renderer.setTechnique(this.sgl_technique);
145    this.sgl_renderer.setGlobals({
146      "PROJECTION_MATRIX": this.projectionMatrix,
147      "WORLD_VIEW_MATRIX": this.stack.matrix,
148      "VIEW_SPACE_NORMAL_MATRIX": SglMat4.to33(this.stack.matrix),
149      "LIGHT0_LIGHT_DIRECTION": this.sunLightDirectionViewSpace,
150    });
151
152    this.sgl_renderer.setPrimitiveMode("FILL");
153    this.sgl_renderer.setModel(this.sgl_car_model);
```

FIGURE 6.15 (SEE COLOR INSERT): Scene illuminated with directional light. (See client *http://envymycarbook.com/chapter6/0/0.html.*)

```
154    this.sgl_renderer.renderModel();
155    this.sgl_renderer.end();
156  };
```

LISTING 6.7: Drawing a model with SpiderGl. (Code snippet from *http://envymycarbook.com/chapter6/0/0.js.*)

At line 144 we assign to the renderer the technique we have defined and at line 145 we pass the uniform values that we want to update with respect to their initial assignent in the definition of the technique. In this example LIGHT0_ LIGHT_ COLOR is not set since it does not change from frame to frame, while all the other variables do (note the sun direction is updated by the server to make it change with time). Finally, at line 154 we invoke this.renderer.renderModel, which performs the redering.

Note that there is nothing in these SpiderGL functionalities that we do not already do for the other elements of the scene (the trees, the buildings). These functions encapsulated all the steps so that it is simpler for us to write the code for rendering a model. Note that this is complementary but not alternative to directly using WebGL calls. In fact, we will keep the rest of the code as is and use SglRenderer only for the models we load from external memory.

Figure 6.15 shows a snapshot from the client with a single directional light.

6.7.3 Point Lights

As the name suggests, point light sources are specified by their position in the scene. These light sources are meant to represent small size emitters in the scene and are approximated as points. If we assume that the point light source is emitting light with uniform intensity I_0 in every direction, then the expression for E_i at the reflector point located at a distance r away from the light source is:

$$E_i = \frac{I_0 \cos \theta_i}{r^2} \tag{6.37}$$

This expression is derived as follows: let dA be the differential area around the reflector point. The solid angle subtended by this differential area from the location of the point light source is $\frac{dA \cos \theta_i}{r^2}$. Intensity is flux per solid angle. So the total flux reaching the differential area is $\frac{I_0 dA \cos \theta_i}{r^2}$. Irradiance is the flux per unit area. So incident irradiance, E_i, on the differential area is $E_i = \frac{I_0 \cos \theta_i}{r^2}$. From the incident irradiance, we can compute exiting radiance as

$$L(\omega_r) = f_r(\omega_i, \omega_r) E_i = f_r(\omega_i, \omega_r) \frac{I_0 \cos \theta_i}{r^2} \tag{6.38}$$

If the reflector is Lambertian then

$$L(\omega_r) = \frac{\rho}{\pi} \frac{I_0 \cos \theta}{r^2} \tag{6.39}$$

Thus the rendering equation for computing direct light from a Lambertian reflector due to a point light source is

$$\frac{\rho}{\pi} \frac{I_0 \cos \theta}{\pi r^2}, \tag{6.40}$$

that is, the reflected radiance from a perfectly diffuse reflector due to a point light source is inversely proportional to the square of the distance of the light source to the reflector and directly proportional to the cosine of the orientation of the surface with respect to the light direction. This is an important result and it is the reason why many rendering engines assume that the intensity of the light decays with the square radius of the distance.

6.7.4   Upgrade Your Client: Add the Street Lamps

In this update we will light a few lamps of the circuit, considered as point lights. Let us add a simple object to represent light sources (see Listing 6.8):

```
7   function Light(geometry, color) {
8     if (!geometry) this.geometry = [0.0, -1.0, 0.0, 0.0];
9     else this.geometry = geometry;
10    if (!color) this.color = [1.0, 1.0, 1.0, 1.0];
11    else this.color = color;
12  }
```

LISTING 6.8: Light object. (Code snippet from *http://envymycarbook.com/ chapter6/1/1.js.*)

Parameter **geometry** is a point in homogeneous coordinates that represents both directional and point lights, and **color** is the color of light. We introduce the function **drawLamp**, which, just like **drawTree**, assembles the basic primitives created in Section 3.9 to make a shape that resembles a street lamp (in this case a thick cylinder with a small cube on the top). The only important change to our client is the introduction of a new shader, called **lambertianMultiLightShader** (see Listing 6.9), which is the same as the **lambertianShader** with two differences: it takes not one but an array of **nLights** and it considers both directional and point lights.

```
36  precision highp float;                                              \n\
37                                                                      \n\
38  const int uNLights = " +  nLamps + ";                              \n\
39  varying vec3 vnormal;                                              \n\
40  varying vec3 vpos;                                                 \n\
41  varying vec4 vdiffuse;                                             \n\
42                                                                      \n\
43  // positional light: position and color                            \n\
44  uniform vec4 uLightsGeometry[uNLights];                            \n\
45  uniform vec4 uLightsColor[uNLights];                               \n\
46                                                                      \n\
47  void main()                                                        \n\
48  {                                                                   \n\
49    // normalize interpolated normal                                 \n\
50    vec3 N = normalize(vnormal);                                     \n\
51    vec3 lambert= vec3(0,0,0);                                       \n\
52    float r,NdotL;                                                   \n\
53    vec3 L;                                                          \n\
54    for (int i = 0; i <uNLights; ++i) {                              \n\
55    if (abs(uLightsGeometry[i].w-1.0)<0.01) {                        \n\
56    r = 0.03*3.14*3.14*length(uLightsGeometry[i].xyz-vpos); \n\
57      // light vector (positional light)                             \n\
58      L = normalize(uLightsGeometry[i].xyz-vpos);                    \n\
59    }                                                                 \n\
60    else {                                                           \n\
61     L = -uLightsGeometry[i].xyz;                                    \n\
62     r = 1.0;                                                        \n\
63    }                                                                 \n\
64     // diffuse component                                            \n\
65     NdotL = max(0.0, dot(N, L))/(r*r);                              \n\
66     lambert += (vdiffuse.xyz * uLightsColor[i].xyz) * NdotL;\n\
67    }                                                                 \n\
68    gl_FragColor = vec4(lambert,1.0);                                \n\
69  }";
```

LISTING 6.9: Light object. (Code snippet from *http:// envymycarbook.com/chapter6/1/shaders.js.*)

In lines 44-45 the arrays of light geometry and color are declared and in lines 59-67 we accumulate the contribution of each light to the final color. For each light we test its fourth component to check if it is a directional light or a position and then we compute the vector L accordingly.

With this implementation the number of lights is limited to the size of the array we can pass to the program shader, which depends on the specific hardware. We will see other ways to pass many values to the shaders using

FIGURE 6.16 (SEE COLOR INSERT): Adding point light for the lamps. (See client *http://envymycarbook.com/chapter6/1/1.html.*)

textures (see Chapter 7). The number of lights may greatly impact on the performance of the fragment shader, which must run over all the array and make floating point computation. This is something that you can test on the device you are using by simply increasing the number of lights and observe the fall of frames per second.

Again, all the light computation is done in view space so all the lights geometry will have to be transformed before being passed to the shader. Figure 6.16 shows a snapshot from the client showing the light of the street lamps.

6.7.5   Spotlights

Spotlights represent a cone of light originating from a point. So they are basically point light sources with directionally varying intensity. These light sources are specified by: the position of the origin of the light source, and the direction of the center axis of the cone. The direction of the axis is also called the spot direction, and the spot intensity is the maximum along that direction, and may fall off away from that direction. So additional specifications are: the intensity fall-off exponent (f), and intensity cutoff angle (β). The cutoff angle is the angle around the spot direction beyond which the spotlight intensity is zero. The exponent determines the factor by which the intensity is reduced for directions away from the spot direction, and is computed as follows:

$$I(\omega_i) = I_0 \left(\cos \alpha\right)^f \tag{6.41}$$

where α is the angle between the cone axis and ω_i, the direction of incidence (see Figure 6.17, on the left). Using derivations from the previous paragraph

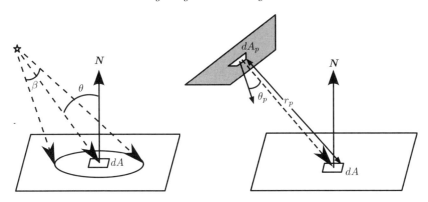

FIGURE 6.17: (Left) Lighting due to *spot* light source. (Right) Lighting due to *area* light source.

we can write the expression for reflected radiance due to spotlight as:

$$L\left(\omega_{\mathrm{r}}\right) = \begin{cases} f_r\left(\omega_{\mathrm{i}}, \omega_{\mathrm{r}}\right) \frac{I_0(\cos\alpha)^f \cos\theta}{r^2} & \text{if } \alpha < \beta/2 \\ 0 & \text{otherwise} \end{cases} \qquad (6.42)$$

If the reflector is Lambertian then

$$L\left(\omega_{\mathrm{r}}\right) = \begin{cases} \frac{\rho}{\pi} \frac{I_0(\cos\alpha)^f \cos\theta}{r^2} & \text{if } \alpha < \beta/2 \\ 0 & \text{otherwise} \end{cases} \qquad (6.43)$$

6.7.6   Area Lights

Area light sources are defined by their geometry, for example a sphere or a rectangle, and by the flux (if spatially and directionally uniform emission), or the exitance function (if spatially varying, but directionally uniform), or the radiance function (if varying both spatially and directionally). We will derive the lighting equation for area light sources by assuming that we know the radiance function at every point on the emitter surface. Let this radiance at point p of the emitter towards the reflector surface be $L_{\mathrm{p}}\left(\omega_{\mathrm{p}}\right)$. Then the expression for the incident irradiance due to a differential area dA_{p} around point p on the light source is:

$$L_{\mathrm{p}}\left(\omega_{\mathrm{p}}\right) \frac{\cos\theta \cos\theta_{\mathrm{p}} dA_{\mathrm{p}}}{r_{\mathrm{p}}^2} \qquad (6.44)$$

This expression is derived as follows (refer to Figure 6.17). Let dA_{p} be the differential area around a point p on the light source. The solid angle subtended by the differential reflector area dA at p is $\frac{dA\cos\theta}{r_{\mathrm{p}}^2}$. The projection of dA_{p} along the direction towards the receiver is $dA_{\mathrm{p}}\cos\theta_{\mathrm{p}}$. Radiance is the flux per projected area per solid angle. So the total flux reaching dA at the reflector is

$$L_p(\omega_p) \frac{dA_p \cos\theta_p dA \cos\theta}{r_p^2} \tag{6.45}$$

and hence, the incident irradiance at the receiver is

$$L_p(\omega_p) \frac{dA_p \cos\theta_p \cos\theta}{r_p^2} \tag{6.46}$$

The reflected radiance dL_r due to this incidence is:

$$dL_r(\omega_r) = L_p(\omega_p) \frac{\cos\theta \cos\theta_p}{r_p^2} dA_p \tag{6.47}$$

The total reflected radiance due to the whole area light source is the integration of dL_r, where the domain of integration is the whole area of the light source. So the irradiance is:

$$L_r(\omega_r) = \int_{p \in A} dL_r(\omega_r) = \int_{p \in A} f_r(\omega_p, \omega_r) L_p(\omega_p) \frac{\cos\theta \cos\theta_p}{r_p^2} dA_p \tag{6.48}$$

If we further assume that the radiance is constant over the light source and the reflecting surface is Lambertian, then the equation simplifies slightly to

$$L_r = \frac{\rho}{\pi} L_p \int_{p \in A} \frac{\cos\theta \cos\theta_p}{r_p^2} dA_p \tag{6.49}$$

As we see here, the computation of lighting due to area light requires integration over area, which means a two-dimensional integration. Except for very simple area lights such as uniformly emitting hemisphere, close form integrations are difficult, or even impossible to compute. Thus, one must resort to numerical quadrature techniques in which an integration solution is estimated as a finite summation. A quadrature technique that extends easily to multidimensional integration divides the domain into a number of sub-domains, evaluates the integrand at the center (or a jittered location around the center) of the sub-domain, and computes the weighted sum of these evaluated quantities as the estimate of the integration solution. A simple subdivision strategy is to convert the area into bi-parametric rectangles, and uniformly divide each parameter and create equi-area sub-rectangles in the bi-parametric space. Such conversion may require domain transformation.

An alternative way to deal with area lights is to approximate them with a set of point lights. This approach is simple but could be computationally expensive, so we will use it in the next example.

6.7.7 Upgrade Your Client: Add the Car's Headlights and Lights in the Tunnel

We can use the spotlight to implement the cars' headlights. First of all we define an object SpotLight as shown in Listing 6.10:

```
8
9   SpotLight = function () {
10      this.pos = [];
11      this.dir = [];
12      this.posViewSpace = [];
13      this.dirViewSpace = [];
14      this.cutOff = [];
15      this.fallOff = [];
```

LISTING 6.10: Light object including spotlight. (Code snippet from *http://envymycarbook.com/chapter6/2/2.js.*)

We define pos and dir of the headlights in model space, that is, in the frame where the car is defined, but remember that our shader will perform lighting computation in view space; therefore we must express the headlights' position and direction in view space before passing them to the shader. The modifications to the shader are straighforward. We proceed in the same way as for the point lights by adding arrays of uniform variables and running over all the spotlights (2 in our specific case, see Listing 6.11).

```
324   for(var i in this.spotLights){
325      this.spotLights[i].posViewSpace = SglMat4.mul4(this.stack.↩
            matrix, SglMat4.mul4(this.myFrame(), this.spotLights[i].↩
            pos));
326      this.spotLights[i].dirViewSpace = SglMat4.mul4(this.stack.↩
            matrix, SglMat4.mul4(this.myFrame(), this.spotLights[i↩
            ].dir));
327   }
```

LISTING 6.11: Bringing headlights in view space. (Code snippet from *http://envymycarbook.com/chapter6/2/2.js.*)

Adding area lights in the tunnel is also very straightforward. We define an area light as a rectangular portion of the XY plane of a local reference frame, with a given size and color. As suggested in the previous section, we implement the lighting due to area lights simply as a set of point lights distributed over the rectangle. In this example we simply use a grid of 3×2 lights. You can play with these numbers, that is, you can increase or decrease the number of point lights, and observe the effect on frame rate.

The implementation is very similar to what we did for the headlights. There are only two differences worth noticing. First, we have to convert an area light into a set of point lights. In our implementation we do this in the fragment shader. That is, we pass the frame of the area light to the shader and then we implicitly consider its contribution as due to 3×2 point lights, as shown in Listing 6.12. Second, the point lights are not really point lights because they illuminate only the $-y$ half space.

```
303   for(int i = 0; i < uNAreaLights; ++i)                        \n\
304   {                                                            \n\
305   vec4 n =  uAreaLightsFrame[i] * vec4(0.0,1.0,0.0,0.0);\n\
306   for(int iy =  0; iy < 3;  ++iy)                              \n\
307     for(int ix =  0; ix < 2;  ++ix)                            \n\
308     {                                                          \n\
309       float y = float(iy)* (uAreaLightsSize[i].y / 2.0 )\n\
310       - uAreaLightsSize[i].y / 2.0;                            \n\
311       float x = float(ix)* (uAreaLightsSize[i].x / 1.0 )\n\
312       - uAreaLightsSize[i].x / 2.0;                            \n\
313       vec4 lightPos = uAreaLightsFrame[i] * vec4(x,0.0,y,1.0);\n↩
                \
314       r = length(lightPos.xyz-vpos);                           \n\
315       L = normalize(lightPos.xyz-vpos);                        \n\
316       if(dot(L,n.xyz) > 0.0) {                                 \n\
317         NdotL = max(0.0, dot(N, L))/( 0.01*3.14 * 3.14 *r*r);  ↩
                \n\
318         lambert +=   (uColor.xyz * uAreaLightsColor[i].xyz) *↩
                NdotL/(3.0*2.0);\n\
319       }\n\
320     } \n\
321   } \n\
```

LISTING 6.12: Area light contribution (fragment shader). (Code snippet from *http://envymycarbook.com/chapter6/2/shaders.js.*)

Figure 6.18 shows a snapshot of the client with headlights on the car.

FIGURE 6.18 (SEE COLOR INSERT): Adding headlights on the car. (See client *http://envymycarbook.com/chapter6/2/2.html.*)

6.8 Phong Illumination Model

6.8.1 Overview and Motivation

As we have seen, solving the rendering equation is a complex task that requires a high computational burden and sophisticated data structures to account for all the contribution of lights coming from the light sources and the reflectors. In order to allow easier computation we have stated that one approach is to consider only the *local* illumination ignoring visibility, taking into account only direct light sources. In other words, the local illumination model evaluates the light contribution at any point on the surface, for example at a vertex, only taking into account the material properties and the lights coming from the light sources. In this context, one of the most used local illumination models for many years has been the so-called *Phong illumination model*, developed by Bui Tuong Phong [35] in 1975. This model was designed empirically and it is a very good tradeoff between simplicity and the degree of realism obtained in the rendering. For this reason, it has been the standard way to compute illumination in the fixed rendering pipeline, until the advent of the programmable rendering pipeline.

This reflection model is composed of three distinct components:

$$L_{\text{reflected}} = k_A L_{\text{ambient}} + k_D L_{\text{diffuse}} + k_S L_{\text{specular}} \qquad (6.50)$$

The constants k_A, k_D and k_S define the color and the reflection properties of the material. For example, a material with k_A and k_S set to zero means it exhibits purely diffusive reflection; conversely, a perfect mirror is characterized by $k_A = 0, k_D = 0, k_S = 1$. The role of the *ambient* component will be clarified in the next section, where each component will be described in depth.

We emphasize that the summation of each contribution can be greater than 1, which means that the energy of the light may not be preserved. This is another peculiarity of the Phong model, since it is not a physical model but is based on empirical observations. An advantage of this independence from physical behavior is that each and every component in the Phong model can be freely tuned to give to the object the desired appearance. Later on, when we will see other reflection models, we will analyze models that follow the rule of conservation of the energy, such as the Cook-Torrance model.

6.8.2 Diffuse Component

The diffuse component of the Phong illumination model corresponds to the Lambertian model seen in Section 6.1.1. So,

$$L_{\text{diffuse}} = L_{\text{incident}}(\boldsymbol{L} \cdot \boldsymbol{N}) \qquad (6.51)$$

where $L_{incident}$ is the amount of light arriving from the direction $\boldsymbol{L} = \omega_i$ at the surface point considered. We remind the reader that for a diffuse material the light is reflected uniformly in every direction.

6.8.3   Specular Component

In specular reflection, the directionally dependent component of the reflected light, the amount of reflected light, depends both on the incident and on the reflection direction. Perfect mirrors reflect only along the mirror reflection direction of the incident light vector. Rough mirrors reflect the most along the mirror reflection direction, and additionally, reflect a reduced amount along the directions close to the mirror reflection direction (as shown in Figure 6.3). The reduction is modeled as a power function of the cosine function of an angle related to the incident direction and the direction along which we wish to compute the amount of reflection. In lighting computation related to rendering, the direction of interest is the direction connecting the surface point to the synthetic camera, also called the *view direction*, $\boldsymbol{V}$. So the amount of reflected light along $\boldsymbol{V}$ is

$$L_{\text{specular}} = L_{\text{incident}} \cos(\alpha)^{n_s} \qquad (6.52)$$

where the exponent $n_s > 1$ is the shininess coefficient of the surface. The role of the exponent is to accelerate the falloff. So the larger the value of n_s, the larger is the falloff of the reflection as the reflection direction differs from the mirror reflection direction, and hence the closer the specular reflection property is to perfect mirror reflection. The exact definition of angle α distinguishes between two variants of the Phong reflection model. The original Phong reflection model uses the angle between the mirror reflection direction of the light vector, $\boldsymbol{R}$, and the view vector $\boldsymbol{V}$. The cosine of such an angle, $\cos\alpha$, may be computed as

$$\cos\alpha = \boldsymbol{R} \cdot \boldsymbol{V} \qquad (6.53)$$

where, according to (6.6),

$$\boldsymbol{R} = \boldsymbol{L} - 2(\boldsymbol{L} \cdot \boldsymbol{N})\boldsymbol{N} \qquad (6.54)$$

James Blinn proposed a variant to the Phong model [4] to avoid the computation of the reflection direction. Such a variant is called the *Blinn-Phong model* and it uses the angle between the normal to the surface point and the so-called *half vector* $\boldsymbol{H}$, which the vector between the light vector and view vector. So, when using Blinn-Phong model $\cos\alpha$ may be computed as

$$\cos\alpha = \boldsymbol{N} \cdot \boldsymbol{H} \qquad (6.55)$$

where

$$\boldsymbol{H} = \frac{\boldsymbol{L} + \boldsymbol{V}}{2} \qquad (6.56)$$

Figure 6.19 shows the difference in the angle α used in the two definitions. Note that all the vectors mentioned up until now are assumed to be normalized.

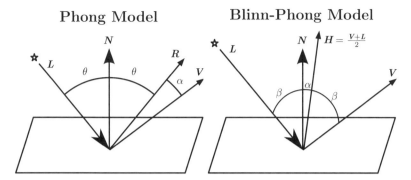

FIGURE 6.19: (Left) Specular component of the Phong illumination model. (Right) The variant proposed by Blinn.

6.8.4 Ambient Component

The ambient component of the Phong illumination model is used to "simulate" the effect of the indirect lighting present in the scene. Secondary light sources, that is, the nearby reflectors, can make significant contributions to the illumination of surfaces. We will see in later chapters that such computation can be very complex and computationally very expensive. Since speed of computation is of prime concern, the inter-reflection component of reflected light is approximated by introducing an ambient term that is simply the product of an *ambient incident light* L_{ambient} and an ambient reflection coefficient k_A. The idea of adding this term to the other terms is that a certain amount of light (coming from all directions) always reaches all the surfaces of the scene because of the inter-reflections between the objects in the scene.

6.8.5 The Complete Model

By putting the ambient, the diffuse and the specular component together, we obtain the final formulation of the Phong model:

$$L_{\text{refl}} = k_A L_{\text{ambient}} + L_{\text{incident}} \Big(k_D \max(\cos\theta, 0) + k_S \max(\cos(\alpha)^{n_s}, 0) \Big) \quad (6.57)$$

The max function in the equation guarantees that the amount of reflected light due to any light source is not less than zero. Equation (6.57) is valid for one light source. In the presence of multiple light sources the reflection due to each individual light is accumulated to get the total amount of reflected light. This is a fundamental aspect of the light: the effect of lighting in a scene is the *sum* of all the light contributions. By accumulating the contributions of the different light sources, Equation (6.57) becomes:

$$L_{\text{refl}} = L_{\text{ambient}}k_{\text{ambient}} + \sum_i L_{\text{incident},i}\Big(k_D \max(\cos\theta_i, 0)$$

$$+ \quad k_S \max(\cos^{n_s}\alpha_i, 0)\Big) \qquad (6.58)$$

where the subscript i in the equation is used to represent the dependence of the corresponding term with the i-th light source. We point out that the ambient term does not depend on the number of light sources since its role is to include just all indirect lighting contributions.

As previously stated, the specular and diffuse coefficients are functions of wavelength of light, but for practical reasons, they are normally represented as triplets consisting of three color components R, G and B. So, the final model, for a single light source, becomes:

$$\begin{pmatrix} R \\ G \\ B \end{pmatrix} = \begin{pmatrix} K_{A,r}L_{A,r} \\ K_{A,g}L_{A,g} \\ K_{A,b}L_{A,b} \end{pmatrix} + \begin{pmatrix} K_{D,r}L_{p,r} \\ K_{D,g}L_{p,g} \\ K_{D,b}L_{p,b} \end{pmatrix}(\boldsymbol{L}\cdot\boldsymbol{N}) + \begin{pmatrix} K_{S,r}L_{p,r} \\ K_{S,g}L_{p,g} \\ K_{S,b}L_{p,b} \end{pmatrix}(\boldsymbol{V}\cdot\boldsymbol{R})^{n_s}$$

$$(6.59)$$

where the cosine of the involved angles has been replaced by the dot product of the corresponding vectors. Figure 6.20 shows the effect of the different components.

FIGURE 6.20 (SEE COLOR INSERT): (Top-Left) Ambient component. (Top-Right) Diffuse component. (Bottom-Left) Specular component. (Bottom-Right) The components summed up together ($k_A = (0.2, 0.2, 0.2)$, $k_D = (0.0, 0.0, 0.6)$, $k_S = (0.8, 0.8, 0.8)$, $n_s = 1.2$).

6.9 Shading Techniques

Shading is the way the computed light is mixed with the color of the surface of the object in order to obtain the final look of the rendered object. This can be achieved in different ways. For example, we can evaluate the illumination model at each vertex, that is, in the vertex shader, and then let the rasterization stage of the rendering pipeline interpolate the color obtained. Another way to shade the object is to evaluate the illumination model for each pixel of the final image, that is, in the fragment shader, instead of for every vertex. In this section we analyze three classic different general shading techniques, particularly important for didactic purposes, *flat shading*, *Gouraud shading* and *Phong shading*.

6.9.1 Flat and Gouraud Shading

The main difference between flat and Gouraud shading is that flat shading produces a final color for each face while Gouraud shading produces a final color for each vertex. Then, the color inside each triangle is generated by interpolation through the rasterization stage. For this reason it is usually said that the *Gouraud shading* computes the object's illumination and color *per-vertex*. Figure 6.21 shows the difference between the two shading techniques. As we can see, Gouraud shading produces a pleasant smooth visual effect that hides the tessellation of the surface. This interpolation effect is very important since it helps us to see less discontinuities on the surface due to an effect named *Match Banding*. Defined briefly, the Match Banding is caused by the fact that our perception tends to enhance the color differences we perceive at the edges. For this reason, Gouraud shading is not only useful to provide a smooth look to our 3D object but it is truly necessary every time we want to reduce the visibility of the faces that compose the object. Obviously, sometimes we would

FIGURE 6.21: Flat and Gouraud shading. As it can be seen, the flat shading emphasizes the perception of the faces that compose the model.

FIGURE 6.22 (SEE COLOR INSERT): Gouraud shading vs Phong shading. (Left) Gouraud shading. (Right) Phong shading. Note that some details result in a better look with Phong shading (per-pixel) due to the non-dense tessellation.

like to visualize clearly the faces of our object; in this cases flat shading is more useful than Gouraud shading.

6.9.2   Phong Shading

First of all, we would like to advise the reader to be aware not to confuse the Phong illumination model, just described, and Phong shading. The first is a local lighting model, the second is a method to interpolate the lighting calculated over our 3D scene.

Phong shading is a shading technique that consists of calculating the contribution of the lighting along the object's surface instead of at the vertex only. To achieve this goal, from a practical point of view, the lighting should be computed in the fragment shader; in this way for each pixel we calculate the lighting equation. This is the reason why such lighting computation is referred to as *per-pixel*, or more precisely *per-fragment*, lighting. The per-fragment lighting computation requires that each fragment knows the normal of the surface at the point visible through the fragment. To calculate such normals we declare a varying variable at the vertex shader that is then interpolated linearly by the rasterization stage, thus providing the normal for each pixel. The rendered effect is shown in Figure 6.22. The visual differences between the Gouraud and the Phong shading are strictly related to the number of triangles rendered in the viewport with respect to the total number of pixels of the viewport. If the object is composed by many triangles, so many that their average screen-size is around one or two pixels, the two renderings will look very similar.

6.9.3   Upgrade Your Client: Use Phong Lighting

The last client of this chapter incorporates only a shading model update. We drop the assumption that every material is Lambertian and use the Phong model explained in Section 6.8. The only modification with respect to the previous client is the way the fragment shader computes the contribution of each light source (see Listing 6.13).

```
74  vec3 phongShading( vec3 L, vec3 N, vec3 V, vec3 lightColor){\n\
75    vec3 mat_ambient = vambient.xyz;                           \n\
76    vec3 mat_diffuse = vdiffuse.xyz;                           \n\
77    vec3 mat_specular= vspecular.xyz;                          \n\
78                                                               \n\
79    vec3 ambient = mat_ambient*lightColor;                     \n\
80                                                               \n\
81    // diffuse component                                       \n\
82    float NdotL = max(0.0, dot(N, L));                         \n\
83    vec3 diffuse = (mat_diffuse * lightColor) * NdotL;         \n\
84                                                               \n\
85    // specular component                                      \n\
86    vec3 R = (2.0 * NdotL * N) - L;                            \n\
87    float RdotV = max(0.0, dot(R, V));                         \n\
88    float spec = pow(RdotV, vshininess.x);                     \n\
89    vec3 specular = (mat_specular * lightColor) * spec;        \n\
90    vec3 contribution =  ambient +diffuse +  specular;         \n\
91    return contribution;                                       \n\
92  }                                                            \n\
```

LISTING 6.13: Function computing the Phong shading used in the fragment shader. (Code snippet from *http://envymycarbook.com/chapter6/3/shaders.js.*)

6.10   Advanced Reflection Models

In the previous section we have seen a local illumination model that has been a reference for many years. With the advent of the possibility to program the rendering pipeline through vertex and fragment shaders, many other illumination models have become widely used to produce realistic renderings of different materials, such as metals, textiles, hair, etc. In the following we briefly describe some of them to increase the expressive tools at our disposal. We suggest that the reader also try to implement other models and experiments on his or her own.

6.10.1   Cook-Torrance Model

We know that the Phong illumination model has several limitations. In particular, it is not able to produce a realistic look for non-plastic, non-diffuse materials, and it is mainly based on empirical observations instead of physical principles.

The first local lighting model based on physical principles was proposed by James Blinn in 1977. In practice, the Blinn's model was based on a physical model of the reflection developed by Torrance and Sparrow. The Torrance and Sparrow reflection model assumes that the surface of an object is composed by thousands of micro-faces that act as small mirrors, oriented more or less randomly. Taking a piece of surface, the distribution of the micro-facets in that part determines, at macroscopic level, the behavior of the specular reflection. Later, Cook and Torrance [5] extended this model to reproduce the complex reflection behavior of metals.

The Cook-Torrance model is defined as:

$$L_r = L_p \frac{DGF}{(\boldsymbol{N} \cdot \boldsymbol{L})(\boldsymbol{N} \cdot \boldsymbol{V})} \tag{6.60}$$

where F, D, and G at the numerator are its three fundamental components.

The D term models the micro-facets assumption of Torrance and Sparrow, and it is called the *roughness* term. This term is modeled using the Spizzichino-Beckmann distribution:

$$D = \frac{1}{m^2 \cos^4 \alpha} \exp^{\frac{-\tan \alpha}{m}} \tag{6.61}$$

where m is the average slope of the microfacets.

G is the geometric term and models the self-shadowing effects. Referring to Figure 6.23, we can note that the micro-facet can create self-shadowing effects, reducing the radiance arriving at a certain point of the surface (shadowing effect) or can block some of the reflected light, reducing the outgoing radiance (masking effect). This term is calculated as:

$$G_1 = \frac{2(\boldsymbol{N} \cdot \boldsymbol{H})(\boldsymbol{N} \cdot \boldsymbol{V})}{(\boldsymbol{V} \cdot \boldsymbol{H})} \tag{6.62}$$

$$G_2 = \frac{(\boldsymbol{N} \cdot \boldsymbol{H})(\boldsymbol{N} \cdot \boldsymbol{L})}{(\boldsymbol{V} \cdot \boldsymbol{H})} \tag{6.63}$$

$$G = \min\{1, G_1, G_2\} \tag{6.64}$$

where G_1 accounts for the masking effects and G_2 accounts for the shadowing effects.

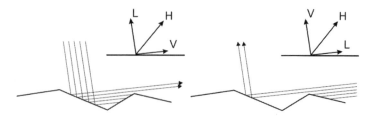

FIGURE 6.23: Masking (left) and shadowing (right) effects.

FIGURE 6.24: A car rendered with different reflection models. (Top-Left) Phong. (Top-Right) Cook-Torrance. (Bottom-Left) Oren-Nayar. (Bottom-Right) Minnaert.

The term F is the Fresnel term and takes into account the *Fresnel law* of reflection. The original work of Cook and Torrance is a valuable source of information about the Fresnel equation for different types of materials. The *Fresnel effect* depends not only on the material but also on the wavelength/color of the incoming light. Even removing this dependency, its formulation is quite complex:

$$F = \frac{1}{2}\frac{(g-c)^2}{(g+c)^2}\left[1 + \frac{(c(g+c)-1)^2}{(c(g-c)+1)^2}\right] \tag{6.65}$$

where $c = \sqrt{V \cdot H}$, $g = \sqrt{c^2 + \eta^2 - 1}$ and η is the refraction index of the material. Due to the complexity of this formula, when no high degree of realism is required, a good approximation can be achieved by the following simpler formulation:

$$F = \rho(1 - \rho)(1 - \boldsymbol{N} \cdot \boldsymbol{L})^5 \tag{6.66}$$

The Top-Left image in Figure 6.24 gives us an idea of how an object rendered with the Cook-Torrance model appears. As we can see, the car seems effectively composed of metal.

6.10.2 Oren-Nayar Model

Oren and Nayar [32] proposed this reflection model to improve the realism of the diffuse component of a Lambertian material. In fact, some diffusive materials are not well described by the Lambertian model; for example, clay and some textiles, which exhibit the phenomenon of *retro-reflection*. Retro-reflection is an optical phenomenon that consists of reflecting the light back in the direction of the light source. Mathematically, the Oren-Nayar model is defined as:

$$L_r = k_D L_p (\mathbf{N} \cdot \mathbf{L}) \, (A + BC \sin(\alpha) \tan(\beta)) \qquad (6.67)$$

Equation (6.67) requires further explanation: α is the angle between the normal of the surface and the incident light, $\alpha = \arccos(\mathbf{N} \cdot \mathbf{L})$, β is the angle between the normal and the viewing direction, $\beta = \arccos(\mathbf{N} \cdot \mathbf{V})$; A and B are parameters related to the roughness of the surface and C is the azimuthal angle between the light vector $\mathbf{L}$ and the view vector $\mathbf{V}$.

The roughness, determined by assuming also in this case a micro-facets model for the surface, is modeled as a Gaussian distribution with zero mean. Hence, in this case the roughness is related to the standard deviation of the Gaussian (σ). With this premise, the parameters A and B are calculated on the basis of σ as:

$$A = 1.0 - 0.5 \frac{\sigma^2}{\sigma^2 + 0.33} \qquad B = 0.45 \frac{\sigma^2}{\sigma^2 + 0.09} \qquad (6.68)$$

The angle represented by the parameter C requires some computational effort to calculate. An intuitive way to compute it is to project on the plane tangent to the surface the light and view vector and then recover the azimuthal angle. In other words we have to compute:

$$
\begin{aligned}
C &= \cos(\phi_V - \phi_L) = (L' \cdot V') & (6.69) \\
L' &= \mathbf{L} - (\mathbf{L} \cdot \mathbf{N})\mathbf{N} & (6.70) \\
V' &= \mathbf{V} - (\mathbf{V} \cdot \mathbf{N})\mathbf{N} & (6.71)
\end{aligned}
$$

It may be noted that this is the first reflection model we describe where the reflected light depends not only on the angle of incidence of the incoming light but also on the azimuthal angle.

6.10.3   Minnaert Model

The last local illumination model to be described was developed a long time ago (1941) by Marcel Minnaert [30]. This model is basically a Lambertian model with the addition of a "darkening factor" capable of describing well the behavior of certain materials, like the reflection behavior of velvet or the visual aspects of the moon. In fact, Minnaert developed such an optical model to try to explain from an optical point of view the visual appearance of the moon. Mathematically, it is defined as:

$$L_r = \underbrace{k_D L_p (N \cdot L)}_{\text{diffuse}} \underbrace{\left((N \cdot L)^K (N \cdot V)^{K-1} \right)}_{\text{darkening factor}} \qquad (6.72)$$

where K is an exponent used to tune the look of the material. For a visual comparison with the Phong illumination model, take a look at Figure 6.24.

6.11   Self-Exercises

6.11.1   General

1. What kind of geometric transformations can also be applied to the normal without the need to be inverted and transposed?

2. If you look at the inside of a metal spoon, you will see your image inverted. However, if you look at the backside of the spoon it does not happen. Why? What would happen if the spoon surface was diffusive?

3. Find for which values of V and L the Blinn-Phong model gives exactly the same result as the Phong model.

4. Consider a cube and suppose the ambient component is 0. How many point lights do we need to guarantee that all the surface is lit?

5. Often the ambient coefficient is set to the same value for all elements of the scene. Discuss a way to calculate the ambient coefficient that takes into account the scene. *Hint*: for example, should the ambient coefficient inside a deep tunnel be the same as the ground in an open space?

6.11.2   Client Related

1. Modify the "Phong model" client by setting the properties of the lighting and the materials to give the sensation of morning, daylight, sunset and night. Then, use the timer to cycle between these settings to simulate the natural light changes during the day.

2. Modify the "Phong model" client in order to add several light sources to it. What happened due to its non-energy-preserving nature? How do you solve this problem?

3. Modify the "Cook-Torrance" client and try to implement a per-vertex and a per-pixel Minnaert illumination model.

Chapter 7

Texturing

Texture mapping is by far the most used technique to make 3D scenes look real. In very simple terms, it consists of applying a 2D image to the 3D geometry as you would do with a sticker on a car. In this chapter we will show how this operation is done in the virtual world where the sticker is a raster image and the car is a polygon mesh.

7.1 Introduction: Do We Need Texture Mapping?

Suppose we want to model a checkerboard. With texture mapping we can make a box with six quads and then stick an image with the black and white pattern on the top (Figure 7.1, Right). However, we could obtain the same result even without texture mapping: we could make a mesh with 5 polygons for the base and the sides, and then 64 black and white quads to model each single tile (Figure 7.1, Left). Therefore, in principle, we could say we do not need texture mapping. However, note that in the second case we had to adapt the geometry of our model to comply with the color we wanted to put on it, by replacing the single top quadrilateral of the box with $8 \times 8 = 64$ quadrilaterals that represent the very same surface, for the sole goal of showing the color pattern. While at this scale it may seem an acceptable computational cost to avoid studying a new subject, consider what this process would be, even for a small image, say 1024×1024: you should modify geometry to introduce $1,048,576$ new quadrilaterals, one for each pixel of the image.

Although the efficiency of the representation alone would be enough, there are many other things that we can do with texture mapping. Back to the sticker on the car example: by using texturing we can move the sticker around, change its size, place a non-color information such as the normal of the surface, and so on.

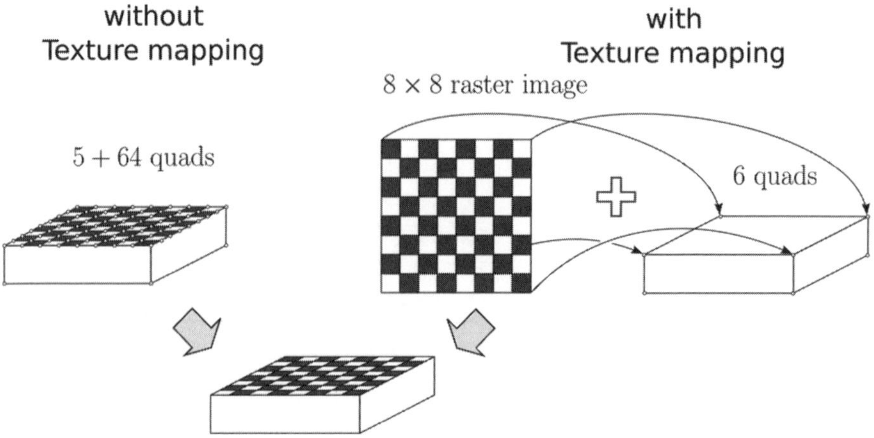

FIGURE 7.1: A checkerboard can be modeled with 69 colored polygons or with 6 polygons and an 8 × 8 texture.

7.2   Basic Concepts

A **texture** is a raster image, and its pixels are called **texels** (**tex**ture **elements**). A position in a texture is conventionally referred to as **texture coordinates**, or **UV-coordinates**, and is expressed in a reference system originating at the Bottom-Left of the image with axis $(sx, 0), (0, sy)$, so that the texture corresponds to the rectangular space between $(0, 0)$ and $(1, 1)$, called **texture space** (see Figure 7.2(a)). A texture may be "stuck" onto a 3D surface providing a function M that maps the 2D texture space to the 3D surface. The way to specify and compute M depends very much on how the surface is represented (a polygon mesh, an implicit surface, an algebraic surface, etc.). In the case of a polygon mesh M is defined by assigning to each vertex of the model a pair of texture coordinates. Inside the each polygon, M is found by interpolating the values assigned to the polygon vertices. Defining a correspondence between texture space and a generic polygon mesh is commonly referred to as *mesh parameterization* and it is a wide topic on its own, on which we will provide some short notes in Section 7.9. In the scope of this book, either we will have simple cases where the parametrization is obvious, or we will use polygon meshes that already specify a parametrization. If you are particularly interested in polygon mesh parametrization, please refer to Floater et al. [12].

What if the value of texture coordinates is outside texture space, for example $(-0.5, 1.2)$? It is useful to define a complete mapping from $[-\infty, -\infty] \times [+\infty, +\infty]$, to $[0, 1]^2$ in order to avoid dealing with exceptions and, as we will

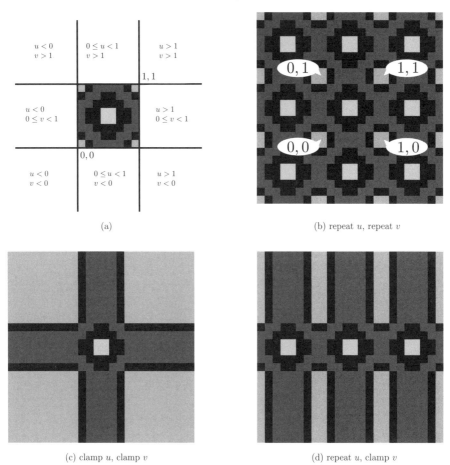

(a)

(b) repeat u, repeat v

(c) clamp u, clamp v

(d) repeat u, clamp v

FIGURE 7.2: Common wrapping of texture coordinates: *clamp* and *repeat*.

see shortly, to achieve some special behaviors. This mapping is usually referred to as **texture wrapping** and it is commonly defined in two alternative modes: *clamp* and *repeat*.

$$\begin{aligned} \text{clamp}(x) &= \min(\max(0.0, x), 1.0) \\ \text{repeat}(x) &= x - \lfloor x \rfloor \end{aligned}$$

where x is the texture coordinate. Figure 7.2.(a) shows the values of texture coordinates outside the region $[0, 1]^2$ and the images in Figure 7.2.(b,c,d) show the effect of applying the repeat mode for both coordinates, the clamp mode for both coordinates or the repeat mode for u and the clamp mode for v.

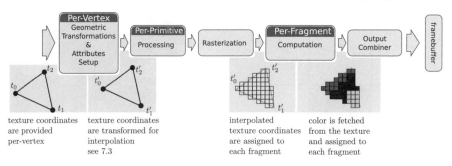

FIGURE 7.3: Texturing in the rendering pipeline.

7.2.1 Texturing in the Pipeline

Texture mapping functionalities are done in two steps:

1. Texture coordinates are assigned to each vertex and then interpolated to obtain a per-fragment value. This involves the GT&AS stage and the Rasterization stage and it will be explained in detail in Section 7.4.

2. Each fragment is colored with the color contained in the texture at the location addressed by the fragment's texture coordinates.

Figure 7.3 shows where texturing related operations take place in the rendering pipeline.

7.3 Texture Filtering: from per-Fragment Texture Coordinates to per-Fragment Color

Let us say we have a fragment and its texture coordinates, which means its corresponding position in texture space: how do we pick the right color? If we were in a continuum, with pixels and texels infinitely small, we should just pick up the color corresponding to the texture coordinates. Unfortunately, resources are limited and we deal with discrete domains, so we do not have a one-to-one correspondence between pixels and texels. The projection of a pixel in texture space is a quadrilateral that can be smaller than a texel, in which case we have texture **magnification**, or it can span over multiple texels, in which case we have texture **minification** (see Figure 7.4). In both cases we need a way to decide which is the color to assign to the fragment.

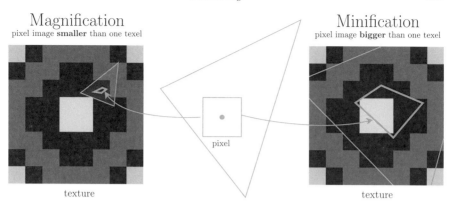

FIGURE 7.4: Magnification and minification.

7.3.1 Magnification

The straightforward solution for magnification is to see in which texel the texture coordinates fall and to pick up its color. This is called **nearest neighbor interpolation**. Obviously the more the texture is magnified (the smaller the projection of the pixels is), the more the texels of the texture are visible.

To obtain a smoother result we can linearly interpolate the color of the four closest neighbors as shown in Figure 7.5. Texture coordinates $(u', v') \in [0, 1]^2$ are expressed in a local reference frame with origin in the center of the lower left texel. The formula in the left part computes the color c by interpolating the color of the four texels c_{00}, c_{10}, c_{11} and c_{01}. The weight assigned to each texel is given by its barycentric coordinates. Since the interpolation is linear both along u and along v, it is called **bilinear interpolation**. The drawing in the right part of Figure 7.5 also shows another geometrical interpretation of the formula: if you center an imaginary texel to the texture coordinates, the weight of each texel corresponds to its intersection with the imaginary texel. Note that, althought the image produced by nearest neighbor interpolation is correct, bilinear interpolation gives in general more realistic results.

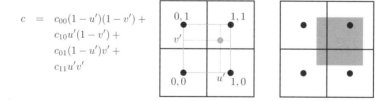

$$
\begin{aligned}
c \;=\; & c_{00}(1 - u')(1 - v') + \\
& c_{10}u'(1 - v') + \\
& c_{01}(1 - u')v' + \\
& c_{11}u'v'
\end{aligned}
$$

FIGURE 7.5: Bilinear interpolation. Computation of the color at texture coordinates (u', v').

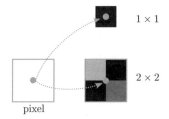

pixel

FIGURE 7.6: The simplest mipmapping example: a pixel covers exactly four texels, so we precompute a single texel texture and assign the average color to it.

7.3.2   Minification with Mipmapping

With minification, the projection of a pixel in texture space spans over several texels. It is obvious that in this case nearest neighbor interpolation would cause adjacent fragments to pick up the color of arbitrarily far texels, so that we would have a meaningless sampling of the texture. Similarly, bilinear interpolation is pointless because we would have sparse sampling of a group of four texels.

What we would like to do is to assign to the pixel the combination of the texels covered by its projection. We could do it in principle but it would require many accesses to the texture, more precisely to all the texels that project on the view plane. A solution producing almost the same result in a much more efficient way is *mipmapping*, where *mip* stays for the latin *multum in parvo*, many in one.

Consider the ideal case depicted in Figure 7.6, where a quadrilateral with a 2×2 texture projects exactly on a pixel. In this case we could access the 4 texels to compute their average value and assign it to the pixel, or we can precompute an alternative version of the texture image made of only one pixel of which color is the average value of the four texels of the original texture and access it. The extension to the general case of an $n \times n$ texture and an arbitrary projection is quite straightforward. When we create the texture, we also create alternative versions of the same texture by iteratively halving its width and height. So if the original texture is, say, 1024×1024, we build a version of the same image with 512×512, 256×256, 128×128, 64×64, 32×32, 16×16, 8×8, 4×4, 2×2 and 1×1 texels, where each texel is obtained by averaging the values of the four corresponding texels at the lower level. Each of these images is a mipmap and the set of mipmaps is referred to as a *mipmap pyramid* (see Figure 7.7). A specific mipmap is indicated by its *mipmap level*, which is 0 for the original texture, 1 for the first mipmap and so on. Note that to build the whole hierarchy we need the original texture size to be power of two.

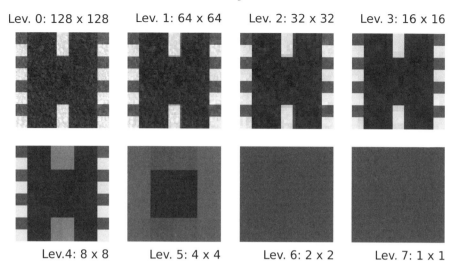

Lev. 0: 128 x 128 Lev. 1: 64 x 64 Lev. 2: 32 x 32 Lev. 3: 16 x 16

Lev.4: 8 x 8 Lev. 5: 4 x 4 Lev. 6: 2 x 2 Lev. 7: 1 x 1

FIGURE 7.7 (SEE COLOR INSERT): Example of a mipmap pyramid.

Choosing the Proper Mipmap Level

In the ideal example (in Figure 7.6) we can "see" that the correct mipmap level is the highest one because the projection of the pixel on the texture exactly matches with the texture. In the general the choice of mipmap level for each fragment is done by calculating how big is the projection of the pixel in texture space. If the pixel is as big as 4 texels the mipmap at level 1 will be used, if it is as big as 16 pixels the level 2 and so on. More formally setting $\rho = texels/pixel$ the number of texels covered by a pixel the mipmap level is found as $L = log_2\rho$.

To compute ρ we could project the four corners of the pixel in texture space and then compute the area of the relative parallelogram, but that would be too computationally demanding. Instead, the implementations of graphics API perform an approximate computation of ρ. Figure 7.8 shows a pixel with coordinates $(x, y)^T$ and its projection in texture space (u, v). For the sake of simplicity, let us say the (u, v) is expressed in textels ($[0,0] \times [sx, sy]$) and not in canonical texture coordinates ($[0,0] \times [1,1]$). If we compute:

$$\begin{pmatrix} \frac{\partial u}{\partial x} \\ \frac{\partial v}{\partial x} \end{pmatrix} = \begin{pmatrix} \frac{u(x+\Delta x, y) - u(x,y)}{\Delta x} \\ \frac{v(x+\Delta x, y) - v(x,y)}{\Delta x} \end{pmatrix}$$

we know how much the texture coordinates change if we move along x in screen space. For $\Delta x = 1$ the length of this vector is a measure of the distance between two adjacent pixels (which is the same as the size of a pixel) in texture space. Of course we can do the same along y and take the maximum of the two lengths:

$$\rho = \max \left(\left\| \begin{bmatrix} \frac{\partial u}{\partial x} \\ \frac{\partial v}{\partial x} \end{bmatrix} \right\|, \left\| \begin{bmatrix} \frac{\partial u}{\partial y} \\ \frac{\partial v}{\partial y} \end{bmatrix} \right\| \right)$$

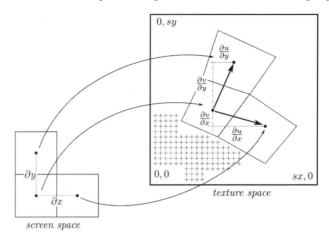

FIGURE 7.8: Estimation of pixel size in texture space.

If, for example, $\rho = 16$, it means that neither the x nor the y side of the pixel spans more than 16 texels, and therefore the level to use is $L = log_2 16 = 4$. If $\rho = 1$ there is one-to-one correspondence between pixels and texels and the level to use is $L = log_2 1 = 0$. Note that $\rho < 1$ means that we have magnification. For example $\rho = 0.5$ means a texel spans over two pixels and the mipmap level would be $L = log_2 0.5 = -1$, which means the original texture with twice the resolution in both sides.

In the general case ρ is not a power of two, therefore $log_2 \rho$ will not be an integer. We can choose to use the *nearest* level or to interpolate between the two nearest levels ($\lfloor log_2 \rho \rfloor$, $\lceil log_2 \rho \rceil$). See Figure 7.9 for an example of mipmap at work.

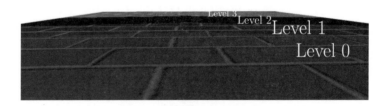

FIGURE 7.9 (SEE COLOR INSERT): Mipmapping at work. In this picture, false colors are used to show the mipmap level used for each fragment.

FIGURE 7.10: Perspective projection and linear interpolation lead to incorrect results for texturing.

7.4 Perspective Correct Interpolation: From per-Vertex to per-Fragment Texture Coordinates

In the previous chapter we have seen how attribute values of the vertices can be linearly interpolated to assign color or normal to the fragment. Considering the UV-coordinates as yet another vertex attribute the problem seems easily solved. Unfortunately it is slightly more complicated: if we linearly interpolate texture coordinates on the checkerboard example and use a perpective projection (see Section 4.6.2.2) we will get a result like that shown in Figure 7.10. The reason is that *perspective projection **does not** preserve ratios between distances* (see Chapter 4.6.2.2), which means that, for example, the middle point of the perspective projection of a segment **is not** the projection of the middle point of the segment. You may wonder if this means that the linear interpolation for color and normal we used for Gourad shading and Phong shading also produces incorrect results with perspective projection. The answer is yes it does, but the resulting artifact is generally not noticeable. We will make a simple example in 2D to find out the correct texture coordinate we should look up for a given fragment. Consider the situation shown in Figure 7.11. The segment $\overline{a'b'}$ is the projection on the view plane of segment $\overline{ab}$ and the point $p' = \alpha'a' + \beta'b', \alpha' + \beta' = 1$ is the projection of the point $p = \alpha a + \beta b, \alpha + \beta = 1$. The vertices (a, b) of the segment are assigned texture coordinates, respectively, 0 and 1. Our problem is, given the interpolation coordinates of point p', to find out its correct texture coordinates, which are just the interpolation coordinates of point p with respect to the segment extremes.

Using homogeneous coordinates and substituting $\frac{a}{a_z/d} \rightarrow a'$ and $\frac{b}{b_z/d} \rightarrow b'$ we have:

$$p' = \begin{pmatrix} \alpha'a' + \beta'b' \\ 1 \end{pmatrix} = \begin{pmatrix} \alpha'\frac{a}{a_z/d} + \beta'\frac{b}{b_z/d} \\ 1 \end{pmatrix} = \begin{pmatrix} \frac{\alpha'}{w_a}a + \frac{\beta'}{w_b}b \\ 1 \end{pmatrix}$$

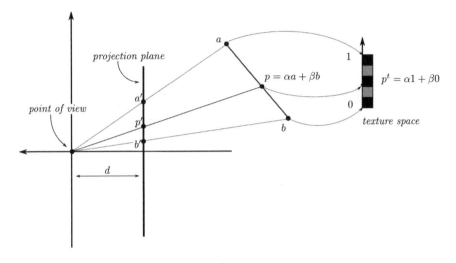

FIGURE 7.11: Finding the perfect mapping.

where we applied $a_z/d \to w_a$ and $b_z/d \to w_b$. We recall that $\begin{pmatrix} a \\ 1 \end{pmatrix} =$
$\begin{pmatrix} aw \\ w \end{pmatrix}$, $\forall w \neq 0$. Multiplying point p' for any non-zero value, we will always
have points along the line passing through the point of view and p', meaning
all the points that project to the same point p'. We choose to multiply p' by
$\frac{1}{\frac{\alpha'}{w_a} + \frac{\beta'}{w_b}}$:

$$p' = \left(\begin{array}{c} \frac{\alpha'}{w_a} a + \frac{\beta'}{w_b} b \\ 1 \end{array} \right) \frac{1}{\frac{\alpha'}{w_a} + \frac{\beta'}{w_b}} = \left(\begin{array}{c} \frac{\frac{\alpha'}{w_a}}{\frac{\alpha'}{w_a} + \frac{\beta'}{w_b}} a + \frac{\frac{\beta'}{w_b}}{\frac{\alpha'}{w_a} + \frac{\beta'}{w_b}} b \\ \frac{1}{\frac{\alpha'}{w_a} + \frac{\beta'}{w_b}} \end{array} \right)$$

Note that the terms multiplying a and b sum to 1, meaning that the point is
on the segment $\overline{ab}$. Since it is also, by construction, on the line L it means
it is the point p, therefore the two terms are the barycentric coordinates of
point p, alias the texture coordinates we were looking for.

$$t_{p'} = \frac{\alpha' \frac{t_a}{w_a} + \beta' \frac{t_b}{w_b}}{\alpha' \frac{1}{w_a} + \beta' \frac{1}{w_b}}$$

Note that another way to write this expression is:

$$t_{p'} = \alpha' \left[\begin{array}{c} t_a \\ 1 \end{array} \right] + \beta' \left[\begin{array}{c} t_b \\ 1 \end{array} \right] = \alpha' \left[\begin{array}{c} t_a/w_a \\ 1/w_a \end{array} \right] + \beta' \left[\begin{array}{c} t_b/w_b \\ 1/w_b \end{array} \right]$$

which is called *hyperbolic interpolation*. The generalization to the interpolation
of n values is straigthforward, so we have the rule to compute perspectively

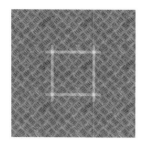

FIGURE 7.12: (Left) A tileable image on the left and an arrangment with nine copies. (Right) A non-tileable image. Borders have been highlighted to show the borders' correspondence (or lack of it).

correct attributes interpolation for the triangle. Consider the triangle (a, b, c) with texture coordinates t_a, t_b, t_c and a fragment with position $p' = \alpha'a + \beta'b + \gamma'c$. The texture coordinates for p' are obtained as:

$$t_{p'} = \frac{\alpha' \frac{t_a}{w_a} + \beta' \frac{t_b}{w_b} + \gamma' \frac{t_c}{w_c}}{\alpha' \frac{1}{w_a} + \beta' \frac{1}{w_b} + \gamma' \frac{1}{w_c}} \tag{7.1}$$

7.5 Upgrade Your Client: Add Textures to the Terrain, Street and Building

Assuming our terrain is a big rectangular square we could just find an image of a terrain to use as texture and map it on the polygon representing the terrain. Say our terrain is a square patch of $512m \times 512m$ and we make a texture map from a 512×512 image. The result would be that a single texel of the texture covers one square meter of terrain. It will hardly look like a grass field and be assured that the texels will be clearly visible from the inside-the-car view. If we want more detail, say that one texel covers only a square centimeter, our image should be $512,000 \times 512,000$ pixels, which would make 786 GB of video memory just for the terrain (considering simple RGB, 8 bits per channel), against the few GBs available on current GPUs.

The real solution to this problem is *texture tiling*, which consists of putting side by side multiple copies of the same image to fill a larger space. If the result does not show noticeable discontinuities, the image used is said to be *tileable*, like the one in Figure 7.12 (Left). To actually place copies of the texture side by side we could change the geometry and transform the single large quadrilateral corresponding to the whole plane to 1000×1000 quadrilaterals, or, more efficiently, to use texture wrapping repeat mode for both coordinates and assign texture coordinates $(0, 0), (512, 0), (512, 512), (0, 512)$.

We start by adding a function that creates a texture, shown in Listing 7.1.

```
12  NVMCClient.createTexture = function (gl, data) {
13    var texture = gl.createTexture();
14    texture.image = new Image();
15
16    var that = texture;
17    texture.image.onload = function () {
18      gl.bindTexture(gl.TEXTURE_2D, that);
19      gl.pixelStorei(gl.UNPACK_FLIP_Y_WEBGL, true);
20      gl.texImage2D(gl.TEXTURE_2D, 0, gl.RGBA, gl.RGBA, gl.↩
          UNSIGNED_BYTE, that.image);
21      gl.texParameteri(gl.TEXTURE_2D, gl.TEXTURE_MAG_FILTER, gl.↩
          LINEAR);
22      gl.texParameteri(gl.TEXTURE_2D, gl.TEXTURE_MIN_FILTER, gl.↩
          LINEAR_MIPMAP_LINEAR);
23      gl.texParameteri(gl.TEXTURE_2D, gl.TEXTURE_WRAP_S, gl.REPEAT↩
          );
24      gl.texParameteri(gl.TEXTURE_2D, gl.TEXTURE_WRAP_T, gl.REPEAT↩
          );
25      gl.generateMipmap(gl.TEXTURE_2D);
26      gl.bindTexture(gl.TEXTURE_2D, null);
27    };
28
29    texture.image.src = data;
30    return texture;
31  }
```

LISTING 7.1: Create a texture. (Code snippet from *http://envymycarbook.com/chapter7/0/0.js.*)

At line 13 we use the WebGL command createTexture() to create a WebGl texture object. Then we add to this object a member Image, that is, a JavaScript image object and assign the path to where the image must be loaded from. Lines 17-27 set how the texture is set up when the image will be loaded.

The first thing is to bound our texture to a *texture target*. A texture target specifies which will be the target of the next calls. Up to now we have only seen textures as bidimensional images but there are other kinds of textures made available in WebGL. For example, gl.TEXTURE_1D for texture made only of one line of pixels, or gl.TEXTURE_3D, which is a stack of bidimensional textures.

With the call at line 18 we say that from now on the gl.TEXTURE_2D is the texture we just created. Then at line 20 we associate the JavaScript image we loaded from disk to our texture. This is the point where the image is created in video memory. The first parameter of gl.texImage2D (and all subsequent calls) is the texture target. The second parameter is the *level* of the texture: 0 indicates the original image and $i = 1 \ldots \log(size)$ the $i - th$ level of mipmapping.

The third parameters tells how the texture must be stored in video memory. In this case we are telling each texture has four channels gl.RGBA. The fourth and fifth parameters tell how the image (the sixth parameter) must be read. In this case gl.RGBA says that the image has four channels and gl.UNSIGNED_BYTE that each channel is encoded with an unsigned byte code (0 . . . 255).

Line 21 indicates how the texture must be sampled when the texture is magnified (linear interpolation) and line 22 when the texture is minified. In the latter case we passed the parameter gl.LINEAR_MIMAP_LINEAR that says that the texture value must also be interpolated linearly within the same level and also linearly in between mipmapping levels. We invite the reader to change this value on gl.LINEAR_MIMAP_NEAREST and look at the differences. At lines 23-24 we specify the wrapping mode for both coordinates to be gl.REPEAT and at line 26 we make WebGL generate the mipmap pyramid. The call gl.bindTexture(gl.TEXTURE_2D,null) *unbinds* the texture from the texture target. This is not strictly necessary but consider that if we do not do this any call to modify a texture parameter with gl.TEXTURE_2D will affect our texture. We strongly advise to end each texture parameter setting with the unbinding of the texture.

We will create 4 textures: one for the ground, one for the street, one for the building facade and one for the roofs, by adding the lines in Listing 7.2 in function onInitialize.

```
398    NVMCClient.texture_street = this.createTexture(gl, ↩
           ../../../media/textures/street4.png);
399    NVMCClient.texture_ground = this.createTexture(gl, ↩
           ../../../media/textures/grass.png);
400    NVMCClient.texture_facade = this.createTexture(gl, ↩
           ../../../media/textures/facade.png);
```

LISTING 7.2: Loading images from files and creating corresponding textures. (Code snippet from *http://envymycarbook.com/chapter7/0/0.js.*)

7.5.1   Accessing Textures from the Shader Program

So far we have seen how to create a texture object. Now we want to use our texture in our shader program. This is done by the *texture mapping unit*s or *texture units*, as they are usually referred. Texture units work in conjunction with the vertex and fragment shader and are in charge to access the textures with the parameters specified in the texture object. Listing 7.3 shows the vertex and fragment shader for texturing. The vertex shader just passes along the texture coordinates just like it does for position, and everything happens in the fragment shader.

```
2    var vertex_shader = "\
3        uniform   mat4 uModelViewMatrix;    \n\
4        uniform   mat4 uProjectionMatrix;   \n\
5        attribute vec3 aPosition;           \n\
6        attribute vec2 aTextureCoords;      \n\
7        varying   vec2 vTextureCoords;      \n\
```

```
 8      void main(void)                        \n\
 9      {                                       \n\
10        vTextureCoords = aTextureCoords;        \n\
11        gl_Position = uProjectionMatrix *       \n\
12        uModelViewMatrix * vec4(aPosition, 1.0);\n\
13      }";
14    var fragment_shader = "\
15      precision highp float;             \n\
16      uniform sampler2D uTexture;        \n\
17      uniform vec4 uColor;               \n\
18      varying vec2 vTextureCoords;       \n\
19      void main(void)                    \n\
20      {                                  \n\
21        gl_FragColor = texture2D(uTexture, vTextureCoords); \n\
22      } ";
```

LISTING 7.3: Minimal vertex and fragment shaders for texturing. (Code snippet from *http://envymycarbook.com/chapter7/0/shaders.js.*)

At line 16 we declare the uniform variable uTexture of type sampler2D. Doing that, we have created a reference to texture unit (uTexture) which will sample value of a bidimensional texture. Then, at line 21, we access the value contained in the texture bound to the texture target gl.TEXTURE_2D of texture unit uTexture at coordinates vTextureCoords. Texture units are identified with an index between 0 and MAX_TEXTURE_IMAGE_UNITS (a hardware dependent value that we can find with function gl.getParameter). On the Javascript/client side we need to do two things: bind our texture to a texture unit and pass to the shader the index to such texture unit. Listing 7.4 shows how these operations are done. At line 318 we set the current active texture unit to 0 and at line 319 we bind the texture this.texture_ground to the gl.texture_2D target. This means that texture unit 0 now will sample the texture this.texture_ground. Finally, at line 320, we set the value of uTexture to 0.

```
318    gl.activeTexture(gl.TEXTURE0);
319    gl.bindTexture(gl.TEXTURE_2D, this.texture_ground);
320    gl.uniform1i(this.textureShader.uTextureLocation, 0);
```

LISTING　7.4: Setting texture access. (Code snippet from *http://envymycarbook.com/chapter7/0/0.js.*)

Figure 7.13 shows a client with textures applied to the elements of the scene.

7.6　Upgrade Your Client: Add the Rear Mirror

In terms of texture mapping, adding a rear mirror only means changing the source of the texture from a still image loaded from somewhere (the hard disk, Internet) to one produced at every frame. The tricky part is how to produce the image to put on the mirror.

FIGURE 7.13 (SEE COLOR INSERT): Basic texturing. (See client *http://envymycarbook.com/chapter7/0/0.html.*)

We have seen in Chapter 6 that the light arriving on a perfectly reflecting surface bounces away in the specular direction, that is in the symmetric direction with respect to the surface normal. This means that referring to Figure 7.14 the image we see in the mirror from the driver's view frame V is the same as the one seen from view frame V', which is V' mirrored with respect to the plane XY containing the rear mirror. Since the mirror is a part of the car it makes sense that its four corners are specified in the frame of the car. Here we assume that these points have been already multiplied by the car's frame and hence $p_i : i = 0 \ldots 3$ are in world coordinates. Also we assume frame V is in world coordinates. Since we want to mirror frame V with respect to the mirror plane we build the frame M as *any* frame whose XY plane contains the mirror. For example, we can take p_0 as origin, $\frac{(p_1 - p_0)}{\|p_1 - p_0\|}$ and $\frac{(p_3 - p_0)}{\|p_3 - p_0\|}$ as x and y axes and $x \times y$ as z axis. The expression to find the mirrored frame is:

$$V' = M Z_m M^{-1} V$$

that is, express frame V in frame M coordinates, then mirror the z component, then again express it in world coordinates.

The next step is perform the rendering of the scene with V' as viewing frame and use the result as texture to be mapped on the polygon representing the rear mirror. Note that we do not want to map the whole image on the such polygon but only the part of the frustum that passes through the mirror. This is done by assigning the texture coordinates to vertices p_i using their projection on the viewing window:

$$t_i = T \ P \ V' p_i$$

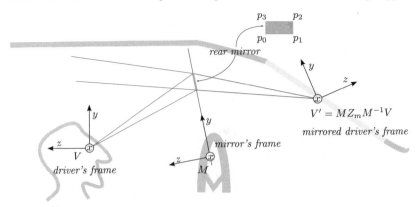

FIGURE 7.14: Scheme of how the rear mirror is obtained by mirroring the view frame with respect to the plane where the mirror lies.

where P is the projection matrix and T is the matrix that maps coordinates from NDC $[-1, 1]^3$ to texture space $[0, 1]^3$, which you can find explained in Section 7.7.5. Note that we actually need only the first two components of the result.

7.6.1   Rendering to Texture (RTT)

Rendering to texture is one of the ways we can do *off-screen* rendering, that is, store the result of the rendering somewhere instead of showing it on the screen.

We introduce a new function to our client, shown in Listing 7.5, that creates an *alternative* framebuffer. The call at line 41 is the most explicative: gl.bindFrameBuffer(gl.FRAMEBUFFER,null) tells WebGl where to redirect the result of rasterization. The default value (that is null) indicates the on-screen framebuffer but we can create new framebuffer to be used. Let us start from the begining, by showing how to create a framebuffer object. Referring to Listing 7.5, at line 13 we create an object TextureTarget, which is a simple container of a framebuffer and its texture. At line 14 we create the WebGl object framebuffer, then we set it as current output buffer and target of all subsequent operations. At lines 17-20 we set the size in pixels. At line 36 we assign to the framebuffer its *color attachment*, that is the buffer to which the color will be written. In this case the color attachment is the texture we create with the lines 22-30. This means that the channels and the bit planes of the new framebuffer are defined by those of the texture textureTarget.texture. This texture is used as output buffer when this framebuffer is to be the current one, but it can be normally bound to show the result in the rear mirror. Please note, and this is an important bit of information and often a source of painful bugs, that when a framebuffer is used for rendering, its color attacment cannot be bound as texture target. In other words you cannot simultaneously read and write the same texture.

At line 37 we specify the buffer to use as depth buffer. This is an object we have not seen yet, a renderbuffer, that is, just another type of buffer like the textures but more generic where data contained is not necessarily the output written by gl_FragColor, for example, stencil or depth buffer (like in this case). With the call at line 34 we declare that its physical storage will be a 16-bit depth value. Note that we may create and use a framebuffer even without depth attachment, if, for the specific purpose of rendering, depth test is not necessary. Finally we return the object TextureTarget.

```
6   NVMCClient.rearMirrorTextureTarget = null;
7   TextureTarget = function () {
8       this.framebuffer = null;
9       this.texture = null;
10  };
11
12  NVMCClient.prepareRenderToTextureFrameBuffer = function (gl, ←
        generateMipmap, w, h) {
13      var textureTarget = new TextureTarget();
14      textureTarget.framebuffer = gl.createFramebuffer();
15      gl.bindFramebuffer(gl.FRAMEBUFFER, textureTarget.framebuffer);
16
17      if (w) textureTarget.framebuffer.width = w;
18      else textureTarget.framebuffer.width = 512;
19      if (h) textureTarget.framebuffer.height = h;
20      else textureTarget.framebuffer.height = 512;;
21
22      textureTarget.texture = gl.createTexture();
23      gl.bindTexture(gl.TEXTURE_2D, textureTarget.texture);
24      gl.texParameteri(gl.TEXTURE_2D, gl.TEXTURE_MAG_FILTER, gl.←
            LINEAR);
25      gl.texParameteri(gl.TEXTURE_2D, gl.TEXTURE_MIN_FILTER, gl.←
            LINEAR);
26      gl.texParameteri(gl.TEXTURE_2D, gl.TEXTURE_WRAP_S, gl.REPEAT);
27      gl.texParameteri(gl.TEXTURE_2D, gl.TEXTURE_WRAP_T, gl.REPEAT);
28
29      gl.texImage2D(gl.TEXTURE_2D, 0, gl.RGBA, textureTarget.←
            framebuffer.width, textureTarget.framebuffer.height, 0, gl←
            .RGBA, gl.UNSIGNED_BYTE, null);
30      if (generateMipmap) gl.generateMipmap(gl.TEXTURE_2D);
31
32      var renderbuffer = gl.createRenderbuffer();
33      gl.bindRenderbuffer(gl.RENDERBUFFER, renderbuffer);
34      gl.renderbufferStorage(gl.RENDERBUFFER, gl.DEPTH_COMPONENT16, ←
            textureTarget.framebuffer.width, textureTarget.framebuffer←
            .height);
35
36      gl.framebufferTexture2D(gl.FRAMEBUFFER, gl.COLOR_ATTACHMENT0, ←
            gl.TEXTURE_2D, textureTarget.texture, 0);
37      gl.framebufferRenderbuffer(gl.FRAMEBUFFER, gl.DEPTH_ATTACHMENT←
            , gl.RENDERBUFFER, renderbuffer);
38
39      gl.bindTexture(gl.TEXTURE_2D, null);
```

FIGURE 7.15 (SEE COLOR INSERT): Using render to texture for implementing the rear mirror. (See client *http://envymycarbook.com/chapter7/1/1.html*.)

```
40    gl.bindRenderbuffer(gl.RENDERBUFFER, null);
41    gl.bindFramebuffer(gl.FRAMEBUFFER, null);
42
43    return textureTarget;
44  }
```

LISTING 7.5: Creating a new framebuffer. (Code snippet from *http://envymycarbook.com/chapter7/1/1.js*.)

Figure 7.15 shows a view from the driver's prespective with rearview appearing in the rear mirror.

7.7   Texture Coordinates Generation and Environment Mapping

Up to now we learned how to stick images to geometry, but the techniques at hand allow us to do it much more. For example, we could do a scrolling sign on a panel by changing the texture coordinates from frame to frame. This is just the most trivial example: once it is assumed that texture coordinates can be a function of something (of time in the example above) and having complete freedom as to the content of the texture, texturing becomes a powerful weapon to achieve more realistic renderings.

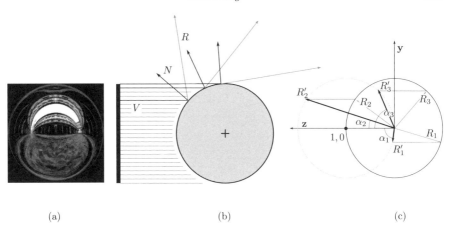

(a)   (b)   (c)

FIGURE 7.16: (a) An example of a sphere map. (b) The sphere map is created by taking an orthogonal picture of a reflecting sphere. (c) How reflection rays are mapped to texture space.

With the term *environment mapping* we refer to texture mapping used to show the reflection of the surrounding environment on the 3D scene to be represented. This is a very general notion that does not specify if the surrounding environment is something different from the 3D scene or if it is part of it. In some of the most common techniques we will see that the environment is represented by images and encoded into textures.

7.7.1 Sphere Mapping

If we take a picture of a perfectly reflecting sphere with a camera we will have a picture like the one shown in Figure 7.16.(a), containing all the surrounding environment except the part exactly behind the sphere. Suppose that the picture is taken at an infinite distance, so that the projection is orthogonal, as illustrated by Figure 7.16.(b). In this way we have established a one-to-one correspondence between the direction of reflection of view rays (rendered in blue) and the image. The idea of sphere mapping is to use the image as texture and use this correspondence for a generic object, computing the texture coordinate as a function of the reflection ray. Note that parallel reflection rays will always map to the same texture coordinates, no matter how far they are from each other, which is the approximation error introduced by sphere mapping. The smaller the distance between parallel rays with respect to the distance of the reflected environment, the less noticeable is the error. If the environment tends to be infinitely far or, equivalently, the sphere and the object tend to be infinitely small, the approximation error tends to 0.

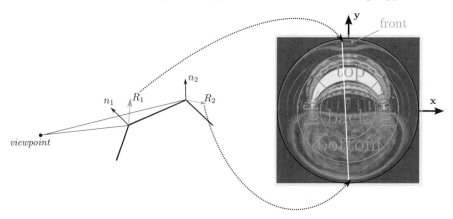

FIGURE 7.17: A typical artifact produced by sphere mapping.

7.7.1.1   Computation of Texture Coordinates

Figure 7.16(c) illustrates how reflection rays are mapped to texture space in the 2D case. Given a normalized ray $R = (y, z)$, consider the angle α formed by $R = (y, z + 1)$ with the $\mathbf{z}$ axis. The texture coordinate t is found as $t = \frac{sin(\alpha)}{2} + \frac{1}{2}$, where the division and summation simply map $[-1, 1]$ to the conventional texture space $[0, 1]$. Writing $sin(\alpha)$ in terms of R we obtain the formula you usually find in the manuals:

$$s = \frac{R_x}{2\sqrt{R_x^2 + R_y^2 + (R_z + 1)^2}} + \frac{1}{2}$$

$$t = \frac{R_y}{2\sqrt{R_x^2 + R_y^2 + (R_z + 1)^2}} + \frac{1}{2}$$

7.7.1.2   Limitations

Sphere mapping is view dependent, meaning that, besides the aforementioned approximation, a sphere map is only valid from the point of view from which it was created. Furthermore, the information contained in the texture is not a uniform sampling of the environment, but it is more dense in the center and less in the boundary. In the practical realization, the tessellation of the object's surface may easily lead to artifacts in the boundary region of the sphere map, because neighbor points in the surface may correspond to faraway texture coordinates, as shown in Figure 7.17.

7.7.2   Cube Mapping

Like sphere mapping, cube mapping works on the assumption that the environment is infinitely far and establishing a correspondence between reflection ray and texture coordinates.

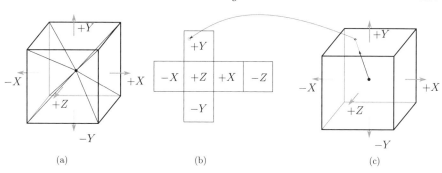

FIGURE 7.18: (a) Six images are taken from the center of the cube. (b) The cube map: the cube is unfolded as six square images on the plane. (c) Mapping from a direction to texture coordinates.

Let us suppose that we place an ideal cube in the middle of the scene and we shot 6 photos from the center of the cube along the three axes and in both directions (as shown in Figure 7.18) so that the viewing window of each photo matches exactly with the corresponding face of the cube. The result is that our cube contains all the environment. Figure 7.18.(b) shows a development of the cube so that each square is a face of the cube.

Computation of Texture Coordinates

Mapping the reflection direction to the texture map, which in this case is referred to as *cube map*, is fairly intuitive: we simply find the intersection between the extension of the reflection direction starting from the center of the cube. This is done by the following formulas:

$$
\begin{aligned}
s &= \frac{1}{2}\frac{R_1}{R_{max}+1} \\
t &= \frac{1}{2}\frac{R_2}{R_{max}+1}
\end{aligned}
\tag{7.2}
$$

where R_{max} is the biggest component in absolute value: $R_{max} = max(|R_x|, |R_y|, |R_z|)$, and R_1 and R_2 are the other two components.

Limitations

Cube mapping has several advantages over sphere mapping: a cube map is valid from every view direction, we do not have the artifact due to the singularity along the $(0, 0, -1)$ direction and the mapping from the cube to the cube maps does not introduce distortion. However, like sphere mapping, the method works correctly on the same assumptions, that is: the environment is far, far away.

7.7.3   Upgrade Your Client: Add a Skybox for the Horizon

Now we are going to add a *skybox* that, as the word suggests, is none other than a huge box containing all our world and on the faces of this box there are images of the environment as it is seen from the scene. Which point of the scene? Any, because the box is so large that only the view direction counts. This is the simplest use of cubemapping and does not even have to do with reflection. The idea is that we just render an infinitely large cube with a cubemap on it. Now, we obviously cannot position the cube vertices to infinite, but consider that if we could, we would have two effects that we can achieve in other ways:

1. The portion of the cube rendered on the screen depends only on the view direction. This can be done by rendering the unitary cube (or a cube of any size) centered in the viewer position.

2. Everything in the scene is closer than the box and therefore every fragment of the rasterization of a polygon of the scene would pass the depth test. This can be done by rendering the cube first and telling WebGL not to write on the depth buffer while rendering the cube, so everything rendered after will pass the depth test.

Creating a cubemap is just like creating a single 2D texture and hence we are not going to comment it line by line. The important thing is that we specify a different target: instead of gl.TEXTURE_2D we have gl.TEXTURE_CUBE_MAP and then we have — gl.TEXTURE_CUBE_MAP _[POSITIVE |NEGATIVE]_[X |Y|Z] to load single 2D textures on the faces.

At line 48 in Listing 7.6 we set the shader to use (that we will see shortly), and then we pass the projection matrix we are using, as usual. Next, we copy the modelview matrix but we put that 0's in the translation which part (that is, the last column), which means that the point of view is now set to the origin. Then, at line 58 we disable the writing on the depth buffer and render the unitary cube.

```
47  NVMCClient.drawSkyBox = function (gl) {
48    gl.useProgram(this.skyBoxShader);
49    gl.uniformMatrix4fv(this.skyBoxShader.↩
        uProjectionMatrixLocation, false, this.projectionMatrix);
50    var orientationOnly = this.stack.matrix;
51    SglMat4.col$(orientationOnly,3,[0.0,0.0,0.0,1.0]);
52
53    gl.uniformMatrix4fv(this.skyBoxShader.uModelViewMatrixLocation↩
        , false, orientationOnly);
54    gl.uniform1i(this.skyBoxShader.uCubeMapLocation, 0);
55
56    gl.activeTexture(gl.TEXTURE0);
57    gl.bindTexture(gl.TEXTURE_CUBE_MAP, this.cubeMap);
58    gl.depthMask(false);
59    this.drawObject(gl, this.cube, this.skyBoxShader, [0.0, 0.0, ↩
        0.0, 1]);
```

```
60    gl.depthMask(true);
61    gl.bindTexture(gl.TEXTURE_CUBE_MAP, null);
62  }
```

LISTING 7.6: Rendering a skybox. (Code snippet from *http://envymycarbook.com/chapter7/3/3.js.*)

The shader, shown in Listing 7.7, is very simple, being just a sampling of the cubemap based on the view direction. The only difference with the bidimensional texture is that we have a dedicated sampler, **sampleCube**, and a dedicated function, **textureCube**, which takes a three-dimensional vector, and accesses the cubemap by using Equation (7.2).

```
2   var vertexShaderSource = "\
3     uniform    mat4 uModelViewMatrix;   \n\
4     uniform    mat4 uProjectionMatrix; \n\
5     attribute vec3 aPosition;           \n\
6     varying vec3 vpos;                  \n\
7     void main(void)                     \n\
8     {                                   \n\
9       vpos = normalize(aPosition);      \n\
10      gl_Position = uProjectionMatrix*uModelViewMatrix * vec4(←
          aPosition, 1.0);\n\
11    }";
12  var fragmentShaderSource = "\
13    precision highp float;              \n\
14    uniform   samplerCube  uCubeMap; \n\
15    varying vec3 vpos;                  \n\
16    void main(void)                     \n\
17    {                                   \n\
18      gl_FragColor = textureCube (uCubeMap,normalize(vpos));\n\
19    } ";
```

LISTING 7.7: Shader for rendering a skybox. (Code snippet from *http://envymycarbook.com/chapter7/3/shaders.js.*)

7.7.4 Upgrade Your Client: Add Reflections to the Car

At this point adding the reflections on the cars is a simple matter of using a shader similar to the one in Listing 7.7, with the difference that the texture is accessed at the position indicated by the reflection direction.

Since we need the normal and the position they are passed as attributes and interpolated as usual (see Listing 7.8). Then the reflection direction is computed with Formula (6.6) by the native function **reflect**, at line 35. We pass the matrix **uViewToWorldMatrix** to the shader, that is, the matrix converting the coordinates from the view reference frame, where the reflection computation is done, to the world reference frame, where the cubemap is expressed.

This is not the only way to do it. We could compute the refraction direction directly in world space and avoid the final transformation in the fragment shader.

```
5   shaderProgram.vertexShaderSource = "\
6     uniform    mat4 uModelViewMatrix;           \n\
7     uniform    mat4 uProjectionMatrix;          \n\
8     uniform    mat3  uViewSpaceNormalMatrix; \n\
9     attribute vec3 aPosition;                   \n\
10    attribute vec4 aDiffuse;                    \n\
11    attribute vec4 aSpecular;                   \n\
12    attribute vec3 aNormal;                     \n\
13    varying   vec3 vPos;                        \n\
14    varying   vec3 vNormal;                     \n\
15    varying   vec4 vdiffuse;                    \n\
16    varying   vec4 vspecular;                   \n\
17    void main(void)                             \n\
18    {                                           \n\
19    vdiffuse = aDiffuse;                        \n\
20      vspecular = aSpecular;                    \n\
21      vPos = vec3(uModelViewMatrix * vec4(aPosition, 1.0)); \n\
22      vNormal =normalize( uViewSpaceNormalMatrix *  aNormal);\n\
23      gl_Position = uProjectionMatrix*uModelViewMatrix * vec4(←
          aPosition, 1.0);\n\
24    }";
25  shaderProgram.fragmentShaderSource = "\
26    precision highp float;             \n\
27    uniform mat4 uViewToWorldMatrix;   \n\
28    uniform  samplerCube uCubeMap;     \n\
29    varying  vec3 vPos;                \n\
30    varying vec4 vdiffuse;             \n\
31    varying vec3 vNormal;              \n\
32    varying vec4 vspecular;            \n\
33    void main(void)                    \n\
34    {                                  \n\
35      vec3 reflected_ray = vec3(uViewToWorldMatrix* vec4(reflect←
          (vPos,vNormal),0.0));\n\
36      gl_FragColor = textureCube (uCubeMap,reflected_ray)*←
          vspecular+vdiffuse;\n\
37    }";
```

LISTING 7.8: Shader for reflection mapping. (Code snippet from *http://envymycarbook.com/chapter7/4/shaders.js.*)

7.7.4.1 Computing the Cubemap on-the-fly for More Accurate Reflections

We recall that the cube mapping works on the assumption that the environment is infinitely far away. The way we implemented reflection mapping, the car surface will always reflect the environment, no matter in which part of the scene the car is, just like if the rest of the scene (the track, the buildings, the trees etc..) were not present. We can have a more convincing reflection computing the cubemap on-the-fly, that is, instead of using the static reflection map used for the skybox, we create a new cube map for each frame, taking 6 views from, say, the center of the car, filling the faces of the cubemaps with the results. We already know how to render to a texture since we have seen it in Section 7.6. The only difference is that in this case the texture will be a face of the cubemap.

The only sensible change to the code is the introduction of function dra-wOnReflectionMap. The first lines of the function are shown in Listing 7.9. First of all, at line 62, we set the projection matrix with a 90 angle and aspect ratio 1 and at line 2 we set the viewport to the size of the framebuffer we created. Then we perform a render of the whole scene *except the car* for each of the six axis aligned directions. This requires to: set the view frame (line 65), bind the right framebuffer (line 66) and clearing the used buffers.

```
61  NVMCClient.drawOnReflectionMap = function (gl, position){
62    this.projectionMatrix = SglMat4.perspective(Math.PI↩
        /2.0,1.0,1.0,300);
63    gl.viewport(0,0,this.cubeMapFrameBuffers[0].width,this.↩
        cubeMapFrameBuffers[0].height);
64    // +x
65    this.stack.load(SglMat4.lookAt(position,SglVec3.add(position↩
        ,[1.0,0.0,0.0]),[0.0,-1.0,0.0]));
66    gl.bindFramebuffer(gl.FRAMEBUFFER, this.cubeMapFrameBuffers↩
        [0]);
67    gl.clear(gl.COLOR_BUFFER_BIT | gl.DEPTH_BUFFER_BIT);
68    this.drawSkyBox(gl);
69    this.drawEverything(gl,true, this.cubeMapFrameBuffers[0]);
70
71    // -x
72    this.stack.load(SglMat4.lookAt(position,SglVec3.add(position↩
        ,[-1.0,0.0,0.0]),[0.0,-1.0,0.0]));
73    gl.bindFramebuffer(gl.FRAMEBUFFER, this.cubeMapFrameBuffers↩
        [1]);
74    gl.clear(gl.COLOR_BUFFER_BIT | gl.DEPTH_BUFFER_BIT);
75    this.drawSkyBox(gl);
76    this.drawEverything(gl,true, this.cubeMapFrameBuffers[1]);
```

LISTING 7.9: Creating the reflection map on the y. (Code snippet from *http://envymycarbook.com/chapter7/4/0.js.*)

Figure 7.19 shows a snapshot from the client with skybox, normal mapping (discussed later) applied to the street, and reflection mapping applied on the car.

7.7.5 Projective Texture Mapping

In this section we will see how to project an image on the scene, like a video projector or the Batman signal does. Like for environment mapping, there are no new concepts involved, just a smart use of texture coordinates generation.

The *projector* is described just like the view reference frame and it is conceptually the same object, with the only difference that instead of projecting the scene on its viewing plane, an image ideally placed in its viewing plane is projected into the scene. What we need to realize this effect is simply to assign to each point of the scene the texture coordinate obtained by projecting its

FIGURE 7.19 (SEE COLOR INSERT): Adding the reflection mapping. (See client *http://envymycarbook.com/chapter7/4/4.html.*)

position to the viewing plane of the projector.

$$
\overbrace{\begin{bmatrix} s \\ t \\ r \\ q \end{bmatrix}}^{t} = \overbrace{\begin{bmatrix} \frac{1}{2} & 0 & 0 & \frac{1}{2} \\ 0 & \frac{1}{2} & 0 & \frac{1}{2} \\ 0 & 0 & \frac{1}{2} & \frac{1}{2} \\ 0 & 0 & 0 & 1 \end{bmatrix}}^{T} P_{proj}\, V_{proj} \overbrace{\begin{bmatrix} x \\ y \\ z \\ 1 \end{bmatrix}}^{p}
$$

where $P_{proj}\, V_{proj}$ are the projection matrix and view matrix of the projector, respectively, and T is the transformation that maps the space from the canonical viewing volume $[-1, +1]^3$ to $[0, +1]^3$. Note that the final values actually used to access the texture will be the normalized ones, i.e. $(s/q, t/q)$, while coordinate r is unused in this case.

7.8   Texture Mapping for Adding Detail to Geometry

Until now we used texture mapping as a way to add color information to the scene. The textures always contained color, which could be a picture or the surrounding environment. In a more abstract way, we added detailed information about the color to a rougher description of a surface (geometry).

If we observe the objects of the physical world, we can see that almost every object can be seen as a rough, let us say a large scale, geometric description and a finer geometric detail applied to its surface. For example, the trunk of

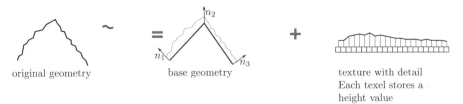

FIGURE 7.20: A fine geometry is represented with a simpler base geometry plus the geometric detail encoded in a texture as a height field.

a tree may be seen as a cylinder (large scale) plus its cortex (the finer detail), the roof of a house may be seen as a rectangle plus the tiles, a street may be seen as a plane plus the rugosity of the asphalt. In CG, the advantage of this way of viewing things is that usually the geometric detail can be efficiently encoded as a texture image and used at the right time (see Figure 7.20). In the following we will see a few techniques that use texture mapping to add geometric detail without actually changing the geometry.

7.8.1 Displacement Mapping

With *displacement mapping* the texture contains, for each texel, a single value encoding how much the corresponding geometric point should be moved (displaced) along the normal in that point. To implement this technique we should, at some point along the pipeline, replace the original geometry with a tessellation having a vertex for each texel in order to displace it accordingly. The way this is done is by implementing a *ray casting* algorithm in the fragment shader and since it is not strictly texture mapping we will explain it in Section 9.3.

7.8.2 Normal Mapping

With normal mapping we use textures to encode the normals and use them during rasterization to compute per-fragment lighting. We refer to these textures with the name of *normal maps*.

Unlike displacement mapping, the geometry is not altered, we just change the value of the normal to be the one that we would have *if* the geometry was actually displaced. This means that the normal we will have on each point of the geometry is inconsistent with the geometry around the point and makes us realize how much the perception of the appearance of a surface is deeply related to its normal, that is, to the lighting which in turn depends on the normal.

Figure 7.21 shows the error committed by using normal mapping instead of the exact geometry. The view ray r_1 hits the base geometry at point p and the normal n_p is used for shading, while if we had the actual geometry the hitting point would have been p' and the normal $n_{p'}$. This is the typical

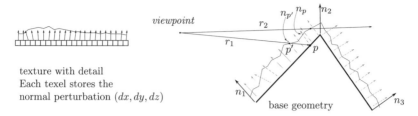

texture with detail
Each texel stores the
normal perturbation (dx, dy, dz)

FIGURE 7.21: With normal mapping, the texture encodes the normal.

parallax error and depends on two factors: how far is the real surface from the base geometry and how small is the angle formed by the view ray and the base geometry.

The view ray r_2 will entirely miss the object, while it would have hit the real geometry. This is the very same parallax error with more evident consequences and it means that we will be able to spot the real shape of geometry on the object's silhouette. In a few words, implementing normal mapping simply means redo the Phong shading we did in Section 6.9.2, perturbing the interpolated normal with a value encoded in a texture.

7.8.2.1   Object Space Normal Mapping

When using normal mapping we must choose in which reference frame we express the perturbation of the normal. If the reference frame is the one where we express the object we speak of **object space normal mapping**. In this case the value stored in the normal maps is simply added to the interpolated normal n:

$$\boldsymbol{n'} = \boldsymbol{n} + \boldsymbol{d}$$

Figure 7.22 shows a classic example of object space normal mapping. On the left is a detailed model of the head of a statue, made of $4M$ triangles. In the middle is the base geometry and on the right the result of using normal mapping.

In order to implement normal mapping, we have to consider in which space the summation is actually done. We recall from Chapter 6 that light is normally specified in world space, while the values in the normal map are expressed in object space. Hence we are left with two options: either we apply to each vector of the normal map the same object-to-world space transformation that is applied to the object, or we apply the inverse transformation, world-to-object space to the light position (or direction for directional lights). With the first option, we will have to perform a matrix multiplication in the fragment shader, while in the second case we can transform the light position/direction in the vertex shader and let the interpolation provide the value for the fragment.

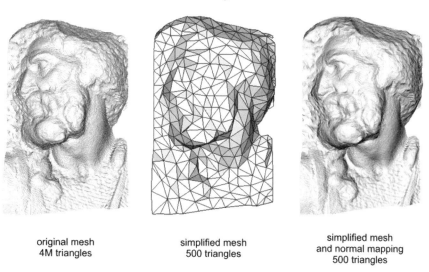

original mesh
4M triangles

simplified mesh
500 triangles

simplified mesh
and normal mapping
500 triangles

FIGURE 7.22: Example of object space normal mapping. (Left) Original mesh made up of 4 million triangles. (Center) A mesh of the same object made of only 500 triangles. (Right) The low resolution mesh with normal mapping applied. (Image courtesy of M. Tarini [39].)

7.8.3   Upgrade Your Client: Add the Asphalt

We interpret the asphalt as a rugosity of the street. Since our street is laying on the horizontal plane we can simply apply object space normal mapping. The modifications to our client are straightforward. We already applied textures to the street in Section 7.5; what we need to add is to load a texture containing a normal map for the asphalt and modify the shader program to take this new texture into account. Figure 7.23 shows a normal map where the three (x, y, z) coordinates are stored as R, G, B color. Note that the color values stored in a texture are in the interval $[0, M]$, while the object space coordinates for the normal are in the interval $[0, 1]$. The reason the texture is all bluish is that the *up* direction is stored in the *blue* channel and for the street it is always in the positive halfspace, while the other two may be both positive and negative, so it will have lower value on average. Listing 7.10 shows the fragment shader that uses normal maps. Note that after we access the normal map we remap the values from $[0, 1]$ to $[-1, 1]$ (lines 25 to 27); then we use this value as normal to compute the shading (line 28). For the sake of readability of the code we use a simple Lambertian material, which is reasonable for the asphalt, but, of course, you can plug every arbitrarily complex shading instead.

FIGURE 7.23 (SEE COLOR INSERT): An example of how a normal map may appear if opened with an image viewer.

```
15    var fragmentShaderSource = "\
16      precision highp float;              \n\
17      uniform sampler2D texture;          \n\
18      uniform sampler2D normalMap;        \n\
19      uniform vec4  uLightDirection;      \n\
20      uniform vec4 uColor;                \n\
21      varying vec2 vTextureCoords;        \n\
22      void main(void)                     \n\
23      {                                                  \n\
24        vec4 n=texture2D(normalMap, vTextureCoords);  \n\
25        n.x =n.x*2.0 -1.0;                             \n\
26        n.y =n.y*2.0 -1.0;                             \n\
27        n.z =n.z*2.0 -1.0;                             \n\
28        vec3 N=normalize(vec3(n.x,n.z,n.y));           \n\
29        float shade =  dot(-uLightDirection.xyz , N); \n\
30        vec4 color=texture2D(texture, vTextureCoords);\n\
31        gl_FragColor = vec4(color.xyz*shade,1.0);      \n\
32      }";
```

LISTING 7.10: Fragment shader for object space normal mapping. (Code snippet from *http://envymycarbook.com/chapter7/2/shaders.js*.)

7.8.4 Tangent Space Normal Mapping

Suppose that we want to define a normal map that is not specific for a predefined mapping M but that can be placed wherever we want, just like we can place a sticker on any part of our car. In this case we cannot simply encode the normal variation as an absolute value, simply because we do not know *a priori* the normal value at the point where each texel will be mapped.

In other words, we want to do with the normal mapping what we do with the color mapping: to create the texture without taking care where it is applied.

The main difference between applying the color from the texture to the surface and applying the normal is that the color encoded in a texel does not have to be transformed in any way to be mapped on the surface: a red texel is red whatever geometric transformation we apply to the object. Not so for the normals, which need a 3D reference frame to be defined. In object space normal mapping, such a reference frame is the same reference frame as for the object and that is why we can write directly the absolute values for the normal.

Let us build a three-dimensional frame C_t centered at a point t in the texture and with axis $\boldsymbol{u} = [1, 0, 0]$, $\boldsymbol{v} = [0, 1, 0]$ and $\boldsymbol{n} = [0, 0, 1]$. What we want is a way to map any value expressed in the frame C_t on the surface at a point where t is projected $p = M(t)$. In order to do this, we build a frame T_f with origin $M(t)$ and axis

$$\boldsymbol{u}_{os} = \frac{\partial M}{\partial u}(p)$$

$$\boldsymbol{v}_{os} = \frac{\partial M}{\partial v}(p)$$

$$\boldsymbol{n}_{os} = \boldsymbol{u}_{os} \times \boldsymbol{v}_{os}$$

therefore we can map a vector expressed in C_t as $[x, y, z]^T$ to T_f as $M_p(x, y, z) = x\, \boldsymbol{u}_{os} + y\, \boldsymbol{v}_{os} + z\, \boldsymbol{n}_{os}$. Note that, by construction, vectors u_{os} and v_{os} are *tangent* to the surface. This is why the set of all vectors generated by them is called *tangent space* and the frame T_f *tangent frame*.

Also note that, since we will only be transforming vectors, the origin of the frame will not come into play in the transformation between C_t and T_f.

It is worth mentioning that historically $\boldsymbol{u}_{os}$, $\boldsymbol{v}_{os}$ and $\boldsymbol{n}_{os}$ are referred to as T (tangent), B (bitangent of binormal) and N (normal). We prefer to use another notation to be more consistent with the rest of this book.

Once we have a way to compute the tangent frame we may apply normal mapping simply by tranforming the light position/direction from object space to tangent space, by multiplying it by the inverse of T_f. As for object space normal mapping, this transformation is done per-vertex and the result interpolated.

7.8.4.1 Computing the Tangent Frame for Triangulated Meshes

If we had an analytic form for M, then computing $\boldsymbol{u}_{os}$, $\boldsymbol{v}_{os}$ would only be a matter of calculating a partial derivative. Instead, we usually have only the texture coordinates of a triangulated mesh like that shown in Figure 7.24. We will now use what we learned about frames in Chapter 4 to compute the tangential vectors $\boldsymbol{u}_{os}$ and $\boldsymbol{v}_{os}$ for the vertex v_0.

Let us consider the frame V_f, with origin in v_0 and axes $v_1 - v_0$ and $v_2 - v_0$, and frame I_f with origin in t_0 and axes $t_1 - t_0$ and $t_2 - t_0$. These frames are

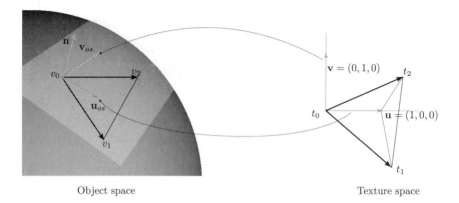

Object space   Texture space

FIGURE 7.24: Deriving the tangential frame from texture coordinates.

known because we know both vertex position and texture coordinates of the vertices of the triangle. The other *important* thing we know is that u_{os} and u have the same coordinates in the respective frames, therefore we can find u_{os} by finding the coordinates u_I of $u = [1, 0, 0]^T$ in the frame I_f and then $u_{os} = u_{Iu} \, v_{10} + u_{Iv} \, v_{20}$.

The end point of vector u is $t_0 + u$. We recall from Chapter 4 that we can express the coordinates of $t_0 + u$ in the frame I_f as:

$$u_{Iu} = \frac{((t_0 + u) - t_0) \times t_{20}}{t_{10} \times t_{20}} = \frac{u \times t_{20}}{t_{10} \times t_{20}} = \frac{[1,0]^T \times t_{20}}{t_{10} \times t_{20}} = \frac{t_{20v}}{t_{10} \times t_{20}}$$

$$u_{Iv} = \frac{t_{10} \times ((t_0 + u) - t_0)}{t_{10} \times t_{20}} = \frac{t_{10} \times u}{t_{10} \times t_{20}} = \frac{t_{10} \times [1,0]^T}{t_{10} \times t_{20}} = \frac{-t_{10u}}{t_{10} \times t_{20}}$$

therefore

$$u_{os} = \frac{t_{20v}}{t_{10} \times t_{20}} \, v_{10} + \frac{-t_{10u}}{t_{10} \times t_{20}} \, v_{20}$$

The same derivation for v_I leads to:

$$v_{os} = \frac{-t_{20u}}{t_{10} \times t_{20}} \, v_{10} + \frac{t_{10v}}{t_{10} \times t_{20}} \, v_{20}$$

Note that doing this derivation we used the fact that the surface at point v_0 is described by the triangle (v_0, v_1, v_2). Specifically, the tangent plane at v_0 contains the triangle. However this is not true because there are other triangles, lying in different planes, which share the same vertex. If we use one of those, we will obtain a different tangent frame. This is the very same consideration we did for vertex normal computation in Chapter 6 and shares the same conclusion: we can find the tangent frame for a vertex by averaging over all the frames computed using the triangles sharing that vertex.

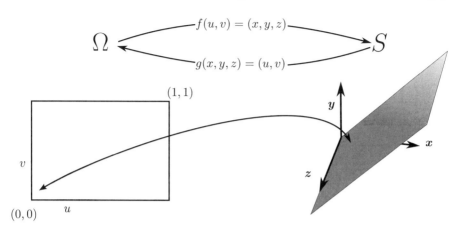

FIGURE 7.25: A parametric plane.

7.9 Notes on Mesh Parametrization

We have seen in Chapter 3 that a 3D parametric surface is a function f that maps the points from a bidimensional domain $\Omega \in \mathbb{R}^2$ to a surface $S \in \mathbb{R}^3$. For example, we may express a plane (see Figure 7.25) as:

$$f(u, v) = (u, v, u)$$

If we had to find the texture coordinates for this plane for the vertex at position (x, y, z) we could simply use the inverse of f:

$$g(x, y, z) = f^{-1}(x, y, z)$$

However, most of the time our surfaces have been modelled manually and are not parametric, so we do not have f. The term *mesh parameterization* indicates the definition of a *bijective* and *continous* mapping from a simple domain to a mesh S. In other words, we want to turn S into a parametric surface in order to use the inverse function g to define the texture coordinates.

When the use of mesh parametrization is limited to uv-mapping we just need an *injective* function g from S to Ω (the difference is that we do not need every point of Ω to be mapped on S). Note that when we specify the texture coordinate we are actually describing g by giving *samples* of its value, that is, its value on the vertices.

We already did some parametrization in the clients of this chapter by defining the texture coordinates for the buildings, the street and the ground. In those cases, however, finding g is straightforward because Ω and S are both rectangles, but consider finding g for the case shown in Figure 7.26. A few questions arise: Does g always exists? There maybe be more than one, and, if so, which is the best?

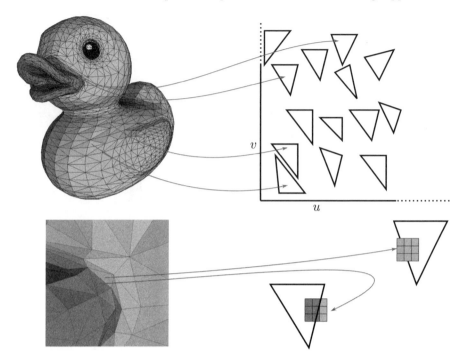

FIGURE 7.26 (SEE COLOR INSERT): (Top) An extremely trivial way to unwrap a mesh: g is continuous only inside the triangle. (Bottom) Problems with filtering due to discontinuities.

7.9.1   Seams

The answer to the first question is yes. Consider just taking each individual triangle of S and placing it onto the plane Ω in such a way that no triangles overlap, as shown in Figure 7.26. In this simple manner we will have our injective function g that maps each point of S onto Ω. Note that the adjacent triangles on the mesh will not, in general, be mapped onto adjacent triangles on Ω, that is, g is not continuous.

Do we care that g is continuous? Yes, we do. Texture sampling is performed in the assumption that close points on S map to close points on Ω. Just consider texture access with bilinear interpolation, where the result of a texture fetch is given by the four texels around the sample point. When the sample is near the border of a triangle (see Bottom of Figure 7.26), the color is influenced by the adjacent triangle on Ω. If g is not continuous, the adjacent texels can correspond to any point on S or just to undefined values, that is, to values that do not belong to $g(S)$.

In parametrization the discontinuities on g are called *seams*. The method we used to build g is just the worst case for seams because it generates one seam for each edge of each triangle.

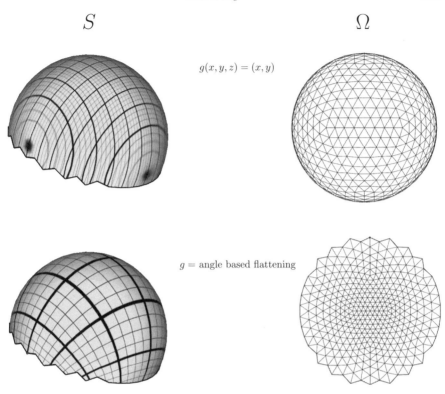

$$S \qquad \Omega$$

$$g(x, y, z) = (x, y)$$

$$g = \text{angle based flattening}$$

FIGURE 7.27: A hemisphere may be mapped without seams.

How do we know if we can avoid seams? Let us assume the mesh S is made of rubber and so we can deform it as we please. If we manage to "flatten" S onto Ω we have a seamless parametrization g. For example if S is a hemisphere and Ω is a plane (see Figure 7.27) we can flatten S onto Ω and define $g(x, y, z) = (x, z)$. Conversely, if S is a sphere, there is no way we can deform it into a plane. What we need is a *cut* to "open" the sphere, that is, we create a seam, and now we can stretch the cut sphere onto the plane. A parametrization g that has no seams, like for the hemisphere above, is called *global parameterization*.

In practice you would rarely encounter global parameterizations on a planar domain for non-trivial shapes; you will always see cases like the one in Figure 7.28. On the other hand, you may find some seamless parameterizations on more complex domains than the plane.

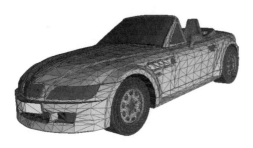

FIGURE 7.28: The model of a car and relative parameterization, computed with Graphite [14].

7.9.2   Quality of a Parametrization

So we know there can be several parameterizations for the same S and Ω, but which is the best one? How can we measure how good a given g is?

Let us consider S and Ω again, and this time assume that S is made of paper, which can bend but cannot be stretched. If we are able to unfold S on the plane we have parameterization g with no distortion. Otherwise we would need to locally stretch the tissue so that it can be flattened. The amount of stretch we do is called *distortion* and it is a characteristic of the parameterization.

Let us consider an (infinitely) small square on the surface S placed at point **p** and its image on Ω. We have three cases for the image of the square on Ω:

- a square with the same area and the same angles, in this case the parametrization is called *isometric*

- a parallelogram with the same area as the square, in this case the parameterization is called *equiareal*

- a square with a different area, and we say the parameterization is called *conformal* or *angle preserving*

Note that every *isometric* parametrization is *conformal* and *equiareal*.

Do we care about distortion? Yes we do. Distortion on parameterization causes uneven sampling of textures. We may have large areas of S corresponding to just a few texels in texture space. A typical way to visually assess the quality of a parameterization is to set a regular pattern as texture image and look how regular it is when mapped on the mesh. The more the parameterization is isometric, the more the areas described by the patterns will be similar over the mesh and the right angles made by the line will stay right on the mesh. Looking again at Figure 7.27, we can see how the parameterization obtained by orthogonal projection (Top row) is okay in the center but degrades towards the borders, while a more sophisticated algorithm (described in [38]) appears more regular everywhere.

As aforementioned, parametrization is a wide topic with a vast literature and there are many proposals on how to achieve a good parameterization. We want to point out that distortion and seams are two related characteristics of a parameterization. For example, the trivial parametrization by triangle has 0 distortion but a large number of seams. On the other hand, the flattened hemisphere has no seams but quite a large distortion that we could reduce by making cuts. Figure 7.29 shows an example of a bad parameterization obtained without allowing any seam and a good one obtained by allowing seams. In fact the seams actually partition the mesh in three separate parts that are then arranged in texture space.

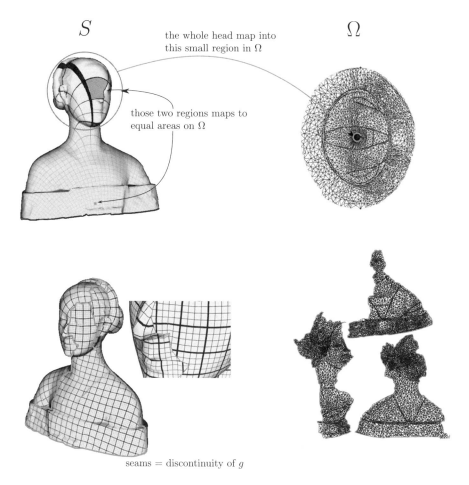

FIGURE 7.29: (Top) Distorted parameterization. (Bottom) Almost isometric.

7.10   3D Textures and Their Use

A *3D texture*, or *volumetric texture*, is none other than a stacked series of sz textures of size $sx \times sy$ that are accessed by specifying three coordinates UVT. Note that filtering (both magnification and minification/mipmapping) is extended to 3D by considering the z dimension, that is, the $2 \times 2 \times 2 = 8$ texels around the access coordinates. So the ith mipmap level is created by taking the average of a group of eight texels. 3D textures are supported in Opengl and OpenGL ES but not (yet) included in the WebGL API so we will not see them at work in our client. Here we briefly mention some use for it.

So far we have always represented volumetric objects by their external surface, but we know from Section 3.5 that the scene may be encoded with voxels and it is clear that a voxel-based representation maps naturally on a 3D texture. If we wanted to visualize a "slice" of volume data we would only need to render a plane and assign the 3D textures' coordinates to the vertices, letting texture sampling do the rest.

A more intriguing matter is what is called *volume rendering*, that is, how to render a volume of data on a 2D device, for which we showed the sample in Figure 3.17. This is a vast topic on its own for which we refer the reader to [45].

With the term *participating media* we indicate those elements that fill a volume without a precise boundary, such as fog and smoke, where light–matter interaction does not stop at the surface. In these cases 3D textures are often updated dynamically by a simulation algorithm that animates the media.

7.11   Self-Exercises

7.11.1   General

1. Suppose we do not use perspective correct interpolation and we see the same scene with two identical viewer settings except that they have different near plane distances. For which setting is the error less noticeable? How much would the error be with an orthogonal projection?

2. If we want to obtain a rendering of a checkerboard with $n \times n$ b/w tiles, how small can the texture be? Do we need an $n \times n$ pixels image or can we do it with a smaller one? *Hint*: Play with texture wrapping

3. Consider the sphere mapping and the cube mapping in term of mesh parameterization. What is S and what is Ω? Which one is the less distorted parametrization? Which one has seams?

4. May a torus be parametrized on a planar domain without seams? And with one seam? How many seams do we need?

5. What is the reason for 3D textures? Is a 3D texture of size $sx \times sy \times sz$ not the same as sz 2D textures?

7.11.2 Client

1. Make a running text on a floating polygon over the car. *Hint*: Make the u texture coordinate increase with time and use "repeat" as wrapping mode.

2. Implement a client where the headlights project a texture. *Hint*: See Section 7.7.5

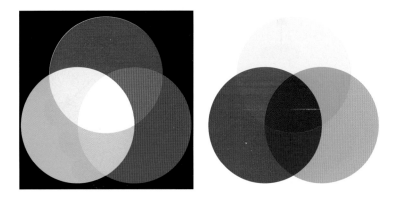

FIGURE 1.2: (Left) RGB additive primaries. (Right) CMY subtractive primaries.

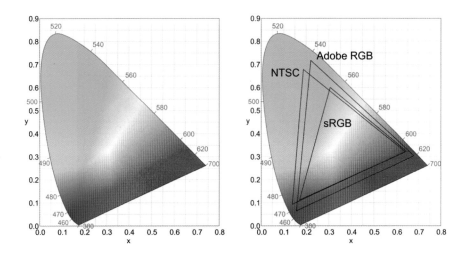

FIGURE 1.4: (Left) Chromaticities diagram. (Right) Gamut of different RGB color systems.

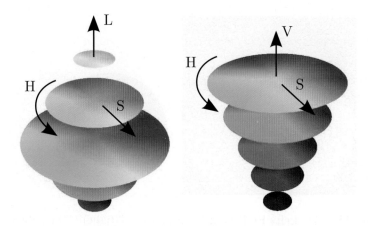

FIGURE 1.5: HSL and HSV color space.

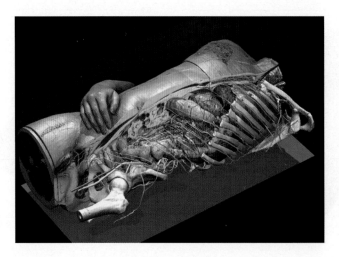

FIGURE 3.17: An example of voxels in medical imaging. (Courtesy of *Voxel-Man* http://www.voxel-man.com.)

FIGURE 5.14: Stenciling example: (Left) The rendering from inside the car. (Middle) The stencil mask, that is, the portion of screen that does not need to be redrawn. (Right) The portion that is affected from rendering.

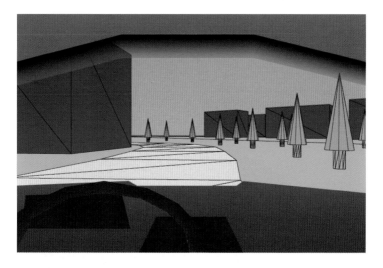

FIGURE 5.18: Adding the view from inside. Blending is used for the upper part of the windshield. (See client *http://envymycarbook.com/chapter5/0/0.html.*)

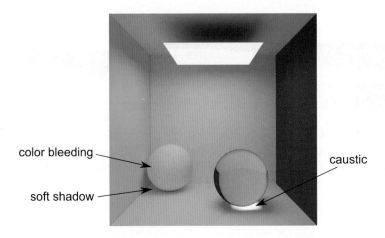

color bleeding

soft shadow

caustic

FIGURE 6.9: Global illumination effects. Shadows, caustics and color bleeding. (Courtesy of Francesco Banterle *http://www.banterle.com/francesco.*)

FIGURE 6.15: Scene illuminated with directional light. (See client *http:// envymycarbook.com/chapter6/0/0.html.*)

FIGURE 6.16: Adding point light for the lamps. (See client *http:// envymycarbook.com/chapter6/1/1.html.*)

FIGURE 6.18: Adding headlights on the car. (See client *http:// envymycarbook.com/chapter6/2/2.html.*)

FIGURE 6.20: (Top-Left) Ambient component. (Top-Right) Diffuse component. (Bottom-Left) Specular component. (Bottom-Right) The components summed up together ($k_A = (0.2, 0.2, 0.2)$, $k_D = (0.0, 0.0, 0.6)$, $k_S = (0.8, 0.8, 0.8)$, $n_s = 1.2$).

FIGURE 6.22: Gouraud shading vs Phong shading. (Left) Gouraud shading. (Right) Phong shading. Note that some details result in a better look with Phong shading (per-pixel) due to the non-dense tessellation.

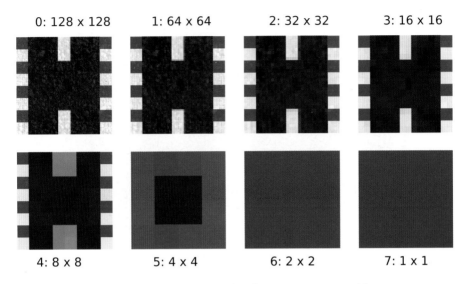

0: 128 x 128   1: 64 x 64   2: 32 x 32   3: 16 x 16

4: 8 x 8   5: 4 x 4   6: 2 x 2   7: 1 x 1

FIGURE 7.7: Example of a mipmap pyramid.

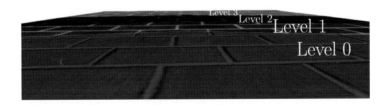

FIGURE 7.9: Mipmapping at work. In this picture, false colors are used to show the mipmap level used for each fragment.

FIGURE 7.13: Basic texturing. (See client *http://envymycarbook.com/chapter7/0/0.html.*)

FIGURE 7.15: Using render to texture for implementing the rear mirror. (See client *http://envymycarbook.com/chapter7/1/1.html.*)

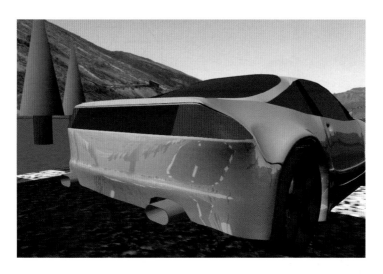

FIGURE 7.19: Adding the reflection mapping. (See client *http://envymycarbook.com/chapter7/4/4.html.*)

FIGURE 7.23: An example of how a normal map may appear if opened with an image viewer.

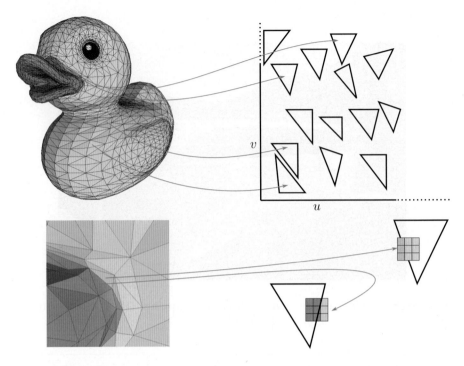

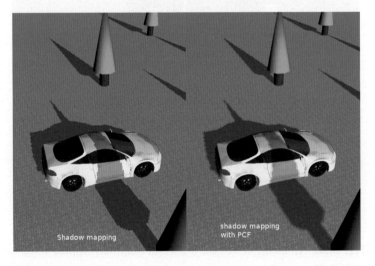

FIGURE 7.26: (Top) An extremely trivial way to unwrap a mesh: g is continuous only inside the triangle. (Bottom) Problems with filtering due to discontinuities.

FIGURE 8.7: PCF shadow mapping. (See client *http:// envymycarbook.com/chapter8/0/0.html*.)

FIGURE 9.4: Client with gadgets added using plane-oriented billboard. (See client *http://envymycarbook.com/chapter9/0/0.html.*)

FIGURE 9.6: (Left) Positions of the lens flare in screen space. (Right) Examples of textures used to simulate the effect.

FIGURE 9.7: A client with the lens flare in effect. (See client *http:// envymycarbook.com/chapter7/4/4.html.*)

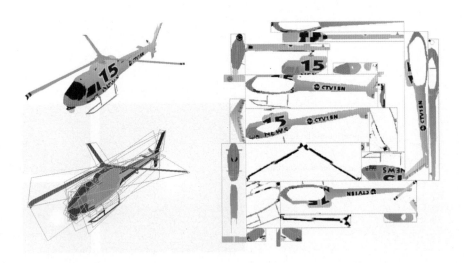

FIGURE 9.10: Billboard cloud example from the paper [6]. (Courtesy of the authors). (Left) The original model and a set of polygons resembling it. (Right) The texture resulting from the projections of the original model on the billboards.

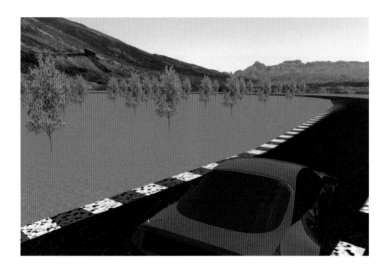

FIGURE 9.11: Snapshot of the client using billboard clouds for the trees. (See client *http://envymycarbook.com/chapter9/3/3.html.*)

FIGURE 10.3: (Left) Original image. (Right) Image blurred with a 9×9 box filter ($N = M = 4$).

FIGURE 10.5: (Left) Original image. (Right) Image blurred with a 9×9 Gaussian filter ($\sigma = 1.5$ pixels).

FIGURE 10.9: (Left) Original image. (Center) Prewitt filter. (Right) Sobel filter.

FIGURE 10.10: Toon shading client. (See client *http://envymycarbook.com/ chapter10/1/1.html*.)

FIGURE 10.12: Velocity vector. (See client *http://envymycarbook.com/ chapter10/2/2.html*.)

FIGURE 10.13: A screenshot of the motion blur client. (See client *http://envymycarbook.com/chapter10/2/2.html*.)

FIGURE 10.14: (Left) Original image. (Right) Image after unsharp masking. The I_{smooth} image is the one depicted in Figure 10.5; λ is set to 0.6.

Chapter 8

Shadows

8.1 The Shadow Phenomenon

In Chapter 6 we learned that many types of interactions between light and matter can occur before photons leaving from emitters eventually reach our eye. We have seen that, because of the complexity of the problem, local illumination models are used in interactive applications. Then, we have seen some techniques for adding some more global lighting effects to the local model in order to improve the realism. For example, in Section 7.7.4 we used cube mapping to add reflections to the car, that is, to add one bounce of light.

In this chapter we will show how to add another global effect: *the shadows*. We all have the intuition of what a shadow is: a region that is darker than its surroundings because of something blocking the light arriving at such a region. The shadow phenomenon is critical in order to create more realistic images. The presence of shadowed areas helps us to better perceive the spatial relations among the objects in the scene, and, in the case of complex objects, the shadows created by the object on itself, known as *self-shadows*, allow for a better understanding of its shape. Now, we give a more formal definition of shadow: *a point* $\mathbf{p}$ *is* in shadow *with respect to a light source if the light rays leaving the source towards* $\mathbf{p}$ *hit a point* $\mathbf{p}'$ *"before" reaching* $\mathbf{p}$.

Figure 8.1 shows three examples with different types of light: point light, directional light and area light. The peculiarity of area lights is that many light rays leaving from the same light source may reach the same point. This means that, potentially, only a portion of the rays that may reach a point on the surface actually do so, while others may be blocked. This is the reason why near the edges of a shadowed area the amount of darkness increases while traveling inward from that area. This phenomenon is called *penumbra* and if you look around it is one of the most commonly observable types of shadow because it is rare to find emitters so small that they can be considered point lights. When the penumbra effect is not considered, due to the type of light or to simplify the implementation, the shadows we obtain are called *hard shadows*.

Note that we gave only a **geometric** definition of shadow without saying anything about how much darker a point in shadow should look, because that depends on the illumination model we are using and the material properties

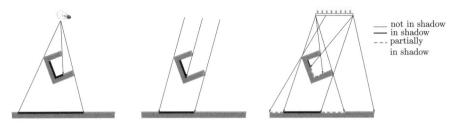

FIGURE 8.1: (Left) Shadow caused by a point light. (Middle) Shadow caused by a directional light. (Right) Shadow caused by an area light.

of our objects. For example, let us consider a complete illumination model, that is, the perfect simulation of reality and a scene made of a closed room, with a light source inside and where all the surfaces are perfectly diffusive with albedo 1, so that they entirely reflect all the incoming light to every direction. In this situation it does not matter if a point is in shadow, it will be lit anyway because even if the straight path from the light source is blocked, photons will bounce around until they reach every point of the scene (with the only neglectable difference that they will not travel the same distance for all the points). Now let us change this setting by assuming that all the surfaces are perfectly specular. In this case, it may not be the case that all the points will be lit, but, again, it does not depend on whether they are in shadow or not. Finally, consider using a local lighting model such as the Phong model. With this model the outgoing light depends **only** on the light coming **directly** from the emitter **and** on the ambient term. So, we can state that a point in shadow will look darker; how much darker depends on the ambient term: if it is 0, that is, no indirect lighting is considered, each point in shadow will be pure black, otherwise the ambient term multiplied by the color is the final darker color.

We discuss the aforementioned examples to underline the fact that the determination of regions in shadow makes sense with a local illumination model, where there is a direct connection between *being in shadow* and *receiving less light*.

In this chapter we will see some of the techniques for rendering shadows in real-time. Because synthesizing accurate shadow phenomena is a difficult task, we will do some assumptions in order to allow us to concentrate on the fundamental concepts. These assumptions are:

- the illumination model is *local* (see Section 6.5): we allow the emitted photons to perform at most one bounce before hitting the camera;

- the light sources are either point light or directional, that is, they are not area lights: this will simplify the shadow algorithms but will not allow us to generate penumbra regions.

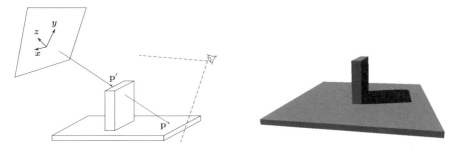

FIGURE 8.2: (Left) A simple scene composed of two parallelepipeds is illuminated by a directional light source. (Right) a rendering with the setup.

8.2 Shadow Mapping

Shadow mapping is a straightforward technique: perform the rendering of the scene and, for each fragment produced, test if the corresponding 3D point is in shadow or not.

The cleverness of shadow mapping resides in how to perform the test. Let us consider the case of directional lights illustrated in Figure 8.2: if we set up a virtual camera with an *orthogonal* projection and with the projectors having the same orientation of our directional light and perform a rendering of the scene from this camera, the result will correspond to the portion of surface visible from the camera (the cyan parts on the central illustration in Figure 8.1). But if a point is visible from this camera, it means that the path from the point to the camera image plane is free of obstacles, and since the camera is modeling the emitter, the visible points are those that are not in shadows. We will refer to this camera as a *light camera*. In this sense we can now restate the definition of being in shadow as follows: *a point* **p** *is in shadow with respect to a light source if it is not visible from the corresponding light camera*. Furthermore, the depth buffer, called *shadow map*, will contain, for each fragment, the distance from the light source of the corresponding point.

After this rendering, if we want to know whether a given point **p** on the scene is lit or not, we can project it to the light camera and compare its distance along the z axis to the value contained in the depth buffer. If it is greater, it means that the point is in shadow because there is another point **p**$'$ along the line from **p** and the light source that generated a smaller depth value than **p** would (see Figure 8.2).

At this point we have all the ingredients for the Shadow Mapping algorithm:

1. [**Shadow Pass**] Draw the scene with the parameters of the light camera and store the depth buffer;

2. [**Lighting Pass**] Draw the scene with the parameters of the viewer's camera and, for each generated fragment, project the corresponding point on the light camera. Then, access the stored depth buffer to test whether the fragment is in shadow from the light source and compute lighting accordingly.

Note that in the practical implementation of this algorithm we cannot use the depth buffer because WebGL does not allow us to bind it for sampling. To overcome this limitation we will use a texture as explained in Section 8.3. Also note that in the shadow pass we do not need to write fragment colors to the color buffer.

8.2.1   Modeling Light Sources

In the introductory example we modelled a directional light source with an orthogonal projection. Here we see more in general how the types of lights described in Section 6.7 are modelled with virtual cameras. What we need from our light camera is that:

- every point that is visible from the light source is seen by the light camera

- the projectors of the light camera are the same as light rays but with opposite direction

Note that the first requirement is actually too much, because we are only interested in the part of the scene seen by the viewer's camera. We will discuss this aspect in more detail in Section 8.4; here we fulfill the first requirement by setting the view volume such that the light camera will include the whole scene.

8.2.1.1   Directional Light

This is the easiest case that we used in the first example. Let d be a unitary vector indicating the direction of the light rays. Set $-d$ as z axis, compute the other two axes as shown in Section 4.5.1.1 and set the center of the scene's bounding box as origin (see Figure 8.3). Set an orthogonal projection so that the viewing volume is a box centered at the origin (please recall that the projection is expressed in view space, so "the origin" is the origin of the light camera frame) and with sides equal to the diagonal of the bounding box, so that we are guaranteed the bounding box of the scene (and hence the scene) is inside the view volume.

8.2.1.2   Point Light

A point light source is only identified by its position, let us call it **c**, from which light rays propagate in every direction. In this case we do the same as we did for adding real on-the-fly reflections in Section 7.7.4.1, that is, we use

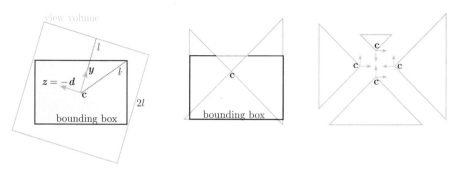

FIGURE 8.3: (Left) Light camera for directional light. (Right) Light camera for point light.

six cameras centered on **c** and oriented along the main axes (both in positive and negative directions). Like we did for the directional light, we could set the far plane to l, but we can do better and compute, for each of the six directions, the distance from the boundary of the bounding box and set the far plane to that distance, as shown in Figure 8.3 (Right). In this manner we will have a tighter enclosure of the bounding box in the viewing volumes and hence more precise depth values (see Section 5.2.4).

8.2.1.3 Spotlights

A spotlight source is defined as $L = (\mathbf{c}, \boldsymbol{d}, \beta, f)$, where **c** is its position in space, $\boldsymbol{d}$ the spot direction, β the aperture angle and f the intensity fall-off exponent. Here we are only interested in the geometric part so f is ignored. The light rays of a spotlight originate from **c** and propagate towards all the directions described by the cone with apex in **c**, symmetry axis $\boldsymbol{d}$ and angle β. We set the z axis of the light camera's frame as $-\boldsymbol{d}$, compute the other two as shown in Section 4.5.1.1 and set the origin to **c** (see Figure 8.4). The projection is in perspective but finding the parameters is slightly more involved.

Let us start with the distance of far plane far. We can set it to the maximum among projections of the vertices of the bounding box on direction $\boldsymbol{d}$ as shown in Figure 8.4 (Left). Now that we have far we can compute the base of the smallest pyramidal frustum containing the cone as:

$$b = 2 \arctan \beta \; far$$

and scale it down to obtain the size of the viewing plane (that is, at the *near* distance)

$$b' = b \, \frac{near}{far}$$

and therefore $left = bottom = -b'/2$ and $top = right = b'/2$. So we computed the smallest trunk of the pyramid containing the cone, not the cone itself. The

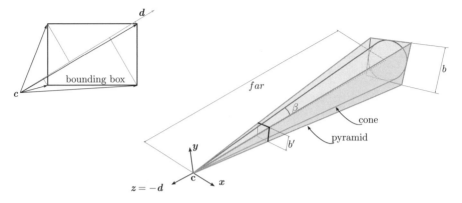

FIGURE 8.4: Light camera for a spotlight.

last part is done in image space: during the shadow pass, we discard all the fragments that are farther away from the image center than $b'/2$.

8.3   Upgrade Your Client: Add Shadows

We will now add to the objects of our scene the ability to cast shadows generated by the sun, which is well modelled as a directional light camera. The first thing to do is to prepare all the necessary graphics resources to perform a render-to-texture operation that will fill our shadow map. As mentioned before, in WebGL we cannot take the depth buffer and bind it as a texture, so what we do is create a framebuffer object that will be used as a target for generating the shadow map in the shadow pass. Ideally, the framebuffer should only consist of a texture that will act as the depth buffer, and that will eventually be accessed in the lighting pass.

Unfortunately, textures with adequate pixel format are not directly exposed from the core WebGL specifications, unless you use extensions.[1] More specifically, a single channel of a color texture is only at most 8 bits while we are commonly using 24 bits for the depth values. In the next subsection we will show how to exploit standard 8 bits per channel, RGBA textures to encode 24 bits depth value.

Listings 8.1 and 8.2 show the code for vertex and fragment shader of the shadow pass, respectively. This is the most basic rendering from the light camera that we do for the sole purpose of producing the depth buffer. Note

---

[1]Probably they will be included in the specification very shortly, but this trick we are going to show is worth knowing anyway.

that the depth buffer is still there; we are just making a copy of it into a texture that will be our shadow map. Let us see the detail of how this is done.

8.3.1 Encoding the Depth Value in an RGBA Texture

We recall that the transformation from NDC space to window space is set with the viewport transformation matrix (gl.viewport(cornerX,cornerY,width, height)) that maps (x, y) from $[(-1, -1), (1, 1)]$ to $[(0, 0), (w, h)]$ and with gl.depthRange(nearval,farval) that maps z from $[-1, 1]$ to $[nearval, farval]$. We assume that nearval and farval are set to the default values, 0 and 1, respectively, and explain how to encode a value in the interval $[0, 1]$ to a four-channel texture. Note that otherwise we can simply encode $z' = \frac{z - nearval}{farval - nearval}$.

So let d = gl_FragCoord.z (gl_FragCoord is a GLSL built-in variable that contains the coordinates of the fragment in window space) be the floating point value to encode in a four-channel texture with eight bits (the number of channels and bits may vary, this is just the most common setup). The idea is that we treat the four channels as the coefficients of a number between 0 and 1 in base B, that is, we want to express d as:

$$d = a_0 \frac{1}{B} + a_1 \frac{1}{B^2} + a_2 \frac{1}{B^3} + a_3 \frac{1}{B^4} \tag{8.1}$$

Let us start with the more intuitive case where $B = 10$, so each channel may store an integer number between 0 and 9, and let us make the practical example where $d = 0.987654$. In this case we would have $a_0 = 9$, $a_1 = 8$, $a_2 = 7$ and $a_3 = 6$:

$$\begin{aligned} d &= 9\tfrac{1}{10} &+& \quad 8\tfrac{1}{10^2} &+& \quad 7\tfrac{1}{10^3} &+& \quad 6\tfrac{1}{10^4} \\ d &= 0.9 &+& \quad 0.08 &+& \quad 0.007 &+& \quad 0.0006 &=& \quad 0.9876 \end{aligned}$$

Obviously, with this simple encoding we are only approximating the value of d but this is more than enough for practical applications. Now what we need is an efficient algorithm to find the coefficients a_i. What we want is simply to take the first decimal digit for a_0, the second for a_1, the third for a_2 and the fourth for a_3. Unfortunately in GLSL we do not have a built-in function for singling out the ith decimal digit of a number, but we have a function frac(x), which returns the fractional part of x, that is, frac(x)=x-floor(x), so we we can write:

$$i^{th} digit(d) = \left(\text{frac}(d10^{i-1}) - \frac{\text{frac}(d10^i)}{10} \right) 10 \tag{8.2}$$

For example, the second digit of 0.9876 is:

$$2^{nd} digit(0.9876) = \left(\text{frac}(\overbrace{0.9876 \cdot 10}^{shift}) - \frac{\text{frac}(\overbrace{0.9876 \cdot 10^2}^{mask})}{10} \right) 10$$

$$= (0.876 - 0.076) \, 10 = 8$$

This is a very simple mechanism to mask out all the digits except the one we want. We first place the dot on the left of the digit $0.9876 \cdot 10 = 9.8765$, then use frac to remove the integer part and remain with 0.8765. Then we mask out the other digits by subtracting 0.0765. The same result can be obtained in many other ways, but in this way we can exploit the parallel execution of component-wise multiplication and subtraction of type vec4.

Now we can comment the implementation of the function pack_depth in Listing 8.2. First of all we have eight bit channels so the value for B is $2^8 = 256$. The vector bit_shift contains the coefficients that multiply d in expression $shift$ of Equation (8.2), while bit_mask contains the ones in expression $mask$. Note that the values in res are in the interval $[0, 1]$, that is, the last multiplication in Equation (8.2) it is not done. The reason is that the conversion beween $[0, 1]$ and $[0, 255]$ is done at the moment of writing the values in the texture. Getting a float value previously encoded in the texture is simply a matter of implementing Equation (8.1) and it is done by the function Unpack in Listing 8.4.

```
84    var vertex_shader = "\
85    uniform   mat4 uShadowMatrix;\n\
86    attribute vec3 aPosition;\n\
87    void main(void)\n\
88    {\n\
89       gl_Position = uShadowMatrix * vec4(aPosition, 1.0);\n\
90    }";
```

LISTING 8.1: Shadow pass vertex shader.

```
92    var fragment_shader = "\
93    precision highp float;\n\
94    float Unpack(vec4 v){\n\
95       return v.x + v.y / (256.0 ) + v.z/( 256.0*256.0)+v.w/ ( ↵
         256.0*256.0*256.0);\n\
96    //   return v.x; \n\
97    }\n\
98    vec4 pack_depth(const in float d)\n\
99    { if(d==1.0) return vec4(1.0,1.0,1.0,1.0);\n\
100      const vec4 bit_shift = vec4( 1.0  , 256.0    ,256.0*256.0   , ↵
         256.0*256.0*256.0 );\n\
101      const vec4 bit_mask  = vec4( 1.0/256.0  , 1.0/256.0 , ↵
         1.0/256.0 , 0.0);\n\
102      vec4 res = fract(d * bit_shift);\n\
103      res -= res.yzwx  * bit_mask;\n\
104      return res;\n\
105    }\n\
106    void main(void)\n\
107    {\n\
108       gl_FragColor = vec4(pack_depth(gl_FragCoord.z));\n\
109    }";
```

LISTING 8.2: Shadow pass fragment shader.

Once we have filled the shadow map with scene depth as seen from the light source in the shadow pass, we are ready to render the scene from the actual observer point of view, and apply lighting and shadowing. This lighting pass is slightly more complicated with respect to a standard lighting one, but it is not difficult to implement, as shown by vertex and fragment shaders code in Listings 8.3 and 8.4, respectively. The vertex shader transforms vertices in the observer clip space as usual, using the combined model, view, and projection matrices (uModelViewProjectionMatrix). Simultaneously, it transforms the same input position *as if it were transforming the vertex in light space*, as it has happened in the shadow pass, and makes it available to the fragment shader with the varying vShadowPosition. The fragment shader is now in charge of completing the transformation pipeline to retrieve the coordinates needed to access the shadow map (uShadowMap) and compare occluder depth (Sz) with the occludee depth (Fz) in the shadow test.

```
150  var vertex_shader = "\
151     uniform   mat4 uModelViewMatrix;                              \n\
152     uniform   mat4 uProjectionMatrix;                             \n\
153     uniform   mat4 uShadowMatrix;                                 \n\
154     attribute vec3 aPosition;                                     \n\
155     attribute vec2 aTextureCoords;                                \n\
156     varying vec2 vTextureCoords;                                  \n\
157     varying   vec4 vShadowPosition;                               \n\
158     void main(void)                                               \n\
159     {                                                             \n\
160        vTextureCoords   = aTextureCoords;                         \n\
161        vec4 position    = vec4(aPosition, 1.0);                   \n\
162        vShadowPosition = uShadowMatrix   * position;              \n\
163        gl_Position      = uProjectionMatrix * uModelViewMatrix\n\
164        * vec4(aPosition, 1.0);                                    \n\
165     }";
```

LISTING 8.3: Lighting pass vertex shader.

```
167  var fragment_shader = "\
168     precision highp float;                                        \n\
169     uniform sampler2D uTexture;                                   \n\
170     uniform sampler2D uShadowMap;                                 \n\
171     varying vec2 vTextureCoords;                                  \n\
172     varying vec4 vShadowPosition;                                 \n\
173     float Unpack(vec4 v){                                         \n\
174        return v.x   + v.y / (256.0) +                             \n\
175        v.z/(256.0*256.0)+v.w/ (256.0*256.0*256.0);                \n\
176     }                                                             \n\
177     bool IsInShadow(){                                            \n\
178        vec3  normShadowPos = vShadowPosition.xyz / ←
              vShadowPosition.w;\n\
179        vec3  shadowPos     = normShadowPos * 0.5 + vec3(0.5);     ←
              \n\
180        float Fz = shadowPos.z;                                    \n\
181        float Sz = Unpack(texture2D(uShadowMap, shadowPos.xy));    ←
              \n\
182        bool  inShadow = (Sz < Fz);                                \n\
183        return inShadow;                                           \n\
184     }                                                             \n\
```

```
185    void main(void){                                           \n\
186        vec4 color = texture2D(uTexture,vTextureCoords);\n\
187        if(IsInShadow())                                       \n\
188            color.xyz*=0.6;                                    \n\
189        gl_FragColor = color;                                  \n\
190    }";
```

LISTING 8.4: Lighting pass fragment shader.

Note that the inclusion of the shadow test only affects the lighting computation, and all other shader machinery is unchanged.

8.4　Shadow Mapping Artifacts and Limitations

When we apply an algorithm to introduce shadow in the scene, we are basically trying to resolve a visibility problem. Even if correct and sound from a theoretical point of view, these techniques must deal with the inaccuracies and limitations of the mathematical tools we use. In particular, with shadow mapping we have to face the inherent issues that arise when using the machine finite arithmetic, and the resolution of the depth map texture.

8.4.1　Limited Numerical Precision: Surface Acne

In the lighting pass, once we calculate the fragment z component F_z in light-space and retrieve the actual value stored in the shadow depth map S_z, we just need to compare them to see if the fragment is in shadow. Note that, theoretically, the two values can relate themselves in only one of two possible ways:

$$F_z > S_z$$
$$F_z = S_z$$

The third comparative relation, $F_z < S_z$, cannot occur because we used depth testing in the shadow pass, hence S_z is the smallest value the whole scene can produce at that particular location of the depth buffer. The real problem comes from the fact that we are using finite arithmetic (that is, floating point numbers) from the beginning of the pipeline to the shadow test. This implies that the calculated numbers incur rounding operations that accumulate over and over, and, in the end, cause two conceptually identical numbers to be different in practice. The visual effect of these numerical inaccuracies is shown in Figure 8.5 and is referred to as *surface acne*: every z component deviates from the exact value by a very small amount, causing the shadow test to behave apparently randomly on fragments that:

1. should be lit but fail the shadow test when compared against themselves

2. are just below lit ones but pass the shadow test.

(a) No Depth Bias   (b) Correct Depth Bias   (c) Too Much Depth Bias

FIGURE 8.5: Shadow map acne. Effect of the depth bias.

A commonly used solution to the acne problem is to give some *advantage* to the fragments being tested, F_z, over the shadow map ones, S_z. This means bringing F_z nearer to light, drastically reducing the misclassification of lit fragments as shadowed ones (false positives). This is accomplished by modifying line 20 in Listing 8.4 with the following:

```
bool  inShadow =  ((Fz - DepthBias) > Sz);
```

By subtracting a small value from F_z (or adding it to S_z), lit fragments are identified more accurately. Note that a *good* value for `DepthBias` that is not dependent on the scene being rendered does not exist, so it must be approximately determined by trial and error.

In this way we have worked against false positives, but unfortunately we have increased the number of false negatives, that is, fragments that are in shadow but are incorrectly classified as lit. Given that this last problem is far less noticeable than the first one, this is often considered an acceptable quality trade-off.

8.4.1.1   Avoid Acne in Closed Objects

We can, however, exploit some properties of the scene being rendered to relieve ourselves of the burden of searching for an adequate amount of depth bias. In particular, if all objects in the scene are *watertight* we can completely abandon the use of depth offseting. The idea is to render in the shadow pass only the *back* faces of the objects, that is, setting the face culling mode to cull away front faces instead of back ones as usual. In this way, we have moved the occurrence of acne phenomena from front faces to back ones:

- the subtle precision issues that caused parts of the surfaces exposed to light to be wrongly considered in shadow are not an issue anymore, because back surfaces are sufficiently distant from front ones, which now do not self-shadow themselves;

- on the other hand, now back surfaces are self shadowing, but this time precision issues will cause light leakage, making them incorrectly classified as lit.

The net effect of this culling reversal in the shadow pass is to eliminate false negatives (lit fragments classified as in shadow) but to introduce false positives (shadowed fragments being lit). However, removing the misclassification in case of false positive back surfaces is easily accomplished: in fact, observing that in a closed object a surface that *points away* from the light source and thus is back-facing from the light point of view is enough to correctly classify that surface as not being lit. To detect this condition, in the light pass we must be able to check if the fragment being shaded represents a part of the surface that is back facing from the point of view of the light: the fragment shader must check if the interpolated surface normal N points in the same hemisphere of the light vector (point and spot lights) or light direction (directional lights) L, that is, if $N \cdot L > 0$.

8.4.2   Limited Shadow Map Resolution: Aliasing

With the shadow mapping technique, what we are doing is approximating the visibility function V with a lookup table, namely, the shadow map: in the shadow pass we construct the table to be used later in the lighting pass. As with all approximation methods based on lookup tables, the quality of the output depends on the table size, which represents its granularity or *resolution*. This means that the shadow test heavily depends on the size of the shadow map texture: the larger the texture, the more accurate the shadow test will be. More formally, the problem that affects the accuracy of the method is the same that causes jagged edges during line or polygon rasterization (see Section 5.3.3), that is, *aliasing*. In particular, this occurs when a texel in the shadow map projects to more than one fragment generated from the observer's point of view: when performing the lighting pass, every F_i will be backprojected to the same location in the shadow map, T, and thus the footprint of T will be larger than one single fragment. In other words we have magnification of the shadow map texture. Figure 8.6 shows a typical example of aliasing for a directional light. Although the problem exists for any type of light source, with perspective light cameras it is more noticeable when the part of the scene rendered is far away from the light camera origin.

8.4.2.1   Percentage Closer Filtering (PCF)

A way to mitigate the sharp boundaries of the footprint of T, that is, *softening* the shadow edges, is to perform not just a single shadow test against the corresponding reprojected texel T, but a series of tests taking samples in

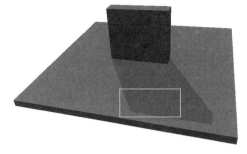

FIGURE 8.6: Aliasing due to the magnification of shadow map.

the neighborhood of T, and then averaging the boolean results and obtaining a value in the interval $[0, 1]$ to use for lighting the fragment. We may compare this technique with the area averaging technique for segment antialiasing discussed in Section 5.3.3 to find out that it follows essentially the same idea.

It is very important to underline that we do not perform a single shadow test with the average depth value of the samples (that would mean to test against a non-existent surface element given by the average depth); instead, we execute the test for every sample and then average the results. This process, known as *Percentage Closer Filtering* (PCF), helps increment the quality of the shadow rendering at the cost of multiple accesses to the depth map.

Softening the shadow edges can also be used to mimic the visual effect of a penumbra (only when the penumbra region is small). At any rate, this should not be confused with a method to calculate the penumbra effect.

Figure 8.7 shows a client using PCF to reduce aliasing artifacts.

8.5 Shadow Volumes

A *shadow volume* is a volume of 3D space where every point is in shadow. Figure 8.8 (Left) illustrates a shadow volume originated by a sphere and a point light. We can define the shadow volume as the volume bounded by the extrusion of the caster's silhouette along the light rays to infinite plus the portion of its surface directly lit (the upper part of the sphere). Since we are not interested in the world outside the scene we consider the intersection with the scene's bounding box. We can use the boundary of the shadow volume to find whether a point is in shadow or not as follows. Suppose we assign a counter, initially set to 0, to each view ray, and follow the ray as it travels through the scene. Every time the ray crosses the boundary *entering* a shadow volume we increment the counter by 1 and every time it crosses the boundary

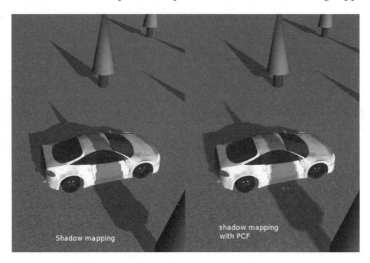

FIGURE 8.7 (SEE COLOR INSERT): PCF shadow mapping. (See client *http://envymycarbook.com/chapter8/0/0.html.*)

exiting a shadow volume we decrement the counter by 1. We know if the ray is entering or exiting by using the dot product between the ray direction and the boundary normal: if it is negative it is entering, otherwise it is exiting. So, when the ray hits a surface, we only need to test if the value of the counter is 0 or greater. If it is 0 the point is **not** in the shadow volume, if it is greater, it is. This may be referred to as the disparity test. Figure 8.8 (Right) shows a more complex example with four spheres with nested and overlapping shadow volumes. As you can verify, the method also works in these situations. The problem with this approach arises when the view point is itself in shadow. The example in Figure 8.9 shows a situation where the view ray hits a surface without having entered any shadow volume, because the ray origin is already inside one. Luckily this problem is solved by counting only the intersections of

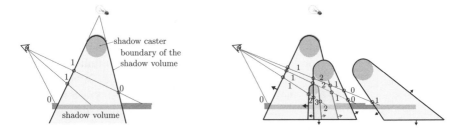

FIGURE 8.8: (Left) Example of shadow volume cast by a sphere. (Right) The shadow volume of multiple objects is the union of their shadow volumes.

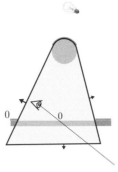

FIGURE 8.9: If the viewer is positioned inside the shadow volume the disparity test fails.

the ray *after* the first hit with a surface: if it exits more times than it enters, the point hit is in shadow, otherwise it is not.

8.5.1 Constructing the Shadow Volumes

As aforementioned, we need to extrude the silhouette edges of the shadow caster along the light rays, so the first step is to find them. Assuming the objects are watertight meshes, we observe that an edge is on the silhouette with respect to a given light camera if and only if one of the two faces sharing the edge is front facing the camera and the other is back facing the camera, as shown in Figure 8.10 (Left).

For each silhouette edge we form a quadrilateral with bases as the silhouette edge itself and its projection on a plane orthogonal to the z direction (and outside the bounding box of the scene). So doing we have swept the silhouette and created a cone-like boundary that we need to cap. The opening nearest

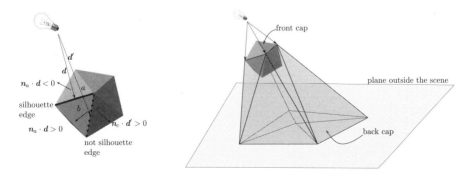

FIGURE 8.10: (Left) Determining silhouette edges. (Right) Extruding silhouette edges and capping.

to the light can be capped by using the front faces of the object, the farthest one by projecting the same faces onto the same plane on which we projected the edges. Note that the projected faces will have to be inverted (that is, two of their indices need to be swapped) so that they are oriented towards the exterior of the bounding volume.

8.5.2   The Algorithm

We described the approach as if we could travel along each single view ray, but in our rasterization pipeline we do not follow rays, we rasterize primitives. Luckily, we can obtain the same result using the stencil buffer (see Section 5.3.1) as follows:

1. Render the scene and compute the shading as if all the fragments were in shadow.

2. Disable writes to the depth and color buffers. Note that from now on the depth buffer will not be changed and it contains the depth of the scene from the viewer's camera.

3. Enable the stencil test.

4. Set the stencil test to increment on depth fail.

5. Enable front-face culling and render the shadow volume. After this step each pixel of the stencil buffer will contain the number of times the corresponding ray has exited the shadow volumes after hitting the surface of some object.

6. Set the stencil test to decrement on depth fail.

7. Enable back-face culling and render the shadow volume. After this step each pixel of the stencil buffer will be decremented by the number of times the corresponding ray has entered the shadow volumes after hitting the surface of some object. Therefore, if the value at the end of the rendering pass is 0 it means the fragment is not in shadow.

8. Set the stencil test to pass on 0, that is, if the number of front face and back face fragments behind the surface hit are equal.

9. Render the scene as completely lit. This is correct because fragments in shadow are masked by the stencil test.

Even if with the shadow volume technique we can achieve pixel-perfect shadow edges and does not suffer from texture magnification aliasing as with shadow maps, it requires an intensive fill rate and it is not prone to easy modifications to soften the resulting shadows' boundaries. Note that the shadow volumes need to be recomputed every time the relative position of light and object casting the shadow change so it may easily become too cumbersome. In fact, the construction of the shadow volume is typically done on the CPU side and it requires great care to avoid inaccuracies due to numerical precision. For example, if the normals of two adjacent triangles are very similar the edge may be misclassified as silhouette edge and so create a "hole" in the shadow volume.

8.6 Self-Exercises

8.6.1 General

1. Describe what kind of shadow you would obtain if the viewer camera and the light camera coincide or if they coincide but the z axes of the view frame are the opposite of each other.

2. We know that the approximation errors of shadow mapping are due to numerical precision and texture resolution. Explain how reducing the light camera viewing volume would affect those errors.

3. If we have n lights, we need n rendering passes to create the shadow maps, and the fragment shader in the lighting pass will have to make at least n accesses to texture to determine if the fragment is in shadow for some of the lights. This will surely impact on the frame rate. Can we use frustum culling to reduce this cost for: directional light sources, point light sources or spotlights?

4. What happens if we enable mipmapping on the shadow map texture?

5. Suppose we have a scene where all the lights are directional and all the objects casting shadows are spheres. How could the shadow volumes technique benefit from these assumptions?

8.6.2 Client Related

1. **UFO over the race!** Suppose there are a few unidentified flying objects over the race. The objects are disk-shaped, completely flat and with 3 meters radius, and they always stay parallel to the ground. Add the disks to the scene and make them cast shadows by implementing a version of the shadow mapping **without** the shadow map, that is, without performing the shadow pass. *Hint*: Think what problem is solved with the shadow map and why in this case the problem is so simple you do not need the shadow map.

Variation 1: The UFOs are not always parallel to the ground, they can change orientation.

Variation 2: This time the UFOs are not simple disks, they can be of any shape. However, we know that they fly so high they will always be closer to the sun than anything else. Think how to optimize the cast shadows with shadow mapping, reducing the texture for the depth value and simplifying the shader. *Hint*: How many bits would be enough to store the depth in the shadow map?

2. Place a 2×2 meter glass panel near a building. On this panel map a texture with an RGBA image where the value for the α channel is either 0 or 1 (you can use the one in http://envymycarbook.com/media/textures/smiley.png). Implement shadow mapping for the car's headlights so that when they illuminate the glass panel, the image on it is mapped on the walls. *Hint:* account for the transparency in the shadow pass.

Chapter 9

Image-Based Impostors

According to the original definition given in Reference [27], "An impostor is an entity that is faster to render than the true object, but that retains the important visual characteristics of the true object." We have already seen an example of impostor technique with the skybox in Section 7.7.3, where a panoramic image of the environment was mapped on a cube to represent the faraway scene. In that case, we are looking at mountains, but, in fact, they are just images.

In this chapter we will describe some *image-based* impostors, which are impostors made of very simple geometry. Images arranged in a way to represent a certain 3D object should be rendered in such a way as to maximize the impression that they look like the geometric representation of the object. The geometry of the imposter is not necessarily related to the geometry of the object but it is the medium to obtain the final rendered image.

Consider the rendering of a tree. A tree has a very intricate geometric description (think about modelling all the branches and the leaves) but most of the time we are not so close to a tree so as to tell one leaf from another, so we can put a rectangle with the picture of a tree mapped onto it, and orient the rectangle towards the point of view, so as to minimize the perception of depth inconsistencies. In this chapter we will describe some simple techniques that are both useful and interesting from a didactic point of view. We will see that these techniques are sufficient to improve considerably the photorealistic look of our client with a little implementation effort.

The Image Based Impostors are a subset of the *Image Based Rendering* techniques, usually shortened to *IBR*. While the impostors are an alternative representation of some specific part of the scene, IBR are in general all the techniques that use digital images to produce a final photorealistic synthetic image. Since a high number of IBR techniques exists, different categorizations have been developed during the last few years to try to better formalize the various algorithms and assess the differences between them well. One of the most interesting categorizations, which is simple and effective, is the so-called *IBR continuum* proposed by Lengyel [23]. This categorization divides the rendering techniques according to the amount of geometry used to achieve the rendering of the *impostor* (see Figure 9.1).

It is important to underline that the definition of impostor also includes pure geometric approximation of the original object, while here we focus only on image-based approximations. According to the IBR continuum, we can

FIGURE 9.1: A categorization of image-based rendering techniques: the *IBR continuum*.

distinguish between techniques that employ a high number of images and no geometric information at all to techniques that use some auxiliary geometry (usually very simple) in conjunction with the images to obtain a final convincing rendering, and techniques that replace in some way a complex geometry with a simpler one plus a set of images. In the following we present some simple but effective techniques starting from the ones that employ no/simple geometry to the ones that rely on more complex geometry to work.

9.1   Sprites

A *sprite* is a two-dimensional image or animation inserted in a scene typically used to show the action of a character. Figure 9.2 shows sprites from the well known video game Pac-Man®. On the right part of the image is the animation of the Pac-Man. Note that since the sprite is overlaid on the background, pixels that are not part of the drawing are transparent. Knowing what we now know, sprites may look naive and pointless, but they have been a breakthrough in the game industry since Atari® introduced them back in 1977. When the refresh rate did not allow the game to show moving characters, *hardware sprites*, circuitry dedicated to light small squares of pixels in a predetermined sequence on any point of the screen allowed for showing an animation as in an overlay mode, without requiring the redraw of the background. As you may note by looking at one of these old video games, there may be aliasing effects in the transition between the sprite and the background

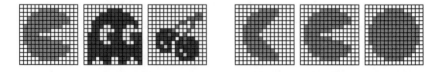

FIGURE 9.2: Examples of sprites. (Left) The main character, the ghost and the cherry of the famous Pac-Man® game. (Right) Animation of the main character.

because sprites are prepared beforehand and were the same on every position of the screen. With 3D games, sprites became less *central* and more a tool for things like *lens flare*, an effect we will see in Section 9.2.4. However, in recent years there has been an outbreak of 2D games on the Web and for mobile devices, and therefore sprites became popular again, although they are now implemented as textures on rectangles and no sprite-specialized hardware is involved.

9.2   Billboarding

We anticipated the example of a billboard in the introduction to this chapter. More formally, a billboard consists of a rectangle with a texture, usually with alpha channel. So, billboards also include sprites, only they live in the 3D scene and may be oriented in order to provide a sense of depth that is not possible to achieve with sprites. Figure 9.3 shows a representation of the billboard we will refer to in this section. We assume the rectangle is specified in an orthogonal frame B. Within this frame, the rectangle is symmetric with respect to the y axis, lies on the XY plane and in the $Y+$ half space.

The way frame B is determined divides the billboard techqniques into the following classes: *static, screen-aligned, axis-aligned* and *spherical*.

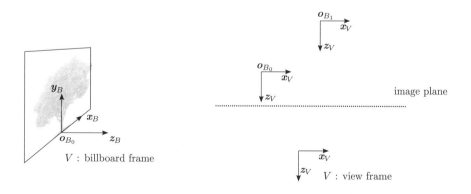

FIGURE 9.3: (Left) Frame of the billboard. (Right) Screen-aligned billboards.

9.2.1   Static Billboards

With static billboards the frame B is simply fixed in world space once and for all. The most straightforward application is to implement real advertisement billboards along the street sides or on the buildings. With some elasticity, the skybox is a form of static billboard, although we have a cube instead of a simple rectangle.

Usually you do not find static billboards mentioned in other textbooks, because if B is static then the billboard is just part of the geometry and that is all. We added this case in the hope of giving a more structured view of billboarding.

9.2.2   Screen-Aligned Billboards

With screen-aligned billboards the axis of frame B and the view reference frame V concide, so the billboard is always parallel to the view plane (hence the name) and only the position (the origin of frame B) moves. These are essentially equivalent to sprites that can been zoomed, and can be used to simulate lens flares, make overlay writing and other gadgets or to replace very faraway geometry.

9.2.3   Upgrade Your Client: Add Fixed-Screen Gadgets

This is going to be a very simple add-on to our client, which will not introduce any new concept or WebGL notion. To keep the code clean, let us define a class OnScreenBillboard as shown in Listing 9.1, which simply contains the rectangle, the texture to map on it and the frame B, and the function to render the billboard.

```
7   function OnScreenBillboard(pos, sx, sy, texture, texcoords) {
8      this.sx = sx;          // scale width
9      this.sy = sy;          // scale height
10     this.pos = pos;        // position
11     this.texture = texture; // texture
12     var quad_geo = [-1, -1, 0, 1, -1, 0, 1, 1, 0, -1, 1, 0];
13     this.billboard_quad = new TexturedQuadrilateral(quad_geo, ↵
          texcoords);
14  };
```

LISTING 9.1: Definition of a billboard. (Code snippet from *http://envymycarbook.com/chapter9/0/0.js*.)

The only interesting thing to point out is how we build the frame B for screen aligned impostors and in which point of our rendering we render them. For things like the speedometer or the image of the drivers's avatar that we always want to overlay the rest, we simply repeat what we did in Section 5.3.4, that is, we express the impostors directly in NDC space and draw it after everything else and after disabling the depth test. We may want fancier effects like to make some writing appear like it is in the middle of the scene, as to say,

FIGURE 9.4 (SEE COLOR INSERT): Client with gadgets added using plane-oriented billboard. (See client *http://envymy carbook.com/chapter9/0/0/html.*)

partially covered by a building or a tree. In this case we may simply express the frame *B* in view space and draw the billboard just after the rest of the scene but before drawing the inside of the cabin.

Listing 9.2 shows the initialization of the speedometer that you can see in Figure 9.4. We create both the analogic version with the needle and a digital one.

```
15  NVMCClient.initializeScreenAlignedBillboard = function (gl) {
16    var textureSpeedometer    = this.createTexture(gl, ↵
          ../../../media/textures/speedometer.png);
17    var textureNeedle         = this.createTexture(gl, ↵
          ../../../media/textures/needle2.png);
18    this.billboardSpeedometer = new OnScreenBillboard([-0.8, ↵
          -0.65], 0.15, 0.15, textureSpeedometer, [0.0, 0.0, 1.0, ↵
          0.0, 1.0, 1.0, 0.0, 1.0]);
19    this.createObjectBuffers(gl, this.billboardSpeedometer.↵
          billboard_quad, false, false, true);
20    this.billboardNeedle      = new OnScreenBillboard([-0.8, ↵
          -0.58], 0.09, 0.09, textureNeedle, [0.0, 0.0, 1.0, 0.0, ↵
          1.0, 1.0, 0.0, 1.0]);
21    this.createObjectBuffers(gl, this.billboardNeedle.↵
          billboard_quad);
22
23    var textureNumbers = this.createTexture(gl, ↵
          ../../../media/textures/numbers.png);
24    this.billboardDigits = [];
25    for (var i = 0; i < 10; ++i) {
```

```
26    this.billboardDigits[i] = new OnScreenBillboard([-0.84, ↩
         -0.27], 0.05, 0.08, textureNumbers, [0.1 * i, 0.0, 0.1 *↩
         i + 0.1, 0.0, 0.1 * i + 0.1, 1.0, 0.1 * i, 1.0]);
27    this.createObjectBuffers(gl, this.billboardDigits[i].↩
         billboard_quad, false, false, true);
28  }
29 };
```

LISTING 9.2: Initialization of billboards. (Code snippet from *http://envymycarbook.com/chapter9/0/0.js.*)

For the analogic version, we use two different billboards, one for the plate and one for the needle. When we render the speedometer, we first render the plate and then the needle, properly rotated on the base of the current car's velocity. For the version with digits, we create 10 billboards, all referring to the same texture textureNumbers, containing the images of the digits $0 \ldots 9$, and making sure that the texture coordinates of the billboard i map to the rectangle of texture containing the number i.

9.2.4   Upgrade Your Client: Adding Lens Flare Effects

When light enters the lens of a camera, light rays are refracted by the lens system to produce the image on the film or CCD. However, when rays come directly from a bright light source, there are also unwanted internal reflection effects that cause artifacts like those shown in Figure 9.5, a real photograph, called *lens flares*. Lens flares typically appear in round or hexagonal shapes principally along a line that goes from the projection of the light source, like the sun in the image, to its opposite position. Another artifact, also visible in the image, is *blooming*, the effect of a very bright source that *propagates*

FIGURE 9.5: Lens flare effect. Light scattered inside the optics of the camera produce flares of light on the final image. Note also the increased diameter of the sun, called *blooming* effect.

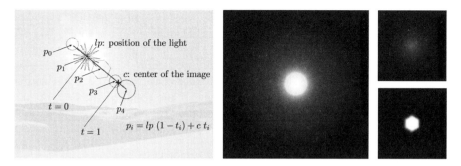

FIGURE 9.6 (SEE COLOR INSERT): (Left) Positions of the lens flare in screen space. (Right) Examples of textures used to simulate the effect.

in the image. These are fairly complex effects to model optically in real time (although there are recent techniques that tackle this problem) but they can be nicely emulated using screen-aligned impostors, and they have been commonly found in video games as far back as the late 1990s. Figure 9.6 illustrates how to determine position and size of the flares. A flare can be done as a *post processing* effect, which means that it happens on the final image after the rendering of the 3D scene has been done. We say that a flare is a *brighter* and *colored* region. Figure 9.6 (Right) shows what is called a *luminance texture*, which is simply a single channel texture. If this image is set as texture on a, say, red rectangle we can modulate the color of the textured polygon by multiplying the alpha value by the fragment color in our fragment shader. Therefore the result would be a shade of red from full red to black. If we draw this textured rectangle enabling blending and set the blending coefficients to gl.ONE, gl.ONE the result will simply be the sum of the color in the framebuffer with the color of the textured polygon, which will cause the red channel to increase by the value of the luminance texture (please note that black is 0). This is it. We can combine more of these impostors and we will obtain any sort of flare we want. For the main flare, that is, the light source, we may use a few star-shaped textures and some round ones. We will have a white patch due to the overlapping between impostors with colors on all the three channels so we also achieve a kind of blooming.

Note that if the light source is not visible we do not want to create lens flares. As we learned in Section 5.2, a point is not visible either because it is outside the view frustum or because it is hidden by something closer to the point of view along the same line of sight.

9.2.4.1 Occlusion Query

Listing 9.3 shows how the test for the visibility of a specific point will be implemented by using the feature called *occlusion query*, which is **not** available in WebGL 1.0 but most likely will be in the near future. With the occlusion query we make the API *count* the number of fragments that pass the depth

test. A query is an object that is created by the function gl.genQueries at line
2. The call gl.beginQuery(gl.SAMPLES_PASSED,idQuery) at line 3 tells WebGL
to start counting and the call gl.endQuery() to stop counting. Then the result
is read by calling gl.getQueryObjectiv(idQuery,gl.QUERY_RESULT,nFragments)
(line 7). In our specific case, we would render a vertex in the light source
position *after* the rest of the scene is drawn. If the result of the query is not
0, it means that the point is visible. Obviously we do not need to actually
render the vertex, so at line 4 we disable the writing on the color buffer.

```
1  isPositionVisible = function(gl,lightPos){
2  gl.genQueries(1,idQuery);
3  gl.beginQuery(GL_SAMPLES_PASSED,idQuery);
4  gl.colorMask(false,false,false,false);
5  this.renderOneVertex(lightPos);
6  gl.endQuery();
7  n_passed = gl.getQueryObjectiv(gl.QUERY_RESULT,idQuery);
8  return(n_passed>0);}
```

LISTING 9.3: Would-be implementation of a function to test if the point at
position lightPos is visible. This function should be called after the scene has
been rendered.

As we do not have occlusion queries in the WebGL 1.0 specification, we
need some other way to test the visibility of a point. We can try to mimic the
occlusion query with the following steps:

1. Render the scene

2. Render a vertex in the light source position, assign an attribute for the
   color with value $(1, 1, 1, 1)$ (that is, white)

3. Use gl.readPixels to read back the pixel correspoing to the vertex projection and check if the color is $(1, 1, 1, 1)$: if so, it means the vertex passed
   the depth test and wrote a white pixel and hence is visible

Unfortunately, this way does not always work. The problem is that maybe
the pixel we test was *already* white *before* the light source was rendered, so
we may have false positives. We will suggest a way around this problem in
the exercise section at the end of the chapter, but as a rule of thumb, it is
alway better to try to avoid readbacks from GPU to CPU memory, because
they are slow and because if you read back data from the GPU it means you
will run some JavaScript code to use it and that is also slow. Here we show a
way that does not require readbacks:

1. Render the scene normally but set the shader to store the depth buffer
   as in the shadow pass of shadow mapping (see Listing 8.2 in Section 8.3)

2. Render the scene normally

3. Bind the depth texture created at step 1 and render the billboards for the
   lens flares. In the fragment shader, test if the z value of the projection of

the light source position is smaller than the value in the depth texture. If it is not, discard the fragment.

Listing 9.4 shows the fragment shader that implements the technique just described. At lines 30-31 the light position is transformed in NDC space and the tests in lines 32-37 check if the position is outside the view frustum, in which case the fragment is discarded. Line 38 reads the depth buffer at the coordinates of the projection of the point light and at line 40 we test if the point is visible or not, in which case the fragment is discarded.

```
20   uniform sampler2D uTexture;          \n\
21   uniform sampler2D uDepth;            \n\
22   precision highp float;               \n\
23   uniform vec4 uColor;                 \n\
24   varying vec2 vTextureCoords;         \n\
25   varying vec4 vLightPosition;         \n\
26   float Unpack(vec4 v){                \n\
27     return v.x   + v.y / (256.0) + v.z/(256.0*256.0)+v.w/ ↩
          (256.0*256.0*256.0);\n\
28   }                                    \n\
29   void main(void)                      \n\
30   { vec3 proj2d = vec3(vLightPosition.x/vLightPosition.w,↩
          vLightPosition.y/vLightPosition.w,vLightPosition.z/↩
          vLightPosition.w);\n\
31     proj2d = proj2d * 0.5 + vec3(0.5);     \n\
32     if(proj2d.x <0.0) discard;             \n\
33     if(proj2d.x >1.0) discard;             \n\
34     if(proj2d.y <0.0) discard;             \n\
35     if(proj2d.y >1.0) discard;             \n\
36     if(vLightPosition.w < 0.0) discard;    \n\
37     if(proj2d.z < -1.0) discard;           \n\
38     vec4 d = texture2D(uDepth, proj2d.xy);\n\
39     if(Unpack(d) < proj2d.z)               \n\
40     discard;                               \n\
41     gl_FragColor = texture2D(uTexture, vTextureCoords); \n\
42   }                                                      \n\
43   ";
```

LISTING 9.4: Fragment shader for lens flare accounting for occlusion of light source. (Code snippet from *http://envymycarbook.com/chapter9/2/ shaders.js.*)

On the Javascript side, Listing 9.5 show the piece of code drawing the lens flare. Please note that the function **drawLensFlares** is called after the scene has been rendered. At lines 65-67 we disable the depth test and enable blending and at line 73 update the position in NDC space of the billboards. Just like for shadow mapping, we bind the texture attachment of the framebuffer where the depth buffer has been stored (**this.shadowMapTextureTarget.texture**) and, of course, the texture of the billboard.

```
64   NVMCClient.drawLensFlares = function (gl,ratio) {
65     gl.disable(gl.DEPTH_TEST);
66     gl.enable(gl.BLEND);
```

```
67    gl.blendFunc(gl.ONE,gl.ONE);
68    gl.useProgram(this.flaresShader);
69    gl.uniformMatrix4fv(this.flaresShader.↩
          uProjectionMatrixLocation, false, this.projectionMatrix);
70    gl.uniformMatrix4fv(this.flaresShader.uModelViewMatrixLocation↩
          , false, this.stack.matrix);
71    gl.uniform4fv(this.flaresShader.uLightPositionLocation, this.↩
          sunpos);
72
73    this.lens_flares.updateFlaresPosition();
74    for(var bi in this.lens_flares.billboards){
75        var bb = this.lens_flares.billboards[bi];
76        gl.activeTexture(gl.TEXTURE0);
77        gl.bindTexture(gl.TEXTURE_2D,this.shadowMapTextureTarget.↩
              texture);
78        gl.uniform1i(this.flaresShader.uDepthLocation,0);
79        gl.activeTexture(gl.TEXTURE1);
80        gl.bindTexture(gl.TEXTURE_2D,this.lens_flares.billboards[↩
              bi].texture);
81        gl.uniform1i(this.flaresShader.uTextureLocation,1);
82        var model2viewMatrix = SglMat4.mul(SglMat4.translation([bb↩
              .pos[0],bb.pos[1],0.0,0.0]),
83          SglMat4.scaling([bb.s,ratio*bb.s,1.0,1.0]));
84        gl.uniformMatrix4fv(this.flaresShader.↩
              uQuadPosMatrixLocation, false, model2viewMatrix);
85        this.drawObject(gl, this.billboard_quad,this.flaresShader)↩
              ;
86    }
87    gl.disable(gl.BLEND);
88    gl.enable(gl.DEPTH_TEST);
89 };
```

LISTING 9.5: Function to draw lens areas. (Code snippet from *http://envymycarbook.com/chapter9/1/1.js.*)

This is just the shadow mapping concept again, in the special case where the light camera and view camera are the same and the test on the depth is always done against the same texel. We can do better than this. We will propose a first improvement in the exercises at the end of the chapter and discuss a major improvement in the exercises of Chapter 10.

Figure 9.7 shows a snapshot of the client implementing lens flares.

9.2.5   Axis-Aligned Billboards

With axis aligned billboarding $\boldsymbol{y}_B = [0,1,0]^T$ and $\boldsymbol{z}_B$ points toward the point of view (see Figure 9.3, Left), that is, toward its projection on the plane $y = \mathbf{o}_{By}$:

$$\boldsymbol{y}_B = [0,1,0]^T$$

$$\boldsymbol{z}'_B = (\mathbf{o}_V - \mathbf{o}_B) \cdot [1,0,1]^T$$

$$\boldsymbol{z}_B = \frac{\boldsymbol{z}'_B}{\|\boldsymbol{z}'_B\|}.$$

$$\boldsymbol{x}_B = \boldsymbol{y}_B \times \boldsymbol{z}_B$$

FIGURE 9.7 (SEE COLOR INSERT): A client with the lens flare are in effect. (See client *http://envymycarbook.com/chapter7/4/4.html*.)

Note that for an orthogonal projection the axes would be the same as for the screen aligned billboards. Axis aligned billboards are typically used for objects with a roughly cylindrical symmetry, which means they look roughly the same from every direction, assuming you are on the same plane (that is, not above or below). This is why trees are the typical objects replaced with axis aligned billboards.

9.2.5.1 Upgrade Your Client: Better Trees

We will now rewrite the function drawTree introduced in Section 4.8.1 to use axis aligned billboards instead of cylinders and cones.

The image we will use as texture for the billboard has an alpha channel and non-zero alpha value on the pixels representing the tree. Figure 9.8 shows the alpha channel remapped to gray scale for illustration purposes. Note that alpha is not only 1 or 0 but it is modulated to reduce the aliasing effect of the discrete representation. The color of the rectangle in this case is unimportant, since we will replace it with the color (and alpha) written in the texture. Just like we did for the windshield in Section 5.3.4, we will use blending to combine the color of the billboard with the color currently in the frame buffer. We recall that in order to handle transparency correctly we need to draw the non-opaque objects back-to-front like in the painter algorithm. Listing 9.6 shows the salient code for rendering the trees, provided that drawTrees is called after having rendered all the rest of the scene. The sorting is done at line 36. Here this.billboard_trees.order is an array of indices where the position i indicates the front-to-back order of tree i. The JavaScript function sort perform the sorting of the array using a comparison function that we define as the comparison between the distance of the billboard to the viewer. Lines 39-47 compute the

FIGURE 9.8: Alpha channel of a texture for showing a tree with a billboard. (See client *http://envymycarbook.com/chapter9/2/2.html.*)

orientation of each billboard as explained above. Writing on the depth buffer is disabled (line 48), blending is set up (lines 49-50) and the billboards are rendered. Note that the order in which they are rendered is determined by the array we sorted (see line 59).

```
33  NVMCClient.drawTrees = function (gl) {
34    var pos = this.cameras[this.currentCamera].position;
35    var billboards = this.billboard_trees.billboards;
36    this.billboard_trees.order.sort(function (a, b) {
37      return SglVec3.length(SglVec3.sub(billboards[b].pos, pos)) -↵
             SglVec3.length(SglVec3.sub(billboards[a].pos, pos))});
38
39    for (var i in billboards) {
40      var z_dir = SglVec3.to4(SglVec3.normalize(SglVec3.sub(pos, ↵
             billboards[i].pos)),0.0);
41      var y_dir = [0.0, 1.0, 0.0,0.0];
42      var x_dir = SglVec3.to4(SglVec3.cross(y_dir, z_dir),0.0);
43      billboards[i].orientation = SglMat4.identity();
44      SglMat4.col$(billboards[i].orientation,0,x_dir);
45      SglMat4.col$(billboards[i].orientation,1,y_dir);
46      SglMat4.col$(billboards[i].orientation,2,z_dir);
47    }
48    gl.depthMask(false);
49    gl.enable(gl.BLEND);
50    gl.blendFunc(gl.ONE, gl.ONE_MINUS_SRC_ALPHA);
51
52    gl.useProgram(this.textureShader);
53    gl.uniformMatrix4fv(this.textureShader.↵
             uProjectionMatrixLocation, false, this.projectionMatrix);
54    gl.activeTexture(gl.TEXTURE0);
55    gl.uniform1i(this.textureShader.uTextureLocation, 0);
```

```
56    gl.bindTexture(gl.TEXTURE_2D, this.billboard_trees.texture);
57
58    for (var i in billboards) {
59        var b = billboards[this.billboard_trees.order[i]];
60        this.stack.push();
61        this.stack.multiply(SglMat4.translation(b.pos));
62        this.stack.multiply(b.orientation);
63        this.stack.multiply(SglMat4.translation([0.0, b.s[1], 0.0]))↵
          ;
64        this.stack.multiply(SglMat4.scaling([b.s[0], b.s[1], 1.0, ↵
          1.0]));
65        gl.uniformMatrix4fv(this.textureShader.↵
            uModelViewMatrixLocation, false, this.stack.matrix);
66        this.drawObject(gl, this.billboard_quad, this.textureShader,↵
            [0.0, 0.0, 0.0, 0.0]);
67        this.stack.pop();
68    }
69    gl.disable(gl.BLEND);
70    gl.depthMask(true);
71  };
```

LISTING 9.6: Rendering axis-aligned billboards with depth sort. (Code snippet from *http://envymycarbook.com/chapter9/2/2.js*.)

As we increase the number of trees, at some point you may wonder if the cost of sorting the billboards in CPU will become the bottleneck. It will. We have two simple options to avoid depth sorting. The first is not to use blending but discard those fragments with a small alpha value instead. So in the fragment shader we would have a test like if (color[4] < 0.5) discard;. The second option for avoiding sorting is: do not sort; just ignore the problem! Both these solutions produce aliasing artifacts but we could find them acceptable to some extent, especially the second one. As a hint, consider that if two fragments with different depths have the same color, it does not matter if they are sorted or not, and since the trees are all copies and they are mostly a shade of green, it makes sense the missing sorting may go unnoticed.

9.2.6 On-the-fly Billboarding

So far we have seen that the image for billboarding is done beforehand, independently from time and view frame. With *on-the-fly billboarding* instead, the image for the billboard is created by rendering the geometry of the object to texture. The advantage of on-the-fly billboarding is better understood with a practical example.

Let us say that our race goes throught a city with many buildings, and we are approaching such a city from a distance. Until we approach the city, its projection on the screen will not change much, so we can render the city on a texture and then forget the geometry and use the texture to build a billboard. As we get closer, the projection of the billboard become bigger and at some point we will start to see magnification (that is, texels bigger than pixels, see Section 7.3.1). Before it happens, we *refresh* the texture re-doing a rendering of the real model and so on. On-the-fly billboarding may help us save a lot of computation but it also requires some criterion to establish when the billboard is *obsolete*.

This technique is often referred to as "impostor" (for example by Reference [1]). We refer to this technique as on-the-fly billboarding, in order to highlight its main characteristic, and keep the original and general meaning of the term *impostor*.

9.2.7   Spherical Billboards

With spherical billboards the axis y_B concides with that of V and the axis z_B points toward the point of view (See Figure 9.9). Note that in general we cannot set $z_B = o_V - o_B$ directly because then z_B and y_B would not be orthogonal, but we can write:

$$y_B = y_V$$
$$z'_B = \frac{o_V - o_B}{\|o_V - o_B\|}$$
$$x_B = y_B \times z'_B$$
$$z_B = x_B \times y_B$$

This is exactly what we showed in Section 4.5.1.1: we built a non-orthogonal frame $[x_B, y_B, z'_B]^T$ and then recomputed z'_B to be orthogonal to the other two axes (see Figure 9.9 (Right)).

This kind of billboard makes sense when the object has a spherical symmetry. You probably cannot think of too many objects of this type except for bushes, balls or planets. However, consider clouds, fog or smoke, entities without a precise, well-defined contour that occupy a portion of volume. These *participating media* can be rendered by combining several spherical bill-

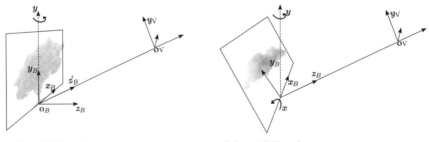

Axis-Aligned Billboard   Spherical Billboard

FIGURE 9.9: (Left) Axis-aligned billboarding. The billboard may only rotate around the y axis of its frame B. (Right) Spherical billboarding: the axis z_B always points to the point of view o_V.

boards, not because they have spherical symmetry but because they have no well-defined shape.

9.2.8   Billboard Cloud

Recently, billboards have been extended to become a more accurate representation of a complex 3D object, preserving at the same time its simplicity in terms of rendering. One of these extensions is the *billboard cloud* [6]. As the name suggests, it consists of a set of freely oriented billboards that form, all together an alternative representation of the object.

The textures for the billboards are obtained by projecting (that is, rasterizing) the original geometry. This can be done by placing a camera so that its view plane coincides with the billboard rectangle, and then rendering the original geometry. The result of the rendering is the texture of the impostor. Note that we need a background alpha initialized to 0. This is an oversimplified explanation since there are several details to ensure all the original geometry is represented and adequately sampled. Figure 9.10 shows an example from the original paper that introduced them and that also proposed a technique to build them automatically from the original textured 3D geometry [6], although they can also be built manually like the one we will use for our client, shown in Figure 9.10.

This kind of impostor has "more 3D" than simple billboards. In fact they can be *direction independent* and therefore are nothing short of alternative representations of the object. In other words, there is no need to rotate the billboards in some way when the camera moves.

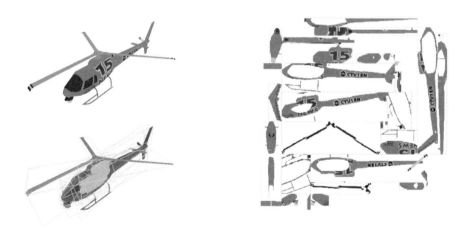

FIGURE 9.10 (SEE COLOR INSERT): Billboard cloud example from the paper [6]. (Courtesy of the authors.) (Left) The original model and a set of polygons resembling it. (Right) The texture resulting from the projections of the original model on the billboards.

FIGURE 9.11 (SEE COLOR INSERT): Snapshot of the client using billboard clouds for the trees. (See client *http://envymycarbook.com/chapter9/3/3.html*.)

9.2.8.1 Upgrade Your Client: Even Better Trees

We do not really have to add anything to render a billboard cloud, since we just encoded it with a textured geometry, just like we did with the car. The only significant news is to remember to discard the fragment with a small alpha as we proposed in Section 9.8 to avoid the sorting. Figure 9.11 shows a snapshot of the corresponding client.

9.3 Ray-Traced Impostors

Since the GPU has become programmable and allowed branching and iterations, a number of new types of impostors techniques has been proposed. Here we will try to show the building blocks of these algorithms and provide a unified view of them.

In Section 7.8.1 we introduced the idea that a texture may contain a displacement value and so encode a height field. Then in Section 7.8.2 we showed how to tweak the normals in order to make it look like the height field was really there, but we know that that solution is limited to front-facing geometry, that is, the height field is not visible on the silhouette. Here we introduce the idea of applying ray tracing in order to show the height map. We recall from Section 1.3.1 that with ray tracing we shoot rays from the point of view towards the scene and find the intersection with the objects. Figure 9.12 shows the rays intersecting the height field encoded in a billboard (shown in 2D for

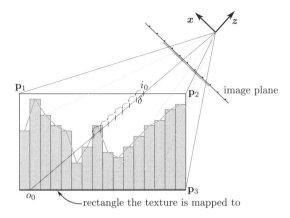

FIGURE 9.12: The way height field is ray traced by the fragment shader.

illustration purposes). We know that the most time-consuming part of ray tracing is finding those intersections, but here we can exploit the rasterization for finding out exactly which rays possibly intersect the height field. The first step is to draw a box whose base is the billboard and whose height is the maximum height value contained in the texture plus a little offset so that the box properly includes the whole height field. Note that the pixels covered by the rasterization of this box are the only ones whose corresponding rays may hit the height field. If we associate to each vertex its position as an attribute, the attribute interpolation will give, for each fragment, the entry point of the corresponding ray (marked with i in the figure). Subtracting the view position to this point and normalizing it we have the direction of the ray. So the fragment shader will have the starting point and direction of the ray and will compute its intersection with the height field encoded in a texture and perform the shading computation. The intersection between the ray and the height map may be found using linear search, that is, starting from the origin of the ray (on the box surface), which is surely outside the height fields, and proceeding by small steps δ or even rasterizing the ray on the texture space. Note that we want to express the ray in the frame of the impostor and therefore the values of the vertex positions $\mathbf{p}_i$ will be specified in this space as well as the viewer position.

Summarizing, we can say there are two "interconnected" building blocks for these techniques:

- what is encoded in the texture, and

- what the ray tracing implementation does to find the intersection and then to shade the intersection point.

Let us consider a few examples. We can use an RGBA texture to include color and store the depth in alpha channel or we can add a second texture to include other material properties, such as diffusion and specular coefficients and the normal.

We can modify the shader to compute the normal by looking at the neighbor texels of the point hit.

We can change the fragment shader to determine if the point hit is in shadow with respect to a certain light. This is simply done by passing the light camera as a vertex attribute and then tracing the ray from the hitting point along the light direction to see if the surface is intersected. Note that if we just do this we only take care of the self shadowing, that is, of the shadows caused by the height field on itself. If we want to consider all of the scene, we should do the two-pass rendering: first render the box from the light source, perform the ray tracing as above and write on a texture which texels are in shadow, and then render from the view.

9.4   Self-Exercises

9.4.1   General

1. Discuss the following statements:

   - If the object to render is completely flat there is no point in creating a billboard.

   - If the object to render is completely flat the billboard is completely equivalent to the original object.

   - The size in pixels of the texture used for a billboard must be higher than or equal to the viewport size.

2. Which are the factors that influence the distance from which we can notice that a billboard has replaced the original geometry?

3. Can we apply mipmapping when rendering a billboard?

9.4.2   Client Related

1. Improve the implementation of the lens flare by changing the viewing window in the first pass so that it is limited to the projection of the light source position.

2. Create a very simple billboard cloud for the car. The billboard cloud is made of five faces of the car's bounding box (all except the bottom one); the textures are found by making one orthogonal rendering for each face. Change the client to use the billboard cloud instead of the textured model when the car is *far enough* from the viewer. *Hint:* For

finding the distance consider the size of the projection of a segment with length equal to the car bounding box's diagonal. To do so proceed as follows:

(a) Consider a segment defined by positions $([0, 0, -z_{car}], [0, diag, -z_{car}])$ (in view space) , where z_{car} is the z coordinate of the car's bounding box center and $diag$ is its diagonal.

(b) Compute the length $diag_{ss}$ of the segment in screen space (in pixels).

(c) Find heuristically a threshold for $diag_{ss}$ to switch from original geometry to billboard cloud.

Note that this is not the same as taking the distance of the car from the viewer because considering also the size of the bounding box we indirectly estimate at which distance texture magnification would happen.

Chapter 10

Advanced Techniques

In this chapter we will cover some advanced techniques to add some fancy effect to our client, mostly using *screen space techiques*. With this term we refer to those techniques that work by rendering the scene, performing some processing on the generated image and then using it to compose the output result.

As practical examples we will see how to simulate the out-of-focus and motion effects of the photo-camera and how to add some more advanced shadowing effects, but, more than that, we will see the basic concepts and tools for implementing these sort of techniques.

10.1   Image Processing

Signal processing is a set of mathematical tools and algorithms aimed at analyzing and processing signals of many natures, such as audio, images and videos. With the advent of digital computers, many signal processing techniques developed in the analog domain have been turned into algorithms and led to the development of the modern digital signal processing. *Digital image processing*, often referred to simply as *image processing*, is about all the algorithms, which, given a digital image in input, elaborate it in order to produce an image with different characteristics or a set of related information/symbols. These processes are oriented to many different goals such as *image enhancement*, for the improvement of the quality of the image (e.g., noise removal, sharpness increase), *image restoration*, to recover some corrupted parts or colors of the input image and *image compression*, to reduce the amount of data of the input image while preserving its appearance, just to name a few.

Image processing was traditionally thought of as a tool for *computer vision*. The goal of computer vision is to analyze an image or a video and extract the information that contributed to its formation, such as the light sources involved, the camera position and orientation, etc. In this sense computer vision can be seen as the inverse of computer graphics. Computer vision is not limited to the extraction of that type of information but it concerns also

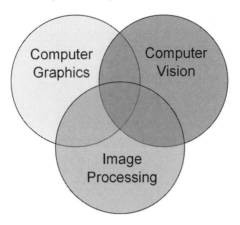

FIGURE 10.1: Computer graphics, computer vision and image processing are often interconnected.

image interpretations, such as the automatic labeling of the object depicted in the image for image search applications.

Since the advent of programmable and parallel GPUs, many image processing algorithms can be executed in a very short time, and therefore image processing also became a tool for computer graphics (and these are the cases we will treat in this chapter). Figure 10.1 schematizes these relationships.

Since the introduction of programmable shading hardware, the modern GPU has become a tool to make computations that are not necessarily related to render a 3D scene. With a somehow drastic statement, we can say that if the first graphics accelerators were circuitry for speeding up some part of the graphics pipeline, modern GPUs are essentially parallel multicore processing units that almost incidentally are used for computer graphics. Of course this is a bit too much of a sentence, because it is true that the architectures are still tailored for graphics computation (the interprocessor communication, the memory model, etc.) but it is a fact that GPUs can be employed to solve big linear systems of equations, to evaluate the Fast Fourier Transform (FFT) of 2D or 3D data, running weather forecasting, evaluating protein alignment/protein folding, computing physical simulations, etc., all those things that were resourced to parallel supercomputers. This way of using the modern GPU is known as *general-purpose computing on GPU (GPGPU)*.

In the following we will focus on some image processing algorithms that can also be used to obtain interesting visual effects on our client. We will see how to blur an image locally, and how to use such operations to obtain a depth-of-field effect, how to extract image edges to obtain some unnatural but interesting-looking effects on our client, and finally how to enhance the details of the rendering by increasing the sharpening of the image generated.

input image I (8×8 pixels)

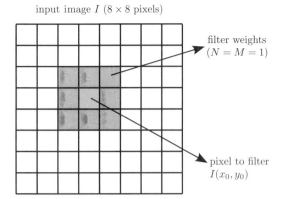

filter weights
($N = M = 1$)

pixel to filter
$I(x_0, y_0)$

FIGURE 10.2: A generic filter of 3×3 kernel size. As we can see, the mask of weights of the filter is centered on the pixel to be filtered.

10.1.1 Blurring

Many image filter operations can be expressed as a weighted summation over a certain region of the input image I. Figure 10.2 shows this process.

Mathematically, the value of the pixel (x_0, y_0) of the filtered image I' can be expressed as:

$$I'(x_0, y_0) = \frac{1}{T} \sum_{x=x_0-N}^{x_0+N} \sum_{y=y_0-M}^{y_0+M} W(x + N - x_0, y + M - y_0) I(x, y) \quad (10.1)$$

where N and M are the radius of the filtering window, $W(x, y)$ is the matrix of weights that defines the filter, and T is the sum of the absolute values of the weights, which acts as a normalization factor. The size of the filtering window defines the support of the filter and it usually called the *filter kernel size*. The total number of pixels involved in the filtering is $(2N+1)(2M+1) = 4NM + 2(N + M) + 1$. We underline that, typically, the window is a square and not a rectangle (that is, $N = M$).

In its simpler form, a blurring operation can be obtained simply by averaging the values of the pixels on the support of the filter. Hence, for example, for $N = M = 2$, the matrix of weights corresponding to this operation is:

$$W(i, j) = \begin{bmatrix} 1 & 1 & 1 & 1 & 1 \\ 1 & 1 & 1 & 1 & 1 \\ 1 & 1 & 1 & 1 & 1 \\ 1 & 1 & 1 & 1 & 1 \\ 1 & 1 & 1 & 1 & 1 \end{bmatrix} \quad (10.2)$$

and T is equal to 25. As we can see, $W(i, j)$ represents a constant weighting function. In this case, Equation (10.1) can be seen as the convolution of the

FIGURE 10.3 (SEE COLOR INSERT): (Left) Original image. (Right) Image blurred with a 9×9 box filter ($N = M = 4$).

image with a box function. This is the reason why this type of blur filter is usually called a *box filter*. Obviously, the blur effect increases as the size of the window increases. In fact, in this way the pixels' values are averaged on a wider support. Figure 10.3 shows an example of applying this filter to an image (the RGB color channels are filtered separately).

The blur obtained by using the box filter can also be obtained with other averaging functions. An alternative option can be to consider the pixels closer to the central pixel (x_0, y_0) more influencing than the ones distant from it. To do so, usually a Gaussian function is employed as a weighting function. A 2D Gaussian is defined as:

$$g(x, y) = \frac{1}{2\pi\sigma} e^{-\frac{(x^2 + y^2)}{2\sigma^2}} \tag{10.3}$$

The support of this function (that is, the domain over which it is defined) is all the $\mathbb{R}^2$ plane, but practically it can be limited considering that when the distance from the origin $\left(\sqrt{(x^2 + y^2)}\right)$ is higher than 3σ, the Gaussian values go very close to zero. So, it is good practice to choose the support of the Gaussian kernel dependent on the value of σ.

By plugging the Gaussian function into Equation (10.1) we obtain the so-called *Gaussian filter*:

$$I'(x, y) = \frac{\sum\limits_{x=x_0-N}^{x_0+N} \sum\limits_{y=y_0-N}^{y=y_0+N} I(x,y) e^{\left(-\frac{(x-x_0)^2 + (y-y_0)^2}{2\sigma}\right)}}{\sum\limits_{x=x_0-N}^{x_0+N} \sum\limits_{y=y_0-N}^{y=y_0+N} e^{\left(-\frac{(x-x_0)^2 + (y-y_0)^2}{2\sigma}\right)}} \tag{10.4}$$

Concerning the kernel size, for what was just stated, it is good practice to set N equal to 3σ or 2σ. For a Gaussian filter, a weighting matrix of 7×7 with

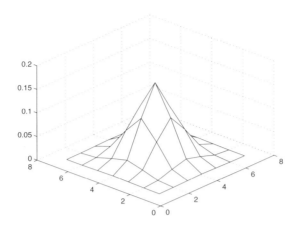

FIGURE 10.4: Weights of a 7×7 Gaussian filter.

$\sigma = 1$ pixels is defined by the following coefficients:

$$W(i,j) = \frac{1}{10000} \begin{bmatrix} 0.2 & 2.4 & 10.7 & 17.7 & 10.7 & 2.4 & 0.2 \\ 2.4 & 29.2 & 130.6 & 215.4 & 130.6 & 29.2 & 2.4 \\ 10.7 & 130.6 & 585.5 & 965.3 & 585.5 & 130.6 & 10.7 \\ 17.7 & 215.4 & 965.3 & 1591.5 & 965.3 & 215.4 & 17.7 \\ 10.7 & 130.6 & 585.5 & 965.3 & 585.5 & 130.6 & 10.7 \\ 2.4 & 29.2 & 130.6 & 215.4 & 130.6 & 29.2 & 2.4 \\ 0.2 & 2.4 & 10.7 & 17.7 & 10.7 & 2.4 & 0.2 \end{bmatrix} \quad (10.5)$$

Note that at the borders of the matrix, where the distance becomes 3σ, the values go quickly to zero. A graphical representation of these weights is shown in Figure 10.4, while an example of an application of this filter is shown in Figure 10.5.

FIGURE 10.5 (SEE COLOR INSERT): (Left) Original image. (Right) Image blurred with a 9×9 Gaussian filter ($\sigma = 1.5$ pixels).

FIGURE 10.6: Out-of-focus example. The scene has been captured such that the car is in focus while the rest of the background is out of focus. The range of depth where the objects framed are in focus is called *depth of field* of the camera. (Courtesy of Francesco Banterle.)

10.1.2   Upgrade Your Client: A Better Photographer with Depth of Field

So far, we have assumed to see the world through an ideal pinhole camera, but a real camera is far from ideal in many senses and one of these is that often we do not see everything *in focus*, that is, with well-defined contours and details. If you try, with a photographic camera, to frame an object very close to the camera, you will note that the background will appear "blurred," that is, *out of focus*. On the contrary, if you try to frame on some far point of the scene, the close objects will appear out of focus. Figure 10.6 shows an example of an out-of-focus background.

The reason why this happens is illustrated in Figure 10.7. The camera lenses make rays leaving at distance d from the lenses to focus on the image plane. Away from this distance, rays leaving from the same point do not meet behind the lenses exactly on the image plane, but they meet closer to the lenses than the image plane (Top) or farther away (Bottom). In both cases the rays coming from the same point in space do not focus on a single point on the image plane but in a circular region, called a *circle of confusion*, causing the image look not in focus. The radius of the circle of confusion grows linearly with the distance of the point from d along the optical axis and its impact on the sharpness of the produced image will be tolerable within a certain range from d. Such a range is called *depth of field*.

In the following we will use blurring to recreate this effect. We indicate with $[z_1, z_2]$ the range of depths from which the 3D objects are in focus. Then, for each z that is not in this range, we add linearly a blurring effect in order to simulate the defocus effect of a real camera. To do this, we express the value of the radius (in pixels) of the circle of confusion, and hence the kernel size of

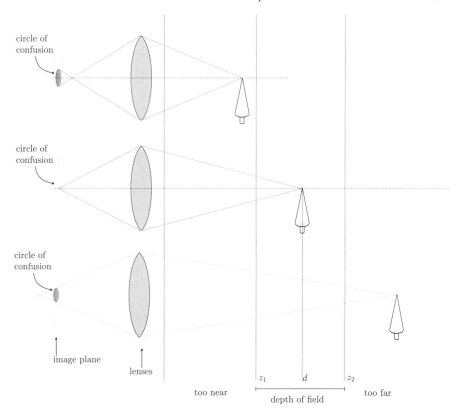

FIGURE 10.7: Depth of field and circle of confusion.

the blurring filter, in the following way:

$$\begin{cases} c = \frac{R_{\max}}{z_1 - near}(z_1 - z) & z < z_1 \\ c = 0 & z_1 \leq z \leq z_2 \\ c = \frac{R_{\max}}{z_1 - near}(z - z_2) & z > z_2 \end{cases} \quad (10.6)$$

The value of c is clamped in the range $[0.0, R_{\max}]$ to prevent increasing the kernel size too much.

10.1.2.1 Fullscreen Quad

Now, we will see a technique that mostly operates in *post processing*: to take the result of the rendering plus some more data and process it to produce the final image. Blurring is the first of several examples of this sort.

The standard way to do this is:

1. Render the scene to a texture.

2. Bind this texture as source.

3. Render a quad covering the screen exactly and with texture coordinates equal to $(0,0), (1,0), (1,1), (0,1)$. Typically this is done by drawing in NDC space and hence the quad has coordinates $(-1,-1,-1)$, $(1,-1,-1), (1,1,-1)$ and $(-1,1,-1)$. This is called the *fullscreen quad*.

By rendering a fullscreen quad we activate a fragment for each pixel and so we have access to all the pixels of the scene rendered at step 1.

Listing 10.1 shows the salient part of the JavaScript code. From line 201 to line 213 we render the scene to store the depth buffer, just like we did in Section 8.3 for shadow mapping. In fact, we reuse the same frame buffer, variables and shader. From lines 215 to 221 we render the scene again, this time to store the color buffer.

In principle we would not need to render the scene twice if we had a *multiple render target*. This functionality, not in the WebGL API at the time of this writing, allows you to output on multiple buffers simultaneously, so that the same shader may write the color on one buffer and some other value on another. The only change in the shader language is that we would have gl_FragColor[i] in the fragment shader, with i the index of the buffer to render to.

Finally, in lines 230-243 we render a full screen quad binding the textures filled in the two previous renderings and enabling the **depthOfFieldShader** that we will comment on next. Note that at line 233 we specify the depth of field with two values that we mean to be in meters. This is an important bit because we must take care of the reference systems when we read the depth from the texture, where we will read the values in the interval $[0, 1]$ and compare them with values in meters. More specifically, we know that the value of z_V (that is, z in view space) will be transformed by the perspective projection as:

$$
z_{NDC} = \overbrace{\frac{f+n}{f-n}}^{A} + \overbrace{2\frac{fn}{f-n}}^{B}\frac{1}{z_V}
$$

(check multiplying $[x, y, z, 1]^T$ by the perspective matrix P_{persp} in 4.10) and then to $[0, 1]$ as:

$$
z_{01} = (z_{NDC} + 1)/2
$$

In the fragment shader, shown in Listing 10.2, we read the depth values from the texture and they are in the interval $[0, 1]$ (see line 40): we have to invert the transformation to express them in view space and test them with the depth of field interval (lines 41-42). This is why we pass to the shader the values A and B, because they are the entries of the perspective matrix necessary to invert the transformation from $[0, 1]$ to view space.

You may wonder why we don't make it simpler and pass the depth of field interval directly in $[0, 1]$. We could, but if we want to be able to express our interval in meters, which is something the user expects, we should at least transform from view space to $[0, 1]$ in the JavaScript side. Consider the function **ComputeRadiusCoC**. As it is, the radius would not increase linearly with the distance from the interval extremes but with the distance of their reciprocals (you can check this by plugging the above equations into the functions). This does not mean it would not work, but we would not have implemented what is described by Equation (10.6).

```
200    if (this.depth_of_field_enabled) {
201        gl.bindFramebuffer(gl.FRAMEBUFFER, this.←
               shadowMapTextureTarget.framebuffer);
202
203        this.shadowMatrix = SglMat4.mul(this.projectionMatrix, this.←
               stack.matrix);
204        this.stack.push();
205        this.stack.load(this.shadowMatrix);
206
207        gl.clearColor(1.0, 1.0, 1.0, 1.0);
208        gl.clear(gl.COLOR_BUFFER_BIT | gl.DEPTH_BUFFER_BIT);
209        gl.viewport(0, 0, this.shadowMapTextureTarget.framebuffer.←
               width, this.shadowMapTextureTarget.framebuffer.height);
210        gl.useProgram(this.shadowMapCreateShader);
211        gl.uniformMatrix4fv(this.shadowMapCreateShader.←
               uShadowMatrixLocation, false, this.stack.matrix);
212        this.drawDepthOnly(gl);
213        this.stack.pop();
214
215        gl.bindFramebuffer(gl.FRAMEBUFFER, this.←
               firstPassTextureTarget.framebuffer);
216        gl.clearColor(1.0, 1.0, 1.0, 1.0);
217        gl.clear(gl.COLOR_BUFFER_BIT | gl.DEPTH_BUFFER_BIT);
218        gl.viewport(0, 0, this.firstPassTextureTarget.framebuffer.←
               width, this.firstPassTextureTarget.framebuffer.height);
219        this.drawSkyBox(gl);
220        this.drawEverything(gl, false, this.firstPassTextureTarget.←
               framebuffer);
221        gl.bindFramebuffer(gl.FRAMEBUFFER, null);
222
223        gl.viewport(0, 0, width, height);
224        gl.disable(gl.DEPTH_TEST);
225        gl.activeTexture(gl.TEXTURE0);
226        gl.bindTexture(gl.TEXTURE_2D, this.firstPassTextureTarget.←
               texture);
227        gl.activeTexture(gl.TEXTURE1);
228        gl.bindTexture(gl.TEXTURE_2D, this.shadowMapTextureTarget.←
               texture);
229
230        gl.useProgram(this.depthOfFieldShader);
231        gl.uniform1i(this.depthOfFieldShader.uTextureLocation, 0);
232        gl.uniform1i(this.depthOfFieldShader.uDepthTextureLocation, ←
               1);
233        var dof = [10.0, 13.0];
234        var A = (far + near) / (far - near);
235        var B = 2 * far * near / (far - near);
236        gl.uniform2fv(this.depthOfFieldShader.uDofLocation, dof);
237        gl.uniform1f(this.depthOfFieldShader.uALocation, A);
238        gl.uniform1f(this.depthOfFieldShader.uBLocation, B);
239
240        var pxs = [1.0 / this.firstPassTextureTarget.framebuffer.←
```

```
              width, 1.0 / this.firstPassTextureTarget.framebuffer.←
              width];
241     gl.uniform2fv(this.depthOfFieldShader.uPxsLocation, pxs);
242
243     this.drawObject(gl, this.quad, this.depthOfFieldShader);
244     gl.enable(gl.DEPTH_TEST);
245   }
```

LISTING 10.1: Depth of field implementation (JavaScript side). (Code snippet from *http://envymycarbook.com/chapter10/0/0.js.*)

```
14     precision highp float;
15     const int MAXRADIUS ="+ constMAXRADIUS+";
16     uniform sampler2D uDepthTexture;
17     uniform sampler2D uTexture;
18     uniform float uA,uB;
19     uniform float near;
20     uniform vec2 uDof;
21     uniform vec2 uPxs;
22     varying vec2 vTexCoord;
23     float Unpack(vec4 v){
24        return v.x   + v.y / (256.0) +
25          v.z/(256.0*256.0)+v.w/ (256.0*256.0*256.0);
26     }
27     float ComputeRadiusCoC( float z ) {
28        float c = 0.0;
29        // circle of confusion is computed here
30        if ( z < uDof[0] )
31          c = float(MAXRADIUS)/(uDof[0]-near)*(uDof[0]-z);
32        if ( z > uDof[1] )
33          c = float(MAXRADIUS)/(uDof[0]-near)*(z-uDof[1]);
34        // clamp c between 1.0 and 7.0 pixels of radius
35        if ( int(c) > MAXRADIUS)
36          return float(MAXRADIUS);
37        else
38          return c;
39     }
40     void main(void)
41     {
42        float z_01 =Unpack(texture2D(uDepthTexture,vTexCoord));
43        float z_NDC = z_01*2.0-1.0;
44        float z_V   = -uB / (z_NDC-uA);
45        int radius = int(ComputeRadiusCoC(z_V));
46        vec4 accum_color = vec4(0.0 ,0.0 ,0.0 ,0.0) ;
47
48        for ( int i = -MAXRADIUS ; i <= MAXRADIUS ; ++i )
49          for ( int j = -MAXRADIUS ; j <= MAXRADIUS ; ++j )
50            if (    (i >= -radius ) && ( i <= radius )
51              && (j >= -radius ) && ( j <= radius ) )
52              accum_color += texture2D( uTexture ,
53                  vec2( vTexCoord.x +float(i) *uPxs[0],
54                        vTexCoord.y+float(j) *uPxs[1]));
55        accum_color /= vec4((radius*2+1)*(radius*2+1));
56        vec4 color = accum_color;
57     //   if(radius > 1) color+=vec4(1,0,0,1);
```

58   `gl_FragColor = color;`

LISTING 10.2: Depth of field implementation (shader side). (Code snippet from *http://envymycarbook.com/code/chapter10/0/shaders.js.*)

Note that we cannot directly use the value of the radius computed at line 45 in the loop of the filter, because the shader compiler must be able to unroll the loop. Therefore, we place the maximum kernel size as cycle limits and test the fragment distance from the kernel center to zero contribution outside the kernel size.

The same operations can be done more efficiently by splitting the computation of the blurred image in a first "horizontal step," where we sum the values only along the x axis, and a "vertical step" where we sum on the result of the previous step vertically. The final result will be the same, but the rendering will be faster because now we apply N + M operations per pixel rather than N × M. Figure 10.8 shows a snapshot from the photographer view with depth of field. As it is, this solution can create some artifacts, the most noticeable of which are due to the depth discontinuities. Suppose we have one object close to the camera and that it is in focus. What happens around the silhouette of the object is that the parts of the object out of focus are influenced by those of the background that are in focus, with the final effect that the border between the two will always look a bit fuzzy. These problems may be partially overcome by not counting pixels whose depth value is too different from the one of the pixel being considered. Another improvement may be to sample more than a single value of the depth map and blur the color accordingly.

FIGURE 10.8: Snapshot of the depth of field client. (See client *http://envymycarbook.com/chapter10/0/0.html.*)

An alternative approach consists of rendering the scene multiple times from positions in a circle around the current point of view and setting the frustum so that it always passes through the same rectangle at the focus distance d. The images so generated are accumulated and the final image is obtained by averaging them. In this manner, everything at distance d will project exactly on the same point on the image plane and the rest will be progressively blurred depending on its distance.

10.1.3   Edge Detection

Many algorithms have been developed to extract salient features from a given image. One of the most important classes of such algorithms is the one that attempts to identify and extract the edges of an image. Here, we describe some basic filters to do this task, in particular the *Prewitt* and the *Sobel* filter. Both these filters are based on the numerical approximation of the first order horizontal and vertical derivatives of the image.

First of all, let say something about the numerical approximations of first order derivatives. It is known that the first order derivative of a real function $f(x)$ is calculated as:

$$\frac{df(x)}{dx} = \lim_{\delta \to 0} \frac{f(x+\delta) - f(x)}{\delta} \tag{10.7}$$

This computation can be approximated as:

$$\frac{df(x)}{dx} = \frac{f(x+\delta) - f(x)}{\delta} \tag{10.8}$$

for some small value of δ. In the discrete case, Equation (10.8) can be rewritten as:

$$\Delta_x(x_i) = f(x_{i+1}) - f(x_i) \tag{10.9}$$

where $f(x_i)$ is the discretized function, that is, the i-th sample of the function $f(.)$. This numerical approximation of the derivative is called *forward differences*. Alternative definitions are the *backward differences*:

$$\Delta_x(x_i) = f(x_i) - f(x_{i-1}) \tag{10.10}$$

and the *central differences*:

$$\Delta_x(x_i) = \frac{f(x_{i+1}) - f(x_{i-1})}{2} \tag{10.11}$$

Considering a digital image, which is defined on a 2D discrete domain, the image gradient is the vector $\Delta = (\Delta_x, \Delta_y)$ where Δ_x is the horizontal derivative and Δ_y is the vertical derivative. Using the central differences the image gradient can be computed as:

$$\Delta(x,y) = \begin{pmatrix} \Delta_x(x,y) \\ \Delta_y(x,y) \end{pmatrix} = \begin{pmatrix} I(x+1,y) - I(x-1,y) \\ I(x,y-1) - I(x,y+1) \end{pmatrix} \tag{10.12}$$

In this case Δ_x and Δ_y represents the discrete version of the partial derivatives $\partial I(x,y)/\partial x$ and $\partial I(x,y)/\partial y$, respectively.

At this point, it is easy to define the "strength" of an edge as the magnitude of the gradient:

$$\mathcal{E}(x,y) = \sqrt{\Delta_x^2(x,y) + \Delta_y^2(x,y)} \ . \tag{10.13}$$

We indicate with $\mathcal{E}$ the resulting extracted edge image.

So, taking into account Equation (10.13), the edge response at pixel (x_0, y_0) given an input image $I(x,y)$ can be easily written in matrix form as:

$$I_h(x_0, y_0) = \sum_{x=x_0-1}^{x_0+1} \sum_{y=y_0-1}^{y_0+1} W_{\Delta_x}(x+1-x_0, y+1-y_0)I(x,y)$$

$$I_v(x_0, y_0) = \sum_{x=x_0-1}^{x_0+1} \sum_{y=y_0-1}^{y_0+1} W_{\Delta_y}(x+1-x_0, y+1-y_0)I(x,y)$$

$$\mathcal{E}(x_0, y_0) = \sqrt{I_h^2(x_0, y_0) + I_v^2(x_0, y_0)} \tag{10.14}$$

where $I_h(x,y)$ is the image of the horizontal derivative, $I_v(x,y)$ is the image of the vertical derivative, and $W_{\Delta_x}(i,j)$ and $W_{\Delta_y}(i,j)$ are the matrix of weights defined as:

$$W_{\Delta_x} = \begin{bmatrix} 0 & 0 & 0 \\ -1 & 0 & 1 \\ 0 & 0 & 0 \end{bmatrix} \qquad W_{\Delta_y} = \begin{bmatrix} 0 & 1 & 0 \\ 0 & 0 & 0 \\ 0 & -1 & 0 \end{bmatrix} \tag{10.15}$$

The filter (10.14) is the most basic filter to extract the edge based on first order derivatives.

Two numerical approximations of the first order derivatives that are more accurate than the one just described are provided, respectively, by exploiting the Prewitt operator:

$$W_{\Delta_x} = \begin{bmatrix} -1 & 0 & 1 \\ -1 & 0 & 1 \\ -1 & 0 & 1 \end{bmatrix} \qquad W_{\Delta_y} = \begin{bmatrix} 1 & 1 & 1 \\ 0 & 0 & 0 \\ -1 & -1 & -1 \end{bmatrix} \tag{10.16}$$

and the Sobel operator:

$$W_{\Delta_x} = \begin{bmatrix} 1 & 0 & -1 \\ 2 & 0 & -2 \\ 1 & 0 & -1 \end{bmatrix} \qquad W_{\Delta_y} = \begin{bmatrix} -1 & -2 & -1 \\ 0 & 0 & 0 \\ 1 & 2 & 1 \end{bmatrix} \tag{10.17}$$

By replacing the matrix of weights in Equation (10.14) we obtain a more accurate result in edge computation. Notice that these kernels have weights similar to the ones of the matrix obtained with the central difference approximation. Figure 10.9 shows the results obtain with these two edge detectors. As in the other filtering examples, the filters are applied separately to each image color channel.

FIGURE 10.9 (SEE COLOR INSERT): (Left) Original image. (Center) Prewitt filter. (Right) Sobel filter.

10.1.4   Upgrade Your Client: Toon Shading

With *toon shading*, or *cel shading*, we refer to a rendering technique capable of making the look of our client similar to the look of a cartoon. This type of rendering has been widely used in videogames (*The Legend of Zelda–The Wind Waker* by Nintendo, to mention one). Toon shading belongs to the so-called *Non-Photorealistic Rendering* (NPR) techniques. NPR aims at producing images that are not necessarily photorealistic in favor of more artistic and illustrative styles. The term NPR is debated, mainly because it tries to define something by saying what it is not and also becase it sounds like a diminishing definition: since in CG we aim at photorealism, then an NPR technique is simply something that does not work?

Most often, NPR techniques try to make a rendering look like it was hand-drawn. In our client, we will do this by combining edge detection and color quantization. More specifically, we will make our toon shading effect by using two simple tricks.

The first trick is to draw black edges on the contour of the objects. Like for the depth-of-field client, we render the scene and then make a fullscreen quad to process the result. Then we calculate the edges in screen-space by using the theory shown in Section 10.1.3 and produce an edge map with the filter described by Equation (10.14) and the kernel of the Sobel operator. The edge map is a single-channel image where the intensity value indicates the "edgeness" of the pixel. By assuming that edges we are interested in drawing are the "strong" ones, we define a threshold over which the pixel is considered to be on an edge and make so that that pixel is drawn in black on the final image. In this code example we use a fixed threshold but an adaptive one may provide better results. The code in Listing 10.3 shows the fragment shader to extract the edge map. colorSample is the texture containing the scene rendered and applied to the fullscreen quad. Note that the strength of the edge is summarized as the mean of the strength of the edge of each color channel.

```
37  float  edgeStrength(){                                          \n\
38    vec2 tc = vTextureCoords;                                     \n\
39    vec4 deltax = texture2D(uTexture,tc+vec2(-uPxs.x,uPxs.y))  \n\
40      +texture2D(uTexture,tc+vec2(-uPxs.x,0.0))*2.0            \n\
41      +texture2D(uTexture,tc+vec2(-uPxs.x,-uPxs.y))            \n\
```

```
42      -texture2D(uTexture,tc+vec2(+uPxs.x,+uPxs.y))            \n\
43      -texture2D(uTexture,tc+vec2(+uPxs.x,0.0))*2.0            \n\
44      -texture2D(uTexture,tc+vec2(+uPxs.x,-uPxs.y));           \n\
45   \n\
46   vec4 deltay = -texture2D(uTexture,tc+vec2(-uPxs.x,uPxs.y))\n\
47      -texture2D(uTexture,tc+vec2(0.0,uPxs.y))*2.0            \n\
48      -texture2D(uTexture,tc+vec2(+uPxs.x,uPxs.y))            \n\
49      +texture2D(uTexture,tc+vec2(-uPxs.x,-uPxs.y))           \n\
50      +texture2D(uTexture,tc+vec2(0.0,-uPxs.y))*2.0           \n\
51      +texture2D(uTexture,tc+vec2(+uPxs.x,-uPxs.y));          \n\
52                                                              \n\
53   float edgeR =sqrt(deltax.x*deltax.x + deltay.x*deltay.x); \n\
54   float edgeG =sqrt(deltax.y*deltax.y + deltay.y*deltay.y); \n\
55   float edgeB =sqrt(deltax.z*deltax.z + deltay.z*deltay.z); \n\
56   return (edgeR + edgeG + edgeB) / 3.0;}                    \n\
```

LISTING 10.3: Code to compute the edge strength. (Code snippet from *http://envymycarbook.com/chapter10/1/shaders.js.*)

The second trick is to quantize the shading values in order to simulate the use of a limited set of colors in the scene. In particular, here we use a simple diffuse model with three levels of quantization of the colors: dark, normal and light. In this way, a green object will result in some parts colored with dark green, in other parts colored in green and in other parts colored in light green. The code that implements this simple quantized lighting model is given in Listing 10.4.

```
23   vec4 colorQuantization( vec4 color ){              \n\
24   float intensity =   (color.x+color.y+color.z)/3.0; \n\
25   // normal                                          \n\
26   float brightness = 0.7;                            \n\
27   // dark                                            \n\
28   if ( intensity < 0.3)                              \n\
29   brightness = 0.3;                                  \n\
30   // light                                           \n\
31   if ( intensity > 0.8)                              \n\
32   brightness = 0.9;                                  \n\
33   color.xyz = color.xyz * brightness / intensity;    \n\
34   return color ; }                                   \n\
```

LISTING 10.4: A simple quantized-diffuse model. (Code snippet from *http://envymycarbook.com/chapter10/1/shaders.js.*)

We follow the same scheme as for the depth-of-field client, but this time we need to produce only the color buffer and then we can render the full screen quad. The steps are the following:

1. Render the scene to produce the color buffer

2. Bind the texture produced at step 1 and render the full screen quad. For each fragment, if it is on a strong edge output black, otherwise output the color quantized version of the diffuse lighting (see Listing 10.5).

Figure 10.10 shows the final result.

FIGURE 10.10 (SEE COLOR INSERT): Toon shading client. (See client *http://envymycarbook.com/chapter10/1/1.html.*)

```
57    void main(void)                         \n\
58    {                                       \n\
59      vec4 color;                           \n\
60      float es = edgeStrength();            \n\
61        if(es > 0.15)                       \n\
62        color = vec4(0.0,0.0,0.0,1.0);\n\
63      else{                                 \n\
64        color = texture2D(uTexture, vTextureCoords);  \n\
65        color = colorQuantization( color );           \n\
66      }                                     \n\
67      gl_FragColor = color;                 \n\
68    } ";
```

LISTING 10.5: Fragment shader for the second pass. (Code snippet from *http://envymycarbook.com/chapter10/1/shaders.js.*)

There are many approaches to obtain more sophisticated toon shading. In this simple implementation we only used the color buffer, but we may consider also performing edge extraction in the depth buffer, and in this case we would need another rendering to produce it like we did in Section 10.1.2. For a complete treatment of them and for an overview of NPR techniques we refer to Reference [1].

10.1.5 Upgrade Your Client: A Better Photographer with Panning

We already left the pinhole camera model in Section 10.1.2 by adding the depth of field. Now we will also consider another aspect of a real photograph: the exposure time. Up to now, we considered the exposure time as infinitely

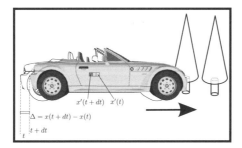

$x'(t + dt)$ $x'(t)$

$\Delta = x(t + dt) - x(t)$

$t + dt$

t

FIGURE 10.11: Motion blur. Since the car is moving by Δ *during* the exposure, the pixel value in $x'(t + dt)$ is an accumulation of the pixels ahead in the interval $x'(t + dt) + \Delta$.

small, so that every object is perfectly "still" *during* the shot, no matter how fast it travels. Now we want to emulate reality by considering that the exposure time is not infinitely small and the scene changes while the shutter is open. Figure 10.11 illustrates a situation where, during the exposure time, the car moves from left to right. What happens in this case is that different points on the car surface will project into the same pixel, all of them contributing to the final color. As a result, the image will be blurred in the regions where the moving objects have been. This type of blur is named *motion blur* and in photography it is used to obtain the *panning* effect, which is when you have the moving object in-focus and the background blurred. The way it is done is very simple: the photographer aims at the moving object *while* the shutter is open, making it so that the relative motion of the object with respect to the camera frame is almost 0. In Section 4.11.2 we added a special view mode to the photographer such that it constantly aims at the car. Now we will emulate motion blur so that we can reproduce this effect.

The most straightforward way to emulate motion blur is to simply mimic what happens in reality, that is, taking multiple renderings of the scene within the exposure interval and averaging the result. The drawback of this solution is that you need to render the scene several times and it may become a bottleneck. We will implement motion blur in a more efficient way, as a post-processing step. First we need to calculate the so called *velocity buffer*, that is, a buffer where each pixel stores a velocity vector indicating the velocity at which the point projecting on that pixel is moving in screen space. When we have the velocity buffer we output the color for a pixel in the final image just by sampling the current rendering along the velocity vector associated with the pixel, as shown in Figure 10.12.

10.1.5.1 The Velocity Buffer

The creation of the velocity buffer is usually treated in two separate situations: when the scene is static and the camera is moving or when some object

FIGURE 10.12 (SEE COLOR INSERT): Velocity vector. (See client from *http://envymycarbook.com/chapter10/2/2.html.*)

is moving and the camera is fixed. Here we deal with a unified version of the problem where all the motion is considered in the camera reference frame.

Note that the basic procedure that we followed to handle the geometric transformation of our primitives coordinates is to pass to the shader program the modelview and the projection matrix. Then in the vertex shader we always have a line of code that transforms the position from object space to clip space:

gl_Position = uProjectionMatrix * uModelViewMatrix * vec4(aPosition, 1.0);

No matter if the camera is fixed or not or if the scene is static or not, this expression will always transform the coordinates from object to clipspace (and hence in window coordinates). Assuming that the projection matrix does not change (which is perfectly sound since you do not zoom during the click of the camera), if we store the modelview matrix for each vertex of the previous frame and pass it along with the one of the current frames to the shader, we will be able to compute, for each vertex, its position on screen space at the previous and at the current frame, so that their difference is the velocity vector.

So we have to change our code to keep track, for each frame, of the value of the modelview matrix at the previous frame (that is, stack.matrix in the code). Since every element of the scene we draw is a JavaScript object of our NVMCClient, we simply extend every object with a member to store the modelview matrix at the previous frame. Listing 10.6 shows the change applied to the drawing of the trees: at line 89, after the tree trees[i] has been rendered, we store the modelview matrix in trees[i].previous_transform. This is the value that will be passed to the shader that computes the velocity buffer.

```
84    for(var i in trees){
85        var tpos = trees[ i].position;
86        this.stack.push();
87        this.stack.multiply(SglMat4.translation(tpos));
88        this.drawTreeVelocity(gl,trees[i].previous_transform);
89        trees[i].previous_transform = this.stack.matrix;
90        this.stack.pop();
91    }
```

LISTING 10.6: Storing the modelview matrix at the previous frame. (Code snippet from *http://envymycarbook.com/chapter10/2/2.js.*)

Listing 10.7 shows the shader program to compute the velocity buffer. We pass both the modelview matrix at the current and previous frame and make the fragment shader interpolate the two positions, so that we can compute the velocity vector for the pixel as the difference between the two interpolated values. At lines 111-112 we perform the perspective division to obtain the coordinate in NDC space, at line 113 we compute the velocity vector; and at line 114 we remap the vector from $[-1, 1]^2$ to $[0, 1]^2$, so that we can output it as a color by writing the x and y component of the velocity vector on the *red* and *green* channel, respectively.

```
90    var vertex_shader = "\
91        uniform    mat4 uPreviousModelViewMatrix;      \n\
92        uniform    mat4 uModelViewMatrix;              \n\
93        uniform    mat4 uProjectionMatrix;             \n\
94        attribute vec3 aPosition;                      \n\
95        varying vec4 prev_position;                    \n\
96        varying vec4 curr_position;                    \n\
97        void main(void)                                \n\
98        {                                              \n\
99            prev_position   = uProjectionMatrix*↵
                  uPreviousModelViewMatrix  *vec4(aPosition, 1.0);\n\
100           curr_position   = uProjectionMatrix*uModelViewMatrix    *↵
                  vec4(aPosition, 1.0);        \n\
101           gl_Position     = uProjectionMatrix*uPreviousModelViewMatrix↵
                  *vec4(aPosition, 1.0);   \n\
102       }                                              \n\
103   ";
104
105   var fragment_shader = "\
106       precision highp float;       \n\
107       varying vec4 prev_position; \n\
108       varying vec4 curr_position; \n\
109       void main(void)              \n\
110       {                            \n\
111          vec4 pp = prev_position / prev_position.w;\n\
112          vec4 cp = curr_position / curr_position.w;\n\
113          vec2 vel= cp.xy- pp.xy;                    \n\
114          vel   = vel*0.5+0.5;                       \n\
115          gl_FragColor =vec4(vel,0.0,1.0);           \n\
116       }                                             \n\
117   ";
```

LISTING 10.7: Shader programs for calculating the velocity buffer. (Code snippet from *http://envymycarbook.com/chapter10/2/shaders.js.*)

Listing 10.8 shows the fragment shader to perform the final rendering with the full screen quad. We have the uVelocityTexture that has been written by the velocityVectorShader and the uTexture containing the normal rendering of the scene. For each fragment, we take STEPS samples of the uTexture along the velocity vector. Since velocity vector is written with only 8 bit precision, the value we read and convert with the function Vel(..) at line 19 is not exactly what we computed with the velocityVectorShader. This is acceptable except when the scene is static (that is, nothing moves at all) and still, because of this approximation, we notice some blurring around the image, so at line 30 we simply set to $[0, 0]$ the too small velocity vectors.

```
13   var fragment_shader = "\
14     precision highp float;                                \n\
15     const int STEPS =10;                                  \n\
16     uniform sampler2D uVelocityTexture;         \n\
17     uniform sampler2D uTexture;                    \n\
18     varying vec2 vTexCoord;                         \n\
19     vec2 Vel(vec2 p){                                   \n\
20       vec2 vel = texture2D ( uVelocityTexture , p ).xy; \n\
21         vel = vel* 2.0- 1.0;                             \n\
22       return vel;                                         \n\
23     }                                                       \n\
24     void main(void)                                     \n\
25     {                                                            \n\
26       vec2 vel = Vel(vTexCoord);                     \n\
27       vec4 accum_color = vec4(0.0 ,0.0 ,0.0 ,0.0);\n\
28                                                                   \n\
29       float l = length(vel);                             \n\
30       if ( l < 4.0/255.0) vel=vec2(0.0,0.0);       \n\
31       vec2 delta = -vel/vec2(STEPS);               \n\
32       int steps_done = 0;                               \n\
33       accum_color= texture2D( uTexture , vTexCoord);\n\
34       for ( int i = 1 ; i <=    STEPS ; ++i )      \n\
35          {                                                     \n\
36          vec2 p = vTexCoord + float(i)*delta;     \n\
37            if( (p.x <1.0) && (p.x > 0.0)            \n\
38               && (p.y <1.0) && (p.y >0.0) ){      \n\
39               steps_done++;                            \n\
40               accum_color += texture2D( uTexture , p);\n\
41          };                                                    \n\
42          }                                                     \n\
43       accum_color /= float(steps_done+1);         \n\
44       gl_FragColor = vec4(accum_color.xyz ,1.0); \n\
45     }                                                           \n\
```

LISTING 10.8: Shader program for the final rendering of the panning effect. (Code snippet from *http://envymycarbook.com/chapter10/2/shaders.js.*)

Figure 10.13 shows the panning effect in action in the client.

10.1.6   Sharpen

There are many image enhancement techniques to increase the sharpness of an image. Here, we describe *unsharp masking*, one of the most used, which

FIGURE 10.13 (SEE COLOR INSERT): A screenshot of the motion blur client. (See client *http://envymycarbook.com/chapter10/2/2.html.*)

consists of improving the visual perception of the image details by extracting them and re-adding them to the original image. Originally, this technique had been developed in the analogical domain by professional photographers. For a complete and interesting description of the original photographing technique we refer the reader to [22].

The extraction of the image details is based on the computation of a smooth/blurred version of I; we call such an image I_{smooth}. The idea is that a blurred/smooth image contains less high-frequency/medium-frequency details than the original image. So, the details can be computed by simply subtracting I_{smooth} to I; the image $I - I_{\text{smooth}}$ represents the details of the input image. The amount and the granularity of the details obtained depends on how the image I_{smooth} is obtained (the kernel size and type, for example if a box filter or a Gaussian filter is used).

The details thus extracted are re-added to the original image so that they are exacerbated, and hence so that our visual system perceives them more clearly than the details of the original image. Mathematically, this can be achieved in the following way:

$$I_{\text{unsharp}}\left(x, y\right) = I\left(x, y\right) + \lambda\left(I\left(x, y\right) - I_{\text{smooth}}\left(x, y\right)\right) \qquad (10.18)$$

where I_{unsharp} is the output image with the sharpness increased. The parameter λ is used to tune the amount of details re-added. High values of λ may exacerbate the details too much, thus resulting in an unrealistic look for the image, while low values of λ may produce modifications that are not perceivable. The choice of these depends on the content of the image and on

FIGURE 10.14 (SEE COLOR INSERT): (Left) Original image. (Right) Image after unsharp masking. The I_{smooth} image is the one depicted in Figure 10.5; λ is set to 0.6.

the effect that we want to achieve. Figure 10.14 shows an example of details enhancement using unsharp masking.

10.2   Ambient Occlusion

The ambient occlusion technique is a real-time rendering solution to improve the realism of a local illumination model by taking into account the total amount of light received by a point **p** of a surface.

As we have just seen and discussed in Chapter 8, a certain part of a scene can receive no lighting or less lighting than another part due to shadows produced by occluders. Also the geometry of the same 3D model can generate self-shadowing effects, causing a point **p** to receive less light than other surface points (see Figure 10.15).

The idea of ambient occlusion is to consider how the light coming from all directions may be blocked by some occluder or by the neighboorhood of **p** on the same surface. We may think of it as a smarter version of the ambient coefficient in the Phong model: instead of assuming that "some light" will reach every point because of global effects, evaluate the neighborhood of **p** to see how much of such light could actually reach **p**.

Ambient occlusion is implemented by calculating the fraction of the total amount of light that may possibly arrive at a point **p** of the surface, and using this quantity, called *ambient occlusion term* ($\mathcal{A}$), in a local illumination model to improve the realism of the overall shading. The term $\mathcal{A}$ is computed in the following way:

$$\mathcal{A}(\mathbf{p}) = \frac{1}{2\pi} \int_\Omega V(\mathbf{p}, \omega) \, (\boldsymbol{n_p} \cdot \omega) \, d\omega \qquad (10.19)$$

where $\boldsymbol{n_p}$ is the normal at point **p** and $V(.)$ is a function, called *visibility function*, which gets value 1 if the ray originating from **p** in the direction

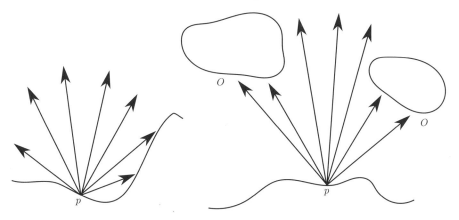

FIGURE 10.15: Occlusion examples. (Left) The point **p** receives only certain rays of light because it is self-occluded by its surface. (Right) The point **p** receives few rays of light because it is occluded by the occluders O.

ω is occluded and 0 otherwise. Since the computation of (10.19) is really computationally expensive, the term $\mathcal{A}$ is usually pre-computed and stored for each vertex or texel of the scene, assuming the scene, itself, is static. The integration is achieved by considering a set of directions on the hemisphere and summing up all the contributions. Obviously, the more directions are considered, the more accurate the value of $\mathcal{A}$. The ambient occlusion term goes from 0, which means that no light is received by the point, to 1, when the areas surrounding **p** are completely free of occluders.

Typically, the ambient occlusion term is used to modulate the ambient component of the Phong illumination model in the following way:

$$L_{\text{outgoing}} = \mathcal{A}L_{\text{ambient}} + K_D L_{\text{diffuse}} + K_S L_{\text{specular}} \qquad (10.20)$$

This local illumination model is able to produce darker parts of the scene where the geometry of the objects causes little lighting to be received. Figure 10.16 shows an example of a 3D model rendered with the standard Phong illumination model and with the per-vertex ambient occlusion term only. Note how using only the ambient occlusion term may greatly increase the perception of the details of the scene (this has been demonstrated by experiments conducted by Langer et al. [21]).

The ambient occlusion term can also be used in other ways and in other illumination models, for example by multiplying a purely diffusive model to make the part exposed to the light brighter than the ones where the light has difficulties in arriving:

$$L_{\text{reflected}} = \mathcal{A}(\boldsymbol{L} \cdot \boldsymbol{N}) \qquad (10.21)$$

We would like to underline that this technique has no cost during the rendering phase, since everything is pre-computed. This is why we describe it as a real-time rendering solution.

FIGURE 10.16: Effect of ambient occlusion. (Left) Phong model. (Right) Ambient occlusion term only. The ambient occlusion term has been calculated with Meshlab (*http://meshlab.sourceforge.net/*). The 3D model is a simplified version of a scanning model of a capital. (Courtesy of the Kunsthistorisches Institut in Florenz *http://www.khi.fi.it/*.)

10.2.1   Screen-Space Ambient Occlusion (SSAO)

The ambient occlusion technique just described has several limitations. One of the most important is the fact that it cannot be applied to dynamic scenes. If an object changes its position in the scene or is deformed by an animation the pre-calculated occlusion term is no longer valid and requires to be re-calculated. Stated in another way, the ambient occlusion previously described can be used only to visualize a static scene. Another limitation is that the pre-computation can require a very long time if the scene is complex and a high number of directions are used to compute the integral (10.19).

Here, we show an alternative way to obtain a visual effect similar to the ambient occlusion but with many advantages: the *screen-space ambient occlusion (SSAO)*. The idea is to compute the ambient occlusion term for each pixel at rendering time instead of pre-computing $\mathcal{A}$ for each vertex. This way of proceeding has several advantages: it is independent of the complexity of the scene because it is calculated in screen-space, hence this allows it to be applied also for dynamic scenes; its computational complexity depends on the screen resolution and not on the complexity of the scene.

Many ideas have been proposed in the last few years to develop an efficient way to calculate the ambient occlusion in screen space [1]. The technique we are going to describe is a simplified version of the SSAO technique proposed by Bavoil et al. [3] and then successively improved by Dimitrov et al. [7]. This technique is based on the concept of *horizon angle*.

Referring to Figure 10.17 (Top-Right), let **p** be a point on the surface $\mathcal{S}$ and $n_{\mathbf{p}}$ be the normal at point **p**. Now let pl_θ be the plane passing by the axis z and forming an angle θ with the plane xy. The intersection between $\mathcal{S}$ with this plane produces the section $\mathcal{S}_\theta$ shown in Figure 10.17 (Bottom). With this notation, we can rewrite equation 10.19 as:

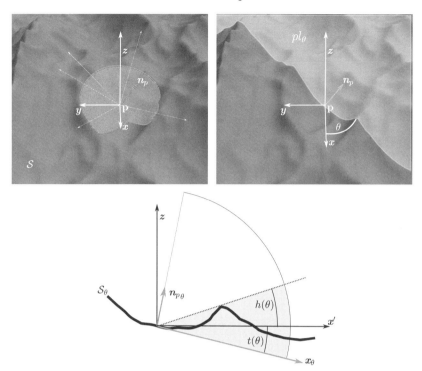

FIGURE 10.17: The horizon angle $h(\theta)$ and the tangent angle $t(\theta)$ in a specific direction θ.

$$\mathcal{A}(p) = \frac{1}{2\pi} \int_{\theta=-\pi}^{\theta=\pi} \overbrace{\int_{\alpha=0}^{\pi/2} V(p, \omega(\theta, \alpha)) W(\theta) d\alpha}^{contribution\ of\ section\ \mathcal{S}_\theta}\, d\theta \qquad (10.22)$$

In the following we will concentrate on the contribution of the inner integral. Let us build a tangent frame on **p** made by n_θ and the tangent vector, which we call x_θ. We want to find the range of elevation angle α so that the ray leaving from **p** *intersects* $\mathcal{S}_\theta$, that is, the values of α for which $V(p, \omega(\theta, \alpha)) = 1$. This range is shown as a darker area in Figure 10.17 (Bottom).

Suppose we know this horizon angle and let us call it Hz. Then we can rewrite equation 10.22 as:

$$\mathcal{A}(p) = \frac{1}{2\pi} \int_{\theta=-\pi}^{\theta=\pi} \int_{\alpha=0}^{Hz} \cos\alpha\ W(\theta) d\alpha d\theta \qquad (10.23)$$

because the contribution of the inner integral is 0 for $\alpha > 0$. Note that we also replaced $n_{\mathbf{p}} \cdot \omega(\theta, \alpha)$ with a generic weighting function $W(\theta)$ (which we will specify later on) that does not depend on α and so can be taken out of the integral.

Now the interesting part. Hz is a value expressed in the tangent frame, but our representation of the surface S is the depth buffer, which means we can have z values expressed in the frame made by $\boldsymbol{x}'$ and $\boldsymbol{z}$. So we find Hz by subtraction of two angles that we can compute by sampling the depth buffer: $h(\theta)$ and $t(\theta)$. $h(\theta)$ is the horizon angle over the $\boldsymbol{x}'$ axis and $t(\theta)$ is the angle formed by the tangent vector $\boldsymbol{x}_\theta$ and $\boldsymbol{x}'$. You can easily see that: $Hz = h(\theta) - t(\theta)$ and hence equation 10.23 becomes:

$$\mathcal{A}(p) = \frac{1}{2\pi} \int_{\theta=-\pi}^{\pi} (\sin(h(\theta)) - \sin(t(\theta)))\, W(\omega) d\omega \qquad (10.24)$$

Given a point **p**, and the knowledge of the horizon angles in several directions, allows us to estimate approximately the region of the hemisphere where the rays are not self-occluded. The greater this region, the greater the value of the ambient occlusion term.

Equation (10.24) can be easily calculated at rendering time with a two-pass algorithm. In the first pass the depth map is generated, like in the depth-of-field client (see Section 10.1.2), and used during the second pass to determine the angles $h(\theta)$ and $t(\theta)$ for each pixel. Obviously, Equation (10.24) is evaluated only for a discrete number N_d of directions $(\theta_0, \theta_1, \ldots, \theta_{N_d-1})$:

$$\mathcal{A}(p) = \frac{1}{2\pi} \sum_{i=0}^{N_d} (\sin(h(\theta_i)) - \sin(t(\theta_i)))\, W(\theta) \qquad (10.25)$$

where $W(\theta)$ is a linear attenuation function depending on the distance r of where the horizon angle is found. In its original formulation, it is set to $W(\theta) = 1 - r/R$. Just 16 directions can provide a good approximation of the real ambient occlusion term. The horizon angle is calculated by walking on the depth map in the specified direction θ and getting the maximum value of it. The walking proceeds in a certain radius of interest R and not on all the depth map. The tangent angle $t(\theta)$ is easily determined from the normal at the pixel (see Appendix B).

10.3   Deferred Shading

In Section 5.2.3 we have seen how depth buffering solves the hidden surface removal problem in a simple and sound manner. However, at this point of our book, we have seen how much is going on besides the pure rasterization. Depending on the specific shader programs, lighting and texture accesses can make creating a fragment computationally expensive. This means that if the depths complexity is high, that is, if many surfaces at different depths project on the same pixels on the screen, then a lot of computation is wasted.

The idea of *deferred shading* is to separate the work for finding out the visible fragments from the work for computing their final color. In a *first pass*, or *geometry pass*, the scene is only rasterized without making any shading computation. Instead we output, on several buffers, the interpolated values for the fragment (such as position, normal, color, texture coordinates, etc.) that are needed to compute the final color.

In the **second** pass, we render a full screen quad and bound this set of buffers, usually referred to as GBuffer, so that for each pixel on the screen we may access all the values written in the first pass and make the shading.

As noted before, since we do not have MRT in WebGL, the first pass will actually consist of at least two renderings: one to store depth and normals and one to store color attribute.

Beside handling depth complexity, another major advantage claimed for deferred shading is that it can easily handle multiple lights. However, we already implemented multiple lights in Section 6.7.4 simply by iterating over all the light sources in the fragment shader and composing their contribution in the final result, so you may wonder why it can be better with deferred shading. The answer is that with deferred shading you can easily combine several shaders, for example one for each light, eliminate iteration and branching in the fragment shader and have a cleaner pipeline. It may not seem like much in a basic example but it will make a world of difference with bigger projects.

There are downsides too. Hardware antialiasing, which we have seen in Section 5.3.3, will be done at rasterization time with the color only and not with the result of shading, so it will simply be plainly wrong. This problem may be alleviated by detecting edges on the image produced at the first pass and blurring them at post processing.

10.4 Particle Systems

With the term *particle system* we refer to an animation technique that consists of using a large population of particles, which we can picture as zero-dimensional or very small entities, that move in space according to either a predefined scripted behaviour or to a physical simulation creating the illusion of a moving entity without a fixed shape. A wide range of phenomena can be effectively represented by particle systems: smoke, fire, explosions, rain, snow and water, to mention the most used, and how a particle is rendered depends on the phenomenon being represented, for example, a small colored circle for fire or a small line segment for rain.

10.4.1 Animating a Particle System

The animation of a particle system is done by defining the *state* of the system and the set of functions to make it progress over time, and they depend on the particular visual effect to achieve.

Typically, the dynamic state of a particle consists ot the acceleration, the velocity and the position . For example, for a particle i we may have $x_i(t) = (a_i(t), v_i(t), p_i(t))$. The evolution of this set of particles can be written as:

$$x_i(t+i) = \left(\begin{array}{c} p_i(t+1) \\ v_i(t+1) \\ a_i(t+1) \end{array} \right) = \left(\begin{array}{c} f(t, a_i(t), v_i(t), p_i(t)) \\ g(t, a_i(t), v_i(t), p_i(t)) \\ h(t, a_i(t), v_i(t), p_i(t)) \end{array} \right) = \left(\begin{array}{c} f(t, x_i(t)) \\ g(t, x_i(t)) \\ h(t, x_i(t)) \end{array} \right)$$

(10.26)

where the functions $f(.)$, $g(.)$ and $h(.)$ provide the acceleration, velocity and position of the particle at the next time step, given the current acceleration, velocity and position of the particle. These functions are basically of two types: physically-based, attempting to simulate the physical behavior of the phenomenon, or scripted to provide the same visual impression of the phenomenon without any connection with the real physics behind it.

The state of the particle can also be characterized by many other parameters, for example, the color of the particle can be evolved as a function of the time or the position, its shape on the acceleration, and so on.

Moreover, the animation of a particle can also be a function of the properties of other particles, for example:

$$\begin{cases} p_i(t+1) = f(t, a_1(t), v_i(t), p_i^1(t), p_i^2(t), \dots, p_i^k(t)) \\ v_i(t+1) = g(t, a_1(t), v_i(t), p_i^1(t), p_i^2(t), \dots, p_i^k(t)) \\ a_i(t+1) = h(t, a_1(t), v_i(t), p_i^1(t), p_i^2(t), \dots, p_i^k(t)) \end{cases}$$

(10.27)

In this case the i-th particle is also influenced by the position of the nearest k particles, indicated with $p_i^1(t), p_i^2(t), \dots, p_i^k(t)$.

The set of particles in a particle system is not fixed. Each particle is *created* by an *emitter* and inserted in the system with an initial state, then its state is updated for a certain amount of time and finally is removed. The lifespan of a particle is not always strictly dependent on time. For example, when implementing rain, the particles may be created on a plane above the scene and then removed when they hit the ground. Another example is with fireworks: particles are all created at the origin of the fire (the *launcher* of the fireworks) with an initial velocity and removed from the system when along their descending parabola. The creation of particles should be randomized to avoid creating visible patterns that jeopardize the final effect.

10.4.2 Rendering a Particle System

The rendering of a particle system also depends on the phenomenon. Often each particle is rendered as a small plane-aligned billboard, which makes sense because there is no parallax to see in a single particle, but we can also have simpler representations like just points or segments. For dense participating media such as smoke, blending will be enabled and set to accumulate the value of the alpha channel, that is, the more particles project on the same pixel the more opaque is the result.

10.5   Self-Exercises

10.5.1   General

1. Imagine that the generateMipmap is suddenly removed by the WebGl specification! How can we create the mipmap levels of a given texture entirely on the GPU (that is, without readbacks)?

2. Suppose we iterate the application of a blurring filter with kernel size 5 on an image of 800×600 pixels. How many times should we apply the filter for the color of the pixel at position $(20, 20)$ to be influenced by the color at pixel $(100, 100)$?

3. Change the Gaussian filter (Equation (10.4)) so that horizontal neighbors of the pixel are weighted more than vertical neighbors.

4. Suppose the objects of the scene were tagged as *convex* and *non-convex*. How could we take advantage of this information to speed up the computation of the ambient occlusion term?

5. Elaborate on this statement: "Ambient occlusion is none other than the implementation of an all-around light camera for shadow mapping."

10.5.2   Client Related

1. For how we implemented it, the rendering of the skybox does not write on the depth buffer. Still, the client implemented in Section 10.1.2 blurs it correctly. How so?

2. Change the client of Section 10.1.2 so that it does not apply the blurring filter for the fragments of the skybox but still shows the skybox blurred when out of the depth of field.

3. Make a view mode that loses the focus away from the center of the image.

4. Improve the toon shading client by also running the edge detection on:

    (a) The depth buffer

(b) The normal buffer. *Hint:* You have to pack the normals as we did for the depth buffer.

5. Improve the toon shading client by also making the black edges **bold**. *Hint:* Add a rendering pass in order to expand all the strong edge pixels by one pixel in every direction.

6. Improve the implementation of the lens flares effect (see Section 9.2.4). *Hint:* Use the fullscreen quad to avoid a rendering pass.

7. Using only the normal map of the street of Section 7.8.3, create an ambient occlusion map, that is, a texture where each texel stores the ambient occlusion term. *Hint:* If the dot product of the normal at texel x, y and every one of the normals on the neighbor texels is negative we can put 1 as an ambient occlusion term (that is, not occluded at all).

Chapter 11

Global Illumination

Global illumination in a 3D scene results from the propagation of light from a light source in the scene through multiple inter-reflections. This chapter presents a few algorithms to compute color due to the global illumination in the scene. Most of these algorithms simulate this propagation in one form or another. Simulation should normally proceed with the distribution of light from the light source to all other surface patches in the environment. The simulation continues by distributing reflected light from those surface patches into the environment. This light distribution process is continued till the equilibrium is reached. Some of the simulation algorithms are designed to compute equilibrium light at only those points that are visible to the camera. Most such algorithms are based on ray tracing. We provided the idea of ray tracing in the first chapter. Here, we come back to it in order to provide more details and insights. Other algorithms compute equilibrium light for the whole scene, and thus compute equilibrium light at every surface of the scene, independent of whether the surface is visible or not. Two algorithms of this type that we describe here are the *Photon Mapping* and the *Radiosity* algorithms.

We would like to underline that this chapter is presented in quite a different way from the previous ones, since no practical implementation of the described algorithms is provided as in the usual **Upgrade Your Client** sections. This is because our main aim is to provide here only the basic ideas behind global illumination algorithms and not to explain how to implement them efficiently. In fact, this is a complex and highly specialized topic. For the readers interested in going deeper into this topic, we refer them to other textbooks such as the book on photon mapping by Henrik Wann Jensen [15], which includes an implementation of photon mapping in C language, and the global illumination books by Dutre et al. [9] and by Pharr and Humphreys [34], the latter of which contains many details about the art of ray tracing.

11.1 Ray Tracing

A ray is defined by an origin $\mathbf{o}$, the point at which it originates and a direction $\boldsymbol{d}$, the direction along which the ray extends. The actual extent of the ray can in principle be infinity. Any point $\mathbf{p}$ on the ray is defined by a scalar parameter t such as $\mathbf{p} = \mathbf{o} + t\boldsymbol{d}$. Every $t \geq 0$ generates all valid points along the ray. If the direction is normalized then t represents the Euclidean distance of the point from the origin of the ray.

Ray tracing plays a very important role in global illumination computation:

(a) For simulating the propagation of light rays originating at the light source through a scene (light ray tracing or photon tracing).

(b) For computing the amount of light reaching the camera through a pixel by tracing a ray from the camera, following the ray through the scene, and collecting all the lighting information (classical ray tracing, Monte Carlo ray tracing, etc.).

Tracing a ray means extending the ray from its origin, and collecting some information along the ray. The exact information collected depends on the application and the type of scene. We restrict our discussion to scenes containing solid opaque objects. Independent of the application, the major computational effort in tracing the ray is the computation of the *ray-scene intersection*. As the scene is assumed to be composed of one or more solid objects, intersecting the ray with the scene involves computation of ray–object intersection. As parameter t represents a point along the ray, computing ray–object intersection can be resolved by computing the ray parameter t. Plenty of research has been devoted to finding efficient ray–object intersection algorithms for a large number of object types. We will restrict our discussion on ray–object intersection to only two classes of objects: algebraic and parametric surfaces.

11.1.1   Ray–Algebraic Surface Intersection

Each point **p** of an *algebraic surface* satisfies an algebraic equation of the type $f(x, y, z) = 0$ where f is a polynomial expression involving the coordinates of the point. For a ray to intersect such a surface there must be at least one point $\mathbf{p}_i$ common between the surface and the ray. Or, in other words:

$$f(p_{i,x}, p_{i,y}, p_{i,z}) = 0 \text{ and } \mathbf{p}_i = \mathbf{o} + t_i \mathbf{d} \qquad (11.1)$$

By substitution we get an algebraic equation of t_i as

$$f(o_x + t_i d_x, o_y + t_i d_y, o_z + t_i d_z) = 0 \qquad (11.2)$$

Any polynomial root-finding method may be used to compute the value of t_i. We detail here a couple of examples: planes and spheres.

11.1.1.1   Ray–Plane Intersection

The plane has the simplest of the algebraic equations:

$$ax + by + cz + d = 0 \qquad (11.3)$$

Substituting the ray equation into the plane equation we get:

$$a(o_x + t_i d_x) + b(o_y + t_i d_y) + c(o_z + t_i d_z) + d = 0 \qquad (11.4)$$

or

$$t_i = -\frac{(ao_x + bo_y + co_z + d)}{(ad_x + bd_y + cd_z)} \qquad (11.5)$$

Thus the ray–plane intersection computation is the simplest of all ray–object intersections.

11.1.1.2 Ray–Sphere Intersection

The sphere has the simplest of the algebraic equations of degree two. The algebraic equation for a sphere whose radius is r and whose center is located at $\mathbf{c}$ is

$$(x - c_x)^2 + (y - c_y)^2 + (z - c_z)^2 - r^2 = 0 \qquad (11.6)$$

which can be easily written as

$$(\mathbf{p} - \mathbf{c}) \cdot (\mathbf{p} - \mathbf{c}) - r^2 = 0 \qquad (11.7)$$

For a ray to intersect a sphere, the point of intersection $\mathbf{p}_i$ must satisfy the following equation:

$$(\mathbf{p}_i - \mathbf{c}) \cdot (\mathbf{p}_i - \mathbf{c}) - r^2 = 0 \text{ and } \mathbf{p}_i = \mathbf{o} + t_i \boldsymbol{d} \qquad (11.8)$$

Substituting of the ray equation into the sphere equation, we get:

$$(\mathbf{o} + t_i \boldsymbol{d} - \mathbf{c}) \cdot (\mathbf{o} + t_i \boldsymbol{d} - c) - r^2 = 0 \qquad (11.9)$$

which on expansion gives us

$$t_i^2 (\mathbf{d} \cdot \mathbf{d}) + 2t_i \left(\boldsymbol{d} \cdot (\mathbf{o} - \mathbf{c}) \right) + \left((\mathbf{o} - \mathbf{c}) \cdot (\mathbf{o} - \mathbf{c}) \right) - r^2 = 0 \qquad (11.10)$$

which is a quadratic equation in t. Quadratic equations have two roots, and hence ray–sphere intersection can result in two intersection points. The smallest of the positive real roots is chosen as the parameter of intersection.

11.1.2 Ray–Parametric Surface Intersection

We remind the reader that parametric objects' surfaces are often expressed as a parametric equations of a form $\mathbf{p} = s(u, v)$, that is, every coordinate of the point on a parametric surface is a function of two parameters u and v. Hence, for a ray to intersect a parametric surface, the equality

$$\mathbf{o} + t_i \boldsymbol{d} = \mathbf{p}_i = g(u_i, v_i) \qquad (11.11)$$

must hold. So we get a system of three equations with three unknown parameters,

$$g(u_i, v_i, t_i) = 0 \qquad (11.12)$$

Depending on the surface the equations can be non-linear. In such a case multivariate Newton iteration may be used to solve the system of equations.

A triangle $T = \{\mathbf{p}_1, \mathbf{p}_2, \mathbf{p}_3\}$ may be considered the simplest of the parametric surfaces whose points satisfy the equation $\mathbf{p} = \mathbf{a} + \boldsymbol{b}u + \boldsymbol{c}v$, where u, v are scalar parameters in the range $[0, 1]$, $u + v$ is also in the range $[0, 1]$ and $\mathbf{a}$, $\boldsymbol{b}$ and $\boldsymbol{c}$ are related to the three vertices of the triangle as: $\mathbf{a} = \mathbf{p}_1$, $\boldsymbol{b} = \mathbf{p}_2 - \mathbf{p}_1$ and $\boldsymbol{c} = \mathbf{p}_3 - \mathbf{p}_1$. For ray–triangle intersection, we get the following system of linear equations:

$$
\begin{bmatrix} -\boldsymbol{d} & \boldsymbol{b} & \boldsymbol{c} \end{bmatrix} \times \begin{bmatrix} t_i \\ u_i \\ v_i \end{bmatrix} = [\mathbf{o} - \mathbf{a}] \tag{11.13}
$$

An often-used method of computing ray–triangle intersection is solving this linear system. If the computed t_i value is greater than zero, and u_i, v_i and their sum $u_i + v_i$ are in the range $[0, 1]$, then the ray intersects the triangle, and the point of intersection $\mathbf{p}_i$ is equal to $\mathbf{o} + t_i \boldsymbol{d}$.

11.1.3 Ray–Scene Intersection

The simplest method of computing ray–scene intersection is intersecting the ray with each and every element of the scene, and choosing the point that corresponds to the smallest positive ray parameter t_i. In this approach, the cost of per-ray intersection is linear in terms of the number of objects in the scene, and is acceptable for scenes composed of only a small number of objects. However, most realistic scenes are composed of hundreds to a hundred thousand or more objects. In such cases the linear approach to computing ray–scene intersection is unacceptably slow. So over the years a number of approaches have been proposed to accelerate this operation. Some of the widely used acceleration approaches (discussed in detail in [34]) are: uniform spatial subdivision (USS) and hierarchical structures such as kD tree and bounding volume hierarchy (BVH). All of these approaches rely on pre-computing *acceleration structures* that reduce the number of ray–object intersection tests, by intersecting the ray with only a few objects that are likely to lie along the ray. Independent of the acceleration approach used, computing an axis aligned bounding box (AABB) for the scene and checking its intersection with the ray is the starting point for every approach. So, we first describe what an AABB is and how the ray–AABB intersection test is calculated. Then, we continue discussing the USS and BVH methods for accelerating ray–scene intersection.

11.1.3.1 Ray–AABB Intersection

As previously stated, the bounding volume of a scene is a simple geometric primitive that entirely covers all the vertices of the scene. An axis-aligned bounding box (AABB) is the simplest bounding volume to compute. As the

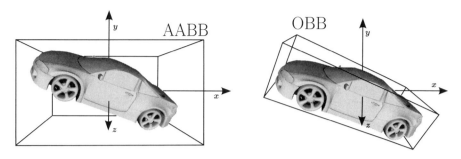

FIGURE 11.1: (Left) Axis-aligned bounding box (AABB). (Right) Oriented bounding box (OBB).

name suggests, this type of bounding volume is a rectangular box with its bounding planes aligned to the axis. In other words, the six bounding planes of an AABB are parallel to the three main axial planes. An oriented bounding box (OBB) is another type of bounding box that is more compact in enclosing the volume of the object, but is not constrained to have its planes parallel to the axial planes. Figure 11.1 shows an example of an AABB and an OBB. In the following we always refer to AABB because this box type is the one used by the algorithm we will describe.

The AABB for a scene is computed by finding the minimum and maximum of the coordinates of the objects in the scene. The minimum and maximum coordinates define the two extreme corner points referred to as $\mathbf{c}_{\min} = \mathsf{AABB.min}$ and $\mathbf{c}_{\max} = \mathsf{AABB.max}$ in the following.

Every pair of the faces of an AABB is parallel to a Cartesian plane. Let us consider the two planes parallel to the XY-plane. The Z-coordinates of every point on these planes are equal to $c_{\min,z}$ and $c_{\max,z}$. So the algebraic equation of the two planes of the AABB parallel to the XY-plane are

$$z - c_{\min,z} = 0 \ , \ z - c_{\max,z} = 0 \tag{11.14}$$

The parameters of intersection of a ray with these planes are simply:

$$\frac{(c_{\min,z} - o_z)}{d_z} \ \text{and} \ \frac{(c_{\max,z} - o_z)}{d_z} \tag{11.15}$$

The smallest of these two parameters, $t_{\min,z}$, corresponds to the nearest point of intersection of the ray with the AABB parallel to the XY-plane and $t_{\max,z}$ corresponds to the farthest point of intersection. Similarly we can compute the ray parameters $t_{\min,x}$, $t_{\max,x}$ and $t_{\min,y}$, $t_{\max,y}$ corresponding to the nearest and farthest point of ray intersection with the planes parallel to the YZ-plane and ZX-plane, respectively. The intersection of a ray with a rectangular box can result in a pair of intersection points. These two points can be computed from the three pairs of ray–box–plane intersection points. If the intersection exists, then the nearest of the farthest intersection points will be the farthest of the ray–AABB intersection points, and the farthest of the nearest intersection points will be the nearest ray–AABB intersection point. Thus the ray parameter for the nearest point of ray–AABB intersection $t_{\min}$ is $\max(t_{\min,x}, t_{\min,y}, t_{\min,z})$, and t_{max}, that of the farthest point of intersection is $\min(t_{\max,x}, t_{\max,y}, t_{\max,z})$. If $t_{\min} < t_{\max}$ then the ray does indeed intersect the AABB and the nearest point of ray–AABB intersection is given by the ray parameter $t_{\min}$. The pseudo-code for ray–AABB intersection computation is given in Listing 11.1.

```
function ray−AABB()
    INPUT ray, AABB

    // ray parameter for the point of intersection
    OUTPUT t_min, t_max
{
    t_min,x = (AABB.min.x−ray.o.x)/ray.d.x
    t_max,x = (AABB.max.x−ray.o.x)/ray.d.x
    if (t_min,x > t_max,x)
        swap(t_min,x,t_max,x)
    endif

    t_min,y = (AABB.min.y−ray.o.y)/ray.d.y
    t_max,y = (AABB.max.y−ray.o.y)/ray.d.y
    if (t_min,y > t_max,y)
        swap(t_min,y,t_max,y)
    endif

    t_min,z = (AABB.min.z−ray.o.z)/ray.d.z
    t_max,z = (AABB.max.z−ray.o.z)/ray.d.z
    if (t_min,z > t_max,z)
        swap(t_min,z,t_max,z)
    endif

    t_min = max(t_min,x,t_min,y,t_min,z)
    t_max = min(t_max,x,t_max,y,t_max,z)
}
```

LISTING 11.1: Ray-AABB intersection finding algorithm.

11.1.3.2   USS-Based Acceleration Scheme

As suggested by the name uniform spatial subdivision, in this scheme the space occupied by the scene is subdivided uniformly, and the objects in the scene are assigned to the created subspaces based on their space occupancy (see Figure 11.2). The actual space subdivided is the AABB of the scene. So the subdivision creates a uniform 3D grid structure. A list of objects is associated with every voxel of the 3D grid. If an object is fully or partially inside a voxel then the object is assigned to the list of objects of that cell. The creation of these object lists for the USS grid voxels is a first and important step in USS-based acceleration schemes. The pseudocode of a simple and often-

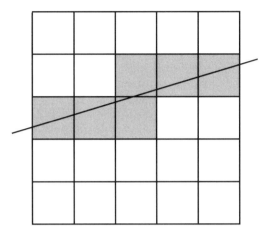

FIGURE 11.2: The idea of a uniform subdivision grid shown in 2D. Only the objects inside the uniform subdivision cells traversed by the ray (highlighted in light gray) are tested for intersections. A 3D grid of AABBs is used in practice.

used algorithm for this objects list computation for a triangle-only scene is given in Listing 11.2.

```
function USSpreProcess()
    INPUT scene: AABB, triangleList
    OUTPUT USS: {AABB, N, objectList[N][N][N]}
            // assumes N³ as the grid resolution
{
    for every T in triangleList
        p_min = min coordinates of the three vertices of T
        p_max = max coordinates of the three vertices of T
        index_min=ivec3((p_min − AABB.min)/(AABB.max − AABB.min))
        index_max=ivec3((p_max − AABB.min)/(AABB.max − AABB.min))
        for i = index_min.x to index_max.x
            for j = index_min.y to index_max.y
                for k = index_min.z to index_max.z
                    append T to USS.objectList[i][j][k]
                endfor
            endfor
        endfor
    endfor
}
```

LISTING 11.2: USS preprocessing algorithm.

For USS-based ray tracing, the ray is first intersected with the AABB associated with the USS. If there is a valid intersection then the ray is marched through the 3D grid of the USS, one voxel at a time. For each voxel it traverses through, the ray is intersected with the list of triangles associated with the voxel objectList. If a valid intersection point is found then that point represents the nearest point of intersection of the ray with the scene, and the ray marching is terminated. Otherwise, the ray is marched through the next voxel, and the process is repeated until the intersection is found or the ray exits AABB. Two crucial steps of the ray marching operation are: find the entry voxel index, and then march from the current voxel to the next voxel along the ray. These operations must be computed accurately and efficiently. Simple use of ray–AABB intersection tests to find the voxel of entry and then finding the next voxel along the path will be highly inefficient. However, an adaptation of that approach has been shown to be very efficient. We describe it below.

11.1.3.3   USS Grid Traversal

Like in AABB, USS is composed of three sets of planes, each of which is parallel to a different Cartesian planes. As we have seen earlier, computing ray intersection with a plane parallel to a Cartesian plane is simple. The ray parameter of intersection with the sets parallel to the YZ, ZX and XY planes are, respectively:

$$
\begin{aligned}
t_{x,i} &= (\mathsf{USS.AABB.min.x} + i\Delta x - \mathsf{ray.o.x})/\mathsf{ray.d.x} \\
&\quad \text{where } \Delta x = (\mathsf{USS.AABB.max.x} - \mathsf{USS.AABB.min.x})/N, \\
t_{y,j} &= (\mathsf{USS.AABB.min.y} + j\Delta y - \mathsf{ray.o.y})/\mathsf{ray.d.y} \\
&\quad \text{where } \Delta y = (\mathsf{USS.AABB.max.y} - \mathsf{USS.AABB.min.y})/N, \\
t_{z,k} &= (\mathsf{USS.AABB.min.z} + k\Delta z - \mathsf{ray.o.z})/\mathsf{ray.d.z} \\
&\quad \text{where } \Delta z = (\mathsf{USS.AABB.max.z} - \mathsf{USS.AABB.min.z})/N.
\end{aligned}
$$

The indices i, j and k are the indices to the USS 3D grid. The starting values of the indices and sign of the index increment depend on the sign of the coordinates of the ray direction. For example: for the set of planes parallel to the YZ plane, the starting value, the increment for index i, the limit of the index, and the coordinate value at the point of intersection are as follows:

$$
(i, \Delta i, i_{limit}, x) = \begin{cases} (N, -1, -1, \mathsf{USS.AABB.max.x}) & \text{if } \mathsf{ray.d.x} < 0 \\ (0, 1, N, \mathsf{USS.AABB.min.x}) & \text{otherwise.} \end{cases} \quad (11.16)
$$

The formula of ray intersection parameters is not only simple, but also lets us write incremental expressions for the parameters of the next intersection along the ray. The incremental expressions along the axes are respectively:

$$
\begin{aligned}
t_{x,i+\Delta i} &= t_{x,i} + \Delta t_x \\
&\quad \text{where } \Delta t_x = (\Delta i \Delta x)/\mathsf{ray.d.x} \\
t_{y,j+\Delta j} &= t_{y,j} + \Delta t_y \\
&\quad \text{where } \Delta t_y = (\Delta j \Delta y)/\mathsf{ray.d.y} \\
t_{z,k+\Delta k} &= t_{z,k} + \Delta t_z \\
&\quad \text{where } \Delta t_z = (\Delta k \Delta z)/\mathsf{ray.d.z}
\end{aligned}
$$

Figure 11.3 shows the intersection points produced by this process in the 2D case. For the ray whose origin is inside the volume of the USS, the starting index values must be adjusted to guarantee the ray parameter values are greater than zero. There are multiple ways of making this adjustment. An iterative method for this adjustment is given in Listing 11.3.

```
t_{x,i} = (USS.AABB.min.x + i Δx − ray.o.x)/ray.d.x
t_{y,j} = (USS.AABB.min.y + j Δy − ray.o.y)/ray.d.y
t_{z,k} = (USS.AABB.min.z + k Δz − ray.o.z)/ray.d.z
while (t_{x,i} < 0 && t_{y,j} < 0 && t_{z,k} < 0)
    if (t_{x,i} < t_{y,j} && t_{x,i}) < t_{z,j})
        t_{x,i} += Δt_x
        i += Δi
    else if (t_{y,j} < t_{z,k})
        t_{y,j} += Δt_y
        j += Δj
    else
        t_{z,k} += Δt_z
        k += Δk
    endif
endwhile
```

LISTING 11.3: Code to take into account the rays originating inside the USS bounds.

Given the start t and index values we can now write a USS-based ray–scene intersection algorithm as shown in Listing 11.4:

```
function USS_ray_traverse()
    OUTPUT t
{
    while(i ≠ i_limit && j ≠ j_limit && k ≠ k_limit)
        [t, intersectFlag] = ray_object_list_intersect(ray, objectList[i][j][k]);
        if (intersectFlag == TRUE && pointInsideVoxel(ray.o+t*ray.d,i,j,k)) ↵
            // intesection found
            return TRUE;
        endif
        if (t_{x,i} < t_{y,j} && t_{x,i} < t_{z,j})
            t_{x,i} += Δt_x
            i += Δi
        else if (t_{(y,j)} < t_{z,k})
            t_{y,j} += Δt_y
            j += Δj
        else
            t_{z,k} += Δt_z
            k += Δk
        endif
    endwhile
    return FALSE
}
```

LISTING 11.4: An incremental algorithm for ray–USS traversal.

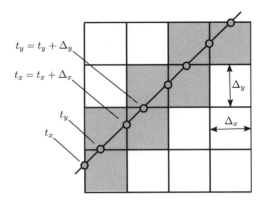

FIGURE 11.3: Efficient ray traversal in USS (shown in 2D). After computing the first intersection parameters t_x and t_y, the Δ_x and Δ_y values are used to incrementally compute the next t_x and t_y values.

The algorithm uses the *ray_object_list_intersect* function where the ray is intersected with each of the objects in the list and returns the nearest point of intersection if there is one or more intersections. In USS an object is likely to be part of multiple voxels. So the intersection of the ray with the object list associated with the voxel may generate an intersection point outside the voxel, and thus could generate an erroneous nearest point detection. This problem is avoided by checking if the point is inside the current voxel or not. Like AABB, the USS voxel boundaries are parallel to the axis plane. So the point-inside-outside test is easily done by checking the coordinates of the point against the coordinates of voxel bounds.

The resolution of the USS grid could be specified by the user directly, or indirectly as average triangle density per voxel. The finer the resolution, the faster the ray–intersection, but this requires longer pre-computation time, a larger amount of memory for the USS storage, and also adds computational overhead for ray-tracing empty parts of the scene. The performance of USS is good in scenes with homogeneous object distribution. However, USS performance can be poor if the extents of the objects in the scene are large and overlap. It also performs poorly for tracing scenes where small but high-triangle-count objects are located, in scenes with large extent, for example a teapot in a football field. To avoid this latter problem, nested USS structures have been proposed. In the next section we describe a hierarchical structure-based ray tracing acceleration technique that better handles this problem.

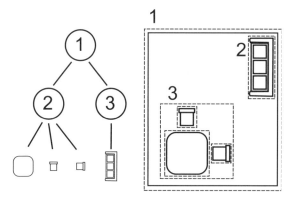

FIGURE 11.4: An example of bounding volume hierarchy. The room is subdivided according to a tree of depth 3.

11.1.3.4 BVH-Based Acceleration Scheme

A bounding volume hierarchy (BVH) scheme uses a recursive partitioning technique to partition objects in the scene into two parts, and continues partitioning till the partitions contain one or a predefined number of objects (see Figure 11.4 for an example). The process creates a binary tree of object lists. As the name suggests, the bounding volume of the objects plays an important role in partitioning the objects. Like in USS, an often-chosen bounding volume is AABB. However, instead of dividing the scene uniformly along each axis as done in USS, the bounding volume is divided hierarchically by a plane parallel to any of the three axial planes. Each division creates two distinct sets of objects. The elements of each set belong to one side of the axial plane of subdivision. The sidedness of the object with respect to the dividing plane is determined by the sidedness of a candidate point of the object. For example, for a scene composed of triangles, the sidedness of a triangle is determined by the sidedness of the centroid point of the triangle. The plane of subdivision is chosen based on a certain heuristic. For example, a simple heuristic could be to choose the plane perpendicular to the longest side of the AABB, and to choose the location of the plane that divides the longest side into two equal halves or to choose the location of the plane such that exactly half of the objects are on one side and the remaining half on the other. After the subdivision, the bounding volume of each subdivision is computed. The two bounding volumes make two nodes of the hierarchy, and the nodes are recursively subdivided till the number of objects in the children nodes reaches a certain predefined minimum. The resulting hierarchy is a binary tree whose every node is a bounding volume. The BVH creation must precede any ray–scene intersection test. A content of the BVH node and sample pseudo-code for BVH creation is given in Listing 11.5.

```
BVHnode
{
    AABB
    objectList or // No object list for intermediate nodes.
    partitionPlane // No Partition plane for leaf node.
}

function BHVCreate() // recursive function.
    INPUT root: BVHnode
          list : list of objects
    OUTPUT left, right: BVHnode
{
    if (list.size < thresholdSize)
    {
        left = right = null
        objectList = list
        return
    }
    P: Choose subdivision plane // based on certain heuristic
    leftList = empty
    rightList = empty
    for each object in objectlist
        if (object is on left of P) insert(object,leftList)
        else insert(object,rightList)
    endfor
    leftAABB = computeAABB(leftList)
    rightAABB = computeAABB(rightList)
    leftNode = (leftAABB, leftList)
    rightNode = (rightAABB, rightList)
    root.left = leftNode
    root.right = rightNode
    root.partitionPlane = P
    BVHcreate(leftNode,leftList)
    BVHcreate(rightNode,rightList)
}
```

LISTING 11.5: BVH creation algorithm.

The partitioning used during BVH creation may be used to sort the object list (partition sorting), and replace the object list in the leaf node by an index to the object and the number of objects in the list. In a BVH-based ray acceleration scheme, ray–scene intersection starts with the intersection of the ray with the root AABB of the BVH tree. If there is an intersection, the ray is recursively intersected with the AABBs of the children nodes till the recursion is complete. The order in which children nodes are intersected depends on the ray direction and the plane of partition associated with the node. The recursion is continued even if intersection is found. It is terminated when the recursion stack is empty. In the case that an intersection is found with the leaf node, the t of the ray is set and is used in the ray–AABB intersection test to

```
function rayBHV() // recursive function
    INPUT ray : Ray,
          node : BVHnode.
    OUTPUT ray.t : nearest point of intersection if any,
           hit   : true/false.
{
    if node==null return
    if (intersect(node.AABB, ray)
    {
        if (node.isLeaf)
        {
            t = intersect(ray,node.objectList)
            if (t < ray.t) ray.t = t
        }
        else
        {
            if (ray.direction[partitionPlane.axis] < 0)
                rayBVH(node.rightNode)
            else rayBVH(node.leftNode)
        }
    }
}
```

LISTING 11.6: Ray–BVH intersection-finding algorithm.

verify if the point of intersection is already closer. A sample pseudo-code for ray–BVH intersection is given in Listing 11.6.

In ray–BVH intersection, ray–AABB intersection plays a dominant role, and hence must be efficiently implemented. While the computational effort required for BVH construction is comparable to USS structure construction, the ray–BVH outperforms ray–USS intersection in most scenes. The performance improvement may vary depending on the heuristic used for choosing the node partition plane. Partitioning by surface area heuristics (SAH) is claimed to provide improved performance as compared to dividing the node by spatial size or by number of objects. However, optimal partition finding is still an open research problem.

11.1.4   Ray Tracing for Rendering

As stated in the introduction of this book, ray tracing is used when high quality rendering is in demand. In ray tracing-based rendering, rays are traced from a virtual camera through every pixel of the rendered image to query the scene color. A general ray tracing algorithm looks something like the code shown in Listing 11.7.

```
function rayTraceRendering()
    INPUT camera, scene
    OUTPUT image
{
    for row = 1 to rows
        for col = 1 to cols
            ray = getRay(row,col,camera)
            image[row][col] = getColor(ray, scene)
        endfor
    endfor
}
```

LISTING 11.7: Fundamental ray-tracing algorithm.

The first function, getRay, computes the ray through every pixel of the image array. How the ray is computed depends on the type of camera used; for the standard pinhole camera used in rasterization-based rendering as discussed earlier, the process is simple. We first compute the rays in camera space, where the image window is parallel to the XY plane and located *near* units away from the coordinate origin 0. Then we transform the ray from camera space to world space using inverse camera matrix (M_{camera}^{-1}). For simplicity we assume that the window is centered around the Z-axis, and the image origin is at the Bottom-Left corner of the image window. Then the ray through the center of the pixel (col,row) is computed as follows:

$$\text{ray.o} = M_{\text{camera}}^{-1} (0,0,0)^T$$

$$\text{ray.d} = M_{\text{camera}}^{-1} \left(w \left(\frac{(col + 0.5)}{cols} - 0.5 \right), h \left(\frac{(row + 0.5)}{rows} - 0.5 \right), -near \right)^T$$

where $M_{camera} = P_{rsp}M$, w and h are the width and height of the image window, and the image resolution is $cols \times rows$. The next function, getColor, gets the color of the light coming along the ray towards the camera. This color is assigned to the pixel. The exact computation carried out in this function distinguishes one ray-traced rendering method from the other. The getColor function may simply return the diffuse color of the object, or may evaluate the direct lighting equation, as explained in Chapter 6, to get the color at the point and return it. The color may be modulated with the texture queried from the texture map associated with the surface. This process is called ray-casting-based rendering. It creates images similar to those created in simple rasterization based rendering. As the rendering using rasterization hardware produces images at a much faster rate, it is uncommon to use ray casting for the same purpose. Most ray-tracing-based rendering methods normally include some form of global illumination computation to get color in their getColor method, and a ray-tracing-based rendering method is distinguished from the others based on what is done in its getColor method. Independent of the methods, the first step in getColor is computing the nearest visible point along the ray originating at the camera, and then computing the color at that visible point. We detail the exact lighting computation technique used in two popular ray-tracing-based rendering methods: classical ray tracing and Monte Carlo ray tracing.

11.1.5 Classical Ray Tracing

Classical ray tracing for rendering was introduced to rendering literature in 1980 by Whitted [41]. This method, like ray-casting-based rendering, computes direct lighting and texturing at the point ray surface intersection, but extends it to include shadows, specular inter-reflections between multiple objects in the scene, and also may include support of transparency. The algorithm given in Listing 11.8 details the method.

```
function getColor()
    INPUT ray, scene
{
    (t, object, intersectFlag) = raySceneIntersect(ray,scene)
    if (intersectFlag==FALSE) return backgroundColor
    color = black
    for i=1 to #Lights
        shadowRay = computeShadowRay(ray,t,object,scene,lights[i])
        if (inShadow(t,ray,scene) == FALSE)
            color += computeDirectLight(t,ray,scene.lights[i])
        endif
    endfor
    if (isReflective(object)) // Interreflection support
        newRay = reflect(ray,t,object)
        color += object.specularReflectance * getColor(newRay,scene)
    endif
    if (isRefractive(object)) // transparency support
        newRay = refract(ray,t,object)
        color += object.transparency * getColor(newRay,scene)
    endif
    return color
}
```

LISTING 11.8: Algorithm for pixel color computation in classical ray-tracing.

As we see from the algorithm, shadow, mirror reflection and transparency are handled naturally by creating additional rays and tracing them. Unlike in rasterization-based rendering, no complicated algorithmic effort is required to support these features. The additional rays are termed secondary rays to distinguish them from the rays originating at the camera, which are called primary rays. For all the secondary rays, the origin is the point of intersection of the primary ray with the scene, but the directions differ.

Shadow ray directions for point light sources are computed by taking the vector difference of the shadow ray origin from the position of the light source. This approach is also extended to area light sources by dividing the surface of the area light source into smaller area patches, and computing the shadow ray directions as the vector differences of the shadow ray origin from the center of (or from randomly chosen points on) the patches. A surface point

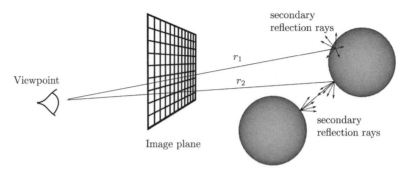

FIGURE 11.5: Path tracing. Every time a ray hits a surface a new ray is shot and a new path is generated.

is under shadow if an object appears between the point and the light source, which translates into finding the t_i of a shadow ray–object intersection and checking for the inequality $0 < t_i < 1$. This ray scene object intersection test, and checking the value of t is done inside function inShadow. Note that inShadow function does not require finding the nearest point of intersection. As soon as an intersection satisfying the condition $0 < t < 1$ is found, there is no more need to continue with the intersection of the shadow ray with the other objects of the scene. That is why sometimes it is preferable to write an inShadow algorithm separately from the standard nearest point-finding ray-Scene intersection algorithm. Furthermore, an object shadowing a point is very likely to shadow the points in the neighborhood. So caching the nearest shadow object information and first checking for the intersection of the shadow ray for the neighboring primary rays with the cached object has been shown to accelerate shadow computation.

Reflection and refraction of light at the nearest point along the primary ray is handled, respectively, by setting the direction of the secondary ray to be the mirror reflection and the refraction of the primary ray and making recursive calls to getColor. The recursion stops when the ray does not intersect any object in the scene, or hits an object that is non-reflective and non-refractive. In a highly reflective/refractive closed environment the algorithm may get into an infinite recursive loop. Though such scenes are uncommon, most algorithms introduce a safety feature by keeping the count of recursive calls, and stopping recursion after the recursion count reaches a certain predefined maximum (often set at 5).

Classical ray tracing is capable of creating accurate rendering with global illumination due to inter-reflection and inter-refraction of light in scenes with mirror-like reflectors and fully or partly transparent objects. Classical ray tracing has been extended to support inter-reflection in scenes with diffuse and translucent surfaces.

11.1.6 Path Tracing

Path tracing is a Monte Carlo-based ray tracing method that renders global illumination effects in scenes with arbitrary surface properties. A path here is a collection of connected rays, starting with primary rays. The rays are recursively generated from the primary rays. So, in effect, path tracing may be considered a simple extension of classical ray tracing algorithm. *The difference is that the secondary reflection rays are not restricted to mirror-like surfaces, and refracted rays are not restricted only to transparent surfaces.* The ray generation from arbitrary surfaces is done by Monte Carlo direction sampling. Unlike in classical ray tracing, instead of generating a primary ray from the camera through the center of the pixel, in path tracing multiple primary rays are normally generating through random positions in the pixel. So a path tracing algorithm for a scene containing opaque surfaces has the form given in Listing 11.9 (see Figure 11.5).

```
function pathTraceRendering()
INPUT camera, scene
OUTPUT image
{
    for row = 1 to rows
        for col = 1 to cols
            for i = 1 to N
                ray = getPathRay(row,col,camera)
                image[row][col] = getPathColor(ray, scene)/N
            endfor
        endfor
}

function getPathColor()
    INPUT ray, scene
{
    (t, object, intersectFlag) = raySceneIntersect(ray,scene)
    if (intersectFlag==FALSE) return backgroundColor
    color = black
    for i=1 to #Lights
        shadowRay = computeShadowRay(ray, t,object,scene,lights[i])
        if (inShadow(t,ray,scene) == FALSE)
            color += computeDirectLight(t,ray,scene.lights[i])
        endif
    endfor
    if (isReflective(object)) // Interreflection support
        (newRay, factor) = sampleHemisphere(ray, t, object)
        color += factor * getPathColor(newRay, scene)
    endif
    return color
}
```

LISTING 11.9: Path tracing algorithm.

As mentioned in the early part of this section, we can see that path-tracing-based rendering and classical rendering are very similar. The difference is in computing the secondary reflection ray direction, which is done by Monte

Carlo sampling of the hemisphere. It generates a random direction on the upper hemisphere of the surface, and computes light along this direction. There exists a number of different ways of sampling this direction: uniform sampling, cosine importance sampling, BRDF importance sampling, etc. Associated with the sampling is a factor that is used to multiply the patch color returned by the getPathColor function. This factor depends on how the sample is generated, and on the BRDF of the surface. Independent of the type of sampling, every Monte Carlo sampling method, also referred to as a stochastic sampling method, depends on a uniform random sampler that samples floating point range [0, 1] uniformly. Many programming language implementations provide us with such a sampler function as a part of their respective libraries. Let us call this function rand(). Using this function we will discuss here a couple of hemisphere samplers and the associated multiplication factors.

Uniform Sampling of Hemisphere: A hemisphere is half of a sphere, and can have infinitely many orientations. The orientation of a hemisphere over a surface point depends on the normal at the surface. For direction sampling on an arbitrarily oriented hemisphere, we first make a uniform sampling of a canonical hemisphere, i.e., a hemisphere of unit radius around Z-axis, and then rotate the direction to match the actual orientation of the hemisphere. A sample vector from the center through the canonical hemisphere surface can be described by spherical coordinates (θ, ϕ), where θ is the angle around the Z-axis, and ϕ is the angle the projection of the direction vector makes with the X-axis. Once the sample vector is generated it is transformed using the TBN matrix. Thus the uniformly sampled direction on this canonical hemisphere is computed as in Listing 11.10.

```
function uniformHemisphereSample1()
    INPUT object, p, ray
    OUTPUT direction, factor
{
    // Uniform sampling the canonical hemisphere
    θ = arccos(rand())
    φ = 2π rand()
    sample_d = (sin(θ) cos(φ), sin(θ) sin(φ), cos(θ))ᵀ
    // Let T, B, N are the unit tangent, bitangent, and
    // normal vectors at the object point p
    (direction, factor) = ([T B N] * sample_d, 2π cos(θ) (object.brdf(ray.d,↵
        sample_d)) ) // Rotation
}
```

LISTING 11.10: Algorithm for uniformly sampling an arbitrarily oriented unit hemisphere.

Another option would be to sample the whole sphere, and discard all those vectors that make an angle greater than 90 degrees with the normal to the surface at the point of interest. In fact the angle checking can be done by checking for the sign of the dot product of the sample vector with the normal, and accepting only those sample vectors that have a positive dot product. As half of the directions are discarded this method may not be considered as efficient, but one advantage of this approach is that no TBN matrix transformation is required. So we also give here (see Listing 11.11) a method based on uniform sampling of the sphere.

```
function uniformHemisphereSample2()
    INPUT object, p, ray
    OUTPUT direction, factor
{
    Let N be the unit normal vectors at the object point p
    while(TRUE)
        θ = arccos(1−2*rand())
        phi = 2π rand()
        sample_d = (sin(θ)cos(φ), sin(θ)sin(φ), cos(θ))^T
        // Uniform sampling the canonical hemisphere
        if (dot(N,sample_d) > 0)
            (direction, factor) = (sample_d, 2π dot(N,sample_d) object.brdf(ray.d,↩
                sample_d) ) // Rotation
        endif
    endwhile
}
```

LISTING 11.11: Rejection-based algorithm for uniformly sampling an arbitrarily oriented unit hemisphere.

Cosine-Based Importance Sampling of Hemisphere: In this approach, sampled directions have a cosine θ distribution on the hemisphere around the normal, which means the density of the samples are maximum closer to the normal, and the density falls according to cosine function away from the normal. Cosine-sampled directions are preferred over the uniform-sampled direction in Monte Carlo lighting computation. It is mostly because the color contributions brought in by the rays traced along directions away from the normal are reduced by a factor of $\cos\theta$. So it is considered better to sample according to cosine distribution and not reduce by a factor, than to attenuate the color contribution by a factor of $\cos\theta$. As the distribution is very much dependent on the angle the sampled direction makes with the normal vector, we cannot use a full sphere sampling method here. Listing 11.12 shows a popular cosine sampling method.

```
function cosineHemisphereSample()
    INPUT object, p, ray
    OUTPUT direction, factor
{
    // Uniform sampling the canonical hemisphere
    θ = arcsin(√rand())
    φ = 2π rand()
    sample_d = (sin(θ)cos(φ), sin(θ)sin(φ), cos(θ))^T
    // Let T, B, N are the unit tangent, bitangent, and
    // normal vectors at the object point p
    (direction, factor) = ([T B N] * sample_d, π object.brdf(ray.d,sample_d) ) // ↩
        Rotation
}
```

LISTING 11.12: Algorithm for cosine importance sampling a hemisphere.

11.2   Multi-Pass Algorithms

Ray-tracing-based lighting computation methods discussed in the above section are view-dependent computations. That means if the view is changed all the lighting-related computation must be repeated. At times it is preferable to compute the lighting distribution in the scene first (global lighting computation pass) and store it in a data structure. Then, access the data structure during the ray casting or rasterization-based rendering time (rendering pass) to compute the color for the pixel. Such approaches create faster rendering. However, global lighting pass can be very time consuming. This approach is preferable when a faster walk through renderings with global illumination is a requirement, for example, in game rendering. Literature abounds with methods to carry out the global lighting computation pass. We describe here two methods: the photon tracing and radiosity methods.

11.2.1   Photon Tracing

Photon tracing is a two-pass rendering technique. Both the passes mostly use ray tracing technique for ray–scene intersection. The first pass of the technique simulates photon behavior of light in which a large number of photons are emitted from the light source and propagated in the scene till they are either completely absorbed, or lost in the space. Each photon is emitted from certain locations of the light source, with a starting direction. The positions are randomly sampled from the surface of the light source and the direction for the sampled photon is randomly sampled from the hemisphere around the normal to the surface of that position. The photon carries with it a power spectrum that is representative of the light source, and is propagated in the scene. During the propagation the photon travels along a ray determined by the propagation direction. If the photon hits a surface during its propagation then it loses part of its power due to the surface absorption, and is reflected with attenuated power. The photon continues its propagation along the reflected direction and continues with its interactions till it no more hits any surface (lost in space) or its power is attenuated significantly. Each hit event of the photons is stored in a data structure associated with the hit surface or with the whole scene. In the second pass, the actual rendering pass, rays are traced from the eye through the view window, and are intersected with the surface. A circular neighborhood around the point of intersection is searched to find the photon hits and a weighted sum of the power spectrum of the points modulated with the surface BRDF is reflected towards the eye.

Photon tracing technique is a relatively simple, but expensive global illumination computation technique. The quality of the rendering of photon-traced scenes normally depends on the number of photons traced: the larger the number, the better the quality. Lighting computation in a relatively simple scene requires tracing hundreds of millions of photons, and even with such high numbers it is not uncommon to see noise in the parts that are indirectly visible to the light source. A lot of recent research has been devoted to increasing the efficiency and quality of photon-traced rendering.

11.2.2   Radiosity

The radiosity method was introduced in 1984 with the goal to compute inter-reflection of light in diffuse scenes. We have described the term radiosity (conventional symbol B) in Section 6.2, as an alternate term for irradiance and exitance. In the context of global lighting computation the term radiosity refers to the method used to compute equilibrium irradiance in a scene. In the radiosity method the propagation of light is modeled as a linear system of equations relating the radiosity of each surface in the scene to the radiosity of all other surfaces in the scene. The equilibrium radiosity over the surfaces are computed by solving this linear system. In the next section we develop this linear system and describe the various solution methods for solving this system. Finally we describe methods for realistic rendering of scenes with a precomputed radiosity solution.

The radiosity method is based on two important assumptions:

1. It is possible to break down the surfaces of any scene into smaller patches in such a way that radiosity is uniform over the patch. So it is assumed that surfaces of the scene have been broken down into a number of such uniform radiosity patches.

2. The surface patches are flat and are diffusely reflecting in nature.

11.2.3   Concept of Form Factor

In the radiosity method every surface patch plays the role of an emitter and a receiver. Of all the patches only a few belong to actual light sources and are inherently emitters. But all other patches emit the reflected light, and hence are secondary emitters. A part of the light flux arriving on a patch from all other patches on the scene is reflected and the rest of the light is lost in absorption. We derive here a relation between the flux emitted by the i-th emitter patch, Φ_i, and the flux received at the receiver patch, j, from the expression derived for lighting due to area light source in Chapter 6. The expression for the irradiance at a differential area around a point on the receiver patch j is

$$E_j = L_i \int_{A_i} \cos\theta_i \cos\theta_j V_{dA_i,dA_j} dA_i / R^2_{dA_i,dA_j} \qquad (11.17)$$

where angle (θ_i) (θ_j) is the angle formed by the line connecting the two patches dA_i and dA_j and the normal at patch $dA_i(dA_j)$, V_{dA_i,dA_j} and R_{dA_i,dA_j} are

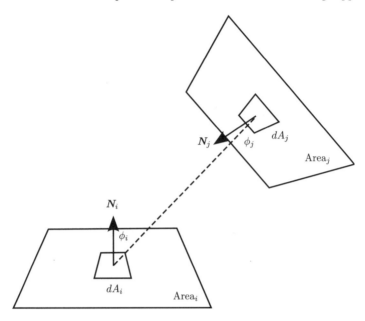

FIGURE 11.6: Form factor.

respectively the visibility and distance between the two differential patches. The visibility term is binary in nature, and takes value one or zero depending on whether the differential areas dA_i, dA_j are visible to each other or not. We assumed that the radiance of the patches is constant over the surface patch, and surfaces are diffuse. Under these conditions the flux and radiance are related by expression $L = \Phi/(\pi A)$. So we will use this relation to replace L_i, the radiance of patch i, by Φ_i. Next we compute an expression for the flux received by the total surface j due to light emitted from surface i. Here we use the relation between irradiance and flux: $d\Phi = EdA$ and integrate the differential flux over the whole area to get the following equation.

$$\Phi_{i \to j} = \int_{A_j} E_j dA_j = \Phi_i/(\pi A_i) \int_{A_j} \int_{A_i} \cos\theta_i \cos\theta_j V_{dA_i,dA_j} dA_i/R^2_{dA_i,dA_j}$$

$$(11.18)$$

Now we can write an expression of the fraction of the flux emitted by patch i that reached patch j as

$$F_{i \to j} = \Phi_{i \to j}/\Phi_i = 1/(\pi A_i) \int_{A_j} dA_j \int_{A_i} \cos\theta_i \cos\theta_j V_{dA_i,dA_j} dA_i/R^2_{dA_i,dA_j}$$

$$(11.19)$$

The expression of this fraction contains terms that depend on the geometry and orientation and is independent of any lighting characteristics of the surface. This fraction is called form-factor, and plays an important role in radiosity computation.

We said earlier that every patch in a scene is an emitter, be it primary or secondary. So if patch i is emitting towards patch j then patch j also must be emitting towards patch i. Using derivations as above we can also write the expression for fraction $F_{j \to i}$, the fraction of flux received by patch i due to emission from patch j. And the expression is:

$$F_{j \to i} = 1/(\pi A_j) \int_{A_i} dA_i \int_{A_j} \cos \theta_i \cos \theta_j V_{dA_i, dA_j} dA_j / R^2_{dA_i, dA_j} \qquad (11.20)$$

We notice that both the fractions are similar except for the area term in the denominator of the right hand side. That means the fractions are related to each other and the relation is: $A_i F_{i \to j} = A_j F_{j \to i}$. This relation becomes useful in the derivation of the radiosity transport equation, and also is useful during form factor computation because if we know $F_{i \to j}$ then we can get $F_{j \to i}$ and *vice versa* by simply applying the relation.

11.2.4 Flux Transport Equation and Radiosity Transport Equation

In this section we derive an expression for total flux leaving any patch i. The total flux leaving a patch has two components: emission term, and a reflection term. Emission is a property of the surface. If the surface is a light source then it has nonzero emission, zero otherwise. We assume that Φ_i^e, the emitting flux for each patch, is known *a priori*. The reflection term Φ_i^r is due to the reflection of the flux received by the patch. In the paragraph above, we defined form factor to express the fractional amount of flux received from elsewhere. Part of that received light is reflection. The fraction reflected is also a material property known as reflectance ρ, and is also known *a priori* for all patches. We use this information to write an expression of flux leaving any patch i in terms of flux leaving from all other patches in the scene as

$$\Phi_i = \Phi_i^e + \Phi_i^r = \Phi_i^e + \rho_i \sum_{j=1}^{N} F_{j \to i} \Phi_j \qquad (11.21)$$

This equation is called *flux transport equation.*

In a uniformly emitting surface the flux is related to its radiosity by the equation $\Phi = BA$. We now use this relation to substitute flux with radiosity to derive a transport equation for radiosity.

$$B_i A_i = B_i^e A_i + \rho_i \sum_{j=1}^{N} F_{j \to i} B_j A_j. \qquad (11.22)$$

Dividing both sides by A_i we get

$$B_i = B_i^e + \rho_i \sum_{j=1}^{N} F_{j \to i} B_j A_j / A_i. \qquad (11.23)$$

Next we use the relation between form factors to replace $F_{j \to i} A_j / A_i$ by $F_{i \to j}$ to get:

$$B_i = B_i^e + \rho_i \sum_{j=1}^{N} F_{i \to j} B_j. \qquad (11.24)$$

This equation is called the *radiosity transport equation*. Note that both the transport equations are very similar. The only difference is the order in which the patch indices are specified in each equation's form factor term. In the flux transport equation the order is from patch j to patch i, and in the radiosity transport equation it is the other way around.

Both the transport equations are written for a patch i and are valid for every patch i from 1 to N. So if we write expressions for all the is, then we get a system of linear equations that expresses flux of every patch in the scene in terms of flux of all other patches. We noticed earlier that form factor $F_{i \to j}$ (or $F_{j \to i}$) depends on the orientation and location of the patches in the scene, and hence can be computed independent of the lighting in the scene. So we should be able to solve this linear system to get the equilibrium flux in the scene due to inter-reflection of the emitted light. Before we describe the radiosity solution methods, we describe a couple of methods for computing form factors.

11.2.4.1   Computation of Form Factor

Many methods have been proposed to compute form factor. Analytical methods of computing form factor between two visible patches have been proposed. However, in real scenes most patches are partly or fully occluded from each other. So visibility must be resolved before using any analytical method. As visibility computation is the most expensive part of the computation, and analytical methods are only useful for completely visible pairs of patches, the use of analytical methods is not popular. So here we discuss a couple of numerical methods that account for visibility during the computation. We mentioned earlier that we can take advantage of the fact that if we have computed $F_{i \to j}$ then $F_{j \to i}$ can be computed by simple arithmetic. So this principle itself reduces the computation cost by half. We describe a couple of methods for the actual form factor computation.

Form Factor by Monte Carlo Quadrature: The form factor between two patches is a four-dimensional integration. So computation of this term by Monte Carlo quadrature proceeds as shown in Listing 11.13.

```
F_{i→j} = 0
for N times
    Let p_i be a randomly sampled point on Patch i
    Let n_i be the normal to the patch at p_i
    Let p_j be a randomly sampled point on Patch j
    Let n_j be the normal to the patch at p_j
    d = p_j - p_i
    R = |d|
    shadowRay = (p_i,d)
    V = inShadow(ray, scene) ? 0:1
    ΔF = dot(d/R, n_j) dot(-d/R, n_j) (V/πR²)
    F_{i→j} += (ΔF/N)
endfor
F_{j→i} = F_{i→j} (A_i/A_j)
```

LISTING 11.13: Algorithm for computing form factor between two patches using Monte Carlo sampling.

As we notice here, we compute visibility between two points using the *inShadow* function described in our ray tracing section. So the algorithm is relatively straightforward. However, we must note that visibility by ray tracing may require full ray-scene intersection, and the form factor must be computed between every pair of the patches, so this method can be expensive.

Hemisphere/Hemicube Method: This is a class of methods that computes form factor between a patch and the rest of the patches in the scene. They are approximate in nature, because the computation is carried out at only one point (mostly the center point) of the patch. So the form factor of the patch is approximated to be the same as the form factor of the differential surface around the point and rest of the scene. As the receiver surface is a differential patch the form factor equation is simplified from a double integration to a single integration.

$$F_{j→i} \approx F_{j→dA_i} = \int_{A_j} \int \cos\theta_i \cos\theta_j V_{dA_i,dA_j} dA_j / R^2_{dA_i,dA_j} \qquad (11.25)$$

Furthermore, patches emitting towards another must all lie on the upper hemisphere of the receiving patch. So if we are interested in computing form factor between all those emitting patches, then we should in principle be integrating only over the surface of the upper hemisphere. We write here an expression for such a form factor.

$$F_{\mathcal{H}_j→i} \approx \int_{\mathcal{H}_j} \int \cos\theta_i V_{dA_i,d\omega_j} d\omega_j \approx \sum_k \cos\theta_k V_{i,k}\Delta\omega_k = \sum_k V_{i,k}factor_k \qquad (11.26)$$

where $\mathcal{H}_j$ represents area of patch j visible to patch i through the unit hemisphere over patch i, and $d\omega_j$ replaces $\cos\theta_j dA_j/R^2_{dA_i,dA_j}$. For a unit hemisphere, $R=1$ and $\cos\theta_j=1$ as well. So the differential areas over the hemisphere itself represent differential solid angles. However, it is not so when we replace hemisphere by hemicube in the numerical method discussed below. The interpretation of the visibility term is slightly different here: it represents whether the patch j is visible through the differential solid angle. The summation terms in the equations approximate the integration over $\mathcal{H}_j$ by the summation of discrete subdivisions of the hemisphere, $V_{i,k}$ is the visibility of patch j to patch i through the solid angle k. The term $factor_k$ represents the analytical form factor of the portion of hemispherical surface area subtended by the k-th discrete solid angle. It is $\Delta\omega_j$ times the cosine of the direction through the k-th solid angle, and can be computed *a priori* for specific discretizations. This approach of form factor computation requires that we find the visibility of patch j through each discrete subdivision of the hemisphere. Instead of finding the discrete subdivisions through which a patch j is visible, if we find the patch j visible through each discrete subdivision k of the hemisphere then this latter becomes the already discussed problem of nearest object finding along a ray. And we can write an expression for computing only a fraction of the form factor for a part of the patch j visible through the discrete solid angle as:

$$\Delta F_{j \rightarrow i} \approx \Delta F_{\mathcal{H}_j \rightarrow i} = factor_k \qquad (11.27)$$

and compute the form-factor for the whole patch j as $F_{j \rightarrow i} = \sum \delta F_{j \rightarrow i}$. Using these formulations we can write the algorithm for computing the form factor between the patches as given in Listing 11.14.

```
for all j
    F_{j→i} = 0
endfor

Let H_i be the unit hemisphere around p_i the center of patch i.
Let N be the number of discrete subdivision of the hemisphere
for k = 1 to N
    // assuming N is the number of discrete subdivision of the hemisphere
    // Let d_k be direction from the center of patch i through the center of the k−↩
        th solid angle ray = (p_i,d_k)
    j = nearestObject(ray, scene)
    F_{j→i} += factor_k
endfor
```

LISTING 11.14: Algorithm for computing form factor between a patch and all other patches using a method based on projection on hemisphere.

Notice that in this algorithm we have replaced the visibility function from the form factor equation by nearest object, that returns the patch visible along the direction through the solid angle. By doing so we are able to update the form factor between the receiver patch and all those patches contributing to the receiver patch. By discretizing the hemisphere sufficiently we can get a good-enough approximation of the form factors.

A variation of the hemisphere-based method is the *Hemicube method*, in which the hemicube replaces the hemisphere. Hemicube covers the whole hemisphere of directions, but has the advantage that its five faces are flat rectangles. So one may use hardware-based visibility computation by projecting the whole scene on each of the hemicube faces, and rendering patch id's on the discrete hemicube pixels. Thanks to hardware acceleration techniques, this method used to be much faster compared to ray tracing, and hence was one of the earliest acceleration methods proposed for form factor computation.

11.2.5 Solution of Radiosity System

We now have all the components required to solve the linear system of radiosity transport and flux transport equation. We can write a matrix form $\mathbf{MA} = \mathbf{B}$ where $\mathbf{A}$ represents the vector of unknown equilibrium flux or radiosity terms, $\mathbf{B}$ represents the vector of emitting flux or radiosity terms, and $\mathbf{M}$ represents a square matrix with terms containing known reflectance and computed form-factors. The size of the vectors and matrix depends on the number of patches in the scene. Solutions for the system $\mathbf{A} = \mathbf{M}^{-1}\mathbf{B}$ can be computed by a matrix inversion followed by a matrix vector multiplication. For a vector size N, the computational complexity of this approach is $O(N^3)$. Because of this complexity, a radiosity/flux system solution for a reasonably complex scene (> 10000 patches) is impractical. One must note here that patches must be small, to satisfy the uniform brightness requirement. So even for a smallish scene the number of patches reaching or exceeding > 10000 is common. An alternate approach to radiosity/flux solution is to use an iterative method for solving linear systems. Any of the three well-known iteration methods, Jacobi method, Gauss-Seidel method and Southwell iteration, may be used. Independent of the exact method used, all the iterative methods start with an initial guess (see Listing 11.15) for radiosity/flux distribution, update radiosity of all patches based on the previous guess, and repeat until converged.

```
for patch i=1 to N // Initialize
    B_i = B_i^e
endfor
```

LISTING 11.15: Initialization for gathering based method.

We first describe Jacobi method (see Listing 11.16) and Gauss-Seidel method (see Listing 11.17)-based algorithms for solving the radiosity system. Same approaches may be applied to solving flux systems as well.

```
// Jacobi Iteration: Radiosity Gathering Method
while (not converged)
    for patch i=1 to N
        $Bnew_i = B_i^e + \rho_i \sum_j B_j F_{i \rightarrow j}$
    endfor
    for patch i=1 to N
        B_i = Bnew_i
    endfor
endwhile
```

LISTING 11.16: Jacobi-iteration-based method for computing equilibrium radiosity.

```
// Gauss–Seidel Iteration: Radiosity Gathering Method
while (not converged)
    for patch i=1 to N
```
$$B_i = B_i^e + \rho_i \sum_j B_j F_{i \to j}$$
```
    endfor
endwhile
```

LISTING 11.17: Gauss-Seidel-iteration-based method for computing equilibrium radiosity.

One may notice that the Jacobi and Gauss-Seidel methods are small variations of each other. The Gauss-Seidel method converges relatively faster, and does not require any intermediate vector *Bnew*. So of the two it is the preferred method.

The third iterative algorithm (see Listing 11.18), like photon tracing, simulates the natural process of light transport. The iteration method distributes light from the brightest patches in the scene. To start with, the emitter patches are the brightest. After light from emitters is distributed, the next brightest patch is chosen and its light that has not been distributed (shot) so far is distributed, and the process is continued till the equilibrium is reached.

```
// Southwell Iteration: Radiosity Shooting Method
for patch i=1 to N // Initialize
```
$$B\_unshot\_i = B_i^e$$
```
endfor
while (not converged)
    // Let j be the patch with highest B_unshot
    for patch i=1 to N
```
$$\Delta B = \rho_i \sum_j B\_unshot\_j \; F_{i \to j}$$
$$B_i \; {+}{=} \; \Delta B$$
```
        B_unshot_i += ΔB
    endfor
    B_unshot_j = 0
endwhile
```

LISTING 11.18: Southwell-iteration-based method for computing equilibrium radiosity.

This algorithm requires an additional vector B_unshot to keep track of the radiosity that is yet to be shot or distributed, and the total radiosity. Every time the light distribution from a surface patch, j, is completed its B_unshot is set to zero. This avoids erroneous repeated distribution of the same light from the patches.

All these iterative algorithms require an equilibrium condition check. The equilibrium condition is assumed to have been reached when the incremental flux on all the patches is reduced below a small threshold. In practice, the iteration is continued for a fixed number of iterations. In such a case, choosing a shooting-based method improves the accuracy of overall lighting computation. In addition to the accuracy-related criterion, this algorithm is also preferred because of a couple of other reasons: less storage requirement and adaptive form factor computation. Note that the form-factor matrix required N^2 storage and a similar order of computation effort. However, we may notice that the iterative solution proceeds with one patch (the brightest one) at a time. So one may choose to compute only the form-factors from this patch to all other patches using a hemisphere or hemicube-based method, and avoid the N^2 computation and storage. However, this approach requires a small modification to the ΔB computation step of the shooting algorithm. The modified step is

$$\Delta B = \rho_i \sum_{j=1} B_j F_{j \to i} A_j / A_i. \qquad (11.28)$$

11.2.5.1 Rendering from Radiosity Solution

The radiosity method computes equilibrium radiosity over every patch of the scene independent of whether the patch is visible or not. For creating rendered images of the scenes, a rendering step must follow a radiosity computation. The goal in this step is to create a realistic-looking visualization of the scene from the computed solution. The simplest approach is to use the patch radiosity directly for color. Radiosity from a uniformly diffuse surface patch is related to its radiance by the relation: $B = \pi L$. This radiance can be used as the color for any point on the patch visible to the virtual camera through a pixel. Such a rendering unfortunately creates a faceted appearance.

A simple approach to get rid of this faceted appearance is to compute radiosity at the vertices of the patches by area weighted averaging of the radiosity values of the connecting patches, followed by Gouraud interpolated rendering. Though the resulting appearance is smooth, it may still suffer from inaccuracy in meshing and will result in blurring of highlights, and leakage of shadow and light. In the following section we discuss a gathering-based approach for creating high-quality rendering.

Final Gathering: In final-gathering-based rendering, radiance at the surface point visible though a pixel is computed by gathering light from the hemisphere surrounding the point. Either of the direct lighting computation algorithms, the one described in Section 2.2.3 for computing from an environment light source, or the one described in Section 2.2.2, can be adapted for use in final gathering.

When using the environment lighting-based approach, the sampling process remains unchanged. Each sampled ray from the point of interest is traced to find the visible surface patch. The radiance from the visible patches along the sample rays are averaged to get the estimated radiance from the point.

The radiosity method computes outgoing equilibrium radiosity at every surface patch in the scene. Thus, every patch in the scene may be considered as a potential light source. The method for direct light computation due to an area light source can be used to compute light at any point on the scene due to each patch. Thus, one can use an area light-based gathering approach for rendering realistic looking images.

One disadvantage to using each and every patch for lighting computation during the gathering process is that in a complex scene only a small fraction of the scene patches are visible from any point in the scene. The contribution of invisible surface patches to the illumination of the point is zero and thus any computational effort spent in gathering light from such patches is wasteful. A hemi-cube-based method removes this problem. In this method a virtual unit hemi-cube is set up over the point of interest. Using the hardware Z-buffer rendering method, the scene is projected onto the faces of this hemicube. The Z-buffer algorithm eliminates invisible surfaces. Each pixel on the hemicube represents a small piece of a visible surface patch and hence can be considered as a light source illuminating the surface point at the center of the hemi-cube.

If the pixel is sufficiently small then the direct lighting due to the pixel can be approximated by $B_j F_{pixel}$ where B_j is the radiosity of the surface patch j projected on the pixel, $F_{pixel} = \frac{\cos \theta_1 \cos \theta_2}{\pi r_{12}^2} \Delta A$, ΔA is the area of the pixel and is mostly the same for all hemicube pixels.

The cosine terms and the r term in the F_{pixel} expression depend on the hemicube face on which the pixel lies and the coordinates of the pixel. For the top face whose pixel coordinate is (x,y,1), $F_{pixel} = \frac{1}{\pi(x^2+y^2+1)^2}\Delta A$. For the side faces, the pixel coordinate is ($\pm$1,y,z) and $F_{pixel} = \frac{z}{\pi(1+y^2+z^2)^2}\Delta A$. For both the front and back side the expression with pixel coordinate (x,$\pm$1,z) is $\Delta F_{pixel} = \frac{z}{\pi(x^2+1+z^2)^2}\Delta A$. In the gathering-based computation, only radiosity, B_j, is projection dependent. The rest of the terms in the equation can be pre-computed and multiplied at the time of final gathering. The final gathering method can be adapted to create noise-free rendering in the photon-tracing-based method. Unlike in the radiosity method, the photon-tracing-based method does not compute equilibrium radiosity. It stores the photon information at the hit points. So radiosity must be computed every time at the surface point visible through the hemicube pixel.

Appendix A

NVMC Class

We have already seen in Section 2.5.1 how the framework is structured and showed a few examples of access to the element of the scene. Here we will give a more detailed description of the framework to serve as reference.

A.1   Elements of the Scene

```
NVMC.Race.prototype = { ...
    get bbox             :  function ...
    get track            :  function ...
    get tunnels          :  function ...
    get arealigths       :  function ...
    get lamps            :  function ...
    get trees            :  function ...
    get buildings        :  function ...
    get weather          :  function ...
    get startPosition    :  function ...
    get observerPosition :  function ...
    get photoPosition    :  function ...
};
```

The class Race contains all the elements of the scene except the participants to the race (that is, the cars). These elements are: the bounding box of the scene, track, tunnels, trees, buildings, area lights, lamps and weather. Obviously more elements can be considered in the scene (for example, people, flags, etc.), but our intention was not to realize a video game, but to learn computer graphics, so we only introduced essential elements to implement the techniques explained.

Bounding box

```
race.bbox = [];
```

bbox is an array of six floating points containing the minimun and maximum corners of the bounding box of the scene: [minx,miny,minz,maxx,maxy,maxz]. It is guaranteed that *every* element of the scene lies inside this bounding box.

Track

```
race.track = new Track()
Track.prototype = {...
    get leftSideAt :  function ...
    get rightSideAt :  function ...
    get pointsCount :  function ...
};
```

The track is described by two arrays of 3D points, race.track.leftSideAt and race.track.rightSideAt, describing the left and right margin, respectively. The layout of the coordinates is: $x_0, y_0, z_0, x_1, y_1, z_1, \ldots, x_{n-1}, y_{n-1}, z_{n-1}$ where the value of n is found as race.track.pointsCount.

Tunnels

```
race.tunnels = [];
Tunnel.prototype = {...
    get leftSideAt  :  function ...
    get rightSideAt :  function ...
    get pointsCount :  function ...
    get height      :  function ...
};
```

A tunnel is described just like a track, with one more member value indicating the height of the entire tunnel.

Buildings

```
race.buildings =   [];
Building.prototype = {...
    get positionAt :  function ...
    get pointsCount :  function ...
    get heightAt    :  function ...
};
```

A building is described by a polygon for its footprint, specified as a sequence of counterclockwise ordered 3D points on the XZ plane and a height value for each point.

Trees

```
race.trees =   [];
Tree.prototype = {...
    get position    :  function ...
    get height      :  function ...
};
```

A tree is described by its position on the ground and its height.

Lamps

```
race.lamps =   [];
```

```
Lamp.prototype = {...
    get position    :    function ...
    get height      :    function ...
};
```

A streelamp, just like a tree, is described with its position on the ground and its height.

Area lights

```
race.arealights     = []
AreaLight.prototype = {...
    get frame       :    function ...
    get size        :    function ...
    get color       :    function ...
};
```

An area light is emitted from a rectangular surface. The rectangle is lying in the XZ plane of the frame specified by frame (a 4×4 matrix), centered on the origin and with size size[0] and size[1]. The color of the area light is specified with color (a 3-value array).

Weather

```
race.weather = new Weather();
Weather.prototype = {...
    get sunLightDirection    :    function ...
    get cloudDensity         :    function ...
    get rainStrength         :    function ...
};
```

The weather is characterized by the sunLightDirection (an array of 3 values), the cloudDensity, a real value ranging from 0 (clear sky) to 1 (very cloudy) and rainStrength, also ranging from 0 (no rain) to 1 (storm). Note that in the Upgrade Your Client sections of this book we only used the sunlight direction. The other properties are hints for additional exercises. Clouds may be rendered with impostors just like the trees and rain by means of particle systems as introduced in Section 10.4.

Initial Positions

The last three members of the object Race are used for initialization purposes and are: the car's starting point position (startPosition), the photographer position (photoPosition) and the observerCamera starting point (observerPosition).

A.2   Players

A player corresponds to a car and it has a PhysicsStaticState and a Physics-DynamicState.

The PhysicsStaticState is the set of the static characteristics of the car, which are all 3-value arrays. The mass is the mass of the car, and the forward-Force (backwardForce) is the magnitude of the force impressed to the car when accelerating forward (backward). The brakingFriction is the friction coefficient imposed to the moving car when the brakes are pressed. These values are set by default to make the car behave as a regular sports car, but you can play with them to obtain different cars.

```
PhysicsStaticState.prototype = {
    get mass                : function ...
    get forwardForce        : function ...
    get backwardForce       : function ...
    get brakingFriction     : function ...
    get linearFriction      : function ...
};
```

The PhysicsDynamicState is the set of characteristics that describe the instantaneous conditions of the car. Frame (a 4 × 4 matrix) is the reference frame of the car and, hence, describes where the car is and how it is oriented. The position and orientation are handy functions to obtain the position of the car (that is, the fourth column of frame) and the orientation (that is, the third column of frame). The linearVelocity, angularVelocity and linearAcceleration are self-explanatory 3-value arrays specifying the current velocity and acceleration of the car.

```
PhysicsDynamicState.prototype = {
    get position            : function ...
    get orientation         : function ...
    get frame               : function ...
    get linearVelocity      : function ...
    get angularVelocity     : function ...
    get linearAcceleration  : function ...
};
```

Appendix B

Properties of Vector Products

This appendix regards the basic properties of vector products and their geometric interpretation.

B.1   Dot Product

The *dot* product, or *scalar* product between two vectors is indicated with the symbol $\cdot$ and is defined as:

$$\boldsymbol{a} \cdot \boldsymbol{b} = \sum_{i=1}^{n} a_1 b_1 + \cdots + a_n b_n \tag{B.1}$$

This equation is a pure algebraic definition where the term vector is intended as a sequence of numbers. When we deal with a geometric interpretation where the vectors are entities characterized by a magnitude and a direction we can write:

$$\boldsymbol{a} \cdot \boldsymbol{b} = \|\boldsymbol{a}\| \|\boldsymbol{b}\| \cos \theta \tag{B.2}$$

where θ is the angle formed by the two vectors. Equation (B.2) tells us a few important things.

One of these things is that two non-zero-length vectors are perpendicular to each other if and only if their dot product is 0. This is easy to verify: since their length is not 0, the only condition for the dot product to be 0 is that the cosine term is 0, which means $\theta = \pm\pi/2$. This notion also gives us a way to find a non-zero vector perpendicular to a given one [see Figure B.1 (Left)]:

$$[\ldots, a_i, \ldots, a_j, \ldots] \cdot [0, \ldots, 0, a_j, 0, \ldots, 0, -a_i, 0, \ldots] =$$
$$= a_i a_j - a_j a_i = 0$$

and we used it in Section 5.1.2.2 to define the edge equation.

If we fix the length of two vectors, their dot product is maximum when they are parallel and equals the scalar product of their lengths. This is because we compute the length of a vector as $\|\boldsymbol{a}\| = \sqrt{(\boldsymbol{a} \cdot \boldsymbol{a})}$.

Given two vectors $\boldsymbol{a}$ and $\boldsymbol{b}$, we can use dot product to find the length of

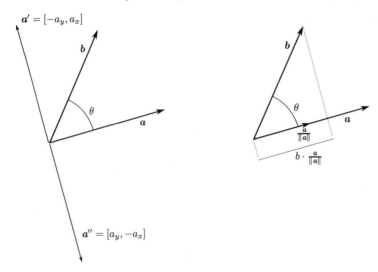

FIGURE B.1: Dot product. (Left) a' and a'' are built from a by swapping the coordinates and negating one of the two. (Right) Length of the projection of b on the vector a.

the projection of b on a:

$$l = b \cdot \frac{a}{\|a\|}$$

as shown Figure B.1 (Right).

The dot product fulfills the following properties:

- Commutative: $a \cdot b = b \cdot a$

- Distributive over vector addition: $a \cdot (b + c) = a \cdot b + a \cdot c$

- Scalar multiplication: $(s_1 a) \cdot (s_2 b) = s_1 s_2 (a \cdot b)$

But **not** associative, that is, $(a \cdot b) \cdot c \neq a \cdot (b \cdot c)$.

B.2   Vector Product

The *vector* (or *cross*) product between two vectors a and b is the vector orthogonal to both a and b and with magnitude equal to the parallelogram formed by $\mathbf{p}, \mathbf{p} + a, \mathbf{p} + a + b$, and $\mathbf{p} + b$ (see Figure B.2).

A typical mnemonic rule to compute the cross product is:

$$a \times b = \begin{vmatrix} \mathbf{i} & \mathbf{j} & \mathbf{k} \\ a_x & a_y & a_z \\ b_x & b_y & b_z \end{vmatrix} =$$

$$= \mathbf{i} \begin{vmatrix} a_y & a_z \\ b_y & b_z \end{vmatrix} + \mathbf{j} \begin{vmatrix} a_x & a_z \\ b_x & b_z \end{vmatrix} + \mathbf{k} \begin{vmatrix} a_x & a_y \\ b_x & b_y \end{vmatrix}$$

$$= \mathbf{i}(a_y b_z - b_y a_z) + \mathbf{j}(a_x b_z - b_x a_z) + \mathbf{k}(a_x b_y - b_x a_y)$$

where $\mathbf{i}$, $\mathbf{j}$ and $\mathbf{k}$ are interpreted as the three axes of the coordinate frame where the vectors are expressed.

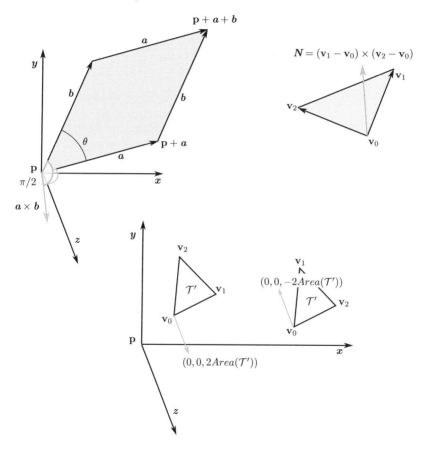

FIGURE B.2: Cross product. (Top-Left) The cross product of two vectors is perpendicular to both and its magnitude is equal to the area of the parallelogram built on the two vectors. (Top-Right) The cross product to compute the normal of a triangle. (Bottom) The cross product to find the orientation of three points on the XY plane.

Like for the dot product, we have a geometric interpretation of the cross product:

$$\|a \times b\| = \|a\|\|b\| \sin \theta \tag{B.3}$$

If we fix the length of two vectors, their cross product is maximum when they are orthogonal and equals the scalar product of their lengths.

Two non-zero-length vectors are *collinear* if and only if their cross product is 0. This is easy to verify: since their length is not 0, the only condition for their cross product to be 0 is that the sin term is 0, which means $\theta = \pi \pm \pi$.

The cross product is typically used to find the normal of a triangular face. Given a triangle $\mathcal{T} = (\mathbf{v}_0, \mathbf{v}_1, \mathbf{v}_2)$, we may define:

$$a = \mathbf{v}_1 - \mathbf{v}_0$$
$$b = \mathbf{v}_2 - \mathbf{v}_0$$

and hence:

$$\boldsymbol{N} = \boldsymbol{a} \times \boldsymbol{b}$$

Note that $\|\boldsymbol{N}\| = 2Area(\mathcal{T})$ so that the magnitude of the normal corresponds to the double of the area of the triangle (we used this property in Section 5.1.3 for expressing the barycentric coordinates).

One of the most used properties of cross product is *antisymmetry*, that is:

$$\boldsymbol{a} \times \boldsymbol{b} = -\boldsymbol{b} \times \boldsymbol{a}$$

If we consider a triangle t' lying on the XY plane and compute its normal, we will obtain the vector $\boldsymbol{N'} = (0, 0, \pm 2Area(\mathcal{T'}))$. The sign of the z component depends on the order of the cross product. If we always perform the product in the same way, that is $(\mathbf{v}_1 - \mathbf{v}_0) \times (\mathbf{v}_2 - \mathbf{v}_0)$, then it depends on whether the vertices are specified in a counterclockwise or clockwise order. In the first case the z component will be positive, in the latter negative, which is the property we used in Section 5.5.1 to distinguish between front-facing and back-facing triangles.

Bibliography

[1] Tomas Akenine-Möller, Eric Haines, and Natty Hoffman. *Real-Time Rendering,* 3rd edition. AK Peters, Ltd., Natick, MA, USA, 2008.

[2] B. G. Baumgart. A polyhedron representation for computer vision. In *Proc. AFIPS National Computer Conference,* volume 44, pages 589–176, 1975.

[3] Louis Bavoil, Miguel Sainz, and Rouslan Dimitrov. Image-space horizon-based ambient occlusion. In *ACM SIGGRAPH 2008 talks,* SIGGRAPH '08, pages 22:1–22:1, New York, NY, USA, 2008. ACM.

[4] James F. Blinn. Models of light reflection for computer synthesized pictures. In *Proceedings of the 4th annual conference on computer graphics and interactive techniques,* SIGGRAPH '77, pages 192–198, New York, NY, USA, 1977. ACM.

[5] R. L. Cook and K. E. Torrance. A reflectance model for computer graphics. *ACM Trans. Graph.,* 1:7–24, January 1982.

[6] Xavier Décoret, Frédo Durand, François X. Sillion, and Julie Dorsey. Billboard clouds for extreme model simplification. In *ACM SIGGRAPH 2003 Papers,* SIGGRAPH '03, pages 689–696, New York, NY, USA, 2003. ACM.

[7] Rouslan Dimitrov, Louis Bavoil, and Miguel Sainz. Horizon-split ambient occlusion. In *Proceedings of the 2008 symposium on interactive 3D graphics and games,* I3D '08, pages 5:1–5:1, New York, NY, USA, 2008. ACM.

[8] Nyra Din, David Levin, and John A. Gregory. A 4-point interpolatory subdivision scheme for curve design. *Computer Aided Geometric Design,* 4(4):257–268, 1987.

[9] Philip Dutre, Kavita Bala, Philippe Bekaert, and Peter Shirley. *Advanced Global Illumination.* AK Peters Ltd, Natick, MA, USA, 2006.

[10] N. Dyn, D. Levin, and J. A. Gregory. A butterfly subdivision scheme for surface interpolation with tension control. *ACM Transaction on Graphics,* 9(2):160–169, 1990.

[11] Gerald Farin. *Curves and Surfaces for CAGD. A Practical Guide*, 5th edition, AK Peters, Ltd, Natick, MA, USA, 2001.

[12] Michael S. Floater and Kai Hormann. Surface parameterization: a tutorial and survey. In Neil A. Dodgson, Michael S. Floater, and Malcolm A. Sabin, editors, *Advances in Multiresolution for Geometric Modelling*, Mathematics and Visualization, pages 157–186. Springer, Berlin Heidelberg, 2005.

[13] Leonidas Guibas and Jorge Stolfi. Primitives for the manipulation of general subdivisions and the computation of voronoi. *ACM Trans. Graph.*, 4(2):74–123, 1985.

[14] INRIA Alice: Geometry and Light. Graphite. `alice.loria.fr/software/graphite`.

[15] Henrik Wann Jensen. *Realistic image synthesis using photon mapping*. A. K. Peters, Ltd., Natick, MA, USA, 2001.

[16] Lutz Kettner. Using generic programming for designing a data structure for polyhedral surfaces. *Comput. Geom. Theory Appl*, 13:65–90, 1999.

[17] Khoronos Group. OpenGL—The Industry's Foundation for High Performance Graphics. `https://www.khronos.org/opengl`, 2013. [Accessed July 2013].

[18] Khronos Group. WebGL—OpenGL ES 2.0 for the Web. `http://www.khronos.org/webgl`. [Accessed July 2013].

[19] Khronos Group. Khronos Group—Connecting Software to Silicon. `http://http://www.khronos.org`, 2013. [Accessed July 2013].

[20] Leif P. Kobbelt, Mario Botsch, Ulrich Schwanecke, and Hans-Peter Seidel. Feature sensitive surface extraction from volume data. In *Proceedings of the 28th annual conference on computer graphics and interactive techniques*, pages 57–66. ACM Press, 2001.

[21] M. S. Langer and H. H. Bülthoff. Depth discrimination from shading under diffuse lighting. *Perception*, 29:49–660, 2000.

[22] M. Langford. *Advanced Photography: A Grammar of Techniques*. Focal Press, 1974.

[23] J. Lengyel. The convergence of graphics and vision. *IEEE Computer*, 31(7):46–53, 1998.

[24] Duoduo Liao. *GPU-Based Real-Time Solid Voxelization for Volume Graphics*. VDM Verlag, 2009.

[25] Charles Loop. Smooth subdivision surfaces based on triangles. Master's thesis, University of Utah, Department of Mathematics, 1987.

[26] William E. Lorensen and Harvey E. Cline. Marching cubes: A high resolution 3D surface construction algorithm. In *Proceedings of the 14th annual conference on computer graphics and interactive techniques*, pages 163–169. ACM Press, 1987.

[27] Paulo W. C. Maciel and Peter Shirley. Visual navigation of large environments using textured clusters. In *1995 Symposium on Interactive 3D Graphics*, pages 95–102, 1995.

[28] Martti Mäntylä. *An introduction to solid modeling*. Computer Science Press, Inc., New York, NY, USA, 1987.

[29] Jai Menon, Brian Wyvill, Chandrajit Bajaj, Jules Bloomenthal, Baining Guo, John Hart, and Geoff Wyvill. Implicit surfaces for geometric modeling and computer graphics, 1996.

[30] M. Minnaert. The reciprocity principle in lunar photometry. *Journal of Astrophysics*, 93:403–410, 1941.

[31] D. Muller and F. P. Preparata. Finding the intersection of two convex polyhedra. Technical report, University of Illinois at Urbana-Champaign, 1977.

[32] Michael Oren and Shree K. Nayar. Generalization of Lambert's reflectance model. In *Proceedings of the 21st annual conference on computer graphics and interactive techniques*, SIGGRAPH '94, pages 239–246, New York, NY, USA, 1994. ACM.

[33] Jingliang Peng, Chang-Su Kim, and C. C. Jay Kuo. Technologies for 3d mesh compression: A survey. *J. Vis. Comun. Image Represent.*, 16(6):688–733, December 2005.

[34] Matt Pharr and Greg Humphreys. *Physically Based Rendering: From Theory to Implementation*, 2nd edition, Morgan Kaufmann Publishers Inc., San Francisco, CA, USA, 2010.

[35] Bui Tuong Phong. Illumination for computer generated pictures. *Commun. ACM*, 18:311–317, June 1975.

[36] R. Rashed. A pioneer in anaclastics: Ibn Sahl on burning mirrors and lenses. *Isis*, 81:464–171, 1990.

[37] Erik Reinhard, Erum Arif Khan, Ahmet Oguz Akyüz, and Garrett M. Johnson. *Color Imaging: Fundamentals and Applications*. AK Peters, Ltd., Natick, MA, USA, 2008.

[38] Alla Sheffer, Bruno Lvy, Maxim Mogilnitsky, and Alexander Bogom Yakov. Abf++: Fast and robust angle based flattening. *ACM Transactions on Graphics*, 2005.

[39] Marco Tarini. *Improving technology for the acquisition and interactive rendering of real world objects.* Universitá degli Studi di Pisa, Pisa, Italy, 2003.

[40] Eric W. Weisstein. Quadratic surface from *MathWorld*–a Wolfram Web resource. `http://mathworld.wolfram.com/QuadraticSurface.html`, 2013. [Accessed July 2013].

[41] Turner Whitted. An improved illumination model for shaded display. *Commun. ACM*, 23(6):343–349, 1980.

[42] Wikipedia. Directx — Wikipedia, the free encyclopedia. `https://en.wikipedia.org/wiki/DirectX`, 2013. [Accessed July 2013].

[43] K. B. Wolf. Geometry and dynamics in refracting systems. *European Journal of Physics*, 16:1417, 1995.

[44] Zoë J. Wood, Peter Schröder, David Breen, and Mathieu Desbrun. Semi-regular mesh extraction from volumes. In *Proceedings of the conference on visualization '00*, pages 275–282, Salt Lake City, UT, USA, 2000. IEEE Computer Society Press.

[45] Magnus Wrenninge. *Production Volume Rendering.* AK Peters/CRC Press, 1st edition, 2012.

[46] D. Zorin. *Subdivision and Multiresolution Surface Representations.* PhD thesis, Caltech, Pasadena, 1997.

[47] D. Zorin, P. Schröder, and W. Sweldens. Interpolating subdivision for meshes arbitrary topology. In *Proceedings of the 23th annual conference on computer graphics and interactive techniques*, pages 189–192, 1996.

[48] Denis Zorin and Peter Schröder. Siggraph 2000 course 23: Subdivision for modeling and animation, 2000.

Index

Commission International de
l'Eclairage (CIE), 8
3D textures, *see* textures
4-point algorithm, 72

spherical billboards, *see also*
billboards

Affine transformation, 96
Algebric surface, 326
Aliasing, 157
ambient occlusion, 316
Antialiasing
Area averaging, 158
Full Screen Antialiasing (FSSA),
159
Super sampling, 159
Area light source, 201
Aspect Ratio, 3
Aspect ratio, 118
axis aligned billboards, *see* billboards
Axis-Aligned Bounding Box
(AABB), 328
Axis-angle rotation, 105

B-Spline, 63
Bézier curves, 59
Bernstein polynomials, 60
Cubic, 61
Back-face culling, 166
Back-to-front drawing, 150
Barycentric coordinates, 146, 147
of a triangle, 148
Barycentric coordinates of a
segment, 147
Bernstein polynomials, 60
Bidirectional Reflectance

Distribution Function
(BRDF), 181
Bidirectional Scattering Surface
Reflectance Distribution
Function (BSSRDF), 183
billboard cloud, *see* billboards
Billboards
on-the-fly billboarding, 287
billboards, 277
axis aligned billboards, 284
billboard cloud, 289
screen aligned billboards, 278
spherical billboards, 288
Blinn illumination model, 211
blurring, 297
Bounding box, 168
Bounding rectangle, 146
Bounding sphere, 168
Bounding volume, 167
Box, 168
Hierarchy, 168
Sphere, 168
Bounding Volume Hierarchy (BVH),
335
BRDF, 181
Bresenham's algorithm, 140
BSSRDF, 183
Building a frame from a single axis,
106

Camera model
Pinhole, 113
Canonical frame, 101
Canonical Viewing Volume, 116
cel-shading, *see* toon-shading
Center of projection, 112
Chaikin's algorithm, 71

Chromaticities diagram, 9
Chromaticy coordinates, 9
CIELab, 11
CIERGB, 9
CIEXYZ, 8
circle of confusion, 300
clamping, *see* texture wrapping
Classic Ray Tracing, 339
Clip space, 117
Clipping, 161
    Cohen-Sutherland algorithm,
        162
    Liang-Barsky algorithm, 164
    Sutherland-Hodgman algorithm,
        165
Clipping polygons, *see also*
        Sutherland-Hodgman
        algorithm
Clipping segments, *see also*
        Cohen-Sutherland
        algorithm
Cohen-Sutherland algorithm, 162
Collinearity, 96
Collinearity of points, 96
color attachment, *see* framebuffer
        object
Color matching functions, 8
Color Model
    Additive, 6
    Subtractive, 7
Color Space
    CIELab, 11
    CIERGB
        Color matching functions, 8
    CIEXYZ, 8
        Color matching functions, 9
    Device-dependent, 9
    Device-independent, 9
    Gamut, 9
    HSL and HSV, 10
    Illuminant, 12
    Standard Observer, 8
Color space, 6
Composition of geometric
        transformations, 97

computational geometry, 3
Computational Photography, 3
Computer Graphics, 1
conformal, *see* mesh parametrization
constructive solid geometry, 70
Cook-Torrance illumination model,
        212
Coordinate frame, 101
creases, *see also* crease angle
CSG, *see* constructive solid geometry
cube mapping, *see* textures
Culling, 165
    Back-face, 166
    Frustum, 167
    Occlusion, 169

deferred shading, 320
Depth sort, 149, 150
Depth-complexity, 170
depth-of-field, 300
Diffuse reflection, 173, 174, *see also*
        Lambertian reflection
Direct light, 172
Directional light source, 192
Directional-Hemispherical
        reflectance, 181
Discrete Difference Analyzer (DDA),
        140
Dot product, 359
    Associative property, 360
    Commutative property, 360
    Distributive property, 360
    Geometric interpretation, 359
    Perpendicularity of two vectors,
        359
    Projection, 359
    Scalar multiplication property,
        360
dsplacement mapping, 243

edge detection, 306
environment mapping, *see* textures
equiareal, *see* mesh parametrization
Euler angles, 108
    Extrinsic rotation, 108

Gimbal, 108
Gimbal lock, 109
Intrinsic rotation, 108
Exitance, 178
Exiting radiosity, 178

Far plane, 115
First person shooter, 130
Flat shading, 209
Flux
    seeRadiant flux, 177
focus, 300
Frame, 101
    Affine transformation, 102
    Canonical, 101
    From a single axis, 106
    Hierarchies of, 102
Frame and affine transformation, 102
Frame rate, *see also*
        Frame-per-second (FPS)
Frame-per-second (FPS), 4
Framebuffer, 21
framebuffer object, 232
Framebuffer Operations, 27
Fresnel effect, 213
Fresnel law, 213
Frustum culling, 167
    Bounding volume, 167
fullscreen quad, 301

Gamma, 13
Gamma correction, 13
Gamut, 9
gaussian filter, 298
Geometric optics, 172
Geometric Processing, 3
Geometric transformation, 92
    3D rotation, 104
    Affine, 96
        Inverse, 100
    Axis-angle rotation, 105
    Composition, 97
    Matrix notation, 94
    Rigid, 96
    Rotation, 93

Rotation about a point, 98
Scaling, 93
Scaling about a point, 99
Shearing, 99
Translation, 92
Gimbal, 108
Gimbal lock, 109
Global and local lighting, 185
Global illumination
    Radiosity, 345
    Ray tracing, 326
Global lighting, 185
global parametrization, *see* mesh
        parametrization
Gouraud shading, 209
GPGPU, 296
Graphics API, 23
    DirectX, 24
    OpenGL, 24
    OpenGL ES, 24
    OpenGL SC, 24
    WebGL, 24

Hemispherical surface reflectance, *see*
        Reflectance
Hidden Surface Removal (HSR), 149
    Culling, 165
    Depth Sort, 149
    Image-space, 149
    Object-space, 149
    Painter's algorithm, 149
    Z-Buffer algorithm, 152
Hierarchical Visibility, 169
Hierarchies of frames, 102
Hierarchy of bounding volumes, 168
Homogeneous coordinates, 95
    Canonical form, 114
    from Cartesian coordinates, 95
    Points, 95
    to Cartesian coordinates, 114
    Vectors, 95
Human Visual System (HVS), 5
    Color stimulus, 5
    Cones, 6
    Metamerism, 6

Illumination, 6
Observer, 6
Opponent channels, 6
Rods, 6
Trichromacy nature of color, 6
hyperbolic interpolation, *see*
perspecive interpolation

IBR, *see* image based rendering
Ideal specular surface, 176
Illuminant, 12
image based impostor, *see also*
impostor
image based rendering, 275
Image plane, 112
image processing, 295
blurring, 297
edge detection, 306
unsharp masking, 314
Image-Based Modeling, 3
implicit surface, 57
impostor, 275
Incident radiosity, 178
Indirect light, 173, 185
Intensity (of light, 178
Interesection of a ray with a plane,
326
International Commission on
Illumination, *see*
Commission International
de l'EclairageCIE)8
Intersection of a ray with a
parametric surface, 327
Intersection of a ray with a sphere,
327
Intersection of a ray with an AABB,
328
Inverse of an affine transformation,
100
Irradiance, 178

Khronos Group, *see also* Graphics
API

Lambertian reflection, 174
lens flares, 280

Liang-Barsky algorithm, 164
Light and matter interaction, 172
Light camera, 259
Light source
Area, 201
Directional, 192
Positional, 197
Spotlight, 200
Light source types, 191
Lighting effects
Diffuse reflection, 173
Direct light, 172
Fresnel, 213
Global, 185
Indirect, 185
Indirect light, 173
interaction with matter, 172
Local, 185
Refraction, 173
Specular reflection, 173
Sub-surface scattering, 173
Lightness, 10
Local illumination model
Blinn, 211
Cook-Torrance, 212
Local illumination models, 185, 205
Minnaert, 214
Oren-Nayar, 213
Local lighting, 185

magnification, *see* textures
Magnitude of a quaternion, 110
manifold, 54
Match banding, 209
Matrix stack, 125
Mesh
fan, 54
Half-edge, 80
Index Data Structure, 78
orientation, 55
quad mesh, 53
strip, 54
triangle mesh, 53
Winged-edge, 80
mesh parametrization, 249

conformal, 252
equiareal, 252
gloabal parametrization, 251
parametrization, 218
seams, 250
Minnaert illumination model, 214
mipmap pyramid, *see* textures
mipmapping, *see* textures
Mirror surface, 176
Multi-pass rendering algorithms
    Photon tracing, 344
    Radiosity, 345
multum in parvo, 222

Near and far plane, 115
Near plane, 115
nearest neighbor interpolation, 221
Non-ideal specular surface, 176
Non-uniform scaling, 93
normal mapping, 243
    object space, 244
    tangent space normal mapping, 246, 247
Normalized Device Coordinates (NDC), *see also* Canonical Viewing Volume
NURBS, 67

object space, *see* normal mapping
Occlusion culling, 169
    Hierarchical Visibility, 169
    Potential Visible Set (PVS), 169
occlusion query, 281
off screen rendering, 232
On-the-fly billboarding, *see* billboards
on-the-fly reflections, *see also* reflections
Oren-Nayar illumination model, 213
orientation, 55
Oriented Bounding Box (OBB), 329
Orthographic projection, 115
Orthonormal matrices, 100
out-of-focus, *see also* focus
Output Combiner, 27

Painter's algorithm, 149
panning, 310
Parallel projection, 114
Parametric curve, 59
    B-Spline, 63
    Bézier curves, 59
Parametric Surface
    Bézier patches, 66
Parametric surface, 58, 64
    NURBS, 67
parametrization, *see* mesh parametrization
particle systems, 321
Penumbra, 257
Per-fragment operations
    Depth test, 155
    Scissor test, 155
    Stencil test, 155
Percentage Closer Filtering (PCF), 268
Perspective division, 114
perspective interpolation, *see* texure
Perspective projection, 112
    Center of, 112
    Image plane, 112
    Projectors, 112
Phong illumination model, 205
    Ambient component, 207
    Diffuse component, 205
    Specular component, 206
Phong shading, 210
Photon Tracing, 344
Pinhole camera, 113
Pixelization effect, 16
Plane of projection, *see* Image plane
Point and vectors
    Common operationss, 91
Point light source, 197
Points, 91
    Collinearity, 96
    Proportions, 96
Points and vectors, 91
Points in homogeneous coordinates, 95
Potential Visible Set (PVS), 169

Primary colors, 6
Primary source (of light), *see* Direct
    light
Primitive Assembler, 26
Projections
    Orthographic, 115
    Parallel, 114
    Perspective, 112
projective texture mapping, *see*
    textures
Projectors, 112

quad mesh, *see* mesh
Quaternions, 110
    Magnitude of, 110
    Summation, 110

Radiance, 179
Radiant flux, 177
Radiometry, 177
    BRDF, 181
    BSSRDF, 183
    Directional-hemispherical
        reflectance, 181
    Exitance, 178
    Exiting radiosity, 178
    Incident radiosity, 178
    Intensity, 178
    Irradiance, 178
    Radiance, 179
    Radiant flux, 177
    Radiosity, 178
    Reflectance, 180
Radiosity, 178, 345
Raster Image, 14
    Alpha channel, 16
    Color Image, 16
    Grayscale Image, 15
    Image channels, 16
    Resolution, 14
    Size in pixels, 14
    Transparent Image, 16
Rasterization, 21
    General Polygons, 142
    Lines, 139

Triangles, 144
Rasterization-based pipeline, 20
    Logical scheme, 20
    Per-fragment computation, 21
    Per-vertex Transformations, 20
    Primitive processing, 20
    Rasterization stage, 21
    WebGL architecture, 25
Rasterizer, 27
Ray optics, *see* Geometric optics
Ray Tracing, 17
    Acceleration structures
        Bounding Volume Hierarchy
            (BVH), 335
        Uniform Spatial Subdivison
            (USS), 330
    Basic form, 17
    Basic idea, 17
    Classic, 18, 339
    Multi-pass algorithms, 344
    Photon tracing, 344
    Ray definition, 326
    Ray-AABB intersection, 328
    Ray-parametric surface
        intersection, 327
    Ray-plane intersection, 326
    Ray-scene intersection, 328
    Ray-sphere intersection, 327
Ray tracing
    Acceleration structures, 328
ray tracing, 290
Ray-parameteric surface intersection,
    327
Ray-Plane intersection, 326
Ray-scene intersection, 328
Ray-sphere intersection, 327
Reflectance, 180
Reflection
    Diffuse, 173, 174
    Lambertian, 174
    Specular, 173–175
        Ideal, 176
        Non-ideal, 176
Reflection law, *see* Snell's law
reflections, 171, *see* textures, 240

Refracted light, 173
Refraction, 173, 176
render to texture, *see* textures
Rendering, 1
    Global illumination, 4
    Illustrative, *see also*
        Non-Photorealistic (NPR)
    Non-Photorealistic (NPR), 4
    Offline, 4
    Paradigms, 17
    Rasterization-based pipeline, 20
    Ray Tracing, 17
    Real-time, 4
    Render Farm, 4
repeat, *see* texture wrapping
Rigid transformation, 96
Rotation, 93
    3D, 104
        Axis-angle, 105
        Euler angles, 108
        Gimbal lock, 109
        Without frame, 106
    Quaternions, 110
Rotation about a point, 98
Rotation in 3D, 104
Rotation with quaternions, 110
RTT, *see* render to texture

Scalar product, *see* Dot product
Scaling, 93
    Non-uniform, 93
Scaling about a point, 99
Scanline algorithm, 143
Scene graph, 124
screen aligned billboards, *see*
        billboards
screen space ambient occlusion, 318
Secondary source (of light), *see*
        Indirect light
Self-shadows, 257
Shading, 209
    Flat, 209
    Gouraud, 209
    Phong, 210
Shading techniques, 209

Shadow map, 259
Shadow Mapping
    Depth Bias, 267
Shadow mapping, 259
    Aliasing, 268
    Depth encoding, 263
    for directional lights, 260
    for point lights, 260
    for spot lights, 261
    Light camera, 259
    PCF, 268
    Shadow map, 259
    Surface acne, 266
Shadow volume, 269
    Construction, 271
    Stencil-based implementation,
        272
Shadowing effects
    Hard shadows, 257
    Penumbra, 257
    Self-shadows, 257
    Shadows, 257
Shadows, 257
sharpen, 314
Shearing, 99
Similar triangles, 113
skybox, *see* textures
Snell's law, 176
Soft-shadows with PCF, 268
Solid angle, 178
    Steradians, 178
Specular reflection, 173–175
sphere mapping, *see* textures
Spotlight light source, 200
Spotlights, 200
sprites, 276
SSAO, *see also* screen space ambient
        occlusion
Stack of matrices, 125
Standard Observer, 8
Steradians, 178
Sub-surface scattering, 173
Subdivision surfaces, 73
    Approximating, 74
    Butterfly scheme, 76

Dual, 73
Interpolating, 74
Loop scheme, 76
Primal, 73
Quadrilateral, 73
Stationary, 73
Triangular, 73
Subdivison surfaces
Continuity, 75
Surface acne, 266
Sutherland-Hodgman algorithm, 165

tangent space normal mapping, *see
also* normal mapping
texture space, 218
texture tiling, *see* textures
texture wrapping
clamping, 218
repeat, 218
textures, 217
3D textures, 254
cube mapping, 236
environment mapping, 234
filtering, 218
magnification, 221
minification, 222
mipmap level, 223
mipmap pyramid, 222
mipmapping, 222
projective texture mapping, 241
reflections, 239
render to texture, 232
skybox, 238
sphere mapping, 235
tiling, 227
The Rendering Equation, 184
toon-shading, 308
Torrance and Sparraw micro-facets
model, 212
Translation, 92
triangle mesh, *see* mesh

Uniform scaling, 93
Uniform Spatial Subdivision (USS),
330

Unit of measure of solid angle, 178
unsharp masking, *see also* image
processing
Unweighted area sampling
seealsoArea averaging, 158
Up direction, 111
UV mapping, *see* mesh
parametrization
UV-coordinates, 218

Vector Graphics, *see also* Vector
Image
Vector Image, 13
PostScript, 14
Scalable Vector Graphics
(SVG), 13
Vector product, 360
Antisymmetry, 362
Collinearity of two vectors, 362
Geometric interpretation, 361
Normal of a triangle, 362
Orientation of a triangle, 362
Vectors, 91
Vectors in homogeneous coordinates,
95
velocity buffer, 311
Vertex Puller, 25
Vertex Shader, 25
View frame, 111
View reference frame, 111
Up direction, 111
Viewing direction, 111
Viewpoint, 111
View transformation, 111
Viewing direction, 111
Viewing volume, 115
Clipping planes, 115
Far plane, 115
Near plane, 115
Viewing window, 115
Viewpoint, 111
Visible light, 5
Volumetric representation, *see also*
Voxel
Volumetric textures, *see* 3D textures

Voxel, 68

watertight, 267
Watertight 3D object, 167
WebGL libraries
    GLGE, 40
    SpiderGL, 40
    Three.js, 40
White point, 12

Z-Buffer algorithm, 152
Z-fighting, 153